The Bible With and Without Jesus

How Jews and Christians
Read the Same Stories Differently

Amy-Jill Levine and Marc Zvi Brettler

HarperOne
An Imprint of HarperCollins*Publishers*

HarperCollins books may be purchased for educational, business, or sales promotional use. For information, please email the Special Markets Department at SPsales@harpercollins.com.

FIRST EDITION

Interior design by Terry McGrath
Cover design by Studio Gearbox
Front cover artwork:
Cover painting: Marc Chagall, Abraham and the Three Angels, 1960–1966
Oil on canvas, 190 x 292 cm. Post-restoration. MBMC6. Photo: Adrien Didierjean
Mark Chagall Artwork © 2020 Artists Rights Society (ARS), New York / ADAGP, Paris
Image © RMN-Grand Palais / Art Resource, NY

Library of Congress Cataloging-in-Publication Data

Names: Levine, Amy-Jill, 1956- author. | Brettler, Marc Zvi, author.
Title: The Bible with and without Jesus : how Jews and Christians read
    the same stories differently / Amy-Jill Levine, Marc Brettler.
Description: 1st edition hardcover. | San Francisco : HarperOne, 2020.
Identifiers: LCCN 2020003441 (print) | LCCN 2020003442 (ebook) | ISBN
    9780062560155 (hardcover) | ISBN 9780062560162 (paperback) | ISBN
    9780062560179 (ebook)
Subjects: LCSH: Judaism—Relations—Christianity. | Christianity and other
    religions—Judaism. | Bible. Old Testament—Criticism, interpretation,
    etc. | Bible. New Testament—Criticism, interpretation, etc.
Classification: LCC BM535 .L3925 2020 (print) | LCC BM535 (ebook) | DDC
    220.6—dc23
LC record available at https://lccn.loc.gov/2020003441
LC ebook record available at https://lccn.loc.gov/2020003442

---

20 21 22 23 24   LSC   10 9 8 7 6 5 4 3 2 1

In memory of our parents,
Miriam and Sidney Brettler, and Anne and Saul Levine.
The Sages taught: There are three partners in the
creation of all people: The Holy One, their father,
and their mother (b. Niddah 31a).

Contents

PREFACE

Our book's cover, Marc Chagall's *Abraham and the Three Angels* (1966), offers readers the choice of multiple interpretations. Some may see an invocation of Genesis 18, the story of three angels or messengers who appear to Abraham and Sarah and announce that Sarah, well into menopause, will soon, miraculously, give birth to a son. For these readers, the picture may bring to mind a main theme of the Bible, expressed through the text's powerful question, "Is anything too wonderful for the LORD?" (Gen 18:14). Those aware of Jewish biblical interpretation may be reminded of the tradition of Abraham as the model of hospitality, who every day "sat at the entrance of his tent in the heat of the day" (Gen 18:1) to greet any passersby and to give them water and food to refresh themselves before they continued on their journey. Christian readers might focus on the meal as representing the Eucharist, or on the angels' haloes, a typical depiction in Christian art, and view this painting as recalling earlier Christian depictions of this scene where the haloes indicate that these three angelic visitors are the Holy Trinity. To complicate matters more: What does it mean that the Jewish Chagall painted this scene from the Hebrew Bible using images that characterize Eastern Orthodox icons, in particular Andrei Rublev's *The Old Testament Trinity*?

We suggest that all of these perspectives—the biblical, the Jewish, the Christian—are important, and all are necessarily partial. The answers we receive, the interpretations we develop, are all dependent on the questions we ask, the experiences we bring, and the preferences we have.

The multiple interpretations of Chagall's picture highlight the intent of this book. Its title is not *The Bible With or Without Jesus*; it is *The Bible With and Without Jesus*. This title offers three subjects that we care about equally: Bible, with Jesus, and without Jesus. We do not claim that only one way of reading Genesis, or any other text in what is called variously the Hebrew Bible, the Tanakh, and the Old Testament, is correct. The questions we bring to the text will yield multiple answers, sometimes mutually exclusive and sometimes complementary and even mutually enhancing. We do not ask only, "What did this text mean in its original context—the time that the author of Genesis wrote the tale?" Nor do we ask only, "What does Genesis 18 mean in a Christian context—with Jesus?" Nor again do we focus only on the various readings of the ancient scripture in the postbiblical Jewish context—without Jesus. Rather, we seek to put these various interpretations into dialogue, for such dialogue helps us understand why, when we read the same text or look at the same painting, we come away with such different views. The better we can see through the eyes of our neighbors, the better able we are to be good neighbors. The more aware we are of the historical settings of the original texts, as best as we can determine them, the better we can see how the texts might have been interpreted by the ancient audience that first heard them. And the more aware we are of the historical settings of those who interpreted the biblical texts, the better we understand our own religious traditions and those of our neighbors.

This multilensed perspective comes from our teaching experience. In both our classrooms and our various programs in churches and synagogues, we have encountered individuals with limited views of their own traditions and even more limited views of interpretations in other religious communities. We have seen not only ignorance but antipathy toward the views of their neighbors. We have met many Christians who wonder about the value of the "Old" Testament, which they see as proclaiming an "Old Testament God of wrath" versus the "New Testament God of love," or which they conclude is about law (seen as a negative) rather than about grace (seen as epitomizing the positive). And we have frequently encountered Jewish audiences who find the "New" Testament irrelevant at best, or a co-optation and even deformation of the Tanakh written by Jews for Jews. Both of these attitudes are unfortunate: ignorance of the other's tradition is not bliss. We live in a multicultural society where we cannot afford to ignore the perspective of others, or indeed to perceive them as "other."

We have thus teamed up, as a scholar who predominantly studies the Hebrew Bible/Old Testament/Tanakh (Brettler) and one who predominantly studies the New Testament (Levine), and who each works in "reception history"—the interpretation of these texts by the communities that hold them sacred—to examine ten well-known passages or themes from Israel's scriptures that are important to the New Testament. Each of our central chapters asks three questions: What did the text mean in its original context in ancient Israel? How do the New Testament authors interpret that text? And how do postbiblical Jews from the time of Jesus (e.g., the Dead Sea Scrolls, the first-century historian Josephus, and the first-century philosopher Philo) through the rabbinic and medieval Jewish tradition and later Christian traditions understand those same texts?

Our chapters highlight how differently different communities interpret the same material. For example, for Jews, the book of Jonah is (predominantly) about the power of repentance, and the postbiblical tradition also finds in the brief book a great amount of humor; meanwhile, for Christians it is a book (predominantly) about the resurrection of Jesus on the third day, and there is nothing funny about that. In other cases, a particular theme or text is important to one community and relatively unimportant to another. For example, Isaiah's depictions of the Servant of the LORD, sometimes called the "suffering servant," are central to Christianity, as already reflected in the New Testament, but most Jews are unaware of this image. Indeed, a number of verses that have enormous import for the New Testament and ongoing Christian theology have become virtually unknown to Jewish readers, just as Jewish interpretations (and there are usually multiple interpretations of the same verse or passage) are generally unknown to Christians. Thus this book is, in part, an act of recovery so that we can all be more familiar with biblical passages that Jews and Christians share, albeit with different emphases.

As biblical scholars, we believe that we have an obligation to provide careful explications of these texts and interpretations in a sympathetic light. Our agenda is not to show how one reading is right and another reading is wrong; it is rather to show how these interpretations developed, how they make sense given the theological presuppositions of their authors and original audiences, and how they are necessarily partial.

We also seek to demonstrate how translation matters: how reading the original Hebrew, the pre-Christian Greek translation (the Septuagint), and different English versions creates substantially different impressions. Translators, sometimes deliberately and often unconsciously, choose readings that fit the needs of their own religious communities. For example, in examining the Bible's very first story, we explain how Genesis 1:2 can be seen as speaking of both "a mighty wind" and the "Spirit of God" hovering over the deep. We see how Isaiah 7 could be speaking of a pregnant young woman, a soon-to-be-pregnant (by usual means) young woman, or a virgin who is also pregnant.

Finally, acknowledging the polemical implications of some of the Jewish and Christian interpretations, we ask of each text or theme, "What might we say about them today, given our knowledge of history and theology, and given our commitment to and respect for differing traditions?" With this approach, we then show how polemic can be turned to possibility.

We have worked together before in editing both the first (2011) and second (2017) editions of *The Jewish Annotated New Testament*, a volume that frequently flags how the followers of Jesus recontextualized and reinterpreted earlier Jewish texts. In each case, we wished we had more pages to develop these readings. We are therefore grateful for the opportunity to collaborate on this volume.

In both editing the *Jewish Annotated* and especially in writing this book, we learned to work together, to sharpen our arguments, to discover how the two of us saw different aspects of the same text. We experienced firsthand how the type of paired study (Hebrew *chevruta*) that is the hallmark of traditional Jewish learning leads to effective understanding, clarity, and sharpness, and we are both grateful for the experience of having sometimes sparred over, but mostly marveled over, even laughed over, almost every interpretation, every word, in the following pages.

A Note on Translations
and Abbreviations

BIBLICAL TRANSLATIONS in this book come from the New Revised Standard Version (NRSV) of the Bible unless otherwise noted. We also use the New Jewish Publication Society *Tanakh* translation of the Hebrew Bible (NJPS), completed in 1985 and last revised in 1999. We recommend this study edition, which includes brief commentary and essays cited in this book: Adele Berlin and Marc Zvi Brettler, eds., *The Jewish Study Bible*, 2nd ed. (Oxford: Oxford Univ. Press, 2014). At times we quote from the Septuagint, the ancient Jewish Greek translation of the Hebrew Bible; for translation we cite the NETS: Albert Pietersma and Benjamin G. Wright, eds., *A New English Translation of the Septuagint* (Oxford: Oxford Univ. Press, 2007).

Each of these translations is available online and will often be referenced in the book by these abbreviations:

- NRSV: https://www.biblegateway.com/
- NJPS: https://www.sefaria.org/texts/Tanakh
- NETS: http://ccat.sas.upenn.edu/nets/edition/

For other ancient sources, we use the following translations unless otherwise noted:

- Philo: C. D. Yonge, trans., *The Works of Philo: Complete and Unabridged* (Peabody, MA: Hendrickson, 1993).

- Josephus: William Whiston, trans., *Josephus: Complete Works* (Grand Rapids: Kregel, 1981), http://penelope.uchicago.edu /josephus/.

- The Mishnah: Jacob Neusner, trans., *Mishnah: A New Translation* (New Haven: Yale Univ. Press, 1988).

- Rabbinic literature (Talmud, midrash): https://www.sefaria.org/.

- Targumim: Various translations in *Targum English Translation* module (Accordance Bible Software); when other translations are used, this will be noted.

- Dead Sea Scrolls: Martin Abegg, *Dead Sea Scrolls Biblical Manuscripts* module (Accordance, 2007).

- Pseudepigrapha: Louis H. Feldman, James L. Kugel, and Lawrence H. Schiffman, eds., *Outside the Bible: Ancient Jewish Writings Related to Scripture* (Philadelphia: Jewish Publication Society, 2013); and James Charlesworth, ed., *The Old Testament Pseudepigrapha,* 2 vols., 3rd ed. (Peabody, MA: Hendrickson, 2013).

Other abbreviations:

- *ANF:* Alexander Roberts and James Donaldson, eds., *The Ante-Nicene Fathers,* 10 vols. (1885–1887; repr., Peabody, MA: Hendrickson, 1994), http://www.ccel.org/fathers.html.

- *DDD:* Karel van der Toorn, Bob Becking, and Pieter W. van der Horst, eds., *Dictionary of Deities and Demons in the Bible,* 2nd rev. ed. (Grand Rapids: Eerdmans, 1999).

- *EBR:* Hans-Josef Klauck et al., eds., *Encyclopedia of the Bible and Its Reception* (Berlin: de Gruyter, 2009–).

- *EDEJ:* John J. Collins and Daniel C. Harlow, eds., *The Eerdmans Dictionary of Early Judaism* (Grand Rapids: Eerdmans, 2010).

- *EDSS:* Lawrence H. Schiffman and James C. VanderKam, *Encyclopedia of the Dead Sea Scrolls,* 2 vols. (New York: Oxford Univ. Press, 2000).

- Heb.: This marks cases where the Hebrew chapter and verse numbers differ from those in the NRSV.

- *JANT:* Amy-Jill Levine and Marc Zvi Brettler, eds., *The Jewish Annotated New Testament: New Revised Standard Version,* 2nd ed. (Oxford: Oxford Univ. Press, 2017).

- *JSB:* Adele Berlin and Marc Zvi Brettler, eds., *The Jewish Study Bible: Jewish Publication Society Tanakh Translation,* 2nd ed. (Oxford: Oxford Univ. Press, 2014).

- KJV: King James Version

- LXX: Septuagint

- MT: Masoretic Text

- *OTB:* Louis H. Feldman, James L. Kugel, and Lawrence H. Schiffman, eds., *Outside the Bible: Ancient Jewish Writings Related to Scripture* (Philadelphia: Jewish Publication Society, 2013).

- *TDOT:* G. Johannes Botterweck and Helmer Ringgren, eds., *Theological Dictionary of the Old Testament,* trans. John T. Willis et al., 8 vols. (Grand Rapids: Eerdmans, 1974–2006).

For Hebrew and Greek, we use a popular phonetic transliteration; our aim is to make the original languages more available to the readers rather than to provide full consistency.

CHAPTER 1

On Bibles and Their Interpreters

SAME STORIES, DIFFERENT BIBLES

THE BIBLE, in the singular, does not exist; different communities have different Bibles. We don't mean that they prefer different translations but that they have Bibles comprised of different books, in different orders, in different languages. The biggest difference is between the Jewish and Christian communities, for only Christians have a New Testament. In fact, only Christians have an "Old Testament," which itself differs among the various Christian communions. Jews have the Tanakh, and although the Old Testament and Tanakh share books, the communities interpret the shared verses differently. The Old Testament and the Tanakh are not, today for Christians and Jews, self-standing books. Christians read their Old Testament through the lens of the New Testament, and Jews read the Tanakh through the lens of postbiblical Jewish commentaries.

These differences raise major interpretive questions. For example, who is the Bible's main character? Is it God? Is it Jesus? Does it lack a main character? What is its main point, or is there one? Does the "original" meaning of a passage, apart from Christian or later Jewish interpretation, still have anything to say to us?

Different interpretive communities answer these questions differently—and that is what this book is about. What does it mean to read, and interpret, sections of the Bible with and without Jesus? What is gained, or lost? We are not advocating for one correct way of reading, but we hope, first, that our book will help all readers to see how and why the Bible is such a contested work. Second, we hope that people with different interpretations—with and without Jesus—will talk to each other and understand each other better. The goal of biblical studies should not be to convert each other or to polemicize. Conversion is a matter of the heart, not of the academy; polemics function more to "speak to the choir" and shore up internal unity rather than to facilitate understanding, let alone to show love of neighbor. Biblical studies, as we understand it, can rather help us better to understand each other, and to move forward in appreciating the Bible's power and importance.

As the early followers of Jesus, reflecting on the proclamation of his resurrection, turned to books such as Isaiah, Jeremiah, and Psalms more fully to understand their risen Lord, they found throughout the ancient sources new meaning. Instead of asking what the texts meant in their original contexts, they asked what the texts meant to them, in their own lives centuries later. Jews throughout the ages have done the same. They looked to their ancient scriptures to understand practices such as honoring the Sabbath and aiding the poor, as well as postbiblical events such as the destruction of the Jerusalem Temple by Rome in 70 CE and later their persecution by Christians. In this turn to scripture, Jews and Christians also fought like family members over the disposition of their parents' legacy. Each claimed the scriptures for themselves, and in doing so they read the texts not only as sources of comfort and inspiration but also as sites of contention and polemic. This book seeks to foster a different future, where Jews and Christians come to understand each other's positions and beliefs, and at the minimum, respectfully agree to disagree.

This is no easy task. It involves appreciating what biblical texts meant in their earliest contexts[1] and then explaining how over the centuries different communities with different concerns developed different interpretations. It also means understanding how these ancient scriptures became weaponized—on papyrus, parchment, vellum, paper, and now online—in the war over the "rights" to their meaning. This war continues today, when a Christian tells a Jew, "You obviously don't understand your Bible because, if you did, you would see how it predicts the Messiah Jesus," and when a Jew responds, "Not only do you Christians see things in the text that are not there, you mistranslate and you yank verses out of context." Neither position is helpful, since neither appreciates how and why Jews and Christians understand their own texts. When read through Christian lenses, what the church calls the "Old Testament" points to Jesus. When read through Jewish lenses, what the synagogue calls the "Tanakh" speaks to Jewish experience, without Jesus. When read through the eyes of historians, these original texts yield meanings often lost to both church and synagogue. Even the terms "Old Testament" and "Tanakh" create problems, as we'll see below.

In this book we focus on texts from ancient Israel that are central in the New Testament. We cannot be comprehensive, for the New Testament either cites directly or alludes to this antecedent scripture from the first verses of Matthew's Gospel to the last verses of John's Revelation. Therefore, we chose texts and ideas most people would know, such as God's speech in Genesis 1:26, "Let us make humankind in our image, according to our likeness"; the meaning of Isaiah 7:14, "A virgin shall conceive" or "a young woman is pregnant"; and the centrality of blood for atonement.

Each of our ten central chapters, Chapters 3–12, attends to a particular text or theme and has the same structure. In most cases beginning with a New Testament citation, we then backtrack to examine that citation in its original context. We do our best to determine when and why that original text was written as well as how to translate the Hebrew words (often a problem). Next we see what the verses meant in Jewish sources earlier to and contemporaneous with the New Testament, such as the Septuagint (the Greek translation of the Hebrew texts) and the Dead Sea Scrolls (scrolls and fragments of biblical and nonbiblical texts, dating from the fourth or third century BCE to the second century CE, found near the Dead Sea). Here we show both how the New Testament draws from Jewish reflections and where it offers distinct readings. The next step is to look at later selected Jewish texts, some of which engage those New Testament readings, and not usually sympathetically. In some cases, we look at how the text was interpreted in early Christian, post–New Testament tradition. We conclude each chapter by seeing what Jews, Christians, and indeed all readers might learn today from those ancient verses. We cover a broad chronological sweep, from the early first millennium BCE, to the first century CE, to the twenty-first century.[2]

We roughly follow the canonical order of the Bible, but to do this precisely is impossible, since the order of books in the Old Testament differs from that of the Tanakh, and we do not want to privilege either.

CHRISTIAN AND JEWISH BIBLES

THE IMPRECISE TERM "Bible" derives from the Greek *ta biblia*, "the books," and it suggests that a particular collection of books has priority. There is no such thing as "*the* Bible"; different religious communities have different Bibles.[3] The Samaritan community has only the Torah, the first five books of the Bible, as its Bible; it lacks works such as Jeremiah and Psalms. Extending scripture, the Orthodox Tewahedo canon used predominantly in Eritrea and Ethiopia includes 1 Enoch and Jubilees and 1, 2, and 3 Meqabyan (which are not, contrary to the sounding of the name, related to 1, 2, and 3 Maccabees, which are found in other Christian canons); additional books have canonical status as well. Other Christian movements, such as the Church of Jesus Christ of Latter-day Saints (commonly called "Mormons") and Christian Science, regard denominationally specific works as also authoritative. It should be obvious that the Jewish Bible does not include a New Testament—and thus reflects a Bible "without Jesus"—although we have often been surprised by our students' unawareness of this fact. Then again, Messianic Jews do include the *brit chadashah*—which is how one would say "the New Testament" in Hebrew—as part of their canon.

Nor is the Old Testament the same for all Christians. The Roman Catholic, Anglican, Eastern Orthodox, and Assyrian Churches include books written by Jews before New Testament times but preserved in Greek, such as Sirach or Judith, as part of their Old Testament. These books are typically called the "Apocrypha" by Protestants or, for those communions that hold them as having the status of scripture, "deuterocanonical" or part of the "second canon."

Part two of the Christian Bible is "the New Testament." The word "testament" is a synonym for "covenant," and the term "New Testament" used for the second part of the Christian canon is first attested by the North African church father Tertullian (ca. 155–ca. 240). The expression refers to Jeremiah 31:31: "The days are surely coming, says the LORD, when I will make a new covenant with the house of Israel and the house of Judah." We return to Jeremiah 31, which the New Testament frequently either cites or evokes, in our concluding chapter.

The terms "New Testament" and "Old Testament" are theologically loaded. In this book, we use "New Testament" in a technical sense to refer to the twenty-seven books from Matthew to Revelation that all Christian churches eventually recognized as canonical.[4]

It is more difficult to know what to call scripture's first section. The early rabbis used the Hebrew terms *mikra'*, "that which is written," or *kitvei hakodesh*, "the holy writings,"[5] but these terms are no longer broadly employed. "Old Testament," first attested in the late second century CE by the church father Melito of Sardis,[6] makes sense only within a Christian context. One needs a "New Testament" in order to have an "Old Testament." Making the expression "Old Testament" even more problematic is a verse from the New Testament, Hebrews 8:13, which says, "In speaking of 'a new covenant' [the Greek can be translated as "new testament"] he [Jesus] has made the first one obsolete. And what is obsolete and growing old will soon disappear." In fact, in the early second century, a fellow named Marcion declared that this first testament should be rejected, along with the God it proclaimed. The nascent Christian Church declared Marcion a heretic—yet the rhetoric of the "Old Testament God of wrath" versus the "New Testament God of love," frequently heard in churches even today, repeats Marcion's heresy and is a misreading of both testaments.

The term "Hebrew Bible," coined by modern biblical scholars seeking a more religiously neutral term than "Old Testament," is inaccurate, since part of this text is in Aramaic, not Hebrew. "Jewish Bible" is problematic for a different reason: it strips this work from the Christian canon.

Some scholars, in the effort to avoid the problem of connecting the term "old" with something outdated or decrepit, speak of the "First Testament."[7] This good-faith effort has its own problems, as Jews don't have a "first Testament" but an "only Testament." Worse, if the earlier material is the "First Testament," then the New Testament becomes the "Second Testament," and there is nothing positive about "second," as second hand, second place, and second rate all suggest.

To refer to the Jewish Bible, we use the medieval term "Tanakh," an acronym of **T**orah (Hebrew "instruction"; the first five books, also known as the Pentateuch), **N**evi'im (Hebrew "prophets"), and **K**etuvim (Hebrew "writings"), the term Jews typically use, and the title for the New Jewish Publication Society translation.[8] "Tanakh" refers to the Jewish Bible in its medieval form, as codified by scholars called the Masoretes, and therefore it is also called the Masoretic Text (MT); these scholars added written vowel points, cantillation marks, and other signs to the consonantal text.[9] When we refer to more or less the same work within a Christian context, we use the term "Old Testament." When we are talking about the books of this corpus, in their original historical setting, we will use, for convenience, both "Hebrew Bible" and "scriptures of Israel."

We say "more or less" because the Christian Old Testament is not identical to the Jewish Tanakh. This is true even within Protestantism, which lacks the Apocrypha. Unlike the three-part division of the Jewish canon, the Christian Old Testament has four sections: Pentateuch, Histories, Poetry and Wisdom, and Prophecy. The last book in the Old Testament is Malachi, and the end of Malachi predicts the return of the prophet Elijah and the coming of the messianic age. Thus, the Christian canon emphasizes prophecy in the Old Testament and fulfillment of that prophecy in the New Testament. By putting the prophets (Nevi'im) in the middle of the canon, the Jewish scriptures appear in comparison to de-emphasize prophecy, although that was not likely the original intent of the canonizers. At least according to some New Testament texts, the canon of the Jews followed the order that became the Tanakh. In Matthew 23:35, following his excoriation of a Jewish movement called the Pharisees, Jesus states, "so that upon you may come all the righteous blood shed on earth, from the blood of the righteous Abel to the blood of Zechariah son of Barachiah whom you murdered between the sanctuary and the altar." This verse is a sweep of biblical history, from Abel in Genesis 4 (the Pharisees were hardly present at the time) to 2 Chronicles 24:20–22, which mentions this death of Zechariah, although identifying him as the son of Jehoiada. Similarly, Luke 24:44–45 reports that the resurrected Jesus told his disciples, "'These are my words that I spoke to you while I was still with you—that everything written about me in the law of Moses, the prophets, and the psalms [likely a reference to the third part of the canon, beginning with Psalms] must be fulfilled.' Then he opened their minds to understand the scriptures." We see here both the continuity and the change: the canonical order remains the same, but for Luke's Gospel only Jesus can provide its correct interpretation.

Although the order of Ketuvim, the Writings, never fully stabilized, most editions end with 2 Chronicles, which concludes with Cyrus of Persia encouraging Jews exiled in Babylonia to return to Israel. The final words of the Tanakh are, "Whoever is among you of all his people, may the LORD his God be with him! Let him go up" (2 Chr 36:23). This ending signals not the coming of the messiah but the centrality of the land of Israel. A few early Jewish canonical collections, such as the famous Aleppo Codex, end with the book of Ezra-Nehemiah. This text concludes, "Remember me, O my God, for good." Perhaps coincidentally, the Hebrew word for "God," *'elohim*, and the Hebrew word for "good," *tov*, echo the first chapter of Genesis, where *'elohim* saw that everything was very good.

The problem of nomenclature is even more complex when we look to scripture in the first century CE, the time of Jesus. Terms like "canon" and "Bible" typically indicate a fixed set of books. During the first century, however, Jews and the followers of Jesus, both Jewish and gentile, had no such canon. To speak of the Tanakh in the time of Jesus would be anachronistic—there was no agreed-upon, three-part Bible to which all Jews then subscribed.[10] Beyond the Torah or Pentateuch, the first five books in all traditions, the order and selection of the books that communities held sacred differed; nor was the text of the various books yet uniform. For this reason, we use the amorphous term "scriptures of Israel" to refer to the writings that were central to Jews during the time of Jesus.[11]

The books comprising this collection were written mostly in Hebrew, with several chapters of some books in Aramaic, a Semitic language also used by many Jews of the sixth and following centuries BCE. But many Jews living outside the land of Israel, such as in Alexandria in Egypt, knew neither Hebrew nor Aramaic: they spoke Greek. Thus, beginning in the third century BCE, they translated the Torah and then other books into Greek. The initial translation is called the Septuagint (from the Latin *Septuaginta*, meaning "seventy"), based on the legend that seventy (or seventy-two) Jewish scholars prepared the translation. The text is abbreviated as LXX, the Roman numeral for 70.[12]

A legend, initially preserved in a circa 250 BCE Greek text called the *Letter of Aristeas* and known to the rabbis (b. Megillah 9a–b), describes the translation of the Torah (not the entire Tanakh) into Greek. In the account, the high priest sent seventy-two scribes from Jerusalem to Egypt to create the Greek translation, and this legend came to sanction the Septuagint for Greek-speaking Jews. Today, "Septuagint" is frequently used to refer to the Greek translation of all the books of the Hebrew Bible as well as the books in the Old Testament Apocrypha or deuterocanonical literature.

The Septuagint encouraged Jews to maintain their identity in the Greek-speaking world. Rather than a prompt for assimilation, it had the opposite effect: it allowed Jews to proclaim and promote their own traditions. The Babylonian Talmud (a collection of Jewish law and lore compiled beginning in the sixth century in Babylonia, present-day Iraq) recognizes the legitimacy of at least some Greek translations (b. Megillah 9a). Eventually, synagogues determined that the Masoretic Text be a unifying factor of all Jewish communities, just as the (Arabic) Qur'an is for the Islamic world. For a time, the Latin translation united the Roman Catholic Church, as the Greek does for Greek Orthodoxy. For Protestants, for whom there is no one recognized translation, unity is more difficult to achieve. What is sacred to one Christian denomination may be consigned to the flames by another.

As evangelists for Jesus began to speak to Jews in the diaspora, the areas outside of Israel, as well as to gentiles, Greek was the preferred language. Thus, the New Testament frequently cites some version of, or versions of, the Septuagint.[13] It is from the Greek translation that we get, for example, Isaiah's prediction of a virginal conception.

As the old Italian proverb goes, all translators are traitors. Words always have connotations, and when they move from one language to another, those connotations often change. Because the New

Testament writers primarily used the Greek translation of Israel's scriptures, some Hebrew nuances are erased or replaced. From the familiar "Beatitudes" of the equally familiar "Sermon on the Mount" (Matt 5–7), Jesus states, "Blessed are the meek, for they will inherit the earth" (Matt 5:5). This is a partial quotation from the Greek translation of Psalm 37:11. However, whereas the Greek (Ps 36:11 LXX) speaks of inheriting the earth (Greek *gē*, as in geology), the Hebrew speaks of inheriting the land (Hebrew *'eretz*), which to its initial hearers would have meant the land of Israel, not all the earth.

Eastern-rite churches, such as the Greek Orthodox Church, to this day regard the Septuagint, rather than the Hebrew Bible, as canonical. Eventually, Greek-speaking Jewish communities produced new Greek translations that were closer to the Hebrew in order to combat Christian claims. Later, the Jewish people decided that for liturgical purposes their sacred texts would remain in the original Hebrew (or Aramaic). Conversely, Christian churches use various vernacular translations in worship.

ON INTERPRETATION

BECAUSE 2 Timothy 3:16 states that "all scripture [the reference was initially to the scriptures of Israel, since there was no "New Testament" at the time 2 Timothy was written] is inspired by God [or "God-breathed"]," the idea developed in Christian circles that all biblical passages are replete with meaning. More, the corollary was that because the text is inspired, it cannot have contradictions: it is "inerrant," containing no error or faults. Jews traditionally have taken the same approach: scripture is divine; it contains revelation.

If we begin with this premise of inerrancy, we will spend ages attempting to harmonize inharmonious texts written by different authors at different times. Genesis 1:1–2:4a (the "a" refers to the first half of the verse) and Genesis 2:4b to the end of the garden of Eden story are different versions of creation, as we see in Chapters 3 and 4. So too, the Gospels give four different versions of the life of Jesus, with major distinctions. Either Jesus died on the first day of the Passover holiday (so Matthew, Mark, and Luke, called the "Synoptic Gospels" because they "see together" or share the same basic plot) or he died the day before, when the Passover lambs were being slaughtered in the Temple (so John's Gospel). Either Joseph's father was named Jacob, like the original Jacob, father of Joseph (he of the *Amazing Technicolor Dreamcoat*) in Genesis, who also dreamed dreams and took his family to Egypt (so Matthew); or Joseph's father was named Heli (so Luke).

In our view, the biblical story is a marvelous tapestry created by many weavers of tales over many centuries, each with a different understanding of history, of the relationship of God to the covenant community, and of how people in that community should believe and act. We celebrate the various perspectives rather than try to harmonize them. Similarly, we celebrate the different Jewish and Christian interpretations rather than try to reconcile them. As mainstream biblical scholars, we respect both views in our work of interpretation, and we recognize that interpretation of texts is a complicated process.

For example, many words have multiple meanings. The English word "port" may refer to a type of fortified wine or to a harbor, and thus the sentence "the sailors enjoyed the port" is ambiguous.[14] Equally ambiguous is the sentence "Roberta likes horses more than Mark," but its ambiguity is syntactic instead of lexical: perhaps Roberta likes horses more than she likes Mark, or perhaps she has a greater liking for horses than Mark does. In most cases, context resolves such ambiguities; however, as we shall see with the biblical texts, the context is often unknown, and different historical contexts yield different interpretations. For example, depending on when it was written, the Tower of Babel story in Genesis 11:1–9 may reflect the hope that Babylon will soon fall, or it may be a story mocking that empire after the Persians conquered it. The words stay the same, but the frame affects what the story means.

Our favorite example of taking a text out of context comes from Ben Witherington's essay on hermeneutics. The term "hermeneutics" comes from the Greek god Hermes, the go-between deity of Olympus and earth and therefore the interpreter of the gods' pronouncements. Hermeneutics today is the art of interpretation. Witherington writes:

I had a phone call over twenty years ago from a parishioner from one of my four N.C. Methodist Churches in the middle of the state. He wanted to know if it was o.k. to breed dogs, 'cause his fellow carpenter had told him that it said somewhere in the KJV [the King James Version] that God's people shouldn't do that. I told him I would look up all the references to dog in the Bible and get to the bottom of this. There was nothing of any relevance in the NT [New Testament], but then I came across this peculiar translation of an OT [Old Testament] verse—"Thou shalt not breed with the dogs." I called my church member up and told him, "I've got good news and bad news for you." He asked for the good news first. I said, "Well you can breed as many of those furry four-footed creatures as you like, nothing in the Bible against it." He then asked what the bad news was. "Well," I said, "there is this verse that calls foreign women 'dogs' and warns the Israelites not to breed with them." There was a pregnant silence on the other end of the line, and finally Mr. Smith said, "Well, I am feeling much relieved, my wife Betty Sue is from just down the road in Chatham county!"[15]

Actually, the "dogs" probably refers to prostitutes, not foreign women; the King James Version does not, in the printed versions we could find, refer to breeding; and the Torah tends to prohibit cross-breeding as part of its concern for placing things in appropriate categories. But the example still holds.

Also complicating interpretation is our incomplete understanding of ancient Hebrew, Aramaic, and Greek language and grammar. These issues affect translation of the Bible's first verse: One reading of the Hebrew is the NRSV's "In the beginning when God created the heavens and the earth"; the "when" connects this opening line to the following clause, "the earth was a formless void and darkness covered the face of the deep." The NRSV translation suggests that God created this world from a formless earth and water. However, the English Standard Version reads, "In the beginning, God created the heavens and the earth," an absolute statement that suggests creation ex nihilo—creation from nothing. In addition, "heavens and earth" may refer to two specific bodies, or the phrase could be a merism, a literary device in which two opposites express the two poles and everything in-between—and thus "heavens and earth" may refer to God's creation of everything.

Features of ancient writing create even more ambiguity. Until the late first millennium CE, Hebrew writing contained only consonants; it had no vowels. If we were to imagine English written in this system, the word "red" would be written "rd." But "rd" could also indicate read, reed, road, raid, rid, rad, ride, rod, ready, or redo. Context will *almost* always clarify what word "rd" represents. A favorite exercise of Bible teachers is to ask students to read, in comprehensible English, the sentence GDSNWHR. Some take the optimistic "God is now here"; others opt for "God is nowhere."

For a biblical example, the first word of Isaiah 9:8 (9:7 Heb.) in Hebrew is *dvr*, which may be vocalized as *davar*, "a thing, word," or *dever*, "pestilence." The Masoretes vocalized it as *davar*, yielding the translation "The Lord sent a word against Jacob," while the Septuagint translators read *dvr* as "pestilence" and so translated it as *thanaton* (Greek for "death"). Both readings make sense in context. It is also possible that the Hebrew author was punning.

Ancient Hebrew and Greek texts also lacked punctuation marks. Psalm 116:15 could be rendered, "Precious in the sight of the LORD is the death of his faithful ones," or "Is the death of his faithful ones precious in the sight of the LORD?" Psalm 121:1 reads, "I lift up my eyes to the hills— / from where will my help come"; the context may suggest that the sentence is a question: "Will my help come from the hills?," and the answer is, "No, you're looking to the wrong place." Help will come from "the Lord, who made heaven and earth" (Ps 121:2). But numerous Christian hymns take the statement as a declarative and then see nature as revealing the divine presence.

Punctuation also matters in the New Testament. A centurion tells Jesus, "Lord, my servant is lying at home paralyzed, in terrible distress" (Matt 8:6). Most translations then have Jesus state, "I will come and cure him." However, given that in Matthew's Gospel Jesus restricts his mission to Jews, the sentence could just as easily be taken as a question, "Shall I come and heal him?"

An example that illustrates the Jewish-Christian interpretive divide appears in how we punctuate Isaiah 40:3–4. As punctuated through the cantillation marks found in the Masoretic Text, Isaiah reads:

> A voice cries out:
>> "In the wilderness prepare the way of the Lord,
>>> make straight in the desert a highway for our God.
>> Every valley shall be lifted up,
>>> and every mountain and hill be made low;
>> the uneven ground shall become level,
>>> and the rough places a plain."

In other words, God will build a road in the desert to facilitate the Jews' return from Babylon.

The Gospel of Mark, however, opens as follows:

> As it is written in the prophet Isaiah,
>> "See, I am sending my messenger ahead of you,
>>> who will prepare your way;
>> the voice of one crying out in the wilderness:
>>> 'Prepare the way of the Lord,
>>> make his paths straight.'"

John the baptizer appeared in the wilderness, proclaiming a
baptism of repentance for the forgiveness of sins. (Mark 1:2–4)

The Hebrew text speaks of a voice telling the people to build a road:
"A voice cries out"—colon, quotation mark—"In the wilderness prepare the way of the LORD." The Gospel speaks of "the voice of one
crying out in the wilderness"—colon, quotation mark—"'Prepare
the way of the Lord.'" Here a dispute over punctuation is interwoven with a major theological issue. This example shows how even
such small matters as commas are significant, as illustrated by the
sentences "Let's eat, Grandma" and "Let's eat Grandma."

The work of scribes, especially before the invention of the print-
ing press, also contributed to interpretive problems. As ancient texts
were repeatedly copied, different versions of the same text developed. For example, the Hebrew of Genesis 22:13, from the story of
the binding and near sacrifice of Isaac, speaks of an 'ayil 'achar, "a
ram after," which is difficult to understand—after what? The Greek
reads, more logically, krios heis, "one ram." The underlying Hebrew
text would have been 'ayil 'echad. In Hebrew, the letters for "r" (ר) and
"d" (ד) are visually similar and apt to get confused. In this case, the
Greek probably reflects the original reading. It is therefore impossible to speak of the original text of the Tanakh, though many Jewish
and some Protestant readers view the medieval Hebrew Masoretic
Text as definitive. The same problems apply to the New Testament.[16]

When we look at ancient, or important, texts, interpretation
becomes even more complex, and often contested. The Second
Amendment to the US Constitution reads: "A well regulated Mili-
tia, being necessary to the security of a free State, the right of the
people to keep and bear Arms, shall not be infringed." But what
rights are enshrined? Does the amendment refer to the individual
or to the state? What types of weapons are regulated—handguns?

Kalashnikovs? Grenade launchers?[17] And how should we decide? Are we restricted by the original intent of the framers, and if we are, how can we securely know this intent? Or do the words take on a meaning of their own, irrespective of their original intent? The latter position is sometimes called "pragmatism"; it claims that it is "both wise and appropriate to change constitutional norms to serve modern needs."[18] Pragmatism is this same process that allows students to find ever-new meaning in literary texts, whether those by Homer or by Hemingway. Because readers always bring their own experiences to the act of interpretation, they will always find new meanings in ancient texts. This we know from our own experiences: no matter how often we teach the biblical texts, our students every year find new interpretations.

Interpreting Divinely
Revealed Texts

INTERPRETING *biblical* texts adds another two layers of complexity. In some cases, religious communities have understood the Bible's proper interpretation to be revealed by divine intermediaries such as angels or inspired teachers. Scholars call this "revelatory exegesis."[19] This type of interpretation is already found in the Bible, when the second-century BCE book of Daniel interprets the late seventh- and early sixth-century prophecies of Jeremiah. The book of Daniel, although containing earlier material, is in its final form a response to the outrages of the Syrian Greek king Antiochus IV Epiphanes, whose defeat is commemorated in the Jewish festival of Hanukkah. Antiochus forbade central Jewish practices, such as circumcision and Sabbath observance, and he and some highly assimilated Jewish priests converted the Jerusalem Temple into a temple for Zeus. For other Jews, these actions contravened Jeremiah's prediction that the Babylonian king Nebuchadnezzar would conquer Judea (which he did in 586 BCE) and rule over the Judeans for seventy (Hebrew *shiv'im*) years (Jer 25:11). Then, Jeremiah predicted, there would be a grand restoration (Jer 29:10–14). Antiochus was not a grand restorer but a tyrant.

Enter the book of Daniel. (Like many biblical books, the book of

Daniel was not written by the sage to whom it is attributed.) When Daniel prays for guidance on this contradiction between ancient prophecy and current reality (Dan 9:2), the angel Gabriel (named angels, both Gabriel and Michael, appear in the Tanakh only in Daniel—one indication of the book's late date) explains that seventy years is not actually seventy years: "Seventy weeks [Hebrew *shavu'im shiv'im*] are decreed for your people and your holy city: to finish the transgression, to put an end to sin, and to atone for iniquity, to bring in everlasting righteousness, to seal both vision and prophet, and to anoint a most holy place" (Dan 9:24). "Seventy weeks" of years means 70 times 7 (since a week has 7 days), or 490 years; thus Jeremiah's prophecy gets a 420-year extension, from 70 years to 490 years, and so it can still be fulfilled.

This extension is based on a manipulation of Jeremiah's words. The Hebrew word for seventy is *shiv'im*, and pronounced this way, it is not ambiguous. But as noted above, Hebrew during this period was written with only consonants, so this word was written *shv'ym*. The same consonants with different vowels yields *shavu'im*, "weeks." Gabriel reads the Hebrew consonants twice—once as *shavu'im* (weeks) and once as *shiv'im* (seventy), yielding his novel interpretation through which 70 equals 490, an interpretation that only an angel can reveal.

The idea that angelic figures know the true meaning of scripture is not unique to Daniel. Jubilees, a text probably written in the second century BCE and thus near the time of Daniel, offers a similar approach. Jubilees presents itself as the words of the Angel of the Presence[20] to Moses, and this angel offers an authoritative interpretation of the first two biblical books, Genesis and part of Exodus. The angel's words constitute a "Second Law" that "amplifies and clarifies the first."[21] For example, Jubilees adds the creation of angels to Genesis 1–3:

For on the first day He created the heavens, which are above, and the
earth, and the waters and all of the spirits which minister before Him:
> the angels of the Presence,
>
> and the angels of sanctification,
>
> and the angels of the spirit of fire,
>
> and the angels of the spirit of the winds,
>
> and the angels of the spirit of the clouds and darkness and snow
> and hail and frost,
>
> and the angels of resoundings and thunder and lightning,
>
> and the angels of the spirits of cold and heat and winter and
> springtime and harvest and summer, and all of the spirits of
> His creatures which are in heaven and on earth.

Jubilees presents itself as revealed by an angel and thus claims that
angels were among the first things created.[22] As we see in our discussion of the Epistle to the Hebrews (Chapter 5), the author ensures
that Jesus is far superior to these angels, who were in early Jewish
literature getting an upgrade.

The idea that later figures offer correct interpretation is also
found in the Dead Sea Scrolls.[23] The Hebrew word *pesher* means
"interpretation," and the pesher literature from Qumran asserts
that ancient texts were actualized in the author's own time.[24] Pesher
Habakkuk interprets the first two chapters of Habakkuk, one of the
twelve minor (in the sense of short) prophets, as applicable to the
author's situation. Interpreting the end of Habakkuk 2:2 the pesher
reads, "When it says, 'so that with ease someone can read it,' this
refers to the Teacher of Righteousness [likely the founder of the
group] to whom God made known all the mysterious revelations of
his servants the prophets" (column 7, lines 3–5). According to this
passage, when Habakkuk uttered his prophecy in the late seventh
century BCE, he did not understand its meaning; only the Teacher

of Righteousness, centuries later, did. The pesher takes biblical verses wildly out of context in order to make them relevant to later readers.[25]

The New Testament makes similar moves when the followers of Jesus reinterpret ancient Jewish texts—turning them into the Bible "with Jesus." For example, Matthew 12:40 states, "For just as Jonah was three days and three nights in the belly of the sea monster, so for three days and three nights the Son of Man will be in the heart of the earth." Jonah the prophet (another book, like Daniel, ascribed to an ancient worthy) was not, several centuries earlier, thinking about Jesus's burial. That was not a message his original readers would have taken either. We return to what Jesus calls "the sign of Jonah" in Chapter 10.

Another example that fits the category of revelatory interpretation appears in the famous Sermon on the Mount. Here Jesus uses the words "You have heard that it was said to those of ancient times" to introduce his own interpretation of such sayings as "an eye for an eye" and "do not commit murder." Rabbinic commentary provides its own interpretations of these passages, as we see in Chapter 6.

These examples from Daniel, Jubilees, Pesher Habakkuk, and Matthew introduce a concern fundamental to our study: what a text *meant* versus what a text *means*.[26] Many biblical scholars seek to reconstruct the earliest form of a text and determine what it meant in its original context—for example, finding (what is closest to) the words uttered by the prophet Ezekiel and understanding how the exiled Judean community in sixth-century BCE Babylonia understood his words.

Other biblical scholars are interested in reception history, in seeing how texts are understood over time.[27] Sometimes these interpretations seem strange to us, even ad hoc. But reception is not always a free-for-all, such that interpreters make a text say anything they want.

Even Daniel's "creative philology"[28] in making 70 mean 490 follows a certain logic.

One scholar of Jewish biblical interpretation, James Kugel, outlines four principles of ancient Jewish exegesis that help explain Daniel's interpretive moves as well as how early Jewish communities understood their scripture:[29]

1. "The Bible is a fundamentally cryptic text." Thus, texts need not mean what they obviously seem to mean.

2. "Scripture constitutes one great Book of Instruction, and as such is a fundamentally *relevant* text." Even were a prophet speaking to his generation, he is not speaking only to his generation. Further, the text may, indeed must, be reinterpreted to remain relevant.

3. "Scripture is perfect and perfectly harmonious." Consequently, texts that appear to be contradictory are not; it is the interpreter's job to make them comport.

4. "All of Scripture is somehow divinely sanctioned, of divine provenance, or divinely inspired." Therefore scriptural language is not quotidian, human language. When a friend says, "I will meet you in seventy minutes," she expects you to be waiting in seventy minutes; but when God says through a prophet, "You will be restored in seventy years," that could mean 490 years.

These four principles characterizing early Jewish biblical interpretation from the second century BCE to the first century CE and continuing in many later Jewish readings[30] also characterize the New Testament, though that collection has an additional assumption: the scriptures of Israel are concerned with the life, death, and resurrection of Jesus.

JEWISH INTERPRETATIONS: TWO JEWS, THREE OPINIONS

AN OLD JEWISH joke proclaims, "two Jews, three opinions." In more mundane terms, the joke correctly indicates that Jewish interpretation is multivocal rather than univocal. We can literally see this appreciation for various interpretations in the Rabbinic Bible, a Tanakh surrounded by commentaries that often disagree with each other yet all live together on the same page.[31] This possibility is due to what Kugel has called the Bible's "omnisignificance."[32] Every detail of the text is meaningful: even seemingly quotidian differences in spelling are divinely intended, and passages that seem insignificant must convey deeper meaning.

Classical rabbinic literature expresses this principle in several ways. The best-known expression is *shiv'im panim latorah*, Hebrew for "The Torah has seventy face(t)s (of interpretation)."[33] The principle of omnisignificance is also found in the rabbinic explanation of Psalm 62:11 (62:12 Heb.), "One thing God has spoken; two things have I heard" (NJPS), which some rabbis interpret to mean, "One verse gives rise to several laws or meanings" (b. Sanhedrin 34a). The same talmudic passage interprets Jeremiah 23:29, "like a hammer that shatters rock" (NJPS), to mean, "Just as the hammer is divided into several sparks, so a single verse gives rise to several laws."[34] Each of these rabbinic interpretations expresses the Bible's omnisignificance.

Another central feature of Jewish biblical interpretation is that it has no single point or goal. As we will see, this approach contrasts sharply with Christian interpretation, which sees Jesus as a main theme of the Old Testament, even though he is never explicitly mentioned there.

Multiple views of a single text can also be found in Jewish translations. These ancient projects, whether Greek (most significantly the Septuagint) or the Aramaic targumim (singular: targum), were produced over several centuries and run the gamut from literal to expansive. For example, Targum Onkelos, a typically literal translation, renders Exodus 23:19 (cf. Exod 34:26; Deut 14:21)—"You shall not boil a kid in its mother's milk"—as "You shall not eat meat in milk," which reflects the rabbinic understanding of this injunction. The takeaway here is that Jews who observe the dietary laws or "keep kosher" will not eat cheeseburgers. Some targumic renderings are even more expansive. The targum to the Song of Songs takes this originally highly erotic book as a historical allegory of the love between God and Israel; the song's second verse, "Let him kiss me with the kisses of his mouth! / For your love is better than wine" (Song 1:2), is transformed into:

> Solomon the prophet said: Blessed be the name of the Lord, who by the hands of Moses the great scribe has given to us the Torah written on two stone tablets and the Six Orders of the Mishnah and the Talmud by oral recitation. And He would speak with us face to face as a man who kisses his friend because of the great love wherewith He loves us, more than seventy nations.

This targum reflects the thinning of the line between translation and exegesis.

Jewish communities living under Hellenistic and Roman rule also produced biblical interpretations. These include not only the Dead

Sea Scrolls but also "pseudepigrapha." A catchall term, "pseudepigrapha" takes its name from the Greek for "false writings," since several of these texts are ascribed to ancient worthies—Moses, Ezra, even Adam and Enoch—but the texts were written much later, in the first few centuries BCE and CE—around and after the time of Daniel. Jewish in origin, most of these texts were preserved and edited by Christians. The great Alexandrian sage Philo (ca. 20 BCE–ca. 50 CE) often interprets biblical texts in an allegorical fashion that would typify later Christianity, while the Jewish historian Josephus (37–ca. 100 CE), in retelling biblical stories in his multivolume *Antiquities of the Jews*, paraphrases, embellishes, or interprets them. We'll return to these writers throughout this book.

The earliest rabbinic texts are preserved from a later period, the third century CE, with the first being the Mishnah, a law-code of sorts compiled in the land of Israel. The Mishnah sometimes cites the Hebrew Bible and interprets it, as does the Tosefta, a slightly later, similar text. The Talmud is an extended commentary on the Mishnah, with many digressions. It takes two forms: the Talmud of the land of Israel, also imprecisely called the Jerusalem Talmud (the Yerushalmi), dates from about the fourth century CE; the longer and more important for later Jewish practice Babylonian Talmud (the Bavli) is from the sixth or seventh century. These rabbinic texts contain the first Jewish readings that directly counter Christian interpretations of the books both communities deem sacred.

The rabbinic period also saw the growth of midrash (plural: midrashim)—that is, elaborations on biblical passages. These commentaries, which do not exposit every biblical verse, often collect a variety of differing, even contradictory, explanations of the same word or phrase. Midrashim typically treat the text atomistically by focusing on single words rather than the broader story. Some even focus on a single letter. For example, the sixth-century midrash Genesis Rabbah

(1:10) speculates on why the Bible begins with the letter *bet*, the second letter of the Hebrew alphabet, which has this shape, ב:

> Rabbi Yonah said in the name of Rabbi Levi: Why was the world created with a "bet"? Just as a bet is closed on all sides and open in the front, so you are not permitted to say, "What is beneath? What is above? What came before? What will come after?" Rather from the day the world was created and after.[35]

The midrash looks to each detail, seen to be infused with meaning. At the same time, it forecloses questions about existence before creation. As we shall see in our discussion of Genesis 1 (Chapter 3), not all rabbis followed this idea. And as we shall also see in Chapter 3, John's magnificent prologue, "In the beginning was the Word . . . ," is a midrash on Genesis 1.

Only in the late first millennium CE does full-fledged commentary develop within Judaism. The greatest medieval commentator was Rashi, an acronym of **Ra**bbi Solomon (Hebrew **Sh**lomo) son of **I**saac, who lived in what is now France (1040–1105) and who compiled earlier interpretations into a brilliant *Reader's Digest* of rabbinic literature in a verse-by-verse fashion. Unlike classical rabbinic commentary, Rashi focused more on the broader story than on individual words. His method of interpretation is often called *peshat*, sometimes rendered "simple," though "contextual" is a better translation for this approach. Other medieval scholars were less dependent on classical rabbinic sources. Some compared Hebrew to Aramaic and to the Arabic of their Muslim-majority cultures, while others were influenced by emerging mystical traditions.

Beginning in the late thirteenth century, Jewish biblical interpretation was often divided into four categories, summarized through the acronym PaRDeS: *peshat*, the simple or contextual meaning;

remez, literally "hint," an allegorical meaning; *derash*, a homiletical meaning; and *sod*, a secret mystical meaning.[36] This term is based on a Persian loanword meaning "orchard" and its use in Song of Songs 4:13. The same Persian word, via Greek, gives us the English "paradise." As the following chapters illustrate, for many commentators, these four modes of interpretation were mutually enhancing rather than mutually exclusive.

Michael Fishbane's Song of Songs commentary, which is formatted like a page from the Rabbinic Bible, visually illustrates these approaches. Instead of offering different commentators on each page, Fishbane offers commentaries from these four main perspectives.[37] We quote selectively from his interpretations of Song 1:2, which opens "Oh, give me of the kisses of your mouth" (NJPS):

> *Peshat:* "The verb . . . articulates the speaker's intense longing for a kiss."
> *Derash:* "At the center of covenant love stands Mount Sinai, the classic site of a revelation whose words are like kisses."
> *Remez:* "'Kisses' boldly express the intensity of the longing for contact with God. . . . The kiss represents the desired infusion of divine reality into the human self—the yearning for spiritual transformation. It is a moment of meeting that silences speech."
> *Sod:* "The spiritual quest begins with great longing, marked by absence and otherness. . . . It wishes for contact with Divinity, symbolized by a kiss. Spiritually understood, the kiss is the co-infusion of breath or spirit between one being and another."

Therefore, "the reader is to consider each level of interpretation in its own right—and to read them interactively as multiple expressions of the human spirit."[38] We note again: such different modes in Jewish tradition are not mutually exclusive; they are mutually enhancing.

We conclude this section with what would have been a surprising statement had we opened with it—but it should now make sense. The Bible itself is less important in Judaism than the Bible *interpreted*. According to Nehemiah 8:8, when the Torah was read publicly as part of the restoration project in the fifth century BCE when the Jews returned to the land of Israel from Babylonian exile, "they read from the book, from the law [the Torah] of God, with interpretation. They gave the sense, so that the people understood the reading." Interpretation in Jewish tradition is an ongoing process, a partnership where humans interpret a divine text.

CHRISTIAN INTERPRETATION: ALIGNED WITH BELIEF

WHEREAS Jewish biblical interpretation tends to celebrate omnisignificance, this is less the case for the New Testament and subsequent Christian commentary, despite its own magnificent diversity. While the present book concentrates on Jewish interpretation before and after Jesus, similar volumes describe how Christian interpreters have, or should, read their Old Testament.[39]

Showing how the Old Testament foreshadows the New is central to Christian interpretation. In addition, maintaining correct doctrine was, and is, more important in Christianity than in Judaism. As Jesus tells Nicodemus, "Very truly, I tell you, no one can see the kingdom of God without being born from above" (John 3:3). The Greek word *anōthen*, here translated "from above," can also mean "anew" and "again," and it is from that last translation that we get the familiar expression "born-again Christian." Nicodemus, identified by John as a ruler of the Pharisees, takes the meaning "again" and asks how he might crawl back into his mother's womb, for how else would one be "born again"? Jesus, however, intends to mean "from above." One is not born into the new movement as one would be born to a Jewish, Egyptian, or Roman parent. Identity is, for the followers of Jesus, defined by belief, not by parentage and so not by ethnicity.

This example from John's Gospel, one of John's many plays on

words, shows not only the potential for language to be misunderstood but also one major way in which the movement of Christ-
followers that later became Christianity diverged from what we know
as Judaism. Neither Paul nor the Gospels use the term "Christianity,"
just as neither Paul nor the Gospel authors knew they were writing
a "New Testament." They were writing to help create and maintain
a community that, in various ways, understood Jesus of Nazareth to
be divine. They were writing to a community brought together by an
emerging set of beliefs, even as they were attempting to standardize
those beliefs.

But Jews were not then, or ever, simply defined by a belief system.
Jews also speak of having a common ancestry traceable to the patriarchs Abraham, Isaac, and Jacob; they claim Hebrew as a common
language and the land of Israel as a homeland; thus Jews, whether
they are of Asian, African, European, Latin American, or any other
geographic origin, are like a single ethnic group or a nationality.[40]
People within such a group can disagree and still maintain membership in the group. No matter how much US citizens disagree over
political issues—and we do disagree!—at the end of the day, we are
all still US citizens. That same point holds for Jews, who do not have
major problems with most alternative readings of scripture. In Judaism, orthopraxy, what one does, is more important than orthodoxy,
what one believes.[41] There are Jewish atheists; technically, however,
"Christian atheist" would be an oxymoron.

If one enters a movement by belief, by being born from above,
disagreement is a greater problem, and thus scriptural interpretation
is more likely to be constrained. If one enters a group by belief, one
also leaves by belief. Christianity therefore developed creeds to as-
sure that its members would all hold the same major beliefs. Otherwise put: orthodoxy, correct belief, is paramount in Christianity. We
have seen this concern for correct interpretation in Luke's story of

Jesus, incognito, meeting two of his disciples on the road to Emmaus. The two, aware of Jesus's death, are despondent. The stranger on the road then "interpreted to them the things about himself in all the scriptures" (Luke 24:27).

The New Testament itself admits that its presentations are both selective and open to multiple interpretations. The Gospel of Luke opens with the observation that others have attempted to tell the story of Jesus, but this Gospel is going to do so accurately and in order (Luke 1:3). Indeed, even having four Gospels instead of harmonizing them into one admits a kind of multiplicity. The Second Epistle of Peter (like Daniel and Jonah, a text probably not written by the figure to whom it is ascribed) says regarding Paul's letters, "There are some things in them hard to understand, which the ignorant and unstable twist to their own destruction, as they do the other scriptures" (2 Pet 3:16). For this author, Paul's letters have scriptural status, and not all agree on what they mean. To this day, debates continue over what Paul meant, whether he changed his mind or displayed remarkable consistency, whether he wrote to specific congregations only or to all followers of Jesus, and so on.

Christians, like Jews, also debate matters of translation. Here are three examples of Christian translations based on theological reasoning, two from antiquity and one from today's headlines. First, in a parable about a tenacious widow and an uncaring judge, Jesus has the widow insist, "*ekdikēson me* against my opponent" (Luke 18:3). Almost all English translations have the widow saying "grant me justice," but the Greek verb asks not for "justice" but for "vengeance," as in the famous phrase, "Vengeance is mine . . . says the Lord" (Rom 12:19, quoting Deut 32:35). Translators were uncomfortable having a morally problematic heroine in a parable or having readers think asking for vengeance was okay, so they modified the original text to comport with their own beliefs.

Second, translators of the parable of the Friend at Midnight betray a similar discomfort with Jesus's words. The parable describes a man who requests from his friend, in the middle of the night, three loaves of bread for a visitor. It concludes with the notice that even though the sleepy friend "will not get up and give him anything because he is his friend, at least because of his *anaideia* he will get up and give him whatever he needs" (Luke 11:8). The Greek term clearly means "shamelessness," but translators from the patristic period (that is, the time of the church fathers) onward, not wanting to commend such behavior, have rendered the Greek "persistence."[42]

The most recent example of theological concern is the 2019 papal approval of a new translation of the "Our Father" prayer that replaces the famous line "lead us not into temptation" with "do not let us fall into temptation." For the Vatican, the new translation avoids the suggestion that "Our Father" would lead his children into temptation (see Jas 1:13); that would be Satan's role. The Greek could also be translated "do not bring us to the test," which would make better sense of the prayer, since in the Bible God does "test" people's fidelity. For example, in Genesis 22:2, God "tests" Abraham by commanding him to sacrifice his son.

Ancient and medieval Christians formulated similar maps of levels of meaning in scripture parallel to the Jewish fourfold typology described above—in fact, Jewish interpreters may have based their fourfold methods on Christian interpretations. Although most interpreters agreed on the need for the literal sense, a variety of other, "fuller" senses emerged: the moral sense, the anagogical sense, the typological sense, the allegorical sense, and so forth.[43] Each of these so-called fuller senses (Latin *sensus plenior*) was typically privileged above the literal sense. Already in 2 Corinthians 3:12–16, Paul writes that Jews are unable to understand their own scriptures. Adducing the notice in Exodus 34:33–35 that Moses wore a veil in order not to frighten the people because his face shone after speaking with God, Paul states that Moses "put a veil over his face to keep the people of Israel from gazing at the end of the glory that was being set aside" (2 Cor 3:13) and affirms, "But their minds were hardened. Indeed, to this very day, when they hear the reading of the old covenant [the phrase can be translated "old testament"; the reference here is to the Torah], that same veil is still there, since only in Christ is it set aside" (3:14). Paul then doubles down: "Indeed, to this very day, whenever Moses [i.e., the Torah] is read, a veil lies over their [i.e., Jews who do not believe in the Christ] minds; but when one turns to the Lord [i.e., Jesus], the veil is removed" (3:15–16). The literal reading, or any reading that does not lead to the Christ, is therefore at best incomplete.

Expanding upon the *peshat* or simple or literal reading, a form of allegorical interpretation known as "typology" shows how some followers of Jesus understood the antecedent scriptures. Typological readings propose that earlier texts offer models, types, or first drafts of what comes to fulfillment with the Christ. For example, Paul reads Adam as, literally, "a type [Greek *typos*] of the one who was to come" (Rom 5:14), and the coming one is the Christ. For Paul, Adam, the first man, brought sin and death into the world; his antitype, the Christ, brings forgiveness and life. We return to diverse readings of Adam and Eve in Chapter 4. Similarly, Jonah's three days in the belly of the fish, the focus of Chapter 10, came to be seen as a type or prefiguration of the Christ, who spent three days in the tomb. The New Testament text that makes the greatest use of typology is the Epistle to the Hebrews, as we'll see in Chapter 5.

The *derash* or homiletical meaning finds its counterpart in Christian concern for a moral interpretation. Here Christians and Jews find some common ground, although the Talmud insists that this type of interpretation cannot lose its connection to the *peshat* (b. Shabbat 63a). A *derash* today might, for example, interpret the story of Abraham's initial sojourn in Egypt (Gen 12)—where he instructs his wife to say she is his sister so that the Egyptians will not kill him—as an example of human trafficking. A *derash* in the New Testament, here one that resembles the *remez* or allegorical reading, would be Paul's interpretation in Galatians 4 of Sarah and Hagar as representing two covenants: Hagar is Mount Sinai, in the wilderness, and in slavery, whereas Sarah, the "mother above," represents the gentile followers of Jesus who do not practice those rituals (understood as enslavement) that mark Jews as distinct from gentiles, such as circumcision. Here, however, Paul has detached the meaning from the literal story.

Finally, the *sod* or secret teaching relates to the Christian concern for the anagogical interpretation. This Christian reading strategy comes from the Greek term *anagoge*, meaning "climb" or "ascent," and it suggests an interpretation that relates to salvation. The connection between *sod* and *anagoge* is not exact, but the two modes function on the same mystical, rather than mundane, level. Daniel's angelic revelations are part of this category as is the Qumran pesher literature, and it extends to the Jewish mystical tradition most familiar from the medieval Kabbalah. The same approach appears in the New Testament. For example, Ephesians 3:3–6 explains how gentiles join the covenant community: "And how the mystery was made known to me by revelation. . . . In former generations this mystery was not made known to humankind, as it has now been revealed to his holy apostles and prophets by the Spirit: that is, the Gentiles have become fellow heirs."

While both the followers of Jesus and the rabbinic tradition on occasion take texts out of context and use them as prooftexts (see the next chapter), it is often the case that knowing the context adds nuance to the verse. According to the Gospel of Matthew, Herod the king seeks to kill Jesus, who, he has heard, is the newborn "King of the Jews." He orders the massacre of all the children of Bethlehem, from infants to age two. Speaking of this "Slaughter of the Innocents," Matthew states:

> Then was fulfilled what had been spoken through the prophet Jeremiah:
>> "A voice was heard in Ramah,
>>> wailing and loud lamentation,
>> Rachel weeping for her children;
>>> she refused to be consoled, because they are no more."
>> (Matt 2:17–18)

Matthew is quoting Jeremiah 31:15, a chapter to which we return at the end of the book.

Jeremiah's context indicates that the verse responds to the Babylonian exile. Rachel, the beloved wife of the patriarch Jacob and the mother of that first Joseph, had died in childbirth and was buried in Ramah, on the outskirts of Jerusalem. In the next two verses, Jeremiah offers comfort to Rachel and so to his readers in exile:

> Thus says the LORD:
> Keep your voice from weeping,
>> and your eyes from tears;
> for there is a reward for your work,
>> says the LORD:
>> they shall come back from the land of the enemy;
> there is hope for your future,
>> says the LORD:
>> your children shall come back to their own country.
> (Jer 31:16–17)

For Jews, the concern of return to the land of Israel surfaces. Christian readers might see this next verse as a promise of the resurrection.

At times, Jewish and Christian readings can complement each other; at times, one community adopts a reading that the other might find impossible. Similar reading strategies can yield substantially different conclusions, since all interpretation depends on a particular starting point, either in Jewish life or in Christian doctrine. If we could better understand how Jews and Christians came to understand the same texts in different ways, we would be in a better position to understand both traditions, and to see the often contingent nature of what each tradition teaches.

CHAPTER 2

The Problem and Promise of Prophecy

PROPHECY

CHRISTIAN evangelists have told us, multiple times, that if we correctly understood the scriptures of Israel, we would see how they all point to Jesus. It is true that when reading these scriptures in light of what Jesus did and said, and of how his followers remembered him, these texts do seem to point to Jesus. Reading the scriptures of Israel retrospectively, believers concluded that Jesus fulfilled prophecies, including texts that were not, until this retrospective reading, understood to be prophetic. For example, Jesus asks his disciples on the Emmaus Road, "Was it not necessary that the Messiah should suffer these things and then enter into his glory?" (Luke 24:26). They would not have previously read their scripture as having made this claim; in the light of Jesus's suffering and death, however, the claim becomes obvious for them. Such after-the-fact reading does not make the conclusion wrong; rather, it makes it contingent on a prior set of beliefs. The person beginning with the view that Jesus is the culmination of the scriptures of Israel, and that all those scriptures point to him, will find confirmation of the view. The person who lacks such a prior belief is unlikely to be convinced by such christological readings.

Understanding how prophecy was understood in ancient Israel and on through Second Temple Judaism (the Second Temple was completed ca. 515 BCE and destroyed by the Romans in 70 CE) serves as important background for understanding both Jewish and Christian interpretation of Israel's scriptures. What some people read as prophecy, others did not; what some people saw as prophecy fulfilled, others saw as false claims or incomplete fulfillment.

Diverse groups can read the same texts—biblical and otherwise—in different ways, with their logical conclusions based on their diverse starting points. Jews and Christians need not agree with each other in terms of biblical understanding, but they should be able to see the logic in both sets of interpretations. Seeing this logic can help all of us develop mutual respect rather than mutual disdain. This chapter moves from prophecy to prooftexting to polemics and concludes with possibilities—especially the possibility of learning to respect the readings of others.

We begin with prophecy. The Gospel writers and Paul, much like the authors of the Qumran pesher texts, regarded the biblical prophets as conveying information about their own time. They understood Isaiah or Habakkuk to be speaking of events fulfilled centuries later.

Contemporary biblical scholars understand these texts differently. We find that biblical prophets, like their ancient Near Eastern counterparts, did not predominantly predict events of the far future. Rather, they mediated between the divine and human worlds with messages for the people of their own times.[1] Many of their "predictions" are better understood as warnings to their contemporaries that if they did not improve their ways, they would be punished. The fulfillment of such proclamations is typically conditional, as several prophecies make explicit. For example, Isaiah 1:19–20 tells its eighth-century Judean audience:

> If you are willing and obedient,
>   you shall eat the good of the land;
> but if you refuse and rebel,

> you shall be devoured by the sword;
>   for the mouth of the LORD has spoken.

For the ancient prophets, like Isaiah and Jeremiah, threats were short-term. People in ancient Israel would not much worry if they were warned, "Straighten up now, or in seven hundred years you will be punished." Nor would they find much comfort in being told by Isaiah that centuries later, a savior would end poverty, sickness, and oppression. By then, their children, and their children's children, would be long dead.

However, much of the Tanakh's prophecy about the future is vague. For that reason, its fulfillment can be seen to take various forms and apply to various dates. For example, Zechariah 9:9, from the postexilic period, predicts:

> Rejoice greatly, O daughter Zion!
>   Shout aloud, O daughter Jerusalem!
> Lo, your king comes to you;
>   triumphant and victorious is he,
> humble and riding on a donkey,
>   on a colt, the foal of a donkey.

This passage offers no clue about when this king is to come, whether immediately, sometime in the prophet's lifetime, or centuries or even millennia later. Terms such as "in days to come" (e.g., Isa 2:2) and "on that day" (Zech 14:9) are open to multiple interpretations. While Zechariah's original audience would have heard a statement that related to them personally, future readers, generation after generation, found a fulfillment of the verse—some with Jesus, some without. Anyone at any time could enter Jerusalem on a donkey, and that person's supporters will see fulfillment of the prediction.

Matthew 21:1–5 (cf. Mark 11:1–11; Luke 19:28–40; John 12:12–19), reading the Bible with Jesus, finds the fulfillment of Zechariah 9:9 in Jesus's triumphal entry into Jerusalem:

> When they had come near Jerusalem and had reached Bethphage, at the Mount of Olives, Jesus sent two disciples, saying to them, "Go into the village ahead of you, and immediately you will find a donkey tied, and a colt with her; untie them and bring them to me. If anyone says anything to you, just say this, 'The Lord needs them.' And he will send them immediately." This took place to fulfill what had been spoken through the prophet, saying,
>
> > "Tell the daughter of Zion,
> > Look, your king is coming to you,
> > > humble, and mounted on a donkey,
> > > and on a colt, the foal of a donkey."

Perhaps Jesus planned his entry in light of Zechariah 9:9. And perhaps Zechariah was influenced by 1 Kings 1:33, 38, in which Solomon, the son of David, signals his claim to the throne by riding on his father's mule.

An example of a postevent reading occurs in John's version of what is known as the "cleansing of the Temple." In the Synoptic Gospels, the scene occurs during the last week of Jesus's life, and it is this incident that sparks the Temple leaders' plot to silence him. John places the event early in the Gospel, in chapter 2, right after Jesus changes water into wine at Cana. John reports: "Making a whip of cords, he [Jesus] drove all of them out of the temple, both the sheep and the cattle. He also poured out the coins of the money changers and overturned their tables. He told those who were selling the doves, 'Take these things out of here! Stop making my Father's house a marketplace!'" (John 2:15–16). The allusion is probably to Zechariah again, this time to the conclusion of the book, which the NRSV and most other translations read, "And there shall no longer be traders in the house of the LORD of hosts on that day" (Zech 14:21b). The Hebrew and Greek do not use the common term for "traders" but read "Canaanites," who in their later incarnation as Phoenicians served as merchants; hence the standard translation. However, the original reference may well have been to actual Canaanites, people representing practices that Zechariah found antithetical to Yahwism.[2]

In retrospect, Jesus's followers make another connection. John's next verse records, "His disciples remembered that it was written, 'Zeal for your house will consume me'" (John 2:17). The citation is to Psalm 69:9 (69:10 Heb.; 68:10 LXX), to which we return in Chapter 11. The psalmist, speaking in the past tense in both the original Hebrew and in the Greek translation, laments that the people are not showing appropriate respect for the holy site: "It is zeal for your house that has consumed me." John takes the verb as a future tense and reads the verse as predictive, as anticipating what Jesus will do, five hundred years later. On the other hand, as our more conservative Christian students sometimes remind us, perhaps John had a version of Zechariah that had a future-tense verb. The scriptures of Israel did not yet have a standardized text in the first century CE.

Jesus's followers were not the only group that saw scriptural prophecies as being fulfilled in their own time, centuries after they were uttered. The Dead Sea Scrolls express similar beliefs, as the pesher texts discussed in the previous chapter make clear. The most famous of these, and among the first scrolls published, is Pesher Habakkuk, which not only sees the Teacher of Righteousness as the only one capable of understanding the ancient prophet but also regards the Chaldeans (Babylonians) of Habakkuk to refer to the contemporary Roman Empire.[3]

Other early first-millennium CE Jewish writers also believed that biblical prophetic texts were fulfilled in their own times. For example, several rabbinic sources take Balaam's prophecy in Numbers

24:17b to refer to Simon bar Kosiba, the leader of the Jewish revolt against Rome in 132–135 CE:

> a star [Hebrew *kochav*] shall come out of Jacob,
>> and a scepter shall rise out of Israel;
> it shall crush the borderlands of Moab,
>> and the territory of all the Shethites.

One tradition records that the great Rabbi Akiva, martyred in this rebellion, changed the leader's name from Bar Kosiba to Bar Kochba to connect him to Balaam's star, *kochav*.[4]

Later Jewish interpreters determined that Balaam's prophecy concerned the coming messiah. Maimonides (1138–1204), the great medieval Jewish teacher, followed earlier commentators in taking the star and the scepter as referring both to King David, who at Balaam's time had not yet been born, and to the messiah.[5] Christians, in turn, see Balaam's prophecy as referring to Jesus. The Epistle to the Hebrews picks up the scepter language in paraphrasing Psalm 45:6 (45:7 Heb.): "Your throne, O God, endures forever and ever. / Your royal scepter is a scepter of equity." Hebrews 1:8 reads, "But of the Son [Jesus] he says, / 'Your throne, O God, is forever and ever, / and the righteous scepter is the scepter of your kingdom.'" Even more explicit is Justin Martyr (ca. 100–165), to whom we shall return in debates over the virginal conception. Justin writes that the Christ "should arise like a star from the seed of Abraham. Moses [i.e., the Torah] showed beforehand when he said, 'A star shall arise from Jacob, and a leader from Israel'" (*Dialogue* 106).

The ongoing interpretation of prophetic texts exemplifies the distinction between what a text *meant* and what a text *means*. As we shall see throughout this book, the two can be quite different. One way to generate that difference is through prooftexting.

Prooftexts

THE TERM "prooftext" and the verb "prooftexting" exemplify Antonio's line "The devil can cite Scripture for his purpose" in Shakespeare's *The Merchant of Venice* (a play relevant for our next topic, polemics). Any biblical text can be manipulated to prove any point, and any text—even one not recited by a prophet—can be taken as "prophetic." The problem with such reading is that often the predictive aspect is apparent only after the event is "fulfilled." We see this approach with works like *The Bible Code* that use computer technology to find hidden messages in the Hebrew wording. With the right programs, and by ignoring all evidence to the contrary, the Bible can be found to have predicted the assassination of John F. Kennedy, the terrorist attacks of 9/11, and pretty much anything else. These ventures, which are sometimes used to persuade both Jews and Christians of the Bible's divine origin, are theologically retrograde. They presume that God is a gamester, a trickster who does not give warning of tragedy but sits back and in effect says, "I told you so."[6] Both Jews and Christians can do more profound theology.

Examples of prooftexting, based on retrospective readings, appear in the New Testament. Here are two examples, one from the Gospel of Matthew and one from Paul's Epistle to the Galatians. Reading a nonprophetic verse as predicting the future,[7] Matthew 2 records that King Herod sought to kill the baby Jesus, a rival king. Warned in a dream (how appropriate for Joseph son of Jacob!) to escape Bethlehem, Joseph takes Mary and the baby and decamps to safety in Egypt. When Herod dies, Joseph receives a dream alerting him that he can return home. Matthew then comments, "This was to fulfill what had been spoken by the Lord through the prophet, 'Out of Egypt I have called my son'" (Matt 2:15). The quotation comes from Hosea 11:1, where it refers to the exodus of Israel, an event in the past. An originally historical recollection becomes, for Matthew, a prediction, and the story of Israel becomes, for Matthew, the story of Jesus.

In Paul's case, the apostle is attempting to explain to this gentile congregation that they should not practice male circumcision or otherwise follow the scriptural laws that kept Jews distinct in antiquity. He therefore needs to cite the scriptures of Israel, which command such practices, in order to show that the practices do not apply to gentiles. In Galatians 3:13 Paul writes, "Christ redeemed us from the curse of the law by becoming a curse for us—for it is written, 'Cursed is everyone who hangs on a tree.'" The citation is to Deuteronomy 21:23 where the original context is capital punishment. According to Deuteronomy, the corpse of an executed person must not "remain all night upon the tree; you shall bury him that same day, for anyone hung on a tree is under God's curse." The verse is, first, not a prophecy but part of a law collection. In addition, Jews at the time of Jesus, who faced crucifixion not infrequently, did not consider victims of this horrific torture to be "cursed by God." To the contrary, they regarded the condemned as victims of injustice if not also as martyrs. We see this approach taken by the Jewish historian Josephus in his *Antiquities of the Jews*, where he describes the crucifixion of eight hundred Pharisees by Alexander Jannaeus, who "did one of the most barbarous actions in the world to [his Pharisaic opponents]; for as he was feasting with his concubines, in the sight of all the city, he ordered about eight hundred of them to be crucified; and while they were living, he ordered the throats of their children and wives to be cut before their eyes" (13.380).

Nor, finally, did Jews consider the Torah to be a curse. But for Paul, writing to gentile Jesus-followers who sought to submit to halakhah (Jewish law), following the Torah and in effect attempting to become Jews via circumcision would be a curse. Paul needed a prooftext to show his gentile converts that they should not engage in Jewish practice; he found it in Deuteronomy 21:23. We return to the question of what the scriptures of Israel say about gentiles in the messianic age in our Conclusion.

Prooftexting, especially when it takes the form of citing verses, often out of context, in order to mandate a certain practice or belief, has received criticism from some Christian writers, who find the practice "unremittingly negative"[8] and even "truly nefarious" and "intentionally deceptive"[9] because it reflects "pulling an authoritative text out of its original context to impose upon it a meaning that advances the interpreter's thesis."[10] Others defend prooftexting by noting how essential it is to the New Testament's interpretation of the Old Testament.[11]

Although we have no interest in participating in this internal Christian debate, we want to be clear: from both Jewish and scholarly perspectives we find no problem with prooftexting—quoting a biblical text to prove something. Prooftexts are so fundamental to Judaism that an important scholarly publication is called *Prooftexts: A Journal of Jewish Literary History*. Prooftexts, central to the New Testament and to the Judaisms of that period, anchor practice and belief in texts that would become the Bible. Prooftexting could be a fifth principle added to Kugel's four approaches of Jewish exegesis.[12]

We illustrate prooftexting with a rabbinic example concerning the grace after meals. The obligation to recite this prayer appears in Tosefta Berachot 6:1; the later Babylonian Talmud (Berachot 48b) offers the following prooftext: "The Sages taught in a Tosefta: From where is it derived that Grace after Meals is from the Torah? As it is stated: 'And you shall eat and be satisfied, and you shall bless the Lord, your God, for the good land that He has given you'" (Deut 8:10).[13] The sages quote a nonlegal speech from Deuteronomy that describes how Israel must act upon entering the land. In Deuteronomy, "And you shall eat and be satisfied and bless" is descriptive rather than prescriptive, but the rabbis take it as legislative: you must bless God by reciting the grace after meals.

In some cases, prooftexts are much more tenuous. For example, the previously mentioned Jewish prohibition against mixing milk and meat is derived from the prohibition of boiling a young goat in its mother's milk.[14] For an example with greater connection to Christian concerns, the rabbis find in Exodus "proof" of the resurrection of the dead. Playing with fine points of Hebrew grammar, Rabbi Judah the Prince notes that Exodus 15:1a, "Then Moses and the Israelites sang [*yashir*] this song to the LORD," uses a verb form that typically refers to the future, "will sing," and concludes, "Thus we are instructed that the resurrection of the dead can be derived from the Torah."[15] Who knew?

Prooftexts rarely appear in the scriptures of Israel.[16] Much more common than quotations of biblical verses are allusions to earlier texts with phrases such as "as is written."[17] For example, 2 Kings 14:6 describes why the Judean king Amaziah does not kill the children of those who killed his father: "But he did not put to death the children of the murderers; according to what is written in the book of the law of Moses, where the LORD commanded, 'The parents shall not be put to death for the children, or the children be put to death for the parents; but all shall be put to death for their own sins.'" The quotation is Deuteronomy 24:16, "Parents shall not be put to death for their children, nor shall children be put to death for their parents; only for their own crimes may persons be put to death."[18] But unlike many of the cases of prooftexting discussed in the following chapters, this citation of Deuteronomy by 2 Kings understands the biblical verse in a straightforward fashion.

The Jewish scholar Michael Marmur highlights the significance of quoting earlier texts, including prooftexting, within Jewish tradition. He notes: "To quote as a Jew is to speak. To speak as a Jew is to quote," and "Quotation both generates and preserves Tradition in general. In quoting, one places oneself within a tradition or network of traditions." Marmur offers three main functions of quotations: "they provide a basis of authority; they stimulate and amplify the text; and they also fulfill an aesthetic and ornamental role."[19] In other words, prooftexting should be appreciated, not criticized, for using creative philology and other methods to anchor the author's present in the authoritative past.[20]

We can appreciate how prooftexting makes sense to those who hold a particular belief, since prooftexting is always retrospective. We should also appreciate how different communities, with different starting points, find different messages in the same texts.

POLEMICS

POLEMIC—"A controversial argument; a strong verbal or written attack on a person, opinion, doctrine, etc."[21]—is a fundamental feature in both the Tanakh and the New Testament, and in the history of interactions between Jews and Christians it has at times had dire consequences. The present book notes numerous polemics, but it also seeks to overcome the venom that turns biblical material toxic.

The Tanakh directs many polemics against Israelites who practice polytheism and idolatry. Isaiah 44:9 declares, "All who make idols are nothing, and the things they delight in do not profit." The polemic continues when the chapter mocks the construction of such images:

> He cuts down cedars [to be used as fuel]. . . . Part of it he takes and
> warms himself; he kindles a fire and bakes bread. Then he makes a god
> and worships it, makes it a carved image and bows down before it.
> Half of it he burns in the fire; over this half he roasts meat, eats it and is
> satisfied. . . . The rest of it he makes into a god, his idol, bows down to it
> and worships it; he prays to it and says, "Save me, for you are my god!"
> (44:14–17)

The unit concludes by stating about anyone who would worship such idols that "a deluded mind has led him astray" (44:20). We suspect, were there a Canaanite Anti-Defamation League, they would protest such claims as bigoted polemic. We have heard these verses deployed against Roman Catholics, for whom art can function as a focus of prayer, and Hindus, who depict their gods through artwork. We find such deployments equally unhealthy.

The main goal of polemic is to persuade. In some cases, the invective is internal: it seeks to persuade those already in a community to adhere to a particular set of beliefs or practices and so helps to strengthen communal identity. It also attempts to preclude alternative views. For example, John Chrysostom (ca. 347–407), whom we discuss below, addressed his caustic polemics primarily to Christians who found certain Jewish practices appealing.[22] At other times polemic is addressed to an outside group with the intent to persuade them to switch their position.

The Tanakh employs both explicit and implicit polemics.[23] The explicit ones populate the prophetic literature, as the speakers condemn beliefs and behaviors they deem inappropriate. With implicit polemic, we need to decide whether a particular passage was written with polemical intent. For example, some scholars believe that the book of Ruth, where Ruth the Moabite is welcomed into the Israelite community, was written as polemic against the policies of Ezra and Nehemiah, which exclude foreigners from the community.[24] Implicit polemic also appears in medieval Jewish commentaries; for example, many scholars think that Rashi's comments on Genesis 1 react to the First Crusade's attempts to recapture the "Holy Land" from Muslims.[25] Rashi writes:

> For should the peoples of the world say to Israel, "You are robbers, because you took by force the lands of the seven nations of Canaan," Israel may reply to them, "All the earth belongs to the Holy One, blessed be He; He created it and gave it to whom He pleased. When

He willed He gave it to them, and when He willed He took it from
them and gave it to us."[26]

For Rashi, the land belonged not to Muslims or to Christians, but to
God, who had given it, for a period of time, to the Jews. Rashi and
his fellow Jewish commentators, especially in Europe, had to present
this idea in a veiled fashion, lest they be persecuted by the dominant
Christian population.

Christianity emerged from Jewish practice and belief, and rabbinic Judaism took shape, in places, in competition with Christian
claims. In the process of self-definition, each side directed polemic
against the other.[27] These polemics were honed especially during
two periods: the emergent period of Christianity, when the need for
self-definition was central; and the Middle Ages, when Jews resisted
Christian pressure to convert.

The earliest polemic found in the New Testament took various
forms, most famously the derogatory depiction of Pharisees and
other Jews in the Gospels. But non-Messianic Jews (that is, Jews who
did not view Jesus as the Messiah) are not the New Testament's only
polemical object. Jesus tells a Samaritan woman, "You worship what
you do not know; we worship what we know, for salvation is from
the Jews" (John 4:22). For John, the "Jews" may have the wrong belief, but at least they, unlike the Samaritans, have the correct text.

John, the author of the book of Revelation, threatens rival leaders,
viscerally. He accuses the church in Thyatira: "But I have this against
you: you tolerate that woman Jezebel, who calls herself a prophet
and is teaching and beguiling my servants to practice fornication
and to eat food sacrificed to idols. . . . Beware, I am throwing her
on a bed, and those who commit adultery with her I am throwing
into great distress, unless they repent of her doings; and I will strike
her children dead" (Rev 2:20, 22–23a). Turning his polemical tone

upon the Roman Empire, John offers, "Babylon the great, mother of whores and of earth's abominations," a description that shortens to the more-familiar "whore of Babylon" (Rev 17:5). John is not writing to Rome; John is writing to fellow believers against what he finds to be internal and external threats.

It is uncertain when Jews began to respond to claims that Jesus was the Messiah, whether in writings predating Constantine's adoption of Christianity in the early fourth century,[28] or in the Babylonian Talmud, composed in a largely Zoroastrian environment where anti-Christian polemic was less of a threat to the writers' safety.[29] We can only tentatively isolate anti-Christian polemic in early Jewish texts.[30]

Polemic as identity formation is found when a weaker group polemicizes against a stronger one—a frequent case in post-Constantinian Jewish polemics against Christianity.[31] A number of our Jewish friends, observing that they have never heard anti-Christian polemic in a synagogue, conclude that therefore Judaism has no anti-Christian polemic. They are wrong. The Talmud makes a few quite negative comments about Jesus, as do several medieval commentators. However, since most Jews have never read the Talmud (just as most Christians have never read the writings of the church fathers or the complete writings of Martin Luther) and since from the early Middle Ages, when Christians burned Talmuds by the cartload, the texts have been censored, such negative comments are not widely known.[32]

Anti-Christian polemic can be bold, as exemplified in the medieval *Toledot Yeshu*, "The Life Story of Jesus,"[33] which ranges from portraying Mary as seduced by a Roman soldier named Ben Panthera to having Jesus perform miracles because he learned the pronunciation of God's ineffable name. Sometimes this polemic was conveyed during formal disputations, where Jews and Christians publicly argued over central issues of their faiths, including many of the verses that we survey in the following chapters.[34] The most famous of these were the Barcelona Disputation of 1263[35] and the Tortosa Disputation of 1412–1415, the result of a serious missionizing campaign of the medieval church. In all such disputations, the odds were stacked against the Jews. Win and face exile; lose and face worse.

Jews never had the political power to initiate disputations, but they did write polemical literature. These tracts, aimed internally, were composed in Hebrew. In the twelfth century, *The Book of the Covenant*[36] by Joseph Kimchi and *Milchamot Adonai* (*The Wars* [*for the Sake*] *of God*) by Jacob ben (son of) Reuben center on what the two authors consider Christian misinterpretation of the Tanakh. This genre finds its culmination in the *Nitzachon Yashan* (*Old Book of Polemic*), a widely circulated book from thirteenth-century Germany that begins with antichristological interpretations of almost 150 passages from the Tanakh, followed by a critique of the Gospels. Its modern editor characterizes the *Nitzachon* as "Jewish disputation in its most aggressive mode."[37] Given that few Jews read Latin and thus few had direct access to the New Testament, the texts and arguments the *Nitzachon* cites are likely from what the Jews heard from neighbors and officials. The following chapters offer more examples of polemic—from both sides.

Whether polemic has any value remains an open question. One of the leading intellectuals of the second half of the twentieth century, Michel Foucault, argued that polemic has no value. In an interview from a month before he died, he insists (polemically!), "Has anyone ever seen a new idea come out of a polemic?" Foucault called polemics "a parasitic figure on discussion and an obstacle to the search for the truth." He viewed polemics as a power game that obstructs the ability to find the truth since the polemicist confronts "not a partner in search for the truth but an adversary, an enemy who is wrong . . . and whose very existence constitutes a threat."[38] The viability of his argument can be demonstrated by some polemical Jewish and Christian texts. In the famous Paris Disputation in 1240, Christians called on rabbis to defend the Talmud against charges of blaspheming the Christ; after Christian judges declared their argument unconvincing, Christians seized and destroyed thousands of Jewish books. Ironically, in this case the Christian judges were correct; the Talmud does, in its unexpurgated form, defame Jesus.[39]

Some critics argue that polemics are "just words," and thus we should not judge harshly polemics of the like of John Chrysostom, who, depicting the Jews as drunk and sick, called them "most miserable of all men" and accused them, saying, "You did slay Christ, you did lift violent hands against the Master, you did spill his precious blood. That is why you have no chance for atonement, excuse or defense."[40] We disagree[41] and instead concur with James Parkes, an Anglican priest who found Chrysostom to have offered "the most horrible and violent denunciations of Judaism to be found in the writings of a Christian theologian."[42] Words matter, and words can do harm.

But polemics can sometimes be constructive.[43] Averil Cameron notes that some polemics help sharpen arguments and consolidate knowledge.[44] Polemics also tell us what is at stake for the individual or group issuing the invectives. We might distinguish among different types of polemics, such as discussion, dispute, and controversy,[45] to determine whether there is constructive material. Polemic gives us stereotype, exaggeration, and often insult; it also tells us what needs to be overcome if we are to have any chance of moving past distrust and hatred.

POSSIBILITIES

ALTHOUGH WE LIVE in a world of polemics, ever more present in social media, we must try to live in a world of possibilities, where we can affirm our own beliefs without negating the beliefs of others. That is the premise of this book: understanding the other is not only good but also necessary for a civil society and for religious commitment.[46] Readers of this book may be more or less sympathetic to a particular perspective—the exploration of what the biblical text first meant, of what it means in Judaism, or of what it means in Christianity—but we ask all readers to be more capacious. We need to do more than read only what we personally find to be relevant or congenial. We believe that it is crucial to understand the texts and beliefs of others—not only because we live in a multicultural society, but also because understanding others helps us better to understand ourselves.

We shall try to avoid polemics, except for one case, where we discuss the polemical position known as supersessionism or replacement theology (Chapter 5). We believe that this theology, which claims that the gentile church replaces the people of Israel as heirs of God's covenants and promises, is harmful for both Jews and Christians. But otherwise we do our best to present historical-critical, Jewish, and Christian positions with equal sympathy and clarity.

In some sense, we are proselytizing—but not in the sense of trying to convert anyone to Judaism, our religion by birth and conviction;

instead, we seek to encourage readers to look at other viewpoints sympathetically. Here we disagree with Jacob Neusner, one of the great figures of Jewish studies in the second half of the twentieth century. Neusner claimed: "My goal is to help Christians become better Christians, because they may come to a clearer account of what they affirm in their faith, and to help Jews become better Jews, because they will realize there—so I hope—that God's Torah is the way (not only our way, but the way) to love and serve the one God, creator of heaven and earth, who called us to serve and sanctify God's name."[47] We do not claim that Jewish interpretation is "the way." It is one way, and Christianity is another. Each is sustaining, inspirational, and based on a logical reading of its scripture.

We do not think that "our" religious beliefs obviate the beliefs of others. Rabbi Menachem Meiri (Provence, 1249–ca. 1315), rejecting the predominant Jewish view of his day, insisted that in terms of Jewish law, Christians were not idolaters and that "the juridical category of brotherhood [is] shared by Jews, Christians, and Muslims."[48] Medieval Jewish commentators typically denied that prophecies were messianic since they sought to undermine any claim that they predicted Jesus, but Rabbi Moshe Hadarshan, a central figure in eleventh-century French biblical exegesis, interpreted those texts messianically without anti-Christian polemic. His work was so infused with messianism that the thirteenth-century Dominican friar Ramon Martini, charged with evangelizing Jews and Muslims (Moors), used it as a major source in his anti-Jewish polemical work *Pugio Fidei*.[49] Until recently the openness of Meiri and Rabbi Hadarshan was exceptional—but we follow in their footsteps.

Several historical factors facilitate our sympathetic understanding of Christian biblical interpretation. These include the development of the academic study of religion; the integration into biblical studies of reception history, that is, how biblical texts were understood, variously and over time, in the postbiblical period; the rise of historical-critical study; and the recognition of ambiguity and multiple understandings of texts. Our readings are also inspired by numerous Christians who have recognized how scriptural interpretation has been used to harm Jews and who have sought alternative messages.

The Roman Catholic Church has played an essential role in encouraging the reading of the entire Christian Bible in a manner that appreciates Jewish perspectives without supersessionist assumptions. From the 1965 Vatican II document *Nostra Aetate* to the 1993 Pontifical Biblical Commission's "The Interpretation of the Bible in the Church"; from the landmark 2001 "The Jewish People and Their Sacred Scriptures in the Christian Bible," also by the Pontifical Biblical Commission, to the 2015 "'The Gifts and the Calling of God Are Irrevocable' (Rom 11:29): A Reflection on Theological Questions Pertaining to Catholic-Jewish Relations," by the Commission of the Holy See for Religious Relations with the Jews,[50] the church has both enriched its own interpretive practices and encouraged mutual respect. We return to this final text in the Conclusion.

The 1993 document, a road map of different ways of reading the Bible in the church, acknowledges that "Jewish biblical scholarship in all its richness, from its origins in antiquity down to the present day, is an asset of the highest value for the exegesis of both Testaments, provided that it be used with discretion." It also highlights the importance of understanding texts in their original contexts, and so understanding the Tanakh without referencing the Christ:

Particular attention is necessary, according to the spirit of the Second Vatican Council (*Nostra Aetate*, 4), to avoid absolutely any actualization of certain texts of the New Testament which could provoke or reinforce unfavorable attitudes to the Jewish people. The tragic events of the past must, on the contrary, impel all to keep unceasingly in mind that, according to the New Testament, the Jews remain "beloved" of God, "since the gifts and calling of God are irrevocable" (Rom. 11:28–29).[51]

For this text, anti-Jewish biblical interpretation is not only historically inaccurate, but theologically and morally wrong. We agree with this conclusion.

Less than a decade later, in 2001, the Pontifical Biblical Commission's "The Jewish People and Their Sacred Scriptures in the Christian Bible" found new ways "to advance the dialogue between Christians and Jews with clarity and in a spirit of mutual esteem and affection." It states: "Christians can and ought to admit that the Jewish reading of the Bible is a possible one, in continuity with the Jewish Sacred Scriptures from the Second Temple period, a reading analogous to the Christian reading which developed in parallel fashion."[52] If the Jewish reading of the Tanakh is "possible," then it is worth studying.

Outside of official religious frameworks, especially in academic circles, such sentiments also appear. *The Oxford Handbook of the Abrahamic Religions* voices the hope "that inasmuch as ignorance is the mother of prejudice this handbook might play a role in fighting religious intolerance in all its forms."[53] Studying different traditions without suggesting which is first, which is better, or which influenced the other was recently advocated as "the parallel spiritual activity model"; it centers around "respectful mutual study and understanding."[54] This same idea is fundamental to a group developed in 1995 by Peter Ochs called "Scriptural Reasoning." As that group's website notes, the process "is not about seeking agreement but rather exploring the texts and their possible interpretations across faith boundaries, and learning to 'disagree better.'"[55]

To understand the New Testament, one must understand the scriptures of Israel. Further, our Christian students are generally happy to "double-dip" when studying a passage from the scriptures of Israel: they can find value in both Jewish and Christian interpretations. But in our experience, most Jews do not feel a need to understand the New Testament. This lack is acknowledged in a 1988 Episcopal statement: "In the case of Christian-Jewish dialogue, a historical and theological imbalance is obvious. While an understanding of Judaism in New Testament times is an indispensable part of any Christian theology, for Jews a 'theological' understanding of Christianity is not of the same significance."[56] We believe, however, that Jews should read the New Testament—that is one of the core reasons we coedited *The Jewish Annotated New Testament*.[57] The New Testament features Jewish figures—Jesus, Mary, Paul, and Peter—and most of its authors are Jewish. It is a crucial source for understanding Jewish practice and belief in the late Second Temple period. Thus the New Testament is both a Jewish and a Christian text, and it tells us how some Jews in the first and early second centuries CE interpreted Israel's scripture.

Our view that Jews should read the New Testament and learn more about Christianity than something about Santa Claus and the Easter bunny is not widespread in the Jewish community. The central Jewish statement on Jewish-Christian relations, the 2000 *Dabru Emet* (*Speak Truth*), sidesteps Jewish (lack of) familiarity with the New Testament.[58] And at least one Christian critic has, fairly, criticized a book based on that statement for not representing Christianity and Christian beliefs well.[59] We Jews can do better. And to this matter we also return in the Conclusion.

Too often interreligious conversation involves highlighting similarities and glossing over differences. In its most problematic form, this approach invokes a common "Judeo-Christian" tradition.[60] Objecting to exaggerating what Jews and Christians share is powerfully expressed by the late Christian theologian George Lindbeck: "Hermeneutical rapprochement has its dangers because Scripture is central to both Judaism and Christianity. The erosion of distinctly Jewish and Christian interpretations cannot help but weaken each community's identity and power, resulting in a tastelessly lukewarm Judeo-Christian tradition good for nothing except to be spewed out."[61] We agree. The point of scriptural interpretation is not to achieve consensus: it is to provide a forum for discussion, for honing our own theological beliefs, for coming to understand our neighbors better.

We live in a time when the search for common ground is less pressing, and the need to acknowledge difference must come to the fore. As we note above, Jews and Christians are not reading the same scriptures; the church's Old Testament is not the same thing as the synagogue's Tanakh. We should acknowledge the logic to each system rather than accuse others of misreading.

It is also essential that we read together not only to see facets of our own traditions that might otherwise go unnoted but also to gain understanding of our neighbors. For example, we can learn to appreciate how different communities create a canon within a canon by highlighting particular books, chapters, and even verses.[62] For Jews, the book of Esther and the related festival of Purim are central; Martin Luther wanted to toss Esther from the canon. Ironically, the Greek text of Esther preserved by the church makes the heroine a much more pious Jew than the Hebrew text read in the synagogue. Conversely, some Old Testament passages well-known in Christian orbits, such as the depiction of the suffering servant in Isaiah 53, which we explore in Chapter 9, are hardly known to most Jews.

This discrepancy derives in part because of different emphases. While the church attends more to the prophetic corpus of Israel's scripture, the synagogue focuses on the Torah. The church stresses the covenant with David; the synagogue concentrates on the covenants with Abraham and Moses. Jews read the entire Torah, every word, Genesis 1 through the end of Deuteronomy; Christian churches who follow a lectionary never hear Numbers (the Bible's fourth book) proclaimed on Sunday morning, and most of Leviticus (the Bible's third book) also goes missing. This Christian focus leads to a difference in theological emphasis, useful though oversimplifying: the church, in terms of scriptural interpretation, focuses on how Jesus fulfilled prophecy in the past and how he will come again in the future; the synagogue focuses on the present.

Indeed, a notable number of Christians are concerned with eschatology—the end-time. The book of Daniel, largely unknown within contemporary Jewish circles, is hugely important especially in conservative Christian circles. But the more the church, at least in antiquity, stressed the world to come, the kingdom of God, or getting into heaven, the more the synagogue stressed sanctification: the making holy of this world through observing the norms of the Torah.

Even when both communities share the same texts or themes, they often emphasize different aspects. Christians and Jews share the story of the exodus, but it contains different messages for each. Jews and Christians have different vocabularies, different orders to their shared scripture, and different translations. They have different cultural memories, different interpretive understandings, and different emphases. Christians and Jews are now sufficiently different, and sufficiently strong on their own ground, that they might want to think about reading together, with a generosity of spirit that the twenty-first century calls for. And that is what we attempt in the chapters that follow. As Rabbi Jonathan Sacks said to Pope Benedict XVI: "We celebrate both our commonalities and differences, because if we had nothing in common we could not communicate, and if we had everything in common, we would have nothing to say."[63]

CHAPTER 3

The Creation of the World

In the Beginning

In the beginning was the Word [Greek *Logos*], and the Word was with God, and the Word was God. He was in the beginning with God. All things came into being through him, and without him not one thing came into being. What has come into being in him was life, and the life was the light of all people. The light shines in the darkness, and the darkness did not overcome it. (John 1:1–5)

THE PROLOGUE to the Gospel of John is a midrash, or elaboration, on the opening verses of Genesis.[1] From John's "in the beginning," to the reference to God, to the celebration of light, echoes of Genesis and other central passages from the scriptures of Israel abound.

Genesis 1:1–3 reads, "In the beginning when God created the heavens and the earth, the earth was a formless void and darkness covered the face of the deep, while a wind from God swept over the face of the waters. Then God said, 'Let there be light'; and there was light." For some Christian readers, that "light" is Jesus, who states, according to John's Gospel, "I am the light of the world" (John 8:12; 9:5). Connections to Israel's scriptures continue with these "I am" statements, which echo God's revelation to Moses at the burning bush of the name YHWH (called the Tetragrammaton, the four-letter name [of God], a name Jews see as too holy to pronounce so it is often written with just the consonants YHWH). The Greek expression "I am," *egō eimi*, is how the Septuagint translates God's reply to Moses there: *'ehye asher 'ehye*, Hebrew for "I shall be what I shall be" or "I am who I am" (Exod 3:14). The Hebrew name YHWH, possibly read as Yahweh, comes into Greek as *kyrios*, "Lord." Thus, Jesus's followers, reading their Greek scriptures, could see *their Lord*, Jesus, throughout, whether they called him "Lord" or, as in John 1:1, "God."

Securing the presence of the *Logos*, the Word, at creation, John's prologue explains that this *Logos* "became flesh and lived [*skenoō*, or better, dwelled or even "pitched a tent"] among us" (John 1:14). The Greek verb may have reminded early readers of the *skēnē*, the tabernacle (Hebrew *mishkan*, [divine] dwelling place), which represented the divine presence (see, e.g., Exod 25:8) until the Jerusalem Temple was built.

John's Gospel is not the only New Testament text to locate the Christ at creation. In 1 Corinthians 8:6, Paul evokes Genesis 1:26 as well as the Wisdom tradition in what looks like a creedal formula: "yet for us there is one God, the Father, from whom are all things and for whom we exist, and one Lord [Greek *kyrios*], Jesus Christ, through whom are all things and through whom we exist."

Colossians 1:15–17 (likely written by one of Paul's followers) not only places Jesus at creation, but it also proclaims that his creative activity distinguishes him from the angels:[2] "He [the Christ] is the image of the invisible God, the firstborn of all creation; for in him all things in heaven and on earth were created, things visible and invisible, whether thrones or dominions or rulers or powers—all things have been created through him and for him. He himself is before all things, and in him all things hold together." The clarification in Colossians that Jesus was not an angel was necessary, for one possible interpretation of Paul's comment in Galatians 4:14, "you did not scorn or despise me, but welcomed me *as an angel* of God, as Christ

Jesus" (emphasis added),[3] is that Jesus was a super-angel. We find this same concern to distinguish Jesus from angels in the Epistle to the Hebrews: The Christ is "the reflection of God's glory and the exact imprint of God's very being" (Heb 1:3), "having become as much superior to angels as the name he has inherited is more excellent than theirs" (1:4). To secure the point, Hebrews produces the well-known prooftext that we discuss in Chapter 11 on Psalm 22: "For to which of the angels did God ever say, 'You are my Son; / today I have begotten you'?" (1:5).

Not only is the *Logos* present at the beginning, so also, in Christian teaching, is the Holy Spirit. This belief finds support at the end of Genesis 1:2, "a wind from God swept over the face of the waters"; the Hebrew word *ru'ach*, translated here as "wind," can also mean "breath" or "spirit." It comes into Greek as *pneuma*, which has the same connotations, as we see in words such as "pneumonia," a disease of the lungs, or "pneumatic," something powered by wind. From wind to spirit, in early Christian texts, the term comes to denote the *pneuma hagion*, the "Holy Spirit." Hence, pneumatology is the technical term for the study of the Holy Spirit. Punning on the various connotations of *pneuma*, Jesus states in John 3:8, "The wind [*pneuma*] blows where it chooses, and you hear the sound of it, but you do not know where it comes from or where it goes. So it is with everyone who is born of the Spirit [*pneuma*]."

The opening verses in Genesis, with their references to the beginning, the light, and the spirit, are not the only places in the chapter where Christology finds an anchor. Toward the end of the chapter, on the sixth day of creation, God speaks in the plural: "God said, 'Let us make humankind in our image, according to our likeness; and let them have dominion over the fish of the sea, and over the birds of the air, and over the cattle, and over all the wild animals of the earth, and over every creeping thing that creeps upon the earth'" (Gen 1:26).

These plural usages suggested for some early Christ-believers the involvement of Jesus and the Spirit not only in the creation of the world, but especially in the creation of humanity.

Although the New Testament never explicitly mentions the Trinity in the technical sense of one God with three manifestations or "persons," already in the second century CE the North African church father Tertullian attests to this perception. His comments are based on claims regarding Genesis 1:26 that he had heard from Jews who rejected both the messiahship of Jesus and teachings regarding the Trinity. These Jews offered an alternative reading of "Let us make . . .":

> If the number of the Trinity also offends you, as if it were not con-nected in the simple Unity, I ask you how it is possible for a Be-ing who is merely and absolutely One and Singular, to speak in plural phrase, saying, "Let us make man in our own image, and after our own likeness" (Genesis 1:26), whereas He ought to have said, "Let me make man in my own image, and after my own likeness," as being a unique and singular Being? In the following passage, however, "Behold the man is become as one of us" (Genesis 3:22). He is either deceiving or amusing us in speaking plurally, if He is One only and singular. Or was it to the angels that He spoke, *as the Jews interpret the passage* [emphasis added], because these also acknowledge not the Son? . . .
>
> It was because He had already His Son close at His side, as a second Person, His own Word, and a third Person also, the Spirit in the Word, that He purposely adopted the plural phrase, "Let *us* make"; and, "in *our* image"; and, "become as one *of us*." For with whom did He make man? and to whom did He make him like? [The answer must be] the Son on the one hand, who was one day to put on human nature, and the Spirit on the other, who

was to sanctify man. With these did He then speak, in the Unity of the Trinity, as with His ministers and witnesses. (*Against Praxeas* 12)[4]

The Jews saw angels in the plural usage; the Christians saw the Trinity. Tertullian was not alone in his claim, for Augustine, Ephrem the Syrian, and other church fathers agreed. At the Council of Sirmium in 351, not only did the Christian participants affirm that God (the Father) was speaking to his Son (the Christ) in Genesis 1:26, they proclaimed this view doctrine and demanded that those who rejected it be excommunicated.[5]

We can see the importance of this Trinitarian teaching in today's *Orthodox Study Bible*. This text glosses Genesis 1:26 thus: "The pronouns 'Us' and 'Our' reveal the plurality of divine Persons. These Persons are the Father, Son, and Holy Spirit operating in complete unity out of the one divine Nature."[6] Reading Genesis in the light of John's prologue, one finds that both the *Logos* that takes on flesh as Jesus of Nazareth and the Holy Spirit are present at creation.

Finding the Trinity in Genesis, or anywhere else in the scriptures of Israel, would not have occurred to anyone before the beginning of the Christian movement. Yet pre-Christian Jewish texts do locate other figures at the beginning of creation, and rabbinic Judaism provides its own, diverse explanations of that problematic "Let us." In the interpretation of Genesis 1, we find both continuity and dissimilarity in how Jews, including Jews who worshiped Jesus as Lord, understood their scriptures.

Making Order from Chaos

Genesis 1–3 can be read as a single narrative, beginning with the creation of the world and ending with Adam and Eve's expulsion from the garden of Eden. But a closer look indicates that these chapters comprise two distinct stories written by different authors.[7] The first, narrating precreation (Gen 1:1–2), the six days of creation, and the origins of the postcreation Sabbath, ends with a summary statement at 2:4a, "These are the generations of the heavens and the earth when they were created"; the second, set in Eden, begins at 2:4b, "In the day that the Lord God made the earth and the heavens."

Attempts to harmonize the two stories create difficulties. According to Gen 1:24–30, first God creates animals and then, as the epitome of creation and in the image of God, male and female humans, together, as equals; in the second account, first God creates a male human being from the clay (2:7), then the animals, and finally, a woman from the "rib" or "side" of the male human being (2:18–23). The first author calls the deity "God" (*'elohim*); the second refers to the "Lord God" (YHWH *'elohim*). In the first, God creates through speaking, while in the second he creates in a hands-on fashion.

Just as the New Testament contains four distinct accounts of the life and death of Jesus, different writers, in different times and settings, understood God, creation, and their place in the world differently. Disentangling these two creation stories requires some detective work.

The first story, Genesis 1:1–2:4a, is from what biblical scholars call the Priestly (P) source, one of several documents that form the Torah.[8] This well-accepted theory posits several recognizable "sources" or traditions that, over time, were woven together into what became the first five books of the Bible. Although this portion of Genesis begins the Bible, it was actually composed later than the Eden story that now follows it. Likely completed during the Babylonian exile in the sixth century BCE, the first creation narrative shares several motifs with a Babylonian epic that narrates the creation of the world, known by its first words as the Enuma Elish, "When on High."[9] The Mesopotamian account, geographically focused, emphasizes the creation of both sacred place, Babylon, especially its temple of the deity Marduk, and sacred kingship, Babylon's central institution. The Israelite story describes the creation of all humanity, male and female, as equal, and it ends with the establishment not of sacred space but of sacred time, the Sabbath. In the Babylonian epic, human beings are created from the blood of a god defeated in battle, and their role is to perform "the work of the gods," to be slaves of the gods "so they shall be at leisure."[10] In Genesis 1, humanity is not defined by slavery[11] but by its connection to the divine and by its dominion, or caretaker status, over creation. For a community whose Temple is destroyed, who has been displaced from their homeland, and whose kingship is disempowered, Genesis 1:1–2:4a provided both stability and hope: it affirms the grandeur of their God, the creation of order out of chaos, the goodness of humanity, and the promise of Sabbath rest. To take the text out of its original context risks losing the import of its comforting and sustaining message.

We also miss part of that message because of translation issues. The opening verse of Genesis is one of the Bible's most discussed, most mistranslated, and therefore most misunderstood texts. The well-known King James Version, which translates Genesis 1:1 as "In the beginning God created the heaven and the earth," is incorrect on several counts. Syntactically, the Hebrew of 1:1 is not an independent sentence. It is an introductory clause, as reflected in the "when" of the NRSV's "In the beginning *when* God created the heavens and the earth" or in the NJPS's "*When* God began to create heaven and earth." Nor does the opening verse describe *creatio ex nihilo*—creation out of nothing, although this idea became prominent in Christian and some Jewish thought.[12] The Hebrew term for "create," *bara'*, which in the scriptures of Israel is only predicated of God, does not mean to create something *from nothing*; it means *to create as only God can create*. It also carries the connotation of "to separate"[13] and so indicates how God brings order to chaos.[14] This concern for separation and organization typifies the Priestly worldview, where every created item belongs to a clearly delineated category. Therefore, the Priestly story ends with the Sabbath, separated from the previous six days of creation, which will be given as a gift to Israel, separated from the other nations.

Not even the King James Version's "heaven and earth" is correct. Hebrew uses the same grammatically plural *shamayim* for both "sky" and "heavens."[15] Ancient Hebrews as well as the Jews of New Testament times thought there were multiple heavens. Paul of Tarsus speaks of being caught up into the "third heaven" (2 Cor 12:2), though he is being modest since many Jews believed there were more than three, and behind the famous Gospel expression "kingdom of heaven" (e.g., Matt 3:2) is a Greek plural: "kingdom of the heavens" (*basileia tōn ouranōn*). Even the famous prayer that begins "Our Father, which art in heaven" (Matt 6:9 KJV) is, in the Greek, "in the heavens." Most English translations of the New Testament follow the King James Version's reading of Genesis 1:1 and so perpetuate the error. Later Jewish literature assumed the existence of seven or ten heavens, and we see a similar view in Dante's *Paradiso*. We can see the vestiges of such beliefs in common expressions of euphoria such as "I'm in the seventh heaven" and even "I'm on cloud nine."

The concern for creating order out of chaos also helps us determine the best translation of that *ru'ach 'elohim* in Genesis 1:2: "spirit of God," "wind from [or of] God," or "a mighty wind."[16] *Ru'ach*, a feminine noun, can mean "wind" or "breeze" or even "gale." Genesis 3:8 describes God as walking in Eden in the evening *ru'ach*, "the evening breeze." In Exodus 10:13, an east *ru'ach* carries away the locusts that plagued the Egyptians; in Exodus 15:10, a *ru'ach* splits the Reed Sea. Related is the translation "breath,"[17] in the sense of life force. In Genesis 6:3, God states, "My spirit [*ru'ach*] shall not abide in mortals forever, for they are flesh; their days shall be one hundred twenty years." Genesis 6:17 refers to the *ru'ach chayim*, the "breath of life" that animates all flesh. *Ru'ach* also describes what fills a person's mind— ideas and attitudes—and in that sense means "spirit." The scout Caleb did not criticize the land of Israel (Num 14:24) "because he has a different spirit [*ru'ach*]" than the other men Moses dispatched for reconnaissance.

The expression for a divine *ru'ach* appears sixteen times in the Hebrew text, where it most frequently describes a quality associated with God. For example, in Genesis 41:38, Pharaoh asks his slaves regarding Joseph's prophetic ability, "Can we find anyone else like this—one in whom is the spirit of God [*ru'ach 'elohim*]?" Joel 2:28 (3:1 Heb.) reads:

> I will pour out my spirit [*ru'ach*] on all flesh;
> your sons and your daughters shall prophesy,
> your old men shall dream dreams,
> and your young men shall see visions.

(This is the verse Luke cites in the Pentecost scene of Acts 2:17; the Greek is *pneuma*.) Isaiah 11:2 describes the various forms of the *ru'ach* that the ideal Davidic king (later called the messiah) will also possess:

> The spirit [*ru'ach*] of the LORD shall rest on him,
>   the spirit [*ru'ach*] of wisdom and understanding,
>   the spirit [*ru'ach*] of counsel and might,
>   the spirit [*ru'ach*] of knowledge and the fear of the LORD.

Related is the expression "spirit of the Lord," which similarly describes special abilities, from military prowess to prophecy to wisdom to an ecstatic state, that "descends" on individuals.

However, the Biblical Hebrew *ru'ach* never refers to "Spirit" in the sense of a separate, divine entity. In the Tanakh, the spirit is something God has, or can bestow, but it is not a deity, an angel, an object of worship, or what in some Christian teachings is called a "person."

Making the translation of *ru'ach* even more confusing is the English language, which like other languages distinguishes between capital and lowercase letters. Translators therefore decide whether to capitalize "spirit" to suggest a deity or supernatural being. The distinction between uppercase and lowercase letters—or what manuscript scholars term "majuscule" and "miniscule"—did not exist for ancient Hebrew, Greek, or Latin texts. Miniscule Greek and Latin letters are an invention of the late first millennium CE, and to this day Hebrew does not have miniscule letters. Thus the most significant early manuscripts of the New Testament, Septuagint, and Hebrew Bible, such as the Christian fourth-century Greek Codex Sinaiticus or the 1008 CE Hebrew Leningrad Codex, do not distinguish between "spirit" and "Spirit," as all modern English translations do. We will return to this point again in this chapter's discussion of "word/

Word" and "wisdom/Wisdom" and in Chapter 12 where we look at "son of man" and "Son of Man."[18]

We can now return to Genesis 1:2 to see how ancient Israelites likely understood what becomes, in Christian interpretation, the Holy Spirit.

The first two verses of Genesis describe an initial chaos with the rhyming phrase *tohu vavohu*; the NRSV offers the translation "formless void," but we prefer Everett Fox's alliterative "wild and waste."[19] The author then accentuates the chaos with related terms: "darkness," "deep," "waters," and "wind" (*ru'ach*). Therefore, the *ru'ach* suggests something chaotic as opposed to ordered.

Nor is this an ordinary *ru'ach*.[20] The second element of the phrase, *'elohim*, can mean "of God" or "from God." But it has other meanings as well. Since Hebrew has no element equivalent to the English "-est," "of God" or "from God" sometimes expresses a superlative.[21] For example, Psalm 36:6 (36:7 Heb.) refers to "mountains of El [= God]," and the NRSV translates "mighty mountains"; 1 Samuel 26:12 speaks of "a sleep of/from Yahweh," which the NRSV renders "a deep sleep." We might compare the English expression "god-awful," that is, really bad, or, according to the *Oxford English Dictionary*, also "really impressive." In its original context, *ru'ach 'elohim* probably indicated a "great wind" or even "awesome wind."[22]

The meaning of *ru'ach 'elohim* can be additionally clarified by the Hebrew participle connected to it, *merachefet*, which the NRSV translates as "swept over"; the King James Version offers "moved upon." The root *r-ch-f* appears here and only two other times in the Bible. In Deuteronomy 32:11, it indicates a bird's fluttering; in Jeremiah 23:9, it refers to the quaking of the prophet's bones. If we imagine the initial chaos as crashing waves and gale-force winds, then "quake" is appropriate; if we think about unresolved chords, as in the beginning of Haydn's "The Creation," or ocean waves lapping upon the shore, "swept over" better fits.

The phrase *ru'ach 'elohim* originally meant "a great wind" or "a wind from God." But like wind itself, the phrase blew in different directions. Connotations of terms always change when their context changes. Such contexts are more than simply "when" and "where" a text was composed or first read; literary contexts can influence how we interpret scripture. Most biblical texts were written independently of each other and not as part of a single, unified book eventually called "the Bible." When distinct accounts that use the same words find themselves on the same scroll, or in the same canon, these words can take on new meanings. Once Genesis 1 became part of the Bible, where the phrase *ru'ach 'elohim* elsewhere holds the connotations of divinely inspired ability, the "wind" becomes a "spirit."

The first-century Jewish philosopher Philo, following the Septuagint, understands Genesis 1:2 as speaking of the divine spirit. In his *On the Creation of the World* he states that the Spirit (*pneuma*) was named "'of God' [Gen. 1:2], because 'spirit is highly important for life and God is the cause of life'" (30).[23] On the other hand, all the targumim speak of "*rucha'* [Aramaic for *ru'ach*] from before God"; the phrasing suggests that the targumim understand *ru'ach* in the sense of "wind."[24]

In the New Testament, the Holy Spirit (*pneuma theou*) is an active agent: present at Jesus's conception, driving him into the wilderness after his baptism, bestowed by Jesus upon his disciples, descending on the followers at Pentecost, and so forth. Consequently, were one to read Genesis in the light of the Gospels, finding the "Holy Spirit" in the first chapter, and elsewhere, is again understandable.

In turn, once one determines that the (Holy) Spirit is in place in Genesis, its role in Genesis then adds additional nuance to the Gospels. For example, as this "Spirit" flutters or hovers over the face of the deep in Genesis, so according to the Gospels will it descend upon Jesus in the form of a dove as he rises from baptism in the River

Jordan (Matt 3:16; cf. Mark 1:10; Luke 3:22; cf. John 1:32). For Mark's Gospel, which starts with the baptism rather than with a nativity, the "beginning" (Mark 1:1) of the story of Jesus echoes the beginning of Genesis, with the appearance of a fluttering spirit. For Mark, a new type of creation, a new way of making order out of chaos, begins when God speaks: "And a voice came from heaven, 'You are my Son, the Beloved; with you I am well pleased'" (Mark 1:11).

Wind, Spirit, Wisdom, *Logos*

A<small>LTHOUGH</small> the *ru'ach* of Genesis 1 originally referred to "wind," the reading of "Spirit" as a distinct figure finds a place in the developing theologies of Judaism and later, Christianity. It also anticipates other figures active with God at the creation. John's Gospel is not the only text to locate what appears to be a second figure together with God in the beginning. Other primordial figures—Wisdom (Hebrew *chochmah*; Greek *sophia*), the Word (Aramaic *memra'*; Greek *Logos*), and even the Torah as preexisting Moses—are attested in Jewish tradition.

Some biblical and other prerabbinic texts speak of Wisdom as a divine entity separate from, and of a lower level than, God.[25] We are again faced with the translation problem: At what point does wisdom become Wisdom? In some verses, the lowercase use is warranted. For example, Proverbs 3:19–20 reads:

> The L<small>ORD</small> by wisdom founded the earth;
>> by understanding he established the heavens;
> by his knowledge the deeps broke open,
>> and the clouds drop down the dew.

Here "wisdom" is simply a synonym for knowledge. Then the tradition develops.

Because the noun "wisdom" is feminine, grammatically, in both Hebrew and Greek, Wisdom came to be imagined as a woman. Proverbs 8:22–23 records Wisdom, here as a separate being, affirming:

> The LORD created me at the beginning of his work,
>> the first of his acts of long ago.
> Ages ago I was set up,
>> at the first, before the beginning of the earth.

The chapter continues:

> . . . I [Wisdom] was beside him [God], like a master worker;
> and I was daily his delight,
>> rejoicing before him always,
> rejoicing in his inhabited world
>> and delighting in the human race. (Prov 8:30–31)

These verses may suggest that Lady Wisdom was a minor deity.[26] Roland Murphy says:

> There can be no doubt about her divine origin, and it is certain that she is somehow associated with creation. Indeed, a specific role in the created world is clearly stated: her delight is to be with human beings (Prov 8:31). Her intercourse with humans is to be gleaned from her preaching to them (Prov 1, 8, 9). She threatens, cajoles, and issues a promise of life that is identified with the divine favor (Prov 8:35). She is a divine gift (Prov 2:16; Wis 9:4) to all who will listen (Prov 1:20–22; 8:4–5, 32; 9:4).[27]

Whether early Hebrew and Greek readers of Proverbs and other texts that depict Wisdom as a female figure active with God at creation understood her to be a goddess, or whether they took the language to be poetic metaphor without the suggestion of a being beside God, cannot be determined.

The third-century BCE book Wisdom of Jesus Ben Sira (or Sirach, also known as Ecclesiasticus) associates personified Wisdom with the *ru'ach/pneuma* that hovered over the deep in Genesis: "I came forth from the mouth of the Most High, / and covered the earth like a mist" (Sir 24:3). The association works well in Hebrew, but less so in Greek and Latin. The Hebrew noun *ru'ach* is feminine (Hebrew, like French, has only masculine and feminine forms); the Greek *pneuma* is neuter (Greek, like German, has masculine, feminine, and neuter forms). When this *pneuma* then comes into Latin, it appears as *spiritus*, a masculine noun. Thus, in Semitic texts, the Spirit can be imagined as female and associated with Wisdom; for Greek and Latin texts, the connection is less secure.

According to the pre-Christian pseudepigraphal book 1 Enoch, Wisdom found no place on earth to live: "Wisdom went out in order to dwell among the sons of men, but did not find a dwelling; Wisdom returned to her place and took her seat in the midst of the angels" (1 En 42:1–2). Baruch, from the second or first century BCE, associates Wisdom with the Torah (also a feminine noun) and so locates her on earth, within the Jewish community: "She appeared on earth / and lived with humankind. / She is the book of the commandments of God" (Bar 3:37–4:1). The idea that the Torah existed before creation, common in rabbinic theology,[28] is a reworking of the notion that God created the world with Wisdom, since for the rabbis, Wisdom (Hebrew *chochmah*) was identical to the Torah.[29]

Given this background, the prologue to John's Gospel reads as a biography of Jesus as Wisdom, who leaves her heavenly abode, tents among humanity, and then eventually, at the end of the Gospel, returns to her true form in heaven. Yet John's *Logos*, the perfect *male* image of the Father, strips from Wisdom her female connotations.

While the *ru'ach 'elohim* of Genesis 1, which we understand as "a great wind," does not achieve the status of a divinelike being in rabbinic Judaism, other figures do. One such entity, associated with God's "glory" (Hebrew *kavod*), begins to appear in the targumim and then in later rabbinic and especially mystical Judaism. Indicating "God's presence in the world,"[30] the Shechinah finds her (yes, feminine) origins in the Hebrew root *sh-ch-n*, "to dwell"; this root is the basis of the word *mishkan*, the tabernacle described in the latter part of Exodus, and John's description of the *Logos* as "tabernacling" with humanity may allude to it.

For example, the Mishnah (Avot 3.2) states that when two people are sitting and discussing the Torah, "the Shechinah" is between them. The Jerusalem Talmud glosses Exodus 19:18 as "Mount Sinai sent up smoke, because the glory of the Shechinah of the Lord was revealed upon it in flame of fire." From the mystical tradition, the first-millennium *Sefer Yetzirah* (*The Book of Creation*) suggests that the Shechinah is one of the *sefirot*, the emanations or attributes of God.[31] Sometimes imagined as God's daughter, the Shechinah will in later mystical Jewish tradition take her place as a feminine aspect of God, yet like Wisdom she is also both independent from and subservient to God. Whether or not for the early rabbis the Shechinah is a manifestation of God or separate from God cannot be determined; it is likely that different rabbis viewed this matter differently.[32]

Jewish writers also had their own version of the "Word" at creation. In the first creation account, God creates through the word— God speaks, and "it was so." This idea of creation through the word is also reflected in Psalm 33:6, which reads, "By the word [Hebrew *davar*; Greek *logos*] of the LORD the heavens were made, / and all their host by the breath [Hebrew *ru'ach*; Greek *pneuma*] of his mouth." The psalm is a good illustration of a common form of poetic parallelism, in which the second part of the verse recapitulates the first; here the psalmist takes "word" and "spirit" as synonyms.

Philo draws from both Genesis and Proverbs to describe the Word (*Logos*) as an "archangel and most ancient ambassador" who mediates between God and humanity: "this same Word is continually a suppliant to the immortal God on behalf of the mortal race, which is exposed to affliction and misery; and is also the ambassador, sent by the Ruler of all, to the subject race." Philo then attributes to this Word Moses's words in Deuteronomy 5:5. The Word states:

> "And I stood in the midst, between the Lord and you" neither being uncreated as God, nor yet created as you, but being in the midst between these two extremities, like a hostage, as it were, to both parties: a hostage to the Creator, as a pledge and security that the whole race would never fly off and revolt entirely, choosing disorder rather than order; and to the creature, to lead it to entertain a confident hope that the merciful God would not overlook his own work. (*Her.* 205–6)[33]

In his *On Flight and Finding* 109, Philo describes the *Logos* as the child of God and Wisdom (Sophia). Given such views, it is not surprising that Christian authors such as Origen and Clement of Alexandria embraced Philo's works, and some even referred to Philo, the Jew from Alexandria, as Philo Christianus, Philo *the Christian*![34]

Philo's *Logos*, a divine intermediary who is both God and not God, was not a fringe idea in Judaism; the Aramaic term for "the word," *memra'*, serves a similar function in the targumim. Where the Hebrew Bible speaks of God, the Aramaic translations sometimes use *memra'*.[35] For example, the Palestinian Targum glosses Exodus 3:12–14, the appearance of God to Moses at the burning bush: "And the *Memra of* YHWH said to Moses, 'He who said to the world from the beginning, Be there, and it was there . . . and he said, Thus you shall say to the Israelites, He has sent me to you.'"[36] Thus, some of the targumim imagine God's *memra'* as participating in creation.[37]

We might imagine a conversation between a Galilean sage, a Hellenized Jew, a gentile Christian, and a pagan sometime in the early second century CE. The Galilean, familiar with the targumic tradition, states that God created the world through his word, his *memra'*. The Hellenized Jew, who has studied Philo's teachings (*Her.* 231), nods approvingly. The Christian cites the Gospel of John, "In the beginning was the *Logos*, and the *Logos* was with God, and the *Logos* was God." And the pagan too finds a connection, saying, "Our great Stoic teachers taught us that the *Logos* animates the universe."

Only when the Christian insists that this *Logos* "became flesh" (John 1:14) do the disagreements begin.

"Let Us Make Humankind . . ."

Finding the Trinity in Genesis 1:1 is a possible reading that has its own internal logic. It is not, however, a necessary reading, as the various Jewish texts indicate. The same point holds for the few places where God speaks in the plural.

In Genesis 1:26, God (*'elohim*) states, "Let *us* make humankind in *our* image, according to *our* likeness." *'Elohim* is grammatically plural, since *-im* is the masculine plural suffix, as in familiar Hebrew words like *cherubim* (cherubs) and *seraphim* (seraphs). However, in reference to the God of Israel, *'elohim* is a masculine singular noun: the verbs and adjectives associated with this noun are almost always masculine singular, and the Hebrew Bible uses the masculine pronoun "he" rather than the plural "they" for God. When *'elohim* does function in the plural, the word refers to the gods of other nations, as in Exodus 12:12, "on all the gods [*'elohim*] of Egypt I will execute judgments," or Exodus 20:3, "other gods" (*'elohim 'acherim*).[38]

In the Hebrew Bible, most plural verbs have plural subjects. But in a few rare cases, singular nouns govern plural verbs. This plural is sometimes called the plural of self-deliberation or self-summons. For example, in Isaiah 6:8, God says, "Whom shall I send, and who will go for *us*?"; in 2 Samuel 24:14, a contrite David says, "I am in great distress; let *us* fall into the hand of the LORD, for his mercy is great."[39] This formulation cannot explain the plural in Genesis 1:26, however, since up to verse 26 God has been speaking in the singular. The claim that Genesis 1:26 uses the "royal we" (as in the famous comment attributed to Queen Victoria, "We are not amused") is likewise impossible, since unlike English, Hebrew verbs are not conjugated in the plural for royalty. To what, then, does "let us make" in Genesis 1:26 refer?

Both the historical context of Genesis 1:1–2:4a and numerous other passages in the scriptures of Israel provide the explanation: God is speaking to his heavenly court. Influenced by various ancient Near Eastern pantheons consisting of a high god surrounded by subsidiary gods,[40] several biblical texts depict a divine council with whom God consults.[41] This council appears in Genesis 3:22, the Adam and Eve story, where "the LORD God said, 'See, the man has become like one of us'"; in reference to the Tower of Babel, God again speaks in the plural in invoking the heavenly host: "Come, let us go down, and [let us] confuse their language there" (Gen 11:7).

Job 1–2 (see especially 1:6) depicts a divine assembly, with God surrounded by the heavenly council called, literally, "children of God" (*benei 'elohim*). Included in this constituency is *hasatan*, "the adversary," who has not yet become Satan, the evil being who opposes God. A less well-known but equally illustrative passage of this divine council appears in 1 Kings 22:19: "Then Micaiah [the prophet] said, 'Therefore hear the word of the LORD: I saw the LORD sitting on his throne, with all the host of heaven [that is, heavenly beings] standing beside him to the right and to the left of him.'"

The Psalms also mention this heavenly court. Psalm 82 opens with, "God has taken his place in the divine council; / in the midst of the gods ['*elohim*] he holds judgment." Psalm 29:1 commands, "Ascribe to the LORD, O heavenly beings [*benei 'elim*, literally "children of God"; cf. Ps 89:7], / ascribe to the LORD glory and strength." The Septuagint, composed in a Hellenistic context of multiple deities, translates the Hebrew *benei 'elim* as *huioi theou*, "sons of God," and correctly understands these passages as describing a divine entourage.

Modern English readers will typically miss this suggestion of a plurality of deities, since translations are often softened, or "monotheized," to conform to later theological proclamations of only one God. For example, the beginning of Exodus 15:11, properly rendered in the NRSV as "Who is like you, O LORD, among the gods?" enters the NJPS as, "Who is like You, O LORD, among the celestials." This verse appears several times in the *Siddur*, the Jewish prayer book, where one version renders it, "Who is like unto thee, O Lord, *amongst the mighty*" (emphasis added).[42] Such (mis)translations obscure the role of the divine council.

They also obscure the fact that theologies develop. The God of Genesis, with his divine council, becomes for Christianity the Triune God; he becomes for Judaism a singular God with an angelic entourage. Both traditions reject the idea that there were other "gods."

Genesis 1:26 depicts God as speaking to the divine council, the "hosts" in the common biblical title "Lord of hosts," and telling them that humanity should look the same as God does and they do.[43] This interpretation comports with Ezekiel's depiction of God as "something that seemed like a human form" (Ezek 1:26). As we see in Chapter 12, Daniel 7:13 similarly claims that the one "like a son of man" looks like a human being, like the divine beings, and like God. And Genesis 18:2 and Judges 13 show that heavenly messengers appear on earth in human form.

Although Genesis 1:26 is typically taken to mean that humans, "in the image and likeness of God," share some type of intellectual or moral features with the deity, its original point is much more prosaic: people look like God and like the heavenly beings. Indeed, the Hebrew words in Genesis 1:26, *tzelem* ("image") and *demut* ("likeness"), almost always refer to physical appearances—as in Ezekiel 23:14, "she saw male figures carved on the wall, images [*tzelem*] of the Chaldeans portrayed in vermilion," and Ezekiel 1:10, describing the heavenly beings: "As for the appearance [*demut*] of their faces."

Later Jewish tradition, which had moved away from the biblical view that there was one God to be worshiped among the other divine beings who inhabited the heavens, will read moral imperatives into the references to image and likeness. This interpretation was inevitable, since by the Middle Ages, most Jews regarded God as both incorporeal and singular. According to the great medieval Jewish philosopher Maimonides, God's incorporeality is one of the tenets of Jewish belief, and this view became accepted in medieval Christian doctrine as well. But that was not the case for most of the Bible, where that deity is depicted in human form.

The shared human appearance of God and the heavenly court explains why in Genesis 1:26 God speaks in the plural. Since people look like these heavenly beings, so God consults them when creating creatures mirroring their appearance.

The plan to create humanity is addressed by God to a plural group in Genesis 1:26, but the next verse refers to God three times, *always in the singular*, to describe this creation: "God created [*bara'*, the singular verb] humankind in his image, in the image of God he created [*bara'*] them; male and female he created [*bara'*] them." God consulted with subsidiary divine beings, but in creating humans, God acted alone.

Interpreted in its original contexts of ancient Israel and the ancient Near East, Genesis 1 depicts no Trinity or cofashioner. There is only consultation with the heavenly council. But when read retrospectively, in light of texts such as John 1:1, the plural "us" and the plural verb open to such interpretations. Some scholars suggest that the idea of the Trinity is not foreign to the Hebrew Bible, and it offers the best explanation of the plural in Genesis 1:26.[44] We find this approach to be theologically understandable but historically untenable. If one believes in the Trinity, Genesis 1:26 can be seen as supporting the belief. But if one reads the text either in its original historical context or through Jewish interpretive approaches, no Trinity appears.

LATER JEWISH INTERPRETATION

THE SEPTUAGINT and most of the targumim read Genesis 1:26 as depicting God speaking to the heavenly host. Later scribes even produced another consultation. In Genesis 2:18, concerning the creation of woman, the Hebrew depicts God speaking in the singular, "I will make him [man] a helper," but the Septuagint, as well as the pre-Christian book of Jubilees (3:4), records a plural, "Let us make." These texts harmonize the second creation story to the first. They infer that since the woman is in the same human form as the man, and since she too is distinct from the animals, God includes the heavenly host in the consultation.

In the first century CE, Josephus and Philo offer opposing understandings of Genesis 1:26. Josephus, describing the creation on the sixth day, notes in *Antiquities of the Jews* 1.32, "On this day *he* also fashioned humanity,"[45] and reasserts, in *Against Apion* 2.192, that God created the world without assistants.[46] Conversely, Philo assumes in *On the Creation of the World* 72–76 that God is speaking to "fellow-workers."[47] Philo was concerned that, since human beings are in the image and likeness of God, readers might conclude that God has an evil component.[48] Humanity's evil must therefore reflect God's fellow-workers.

Although all ancient citations of the Septuagint agree with the plural Hebrew "let us make" of Genesis 1:26, rabbinic literature in several places (e.g., b. Megillah 9a) suggests that the seventy-two elders King Ptolemy invited to write the Septuagint rendered the plural as a singular, "I shall make a human in image and likeness." This tradition may reflect a lost version of the Septuagint,[49] but it could also be a polemic against sectarians or Christians who either were claiming early Trinitarian thought or argued that there were two powers in the heavens.[50] For example, the Babylonian Talmud, knowing of Jewish interpreters who find two (or more) gods at the creation, insists: "In all the passages which the heretics [Hebrew *minim*; i.e., sectarians] have taken as proofs, their refutation is near at hand. Thus: 'Let us make man in our image' 'And God created man in His own image' [Gen 1,27]; 'Come, let us go down and confound their language!' [Gen 11,7] 'And the Lord came down' [Gen 11,5]" (Sanhedrin 38b). In other words, when plural verbs are predicated of God, singular verbs used nearby clarify that God is acting alone. Genesis Rabbah (8:8) cites a tradition responding to the same issue: "When Moses was engaged in the writing of the Law, he had to write the works of each day. When he came to the verse, 'And God said: "Let us make man,"' he said: 'Sovereign of all, why do you provide the heretics with an argument?' God replied: 'Write! Whoever wishes to err, let him err!'" Whether the author of this midrash was polemicizing against Christian readings or whether the concern is with sectarian Jews who held to a binitarian theology of two powers in heaven cannot be determined.

Most Jewish works through the third century CE insist that the plural refers to God in conversation with the angels. One tradition, attributed to a third-century sage, expresses this idea through an imagined dialogue:

When the Holy One, blessed be He, wished to create man [Hebrew *'adam*; i.e., "humanity"], He [first] created a company of ministering angels and said to them, "Is it your desire that we make man in our image?" They answered: "Sovereign of all, what will be his deeds?" He replied that such and such will be his deeds. Thereupon, they exclaimed: "What is man that You are mindful of him and the son of man that You think of him?" [Ps 8:5]. Thereupon, He stretched out His little finger among them and consumed them with fire. The same thing happened with the second company. The third company said to Him: "Sovereign of the universe, what did it avail the former [companies of angels] that they spoke to You [as they did]? The whole world is Yours, and whatever You wish to do therein You do." (b. Sanhedrin 38b)

The angels, realizing that protest is not likely to be met with happy consideration, yield to the divine plan. God would create humanity, regardless of the warning that human beings would sin.

Classical rabbinic interpretation is not, however, unanimous concerning this plural as referring to the angels of the heavenly host. Other rabbis propose that God was speaking to "the works of heaven and earth," "the works of each day," "his heart," or even "the preexisting souls of the righteous."[51] According to one midrash, the plural phrasing indicates God's internal debate. Genesis Rabbah 8:3–4 records in the name of Rabbi Berekhiah: "When the Holy One was about to create Adam, He saw both the righteous and the wicked who were to issue from him. So He said, 'If I create him, wicked men will issue from him; if I do not create him, how are righteous men to be born?'" The midrash concludes by claiming that God "diverted the way of the wicked before His sight, partnered the quality of mercy with Himself, [saying to it, 'Let us make man'], and then created him."[52] It is likely that an early Jewish synagogue prayer, in Greek, preserved in the Christian fourth-century *Apostolic Constitutions*, explained the plural by assuming that God was speaking to Wisdom, with whom he cocreated humanity: "Thereafter the various kinds of animals were formed, those on dry land, those living in water, those traversing the air, and the amphibians; and the skillful Wisdom [*sophia*] of your providence imparts to each of them the corresponding provisions. For just as she was strong enough to produce different kinds (of animals), so too she did not neglect to make different provisions for each."[53] This idea fits well with traditions that we saw above about Wisdom/Sophia as a deity alongside God in a wide variety of Jewish texts. Offering the Torah as God's conversation partner at creation, Pirkei de-Rabbi Eliezer, a Jewish work redacted after the rise of Islam,[54] notes:

> The Holy One, blessed be He, spoke to the Torah: "Let us make man in our image after our likeness" (Gen 1:26). (The Torah) spoke before Him: Sovereign of all the worlds! The man whom You would create will be limited in days and full of anger, and he will come in to the power of sin. Unless You will be long-suffering with him, it would be well for him to not come into the world. The Holy One, blessed be He, rejoined: And is it for naught that I am called "slow to anger" and "abounding in love"?[55]

The lack of unanimity in classical rabbinic interpretation suggests the theological difficulty of this verse. It may also suggest ongoing debates with sectarians and Christians.

Medieval Jewish interpretations largely follow the rabbinic notion that God is talking to the angels. Rashi uses this notion to illustrate God's humility, for God consulted the angels before creating a being like them: "The meekness of the Holy One, blessed be He, they (the rabbis) learned from here: because the man is in the likeness of the angels and they might envy him, therefore He took counsel with them."[56]

These interpretations all assert that God created humanity alone—even if engaged in consultation. The rabbis found it necessary to emphasize that God, although happy to consult with angels, with Wisdom, or with the Torah, created humanity without the help of any partner.

The answer to "Who is 'us' in Genesis 1:26?" depends on the question we ask. Historical critics, concerned with the original or early meaning of the Bible, see the divine court in "us," and so God as taking counsel with the heavenly host. For some Jews, God is in consultation with the Torah. Christians typically see the Trinity, as reflected in Martin Luther's comments—though many would reproduce his ideas without their strong polemical edge:

> The word "Let Us make" is aimed at making sure the mystery of our faith, by which we believe that from eternity there is one God and that there are three separate Persons in one Godhead: the Father, the Son, and the Holy Spirit. The Jews indeed try in various ways to get around this passage, but they advance nothing sound against it. . . . It is utterly ridiculous when the Jews say that God is following the custom of princes, who, to indicate respect, speak of themselves in the plural number. The Holy Spirit is not imitating this court mannerism . . . nor does the Holy Scripture sanction this manner of speech.[57]

Luther was correct: the text is not speaking of the plural of majesty. Whether he is correct on the presence of the Trinity depends on the lenses through which one sees.

People seeking a pastoral teaching may determine that God is modeling cooperation—Genesis Rabbah offers a beautiful precedent for anyone who wants to adopt this reading, as does the Trinity. Feminists may locate Lady Wisdom here, or the Shechinah, and thereby bring female presence to the very beginning of the very beginning. Nor are these explications mutually exclusive.

Our exposition of these difficult verses—what they originally meant and what they mean to different religious communities—should not be used for continuing the late antique and medieval polemic. There is room enough in Jewish and Christian discussion today to be open enough to state, "I may not agree with you, but I understand how you came to your conclusion." Possibilities, not polemics.

We hope that our readers will look beyond these fraught verses and read the first creation story as a whole—a marvelously structured story that makes a strong claim for an ordered, good world, in which people can play a central and constructive role.

CHAPTER 4

❧

Adam and Eve

DEATH, DOMINATION, AND DIVORCE

THE STORY of Adam and Eve is essential to the New Testament. For Paul, Jesus is the antithesis of Adam; what Adam broke, Jesus fixed. As Adam introduces sin into the world, so Jesus introduces being in a right relationship with God. Paul proclaims, "For just as by the one man's disobedience the many were made sinners, so by the one man's obedience the many will be made righteous" (Rom 5:19). As Adam brings death into the world, so Jesus offers the opportunity for new life: "For since death came through a human being, the resurrection of the dead has also come through a human being; for as all die in Adam, so all will be made alive in Christ" (1 Cor 15:21–22; cf. 15:45).

Romans 5:12, "Therefore, just as sin came into the world through one man, and death came through sin, and so death spread to all because all have sinned," then becomes the prompt for seeing all humanity as participating in Adam's sin. The Greek expression *eph'ō*, which the NRSV translates as "because," indicates simply that all people sin. The Old Latin and Vulgate translations read "*in quo omnes peccaverunt*"—"in whom all have sinned."[1] This translation led Augustine to conclude that all people, as descendants of Adam, are born with the taint of this "original sin" and so are guilty and deserving of damnation—an idea found in neither the Hebrew nor the Greek versions of Genesis. Christian tradition reads the Adam and Eve story as indicating the "fall of man." As we shall see, Jewish interpreters had other readings.[2]

Regarding gender roles, Eden informs the New Testament as well. For Paul, the order of creation in Genesis 2—first the man and then the woman—establishes a hierarchy, with woman in the subordinate role; this hierarchy based on the order of creation is absent in Genesis 2 itself. Combining Genesis 2 with Plato's concern for ideal types and then derivatives, Paul sees that woman, created from the body of the man, is a step removed from the original, better creation:

> For a man ought not to have his head veiled, since he is the image and reflection of God; but woman is the reflection of man. Indeed, man was not made from woman, but woman from man. Neither was man created for the sake of woman, but woman for the sake of man. For this reason a woman ought to have a symbol of authority on her head, because of the angels. Nevertheless, in the Lord woman is not independent of man or man independent of woman. For just as woman came from man, so man comes through woman; but all things come from God. (1 Cor 11:7–12)

Reinforcing hierarchy rather than the mutuality with which the Corinthian quotation ends, 1 Timothy, a New Testament letter ascribed to Paul, depicts Eve as the original transgressor, whose sin has ongoing implications for all women: "Let a woman learn in silence with full submission. I permit no woman to teach or to have authority over a man; she is to keep silent. For Adam was formed first, then Eve; and Adam was not deceived, but the woman was deceived and became a transgressor. Yet she will be saved through childbearing, provided they continue in faith and love and holiness, with modesty" (1 Tim 2:11–15). The NRSV's "through childbearing" is a possible but generous translation. The text does not mean that women will not die in childbirth; the Greek suggests rather that women *must bear children* in order to gain salvation. In the late first and early second centuries, as many followers of Jesus came to the realization that he was not necessarily returning during their lifetimes, they determined to follow Paul's suggestion from 1 Corinthians 7:7–9: "I wish that all were as I myself am," says Paul, referring to celibacy. But as he states, celibacy is a spiritual gift: "Each has a particular gift from God." Therefore, he concludes, "To the unmarried and the widows I say that it is well for them to remain unmarried as I am. But if they are not practicing self-control, they should marry. For it is better to marry than to be aflame with passion." They may also have known Jesus's commendation of celibacy in Matthew 19:12, or apocryphal Acts, such as the Acts of Paul and Thecla, which promote celibacy. For the later communities, in which wives accepted not only Paul's message about the Christ but also about the flesh, 1 Timothy's exhortation to produce children, and so to give husbands their conjugal rights, becomes explicable.[3]

The Gospels do not mention Eve, and Adam appears only in Luke's genealogy, which begins with Jesus and ends with "son of Enos, son of Seth, son of Adam, son of God" (Luke 3:38). For Luke, all people, descended from Adam, are also children of God. But in the Gospel tradition, Jesus does cite the garden of Eden story together with the first creation story in Genesis 1. His focus is not on sin, or death, or resurrection; it is on rejecting the practice of divorce: "But from the beginning of creation, 'God made them male and female.' 'For this reason a man shall leave his father and mother and be joined to his wife, and the two shall become one flesh.' So they are no longer two, but one flesh" (Mark 10:6–8; cf. Matt 19:4–5). These and other New Testament interpretations of the garden of Eden story are fundamental to Christianity: they contribute to teachings concerning original sin, the "fall of man," the subordination of women, and the restriction of divorce. None of these ideas is explicit in the text of Genesis 2–3; while each is a possible reading, none is a necessary one. Returning to Eden, we can discern what the second creation story might have meant in its original context, and then see not only why Jesus and his followers emphasized certain interpretations but also how the Jewish tradition came to regard this same text.

THE GARDEN OF EDEN

T HE GARDEN of Eden story is part of the Torah's larger J source (from the German Jahwe, equivalent to English YHWH), or Yahwistic source, another one of the recognized sources of the Torah, which most scholars think antedates both the Priestly source and the Babylonian exile of 586 BCE.[4] This story of the creation of man and woman—their original innocence, the encounter with the snake, their eating the forbidden fruit, and their expulsion from the garden of Eden—is a "myth," by which we mean a metaphorical tale designed to explain why life is the way it is. A myth does not, however, explain how life *should* be. Genesis 2:4b–3:24 follows a cross-cultural mythic pattern, which describes a descent from the ideal to the actual. Similarly, the Greek writer Hesiod, in his eighth-century BCE *Works and Days*, speaks of a "golden age" from which humanity continued to decline. When we think of the "good old days," we are often appealing to a myth that romanticizes the past and ignores its problems.

Such mythic understandings of the past are more than traces of nostalgia; they help us deal with the present. We sometimes find ourselves projecting an image of the perfect past into the future so that, if we can find the right key, we can return to the garden of Eden, or the golden age. But if we confuse "myth" with "history" in the sense of what actually happened, we miscue the genre.

Genesis 2:4b reads, "In the day that the LORD God made the earth and the heavens." Creation here is a one-day effort, not the six-day effort described in Genesis 1:1–2:4a. This second creation story begins with a reference to plants and herbs and the lack of anyone to till the ground (Gen 2:4b–5). We should not pass over this notice too quickly. A major theme of the end of the story, and of life in ancient Israel, is agricultural hardship. Eden is a place where gardening is, in all senses of the term, fruitful; outside, in the real world, humanity faces drought and locusts and fire. Whereas Genesis 1, from the Priestly source, presents the ordering of plants and animals and then gives them to humanity for appropriate use, Genesis 2–3, from the Yahwistic (J) source, reveals how humanity and the natural world, which are initially in harmony, became alienated.[5]

Genesis 1 describes the creation first of plants and animals and then, on the sixth day, of humanity, male and female as equals. In Genesis 2, the creation of the first human, called *ha'adam* (Gen 2:7), precedes the time when there were any plants or animals. More, we do not have here the simultaneous creation of male and female.

The Hebrew prefix *ha-* of *ha'adam* is the definite article "the." In Hebrew, "the" cannot precede personal names; Hebrew has no formula for speaking of "the Deborah" or "the David." Therefore, Genesis 1–3 does not describe the creation of a fellow named "Adam."[6] "Adam," in the sense of a proper name, does not appear until Genesis 4:25, after the expulsion from Eden and the murder of Abel by Cain.

This human of Genesis 2 has two parts. The first, a physical part, is formed from earth or clay, *ha'adamah*. The wordplay highlights the close connection between humanity (*ha'adam*) and earth (*ha'adamah*). The translation "earthling" is appropriate—or perhaps "clod," given the man's passive behavior later in the story.[7] The verb "to form" (Hebrew *y-tz-r*) describes what potters do (see especially Jer 18:4), and thus the "LORD God," the name for the deity in the

J account, is envisioned as a master potter. The J source makes no mention, however, of this human being in the divine image.

The second part, "the breath of life" (Hebrew *nefesh chayah*), connotes the life force; it is what allows this earth creature to breathe. The *nefesh chayah* is not "the soul" in the sense of the part of us that survives physical death. The Septuagint translates *nefesh* as *psychē*, which in this text as well as in the New Testament means the "self" or the "inner life" or even "very being" rather than an "immortal soul." When we start thinking of this "soul" as something immortal, we have added to the original myth. The garden story has much to say about immortality, but surviving death through the immortality of the soul is not initially part of its teaching.

The LORD God then places *ha'adam* in "a garden in Eden" (Gen 2:8). The name "Eden" most likely derives from the Hebrew root *'-d-n*, "bliss, delight," as found, for example, in Psalm 36:8: "They feast on the abundance of your house, / and you give them drink from the river of your delights (*'adanecha*)." A cognate is the noun *'ednah*, meaning "pleasure," including sexual pleasure. When Abraham's wife Sarah hears that she, well past menopause, will conceive a child, she laughs and exclaims, "After I have grown old, and my husband is old, shall I have pleasure [*'ednah*]?" (Gen 18:12).

The Septuagint translates the Hebrew term *gan*, "garden," in Genesis 2–3 as *paradeisos*, which means "garden" but can have the connotation of "paradise." Thus, later texts will collapse, linguistically, the "paradise" of Eden with the "paradise" of heaven. Conflating Eden and heaven, and so projecting the myth of the past into the future, Revelation 2:7b announces, "To everyone who conquers, I will give permission to eat from the tree of life that is in the paradise of God." Similarly, the (probably) first-century Jewish author known as Pseudo-Philo suggests that the garden has been preserved and will be inhabited by the resurrected righteous.[8] Other New Testament references to "paradise" may also suggest the garden of Eden. For example, in Luke 23:43 Jesus tells the repentant thief hanging on a cross, "Truly I tell you, today you will be with me in Paradise." Paul's "third heaven" comment speaks of his being caught up into "Paradise" (2 Cor 12:2, 4).

Eden is, for Genesis, not in heaven but "in the east"—that is, in Mesopotamia, northeast of Israel, at the confluence of four rivers (Gen 2:10–14). The first river, Pishon in the land of Havilah, is in southwest Arabia; the second, Gihon, is in Cush, another name for Ethiopia. Yet Pishon is not otherwise attested, and Gihon is elsewhere in the Bible a spring in the land of Israel. The other two rivers are the well-known Tigris and Euphrates, both in Mesopotamia. The four rivers do not meet, and no geological data indicate that they ever did. Consequently, the setting is everywhere and nowhere.

In this locale, "in the midst of the garden," are two trees: "the tree of life . . . and the tree of the knowledge of good and evil" (Gen 2:9), but until chapter 3, their import for the plot remains unknown.

The role of *ha'adam* in the garden is "to till it and keep it" (Gen 2:15). Eden is not a place of perpetual rest; instead, it is a place where the work is both easy and fulfilling: we might compare the joy of weekend gardening to the backbreaking work of picking crops by hand.

The LORD God then sets up dietary regulations. *Ha'adam* may eat any of the garden's fruits. In this garden setting, humanity is vegetarian. Permission to consume animal flesh will not be given until Noah and his family exit the ark (Gen 9:3–4), and even then, blood is forbidden. One additional restriction prevails for Eden: "of the tree of the knowledge of good and evil you shall not eat, for in the day that you eat of it you shall die" (Gen 2:17). The Hebrew of the last phrase, *mot tamut*, using the same verb *m-w-t* ("to die") twice, can mean "you shall surely die" or "you will drop dead"; it can also mean, "you will become mortal," as in Psalm 82:7, where God tells the heavenly court (Hebrew *benei 'elyon*, literally "children of the Most High"), "You shall die [*temutun*] like mortals."

Whether God intended for humanity to be immortal is never explicitly stated. It seems likely to us that God intended *ha'adam* to live forever, and thus the warning concerning eating from the tree meant "you shall surely die." At this point, no prohibition is made regarding eating fruit from the tree of life, which conferred immortality—most likely because the text is imagining this first human as immortal. The mention of the tree of life is anticipatory.

The LORD God, who cares about this creature, then realizes, "It is not good that the man [*ha'adam*] should be alone; I will make him a helper as his partner" (Hebrew *'ezer kenegdo*) (Gen 2:18). The first word, *'ezer*, "helper," does not imply subordination; it may be used of an equal or even someone superior. It appears in popular personal names such as Ezra (helper) and Azariah (or its variant, Azaryahu), meaning "the Lord (Yah[u]) is [my] helper"; it also describes God in Psalm 121:2: "My help [*'ezer*] comes from the LORD, / who made heaven and earth." The second word, *neged*, means "in front of," "corresponding to," and even "opposite." Thus, this helper should be understood as a partner for *ha'adam*.

Neither is the role of the helper to provide *ha'adam* offspring. "Be fruitful and multiply" is the P version of the story, not the J version. Nor would procreation be advisable for immortal beings; the garden would quickly become overpopulated. The concern for overpopulation might seem anachronistic, but the Mesopotamian epic *Atrahasis*, written centuries earlier than the garden story, mentions the great noise caused by overpopulation and presents mortality as a remedy.[9]

The role of the helper, created as *ha'adam*'s equal, is to alleviate *ha'adam*'s solitary state in Eden. However, as we shall see, this original meaning did not discourage either the Jewish or the Christian tradition from considering this "helper," this woman, as created sub-ordinate to *ha'adam*, the man.

Genesis 2:19 describes the LORD God's initially unsuccessful attempt to create the partner from "every animal of the field and every bird of the air": "but for the man [*ha'adam*] there was not found a helper as his partner" (Gen 2:20). The LORD God tries again. Putting *ha'adam* into a deep sleep, he takes from him a *tzela'* and from it constructs a woman (2:21–22). Although traditionally rendered "rib" (a meaning this noun has in Akkadian and Arabic), in Biblical Hebrew *tzela'* typically means "side"—a meaning it also has in those languages—as in the construc-tion of the tabernacle: "two rings on the one side [*tzela'*] of it" (Exod 25:12). Ziony Zevit, a biblical scholar, and Scott Gilbert, an evolution-ary biologist, argue that this *tzela'* meant, for the J source, the baculum, or penis bone, that all male mammals with the exception of humans possess.[10] (Others take this thesis to be a "phallacy.")

The woman being created second, after the man and the animals, does not imply her—or any woman's—secondary status.[11] For the Bible, what is done last, not first, can be more important. This obser-vation on the order of creation is already noted in *The Women's Bible*, edited by Elizabeth Cady Stanton (1815–1902). Lillie Devereux Blake writes there: "In the detailed description of creation we find a gradu-ally ascending series. Creeping things, 'great sea monsters' . . . 'Every bird of wing,' cattle and living things of the earth . . . then man, and last and crowning glory of the whole, woman."[12]

Ha'adam, waking up and delighted upon seeing this new creation, speaks for the first time, and in poetry:

> This at last is bone of my bones
>   and flesh of my flesh;
> this one shall be called Woman,
>   for out of Man this one was taken. (Gen 2:23)

The word for "man" is *'ish*, and the word for "woman" is *'ishah*. The two words, which sound similar, express the idea that the two created beings are, at this point, closely and harmoniously related: "Therefore a man leaves his father and his mother and clings to his woman, and they become one flesh" (Gen 2:24, authors' translation). This "one flesh" reunites *ha'adam* with his missing piece, and so the two, together, are whole and become a new family. The comment anticipates procreation—when people *have* fathers and mothers—after the expulsion from Eden. The text does not state or even suggest that the man and woman were married, for such an institution did not exist in Eden. The Hebrew term *'ishah*, which we translate "woman," can also indicate "wife"; the same translation holds for the Greek term *gynē* (whence "gynecology"), but the translation "wife" for Genesis 2 would be an overread.

To this point, we have a happy, naked couple in the garden, where their task is to till it and keep it. The problem of human solitude is resolved. But the two trees indicate that problems lie ahead.

EATING FORBIDDEN FRUIT

THE LAST VERSE of Genesis 2 reads, "And the man and his wife were both naked, and were not ashamed" (v. 25). The chapter division is off, however. The verse actually introduces the next scene, in which the woman has her conversation with the snake. That the verse belongs with what follows is seen in the wordplay between 'arumim, "naked," used to describe the man and woman in 2:25, and the introduction of the snake as 'arum, "crafty," in 3:1. This description shows that the common stereotype of the woman as easily enticed is incorrect—craft was needed to persuade her to eat the forbidden fruit. Only in Genesis 3 is 'arum, craftiness, a negative trait; elsewhere it reflects positive cleverness or prudence, as in Proverbs 13:16: "The clever ['arum] do all things intelligently, / but the fool displays folly."

The snake (Hebrew nachash) is exactly that: sometimes a snake is just a snake. The same Hebrew term describes snakes elsewhere, such as Exodus 4 where Moses's and Aaron's staffs miraculously turn into snakes. Nothing in Genesis suggests that this creature is the devil, but we can see the connection in later texts. Paul may be thinking of Satan when he tells the Corinthian assembly, "But I am afraid that as the serpent deceived Eve by its cunning, your thoughts will be led astray from a sincere and pure devotion to Christ" (2 Cor 11:3), and the book of Revelation mentions "the dragon, that ancient serpent, who is the Devil and Satan" (Rev 20:2). The idea that the devil participated in causing Adam's sin is first made explicit by the second-century Christian writer Justin Martyr.[13]

Multiple reasons can be suggested for why the J author chose a snake to entice Eve. Perhaps there is an implied polemic against the worship of snakes or the view that snakes, because they shed their skin, are immortal. Perhaps the author picked up the connection between snakes and immortality, already noted in the Gilgamesh story, an ancient Mediterranean epic about the hero's (failed) search for immortality. Or perhaps the motivation was a pun, since the word for "snake" in several Semitic languages is *chivya*, close to the name of Eve, *chavah*. Perhaps the phallic shape of the snake, or the fact that snakes can be poisonous, made it the ideal character to entice her.[14]

In Genesis 3:1–5, this snake approaches the woman, still unnamed, and inquires about the forbidden tree: "Did God say, 'You shall not eat from any tree in the garden'?" (v. 1). We do not know what the snake's motive is: To gain the fruit for itself? To alienate the human couple from God? To see whether the woman would in fact die?

The woman explains that she and *ha'adam* should neither eat the tree's fruit nor touch it, lest they die. The narrator does not tell us who gave the woman these instructions, or where the comment about touching originated. One midrash fills in the story by suggesting that at this point, the snake pushed the woman into the tree. When she did not die, she determined that since the touch would not kill her, neither would the taste.[15] The snake counters: "You will not die," but "your eyes will be opened, and you will be like God [or "gods"; Hebrew *'elohim*], knowing good and evil" (Gen 3:4–5). Although the NRSV has the singular "God," the designation *'elohim* here is a plural, since the verb "knowing," describing these gods in the heavenly court, is in the plural.

The woman makes a careful decision: "So when the woman

saw that the tree was good for food, and that it was a delight to the eyes, and that the tree was to be desired to make one wise, she took of its fruit and ate; and she also gave some to her husband [Hebrew 'ish, "man"], who was with her, and he ate" (Gen 3:6). We could read this woman as a "theologian, ethicist, hermeneut, rabbi, [who] speaks with clarity and authority"[16] and who eats because she "finds the tree physically appealing, aesthetically pleasing, and above all, sapientially transforming. . . . Moreover, she does not discuss the matter with her man. She acts independently . . . she is not secretive, deceptive or withdrawn."[17] Or, we could see her as deliberately transgressing the one commandment she and her man received, as failing to engage in consultation, and as overstepping her role by seeking to become like the gods. The text could be read either way. As seen above, the author of 1 Timothy blames the woman by stating that the "man was not deceived." For 1 Timothy, the man was not "deceived" because *he realized what he was doing*. As soon as the woman took a bite from the forbidden fruit, she was, the man knew, doomed. By eating, he sacrificed his immortality for her sake.

The couple do not die. After eating the fruit, "the eyes of both were opened, and they knew that they were naked; and they sewed fig leaves together and made loincloths for themselves" (Gen 3:7). No longer like animals, who lack shame in nudity, they realize that their naked bodies should not be on public display. The man and the woman move from the world of nature to what might be called the world of civilization.

They have also become "like gods, knowing good and evil" (Gen 3:5, authors' translation; *ke'lohim*—again, the NRSV mistranslates as "like God"). As the context suggests, "knowing" here has a sexual sense—it is knowing in the biblical sense, and indeed as soon as they are expelled from the garden, "the man knew his wife Eve" (4:1). The type of knowledge the tree of knowledge of good and evil provides is ultimate, sexual knowledge. This couple has become sexual like the "sons of gods" mentioned in Genesis 6:1–3, who father children with human women. Yet unlike the gods, they have become mortal. Like the demoted gods of Psalm 82, they will die. They have a new means of immortality: through children.

The story continues with the repercussions that stem from the couple's disobedience: the man blames the woman but places primary responsibility on God; the woman blames the snake; the snake has no one to blame. It is in God's comments to the woman and the man that we find substantial differences among historical-critical, Jewish, and Christian readings.

The NRSV translates Genesis 3:16 thus:

To the woman he said,
> "I will greatly increase your pangs in childbearing;
>> in pain you shall bring forth children,
> yet your desire shall be for your husband,
>> and he shall rule over you."

Genesis 3 does *not* speak of the woman as cursed, although it does describe the snake as "cursed" (3:14–15), and, regarding the man, the earth is cursed (3:17–19). Rather than a curse, Genesis 3:16 is a description of the woman's new status. Pregnancy and childbirth required women to have twice the amount of work to do, since women are responsible not only for some agriculture work, textile production, culinary activity, and so forth, but also for pregnancy, parturition, lactation, and childcare. Thus, the first part of Genesis 3:16 might be better translated, "I will make great your toil and many your pregnancies; with hardship shall you have children."[18] The Hebrew root the NRSV translates as "pain" and "pangs" is the same term it uses, in the next verse, to describe the man's situation regarding the land, but here the term is rendered "toil": "in toil you shall eat of it all the days of your life."[19] While the final clause, "and he shall rule over you," could be a reference to the male as the dominant sexual partner,[20] the verb "will rule" (Hebrew *yimshol*) suggests a broader understanding: women's subordination. Until this point, the second creation story saw the man and the woman as having equal standing—no more. When they enter into civilization, gender roles, with their built-in hierarchies, enter as well. There is no "separate but equal" outside Eden. The same idea, using the same crucial verb, *m-sh-l,* that men should rule over women, is implied by Isaiah 3:12, where the prophet describes a topsy-turvy world: "My people—children are their oppressors, / and women rule over [*mashelu*] them."

God next curses not the man, but the earth:

> And to the man he said,
> "Because you have listened to the voice of your wife,
> and have eaten of the tree
> about which I commanded you,
> 'You shall not eat of it,'
> cursed is the ground because of you;
> in toil you shall eat of it all the days of your life;
> thorns and thistles it shall bring forth for you;
> and you shall eat the plants of the field.
> By the sweat of your face
> you shall eat bread
> until you return to the ground,
> for out of it you were taken;
> you are dust,
> and to dust you shall return." (Gen 3:17–19)

Originally, while the man had agricultural obligations in the garden (2:15), *ha'adam*, "the man," and *ha'adamah*, "the earth," worked in harmony. Now, *ha'adam* and *'adamah* will have a new relationship: man will eat the earth's produce only through toil and will return to earth by decomposing.

In Genesis 2, the man (*'ish*) identified the woman as *'ishah*. Their similar names demonstrated their connection, as did the man's comment about "bone of my bones and flesh of my flesh." Now, having tasted the forbidden fruit, *ha'adam* names the woman "Eve" (Hebrew *chavah*), which the narrator explains through "she was [to become] the mother of all living" (3:20); *chavah* is connected to the Hebrew word *chai*, "to live." Her naming is appropriate, since only at this point is the couple "knowing" or sexually active. But this naming also signals a distance between them. Not only do their names no longer sound alike, but the woman is now identified not as the man's partner but biologically as a mother.

Despite the disobedience of the man and the woman, the LORD God remains compassionate. Not wanting the couple to wander around wearing fragile fig leaves (3:7), "the LORD God made garments of skins for the man and for his wife, and clothed them" (3:21). We cannot determine whether animals were slaughtered for this purpose, or whether the skins were from animals that had died; later sources suggest that Leviathan hide, or the skin of the crafty serpent, served this purpose.[21]

But the story cannot end here. The garden also contains a tree of life, a tree that grants immortality. God anticipated that the original commandment might be broken. Therefore, God expels the couple from Eden not as punishment but rather out of the concern that "he [the man] might reach out his hand and take also from the tree of life, and eat, and live forever" (3:22). This concern is so great that God places at the entrance to the garden "the cherubim, and

a sword flaming and turning to guard the way to the tree of life"
(3:24).

This is the story—no more, no less. No identification of the garden with paradise where righteous people reside after death, no immortal soul, no Satan, no irreparable breach between humanity and divinity. The fruit, not specified, is unlikely to be an apple—apples were common in the Mediterranean world only centuries after this story was written. The connection likely began with the church father Jerome, whose translation of the Hebrew Bible into Latin (the Vulgate) rendered the fruit as *malus*, the Latin word meaning "evil" but also a term for fruits such as apples and figs. The specification of the fruit as an apple became popular around the twelfth century.

Most significant for later interpretations, the word "sin" is absent from this story. Instead, the story describes how people became both sexually aware and mortal. Like many stories of origin, it explains how the world as we know it came into being. But this new reality, according to Genesis 2–3, is not a state of alienation from God. God is outside the garden, with Adam and Eve, and with their descendants.

THE GARDEN OF EDEN IN THE BIBLE
OUTSIDE OF GENESIS

ALTHOUGH Adam and Eve are among the best-known biblical figures, the Torah never refers to them again.[22] Outside of the initial chapters of Genesis, the name Adam does not appear again other than in a genealogy in 1 Chronicles (1:1).[23] Several prophetic texts mention the luxuriousness of the garden, which Genesis does not emphasize, but they ignore Adam and Eve, the snake, and the trees.[24] For example, Isaiah 51 consoles the exiles in Babylon by promising,

> For the LORD will comfort Zion;
>> he will comfort all her waste places,
>> and will make her wilderness like Eden,
>>> her desert like the garden of the LORD. (51:3a)

These prophetic accounts, which often use the phrase "the garden of God," emphasize the garden's luxurious nature. How exactly this location was "the garden of God" is never clarified. For example, Ezekiel, writing in the early exilic period, uses Eden imagery more frequently than any other prophet. In 28:13, he raises a lamentation against the unnamed king of Tyre—the Phoenician city well known for its luxury goods:

You were in Eden, the garden of God;
 every precious stone was your covering,
carnelian, chrysolite, and moonstone,
 beryl, onyx, and jasper.

Genesis 2:12 associates gold, bdellium, and onyx with Eden. Ezekiel then describes the king's downfall, but because his depiction shares little vocabulary with Genesis 2–3, it is unlikely that he patterned this king's "fall" after that of Adam. In chapter 31, an oracle to Pharaoh, Ezekiel mentions Eden three times (vv. 9, 16, 18), again as symbolic of luxury.[25]

Joel 2:3, by noting "Before them [the ravaging locusts] the land is like the garden of Eden, / but after them a desolate wilderness," similarly depicts Eden as the antithesis of the wilderness. Later tradition conflates these edenic markers: luxury, wealth, fecundity, celebration, and joy. This imagery will inform the book of Revelation, which promises, "To everyone who conquers, I will give permission to eat from the tree of life that is in the paradise of God" (Rev 2:7b). But we should not retroject these ideas into an earlier period.

Original Sin in the Hebrew Bible?

ALTHOUGH the Christian idea of original sin, a genetic marker inherited from Adam (see below), is not made explicit in Genesis 2–3, the view that humans have an innate tendency to sin is found elsewhere in the Bible and is especially common in Psalms and wisdom literature. People are expected to control this tendency, and when they do sin, they are expected, depending on the biblical source, to repent, to confess, to pray, and/or to offer sacrifices. The clearest articulation of humanity's propensity to sin is in Psalm 51:5 (51:7 Heb.; 50:7 LXX), where the psalmist, identified in the superscription as David after he sinned with Bathsheba, claims, "Indeed, I was born guilty, / a sinner when my mother conceived me," and then asks for divine mercy.[26] In Psalm 130:3, another lament, the supplicant pleads, "If you, O LORD, should mark iniquities, / Lord, who could stand?"; and Psalm 143:2 states, "Do not enter into judgment with your servant, / for no one living is righteous before you." According to 1 Kings 8:46, upon dedicating the Jerusalem Temple, Solomon asks God to forgive true supplicants, "for there is no one who does not sin." None of these texts, however, suggests that humanity's propensity to sin was inherited from Adam.

For all of these texts, this human desire to sin should prompt divine compassion and therefore forgiveness; the same idea appears in Genesis 8:21, when Noah offers a sacrifice after the flood: "the LORD said in his heart, 'I will never again curse the ground because of humankind, for the inclination of the human heart is evil from youth; nor will I ever again destroy every living creature as I have done.'"

Similar ideas appear often in Wisdom literature. The sage observes in Ecclesiastes 7:20, "Surely there is no one on earth so righteous as to do good without ever sinning," and Proverbs 20:9 quotes a wisdom saying: "Who can say, 'I have made my heart clean; / I am pure from my sin'?" Job's "friend" Eliphaz asks, "What are mortals, that they can be clean? / Or those born of woman, that they can be righteous?" (Job 15:14). Bildad, another of Job's "friends," notes similarly:

> How then can a mortal be righteous before God?
>> How can one born of woman be pure?
> If even the moon is not bright
>> and the stars are not pure in his sight,
> how much less a mortal, who is a maggot,
>> and a human being, who is a worm! (Job 25:4–6)

While the Psalms and Genesis focus on divine compassion and forgiveness, the Wisdom texts suggest that God is free to punish people, since they always sin.

ADAM AND EVE IN EARLY JUDAISM

NONE OF THESE early sources elaborating upon Genesis 2–3 contains any speculation about the fall of humanity or original sin.[27] Little is said about Eve's particular responsibility, and little is made of the snake. Such negative evidence suggests that these ideas may be original to the early Christ-believing community. The early Jewish focus is rather on the garden itself, the gaining of sexual knowledge and the concurrent loss of immortality, and the regaining of the garden in the future.

Following the few references to him in the Hebrew texts, Adam next appears in the second-century BCE book of Tobit, extant fully in Greek, with some passages found in Hebrew and Greek among the Dead Sea Scrolls. Tobit's son Tobias, having married his several-times widowed yet still virginal cousin Sarah, prays: "You made Adam, and for him you made his wife Eve as a helper and support. From the two of them the human race has sprung. You said, 'It is not good that the man should be alone; let us make a helper for him like himself.'" In this story, Adam and Eve are marital role models, not negative exemplars. This positive view of Adam and Eve continues in the Jewish tradition. One of the seven blessings recited at a traditional Jewish wedding begins, "Bring great joy on these loving friends, as You gave joy to Your creations in the Garden of Eden."[28]

There may be a reference, and a negative one, to Eve in the writings of Jesus ben Sira. The author of the original Hebrew version lived in the first half of the second century BCE; the Greek translation by the author's grandson was completed in "the 38th year of the reign of Euergetes" of Egypt, that is, 132 BCE. The original Hebrew was discovered only in the late nineteenth century in the Cairo Geniza, a repository for old Jewish writings. Since then, additional Hebrew fragments were discovered among the Dead Sea Scrolls and at Masada. These finds attest to the importance of this book in early Judaism. Sirach 25:16–26, which begins, "I would rather live with a lion and a dragon than live with an evil woman," is a speech concerning the evils of women. The Hebrew continues, "From a woman is the beginning of guilt, and because of her we die together"; the Greek version translates, "From a woman is the beginning of sin, and through her we all die."[29] This verse is plausibly a reference to the woman eating the forbidden fruit, feeding her husband, and thus bringing mortality, hard work, and antagonism into the world. Whether Sirach 25:24 refers to Eve is, however, debated. While the verse may refer to Eve, John Levison offers an alternative translation: "From the [evil] wife [*gynē*] is the beginning of sin, and because of her we [husbands] all die."[30]

Other texts do not hesitate to blame Eve. Sibylline Oracles 1:42–43 states: "But the woman first became a betrayer to him [Adam]. She gave, and persuaded him to sin in his ignorance." First Enoch mentions Eve once (69:6), in reference to the angel Gader'el (or Gadre'el) "who misled Eve" and created other acts of mischief among humans.[31] We see here the beginnings of the eventual association of the snake with Satan.

Philo explains that women's creation led to love, which led to physical attraction, which led to carnality, which leads to sin. He begins by associating change, which is a necessary part of the mortal life, with disaster, and then maps this concern onto Adam and Eve. Speaking of the first man, Philo observes:

> As long as he was single, he resembled, as to his creation, both the world and God. . . . But when woman also was created, man perceiving a closely connected figure and a kindred formation to his own, rejoiced at the sight, and approached her and embraced her. And she, in like manner, beholding a creature greatly resembling herself, rejoiced also, and addressed him in reply with due modesty. And love being engendered . . . And this desire caused likewise pleasure to their bodies, which is the beginning of iniquities and transgressions, and it is owing to this that men have exchanged their previously immortal and happy existence for one which is mortal and full of misfortune. (*Creation* 151–52)

For Philo, it is not the woman's disobedience that creates the problem, but her very existence. Genesis becomes the rationale for Philo's promotion of women's subordinate status, for they are of "lesser dignity."

Likely influenced by Aristotle, who proclaimed that women were naturally inferior to men, Philo asks, "Why, as other animals and as man also was made, the woman was not also made out of the earth, but out of the rib of the man?" (*Questions and Answers to Genesis* 1, 27). He posits, first, that the rib indicates that the woman lacks the same dignity her husband possesses. Second, the creation from his rib suggests that wives, naturally, should be younger than their husbands. From this he concludes both that husbands should care for their wives as they do their daughters, just as women should honor their husbands as they do their fathers. The story of the rib, in Philo's imagination, reduces the wife to a subordinate state of childhood.

The Life of Adam and Eve, a Jewish writing whose origins likely date to the first century CE, condemns Eve alone: "Oh evil woman, why have you wrought destruction among us?" (21:6). In 32:2 Eve states, "All sin in creation has come about through me." The strongest negative depiction of Eve is found in 2 Enoch, whose date is uncertain: "I [God] created for him [Adam] a wife, so that death might come [to him] by his wife" (2 En 30:17). This text complements 1 Timothy in observing that the devil "entered paradise and corrupted Eve. But he did not contact Adam" (2 En 31:5; cf. 1 Tim 2:14). For 2 Enoch, "Eve is created only to lure Adam into the trap of his ignorance."[32]

Jewish texts from the Hellenistic period repurpose Eden into an eschatological, postmortem paradise. The section of 1 Enoch known as the Book of Watchers, found among the Dead Sea Scrolls, describes the tree of life as "this beautiful fragrant tree—and no [creature of] flesh has authority to touch it until the great judgment when he will take vengeance . . . this will be given to the righteous and humble" (1 En 25:4).[33] Related is the traditional Jewish prayer concerning the dead, 'el maleh rachamim ("God full of mercy"), which asks, "may his/her resting place be in the garden of Eden."

On the more mundane level, the Torah becomes for the community the tree of life. To this day, in synagogue services, when the Torah scroll is returned to the ark where it is housed, the congregation sings Proverbs 3:18: "She [in this liturgical context, the Torah] is a tree of life to those who lay hold of her; / those who hold her fast are called happy."

The earliest Jewish source outside Paul's letters that speaks to Adam's sin is late first-century CE 4 Ezra, which asks: "O Adam, what have you done? For though it was you who sinned, the misfortune/fall[34] was not yours alone, but ours also who are your descendants" (4 Ezra 7:118). This sentiment is also expressed in 4 Ezra 3:21–26 where Ezra says to God, "For the first Adam, burdened with an evil heart, transgressed and was overcome, as were also all who were descended from him," and then associates Adam with the inhabitants of Jerusalem, who "transgressed, in everything doing as Adam and all his descendants had done, for they also had the evil heart."

A contrary view in the contemporaneous 2 Baruch shows that 4 Ezra's conclusions were far from universal in the late first century CE. For this text, Adam's descendants inevitably disobey God, but they do not inherit sin from him.[35] In 48:42, 2 Baruch appears to echo the lament in 4 Ezra 7:118, "O Adam, what have you done?" by asking, "O Adam, what did you do to all who were born after you?" But 2 Baruch 54:19 then explains, "Adam is therefore not the cause, save only of his own soul, but each of us has been the Adam of his own soul."[36]

Here, as in much of the scriptures of Israel and other postbiblical Jewish sources, sin is part of the human condition, the result of bad choices. Without proclaiming original sin in the sense of an inheritance from Adam, an indelible stain that can be washed clean only through Jesus's blood, these verses find their way into arguments for that position.

Some texts in the scriptures of Israel recognize that sin, while not inherited from Adam or Eve, may be inherited intergenerationally. The Decalogue, for example, suggests that God visits "the guilt of the parents upon the children, upon the third and upon the fourth generations" of those who reject him (Exod 20:5 and Deut 5:9 NJPS). Yet other texts dispute this idea of inherited guilt. Ezekiel cites a proverb, "The parents have eaten sour grapes, and the children's teeth are set on edge" (Ezek 18:2), but then he immediately rejects the concept. Similarly, Jeremiah 31:30 states that in the ideal future, "all shall die for their own sins; the teeth of everyone who eats sour grapes shall be set on edge."

LATER JEWISH TRADITION

S OME CHRISTIANS later deemed the act of eating the forbidden fruit the felix culpa, "fortunate guilt"—because of this "blessed fault," the Christ enters the world. This term appears as early as Ambrose, Augustine's mentor, at the end of the fourth century CE. But the dominant view of the Eden story was that it created a state of alienation between humanity and divinity, with the guilt of Adam and Eve inherited by all their descendants. In Augustine's formulation, the inheritance was biological: Adam's sin caused his "seed to become vitiated" (*Against Julian* 3.33)—or, in modern terms, his semen contained the genetic marker of original sin. Thus, all humanity inherits, literally, the sin of Adam, and this sin is manifest through our desire to do evil or our involuntary sexual longings; this is what Augustine called "concupiscence."[37]

Several rabbinic interpretations polemicize against this view, highlighting God's forgiveness instead of Adam's sin.[38] Leviticus Rabbah 29:1 states, "God tells Adam: 'Just as you came before the divine court and I pardoned you, so too will your descendants come before the divine court, and I will pardon them.'" According to Genesis Rabbah 21:6, God shows Adam "the door to repentance."

Genesis Rabbah 19:7 not only dismisses the idea that we inherit Adam's sin, but it also regards sin as no worse than any in the long line of human evil, including Cain's fratricide, the generation of the flood, the building of the Tower of Babel, the sins of Sodom, and so on. With each sin, the Shechinah, the divine presence, moved farther away from humanity. "But as against these there arose seven righteous men: Abraham, Isaac, Jacob, Levi, Kohath, Amram, and Moses, and they brought it [the Shechinah] down again to earth."[39] Sin is inevitable, but the activities of the righteous can return the Shechinah to earth.

This midrash also introduces an important theme of rabbinic literature: Sinai (and not Jesus) is the antidote to sin.[40] A later midrash quotes God:

> If I gave Adam but one commandment that he might fulfill it, and I made him equal to the ministering angels, for it says *behold the man was one of us* (Gen 3:22)—how much more so should those who practice and fulfill all the six hundred and thirteen commandments [the number of commandments found in the Torah according to the rabbis]—not to mention their general principles, details and minutiae—be deserving of eternal life?[41]

The point here is not the dreaded "works righteousness," that is, the idea that Jews follow the commandments in order to earn God's love or postmortem salvation. This idea is a mistaken view of Jewish thought. Jews do not follow the Torah in order to "earn" divine love. Jews lovingly follow the Torah in response to the love God showed Israel by giving the Torah to them.

Although Augustine's notion of vitiated seed does not appear in Jewish teaching, some rabbis did imagine that the events in Eden caused the human body to change. Genesis Rabbah 12:6 suggests that Adam had a gigantic body (as Isaiah 6 depicts God as having a gigantic body), but that body was diminished as a result of eating the forbidden fruit. A later midrash, Tanhuma,[42] suggests that in addition to losing stature and becoming mortal because of the Eden incident, people lost four other traits: a radiant face, easy access to food, residence in the garden, and the original great luminosity of the sun and the moon.

For the rabbis, the idea of an edenic fall is a minority opinion. More popular are countervailing claims suggesting that everything, including death, was part of the divine plan. Genesis Rabbah 9:5 reports that Rabbi Meir's Torah scroll, instead of saying at the end of creation that everything was "very good" (Hebrew *tov me'od*), read "death was good" (Hebrew *tov mavet*). This fanciful claim implies that the mortality bestowed upon all of Adam's descendants cannot be seen as a curse.

Indeed, the predominant rabbinic opinion is that Adam is *not* guilty of any "original sin," as in the following midrash from Tanhuma:

> Though death was brought into the world through Adam, yet he cannot be held responsible for the death of men. Once on a time he said to God: "I am not concerned about the death of the wicked, but I should not like the pious to reproach me and lay the blame for their death upon me. I pray Thee, make no mention of my guilt." And God promised to fulfil his wish. . . . As soon as life is extinct in a man, he is presented to Adam, whom he accuses of having caused his death. But Adam repudiates the charge: "I committed but one trespass. Is there any among you, and be he the most pious, who has not been guilty of more than one?"[43]

Adam is guilty of sin—but only his own.

Concerning the woman, the rabbis, as to be expected, present a variety of evaluations of Eve herself, and of Eve as a prototypical woman.[44] Genesis Rabbah 18:1 expresses women's superiority over men by punning. The Hebrew *vayiven*, in the expression "the rib that the LORD God had taken from the man he made [*vayiven*—literally "he built"] into a woman" (Gen 2:22), sounds like the word *binah*, "understanding"—in Hebrew the two words share several common letters. Thus Rabbi Ele'azar concludes: "She was given more understanding [*binah*] than the man."[45] Another midrash there (17:2) lauds the importance of marriage by seeing Eve as the answer to Genesis 2:18, "It is not good that the man should be alone"; the midrash states, "anyone who is in a wifeless state is without goodness, without help, without happiness, without blessing and without atonement." After bringing biblical prooftexts for each point, other sages chime in by noting that an unmarried man is also without peace and without life. The passage ends audaciously, with one sage proclaiming that a man without a wife is "not a complete person" and according to some, "even diminishes the [divine] likeness."[46]

Yet the rabbis were also realists who knew of difficult, and failed, marriages. Using the phrase *'ezer kenegdo* (Gen 2:18, 20), where *'ezer* in rabbinic Hebrew means a (subservient) helper and *kenegdo* has a range of meanings, including "opposite," the rabbis adduced, "if he is worthy, she [his wife] is a help; if he is not worthy, she opposes him" (b. Yevamot 63a, also cited by Rashi on Gen 2:18).

Still other rabbinic texts understand Eve, and all women, along the same lines as Ben Sira. Although no rabbinic texts declare women to be of second-class status because they were created second, some texts do draw derogatory conclusions concerning Eve as a result of her creation from a rib. Because man was created from soil and woman from a rib, Genesis Rabbah 17:8 concludes that men do not need to perfume themselves, since soil smells good, while bones stink after a few days.

A later midrash, Pirkei de-Rabbi Eliezer 18, uses negative views about women to explain why the snake chose the woman to entice:

"The serpent had a discussion with itself, saying, 'If I talk to the *'adam*, I know that he will not listen to me, for it is always hard to get a man to change his mind . . . ; but I will talk to the woman, whose thoughts are frivolous, for I know that she will listen to me; for women listen to all creatures, as it is said, "She [the stupid woman] is simple and does not know anything"' (cf. Proverbs 9:13)."[47]

Similar to 1 Timothy, some rabbinic texts find that the woman's disobedience has lasting repercussions. Genesis Rabbah 17:8 takes this viewpoint but at the same time explains why women are entrusted with the commandments to keep the laws of menstrual purity, remove in baking the first part of the dough (*challah*) that is due the priest, and light Sabbath candles.[48] Other texts suggest that women must cover their hair out of shame for the sin they committed and they walk first near the corpse as it is led in procession to be buried because they brought death into the world.[49] Many Jewish women to this day do not, while they are menstruating, have sexual relations with their husbands; they toss a bit of dough into the oven before baking; and they light Sabbath candles. Most, however, do not see themselves as cursed because of Eve. To the contrary, they see these activities as a form of sacralizing their lives.

The Jewish tradition does not depict a perfect woman, such as Mary plays in some Christian traditions, any more than it depicts a sinless man. However, in attempting to harmonize Genesis 1 and Genesis 2, it does offer a negative female figure, Lilith, Adam's first wife. According to this legend, first fully developed in the ninth-century CE *Alphabet of Jesus ben Sira* (unrelated to the much earlier book of Ben Sira or Sirach), "When the first man, Adam, saw that he was alone, God made for him a woman like himself, from the earth. God called her name Lilith, and brought her to Adam. They immediately began to quarrel. Adam said: 'You lie beneath me.' And Lilith said: 'You lie beneath me! We are both equal, for both of us are from the earth.' And they would not listen to one another." Lilith eventually flees to Egypt. As the legend developed, Lilith is the cause of the death of infants and of nocturnal emissions. To prevent her from exerting her power, Jewish women are to do what the Talmud had already suggested: observe the laws of menstrual purity, toss dough into the oven before baking, and light the Sabbath candles.[50]

———————

Today, Adam and Eve are back in the news with debates over biblical literalism coupled with "young earth" theorists. Some people insist that the story of Adam and Eve must be historically true: for Jesus to redeem humanity from sin requires Adam and Eve to introduce it. Some insist there must be a garden of Eden because that is where the righteous dead inherit eternal life. Eve becomes the reason why, in some Christian settings, women do not teach or have authority over men. As we have seen, there are other readings that do not require original sin, the fall of man, or even a historical Adam and Eve.

The story of Eden is a myth of how things came to be. It is not, however, a prescription for how things must be. Instead, it prompts us to ask the necessary questions about how things *should be*. First, it demands we attend to our relation to the earth, to plants and animals. It states we have a natural connection to the ground, since we are all earth creatures, and to the earth we will return. How then should we care for it? Second, although Genesis depicts God as cursing the ground, we nevertheless do what we can to lift that curse, using machinery, or pesticides, or genetic engineering. If we can combat the curse of the ground, there is no reason to derive from Genesis 3 an insistence on women's subordination or their experiencing pain or additional labor during childbirth.

Third, the creation narratives have led to different understandings of human nature: Are we just a bit lower than the angels, cared for by a compassionate God, and given free will, or are we depraved from the moment of conception and worthy of eternal damnation? Do we emphasize original sin, or original opportunity?

Genesis 2–3 asks us to think about immortality. Faced with returning to dust, how do we make each moment count? Are our children, or the works of our hands, or the contributions of our thoughts, a substitute for immortality? Or do we require immortal souls in a mythical future to match the mythical past? Is Eden our true home, such that we are always in exile, or is our true home wherever we make it?

For some, seeing these multiple voices diminishes the Bible's power, and these differences must somehow be reconciled. For others, including us, it is precisely the multivocality of the Bible, its interest in offering multiple, often conflicting perspectives, that gives it its power. Already in the first chapters of the Bible, we see these multiple perspectives in the two creation stories from the Yahwist (J) source and the Priestly (P) source. For some, asking questions about the text is dangerous because the answers could lead to new choices, to different religious beliefs. For us, the text prompts us to ask these questions and others, and it is through our answers that we discover ourselves and our place in the world.

CHAPTER 5

"You Are a Priest Forever"

PRIESTHOOD IN ANCIENT ISRAEL

THE NRSV introduces our text with the heading "The Letter to the Hebrews"; traditionally, it is ascribed to Paul. The text does not claim to be written by Paul, is more a sermon than a letter, and is addressed not to Hebrews in the sense of Jews but to the followers of Jesus, whether Jewish or gentile.

Nevertheless, Hebrews is a rhetorically sophisticated text that offers many delights. Filled with alliteration and assonance, already the first line plays on the "p" sound, *polymerōs kai polutropōs palai* (alas, the English translation of Heb 12:2, identifying Jesus as the "pioneer and perfecter" of the faith, adds alliteration that is missing in the Greek). The epistle also offers amusingly coy comments: it introduces its citation of Psalm 110, the New Testament's most-cited text from the Hebrew scriptures, with the understated phrase "someone has testified somewhere" (2:6). Not only does Hebrews draw on Israel's scriptures, but also it alludes to Hellenistic philosophy, most famously Plato's allegory of the cave (*Republic* 7.514a–520a) by speaking of earthly items such as the wilderness sanctuary (Heb 8:5) and the law (10:1) as "shadows" that portend the true reality manifest in Jesus, the Christ. For Hebrews, Jesus is superior to any other figure: Abraham and Moses, Aaron and the priests descended from him, even angels. More, he is both the preeminent and perfect sacrificial victim as well as the preeminent and perfect high priest. This surprising sacerdotal role is expressed through the equally surprising claim that Jesus is "designated by God a high priest according to the order of Melchizedek" (5:10), a possible translation of Psalm 110:4.

By reinterpreting a number of Israel's texts—including eighteen references to the Psalms, fourteen to the Pentateuch, and seven to the Prophets—Hebrews suggests that the only way to understand these texts, to bring their meaning out of the shadows, is through the lens Jesus provides. Along with recapitulating passages found elsewhere in the New Testament, such as "You are my son; / today I have begotten you" (Heb 1:5; 5:5; citing Ps 2:7 and alluding to 2 Sam 7:14, quoted in Acts 13:33) and "I will proclaim your name to my brothers and sisters, / in the midst of the congregation I will praise you" (Heb 2:12; citing the oft-quoted Ps 22, here 22:22), Hebrews accentuates Jesus's priestly role by connecting him to the only chapters in Israel's scriptures where the priest-king Melchizedek appears: Psalm 110 and Genesis 14. These two enigmatic texts were to become contested sites in the separation of Judaism and Christianity.

Today, the Epistle to the Hebrews figures largely in debates over the pressing question of supersessionism: the belief that the gentile church replaces the people of Israel as heirs of God's covenants and promises. Sometimes called "replacement theology," supersessionism functions as a zero-sum game: if one group is God's elect, the other group cannot be. While Paul insists that the "gifts and calling" of Israel, by which he means the Jewish people, are "irrevocable" (Rom 11:29), not all of Jesus's followers adopted this approach.

Hebrews, as we shall see, can be seen as supersessionist. At the same time, later Jewish tradition, substantially in reaction to Christian teachings, will offer counterreadings that promote Jewish views at the expense of Christian ones. Multivalent texts necessarily give rise to multivalent readings. Not all readings that can be supported by the Greek and Hebrew texts are ethically or theologically desirable. Hebrews reads various texts as prophetic, uses them as prooftexts to support claims for Jesus's superior role, and polemicizes against any who would disagree. But Hebrews also offers a model to move forward in terms of better relations between Jews and Christians. The possibilities are not precluded.

Let us now turn to how ancient Israel understood priesthood.

The mysterious priest-king Melchizedek appears by name eight times in the Epistle to the Hebrews, which is six more times than he appears in the Tanakh. In Hebrews, he has three functions. First, Melchizedek anchors Jesus into the priestly line despite the fact that, as Hebrews acknowledges, Jesus is a "son of David" and therefore not in the priestly lineage of Aaron or Levi.[1] Second, Hebrews argues that because Melchizedek is superior to Abraham, Jesus, who is in Melchizedek's priestly line, is superior to any of Abraham's descendants, including all Jewish priests. Third, because Melchizedek is an eternal priest, Jesus is eternal as well. The arguments all rely on exegetical choices, especially since Genesis 14 and Psalm 110 are two of the most textually problematic passages in Israel's scriptures.

Understanding the claims Hebrews makes requires understanding of the Israelite, and later Jewish, priesthood. During the time of Jesus and subsequently to today, only descendants of Aaron can be priests and only Levi's descendants are Levites. That role is maintained, despite the fact that since 70 CE, there has been no Temple at which priests could perform liturgical rites. That inherited role is not, however, the only way that ancient Israel understood its priesthood.

Early in Israel's history, priesthood did not require any particular familial or tribal membership, so various individuals, including firstborn sons, served as priests (Hebrew kohanim; singular kohen).[2] For example, David and his sons are from the nonpriestly tribe of Judah, but according to 2 Samuel 8:18, "David's sons were priests," and Solomon acts as a priest by offering sacrifices, sanctifying the Temple, and proclaiming a religious festival (1 Kgs 8:63–65).

At some point, well before the first century CE, priesthood became restricted to members of the tribe of Levi. We can see the shift in Numbers 3:12 when God, speaking through Moses, states: "I hereby accept the Levites [Hebrew *leviyim*; singular *levi*] from among the Israelites as substitutes for all the firstborn that open the womb among the Israelites.³ The Levites shall be mine." The priesthood was then further restricted to one group within this tribe: the descendants of Aaron, Moses's brother. While the Levites—who were not descendants of Aaron—came to function as second-tier officials in the Jerusalem Temple by helping with the sacrificial offering or serving in the choir, priests, who claimed Aaron as their ancestor, had specialized roles such as offering the sacrifice itself and receiving designated sections of many offerings (i.e., meat for dinner). Only Aaron's direct descendant could serve as the high priest. Only he could enter the most sacred part of the Temple, the holy of holies—only after extensive preparation and only once a year, on the Day of Atonement (Lev 16). Unlike Christianity, where priesthood is a vocation, in the Israelite and subsequent Jewish tradition, priesthood became an inherited role, carried on the paternal line.

We see this concern for lineage in Luke 1:5, which describes the parents of John the Baptist: "there was a priest named Zechariah, who belonged to the priestly order of Abijah. His wife was a descendant of Aaron, and her name was Elizabeth." Luke also reports that Elizabeth is related to Mary the mother of Jesus, so Mary too may have had a priestly lineage. However, the Gospels focus on Jesus's Davidic descent. The opening verse, Matthew 1:1, reads, "An account of the genealogy of Jesus the Messiah, the son of David, the son of Abraham." Even Hebrews acknowledges: "it is evident that our Lord was descended from Judah, and in connection with that tribe Moses said nothing about priests" (Heb 7:14). Since Jesus is not of Levitical descent, he is not a priest by Jewish norms.

JESUS THE HIGH PRIEST,
AFTER THE ORDER OF MELCHIZEDEK

Yet according to his followers, Jesus is more than just the son of David. He is also the unique Son of God. The second verse of Hebrews makes that point: "But in these last days, he [God] has spoken to us by a Son, whom he appointed heir of all things" (Heb 1:2). Within a few verses, the author confirms the claim in 1:5 by citing Psalm 2:7—"For to which of the angels did God ever say, 'You are my Son; / today I have begotten you'?"[4] (The verse may also be an allusion to 2 Sam 7:14: "I will be a father to him, and he shall be a son to me.") Hebrews 4:14 reinforces the title "Son of God" by connecting it to sacerdotal authority: "we have a great high priest who has passed through the heavens, Jesus, the Son of God."

To claim the high priesthood for Jesus, Hebrews repeats and glosses the reference in Psalm 110:4 to the enigmatic "order of Melchizedek." First, Hebrews 5:6 quotes Psalm 110:4 directly: "as he says also in another place, 'You are a priest forever, / according to the order of Melchizedek.'" No other ancient text describes an "order of Melchizedek" or any descendant Melchizedek might have, physical or metaphorical. Even the word for "order" is clear only in the Greek. The Septuagint (Ps 109:4) uses the term *taxis* (whence "taxonomy") to describe this "order," but as we demonstrate below, "order" does not reflect the meaning of the original Hebrew, *divrati*.

About Jesus's role in this order, Hebrews offers the rhetorical flourish, "About this we have much to say that is hard to explain" (Heb 5:11a). After a chapter of digression, which keeps the audience waiting for the evidence proving Jesus's priestly role, Hebrews returns to its sacerdotal argument. In a discussion both elegant and complex, the author states in 6:19–20, "We have this hope, a sure and steadfast anchor of the soul, a hope that enters the inner shrine behind the curtain, where Jesus, a forerunner on our behalf, has entered, having become a high priest forever according to the order of Melchizedek." By this point, references to high priest, eternity, and the order of Melchizedek sound like a chorus.

The reference to the "inner shrine behind the curtain" refers to the architecture of the tabernacle used for worship in the wilderness before the construction of the Jerusalem Temple. The curtain hid from view the innermost sanctum, which the high priest entered only on Yom Kippur. This same curtain became part of Temple architecture. Describing the events that occurred at Jesus's crucifixion, the Synoptic Gospels recount, "the curtain of the temple was torn in two, from top to bottom" (Mark 15:38; cf. Matt 27:51; Luke 23:45), a report less likely historical than a narrative foreshadowing of the Temple's destruction in the next generation. The tearing could also indicate divine mourning, given the tradition of tearing a garment to signify grief, as when Jacob tears his garments upon hearing the false report that his beloved son Joseph is dead (Gen 37:34).

Some Christian interpreters claim that the rending of the veil in the Synoptic accounts indicates that now all people have access to God. This interpretation incorrectly presupposes that access to the divine was restricted. Worship of Israel's God was never restricted to the Temple, as Genesis 2:1–3, with its concern for sacred time versus sacred space, already indicates. Moreover, sections of the Temple were open to all for worship, gentiles as well as Jews, men as well as women.

Hebrews never mentions the Jerusalem Temple, let alone the "tearing" of the veil, and so we do not know whether it originally sought to replace that Temple. But Hebrews does show how Jesus replaces the wilderness sanctuary. Hebrews suggests that there is a better, a more true, temple in heaven, complete with veil, where Jesus serves at that altar.

In the next chapter, Hebrews provides the lyrics for the chorus "high priest, forever, and order of Melchizedek" by a selective reading of Genesis 14 that is, as we shall see, not evident in the Hebrew original. Hebrews 7 begins by introducing "King Melchizedek of Salem, priest of the Most High God" (7:1a; referencing Gen 14:18). In Biblical Hebrew, written with consonants only, the words *shalem* (a place—traditionally rendered in English "Salem," as in the site of the infamous witch trials) and *shalom* ("peace") are identical. Given this wordplay, Melchizedek can also be understood, as Hebrews 7:2 tells us, as "king of peace."

Since Salem suggests Jeru*salem*, Melchizedek then becomes the prompt for Hebrews' interest in the city. Consistent with its presenting ancient Israel as the shadow or prototype, Hebrews views the earthly Salem/Jerusalem as anticipating something better that the followers of Jesus will possess: "But you have come to Mount Zion and to the city of the living God, the heavenly Jerusalem, and to innumerable angels in festal gathering" (Heb 12:22). This heavenly Jerusalem, which neatly matches the Platonic idea of ideal essences and contingent earthly manifestations or "accidents," appears in contemporaneous Jewish texts[5] as well as Revelation 21:2. In Hebrews, the earthly wilderness sanctuary, the Jerusalem Temple, and the city of Jerusalem itself are all replaced—all superseded—by the heavenly Christ.[6]

Claims for the eternal nature of this altar and its priest find their support in Melchizedek. According to Hebrews 7:3, Melchizedek is "without father, without mother, without genealogy, having neither beginning of days nor end of life, but resembling the Son of God, he remains a priest forever." The author takes absence of evidence (Genesis does not describe Melchizedek's ancestry or death) as evidence of absence (there was no ancestry or death).

Next comes the explication of why Melchizedek is superior to Abraham and, consequently, why Jesus, in Melchizedek's priestly order, is superior to Abraham's descendants. According to Genesis 14, Melchizedek meets Abram (whose name will be changed to Abraham) as the patriarch was returning from his military victory over several local kings who had captured his nephew Lot. Hebrews 7:1b–2, alluding to Genesis 14:19–20, states that Melchizedek "blessed him" and that to Melchizedek "Abraham apportioned 'one-tenth of everything.'" This is one plausible reading of Genesis—although, as we shall see, the Hebrew does not specify who blesses whom.

Hebrews continues by extrapolating from Abram's tithe to Melchizedek to the relationship between Abram's descendants and Jesus as the reigning priest in Melchizedek's order. The argument is complex and clever. It observes first that while Levites collect tithes, Melchizedek, a man "who does not belong to their ancestry" (Heb 7:6), collects them from Abram. Here Hebrews begins to raise the question of the priestly line. Second, since "it is beyond dispute that the inferior is blessed by the superior" (7:7) and since Melchizedek, according to Hebrews, blesses Abram, Melchizedek's superiority is guaranteed. Third, extending this point through the generations, Hebrews proposes, "One might even say that Levi himself, who receives tithes, paid tithes through Abraham, for he was still in the loins of his ancestor when Melchizedek met him" (7:9–10). This notice places Levi, who will not be born for another three generations, and all his descendants in a subordinate position to Melchizedek and so to Jesus.

Having established the relative rankings between Abram (and his family) and Melchizedek (and Jesus, the singular person in his line), Hebrews now explains Jesus's perfect priesthood and perfect sacrifice. First it claims that perfection could not be attained through the law (i.e., the Torah), which "made nothing perfect" (Heb 7:19). This is not a controversial claim. Generally, Jews did not think the point of the Torah was to "perfect" human beings. Our very human nature would preclude this. Ecclesiastes 7:20 confirms: "Surely there is no one on earth so righteous as to do good without ever sinning." The deuterocanonical Sirach concurs: "A person may make a slip without intending it. / Who has not sinned with his tongue?" (Sir 19:16). The Torah is rather a guide to help us make the right choices—to "choose life" (Deut 30:19).

Next comes the claim that Jesus became "a priest, not through a legal requirement concerning physical descent, but through the power of an indestructible life" (Heb 7:16). This verse is one of several Hebrews adduces to show that the Torah's commandments, because they do not create a permanent state and must be continually repeated, are imperfect.

For a fourth time, in 7:17, Hebrews sounds the chorus from Psalm 110:4, "For it is attested of him, 'You are a priest forever, / according to the order of Melchizedek.'" In Hebrews 7:21, the author again writes, "You are a priest forever," and we can easily imagine the congregation responding, "after the order of Melchizedek."

The argument about imperfection because of repetition continues with another point: the former (Levitical) priests cannot continue their roles because they die (Heb 7:23). Jesus holds the office permanently because he is, like Melchizedek, eternal. Further, unlike Levitical priests, or any other human being, Jesus is "holy, blameless, undefiled, separated from sinners, and exalted above the heavens" (7:26). Therefore, while regular priests must offer sacrifices for their own sin (5:3; see Lev 4:3; 16:11), Jesus does not: Hebrews, uniquely among the New Testament books, explicitly claims that Jesus is "without sin." His single sacrifice, of his own flesh and blood, is then sufficient to create atonement for all.

Moreover, Hebrews claims that Jesus is the "mediator of a better covenant," for "if that first covenant had been faultless, there would have been no need to look for a second one" (Heb 8:6–7). Here the author cites the famous "new covenant" passage from Jeremiah 31:31–34:

> The days are surely coming, says the Lord,
>> when I will establish a new covenant with the house of Israel
>> and with the house of Judah;
> not like the covenant that I made with their ancestors,
>> on the day when I took them by the hand to lead them out of the
>> land of Egypt. . . .
> For I will be merciful toward their iniquities,
>> and I will remember their sins no more. (Heb 8:8–9, 12)

The citation concludes, "In speaking of 'a new covenant,' he has made the first one obsolete. And what is obsolete and growing old will soon disappear" (8:13).[7] Just as permanence replaces impermanence, just as perfection replaces repetition, so the Christ replaces the Torah.

Along with permanence and perfection comes replacement. Hebrews argues that not only is Jesus the perfect high priest, he is the perfect sacrificial offering. The argument begins with the premise that "without the shedding of blood there is no forgiveness of sins" (Heb 9:22). Therefore, Jesus's sacrifice is, after the cessation of Temple sacrifice, the only means to obtain forgiveness. (This question of sacrifice, so important for the understanding of how Jews and Christians interpret the Bible, receives a full discussion in Chapter 7.) We simply note here that Jews have not claimed that blood is the sine qua non for restoring any broken relationship between God and humanity.

This discussion ends by returning to Psalm 110, "and since then [the time when he 'sat down at the right hand of God,' the Christ] has been waiting 'until his enemies would be made a footstool for his feet'" (Heb 10:13, citing Ps 110:1), and the affirmation, "For by a single offering he has perfected for all time those who are sanctified" (Heb 10:14). According to Hebrews, Jesus, through his perfect sacrifice, sanctifies and cleanses from sin any who follow him. To participate in any other sacrificial system would be retrograde.

Given such arguments, it is not surprising, as Alan Mitchell notes, that "from the second century C.E., Christians have used [the Epistle to the Hebrews] to promote the view that Christianity, according to God's plan, has replaced Judaism" and that "the language of Hebrews and its author's style lend themselves to this kind of interpretation."[8] The Hebrew of Genesis 14 and Psalm 110 and the later Second Temple and rabbinic interpretation of these passages offer alternative readings. It turns out that both Jewish and Christian traditions rely on select interpretations of these antecedent texts; it also turns out that both of these earlier texts are themselves unclear and open to multiple, often mutually exclusive readings.

GENESIS 14: THE FIRST APPEARANCE
OF MELCHIZEDEK

GENESIS 14 is anomalous, and not simply because only here in the Pentateuch does the priest-king Melchizedek appear. The chapter cannot clearly be assigned to any of the traditional scriptural sources (the J and P sources, as well as the "Elohist" [E] and "Deuteronomist" [D] sources), so we cannot determine its time of composition.[9] Even its description of Abram is anomalous, for only here does the patriarch appear as a "noble warrior."[10]

The chapter opens by describing a war among several Canaanite kings, some known from elsewhere and many listed only here. The names do not advance the broader narrative, and the section leaves the impression that the details were spliced in, somewhat awkwardly, from another source. We next learn that "the enemy" (Gen 14:11–12) has captured Abram's nephew Lot, who had been living in Sodom (the famous account of the destruction of Sodom and Gomorrah occurs five chapters later, in Gen 19). Abram enters the battle, rescues Lot, and obtains substantial spoils for his efforts. Genesis 14:17 recounts, "After his [Abram's] return from the defeat of Chedorlaomer and the kings who were with him, the king of Sodom went out to meet him at the Valley of Shaveh (that is, the King's Valley)."

Then, Genesis 14:18–20 drops the reference to the king of Sodom and suddenly introduces Melchizedek, the king of Salem. It is possible that Salem originally read "Sodom" so that Melchizedek was "king of Sodom"; without this connection between the terms, the passage about Melchizedek is at best abrupt:

> And King Melchizedek of Salem brought out bread and wine; he was priest of God Most High. He blessed him and said,
>> "Blessed be Abram by God Most High,
>>> maker of heaven and earth;
>> and blessed be God Most High,
>>> who has delivered your enemies into your hand!"
> And he [NRSV's "Abram" is an interpretive gloss] gave him one-tenth of everything.

At this point, the Hebrew is unclear about who paid tithes to whom.

At the end of this brief episode, the narrative picks up where it left off in verse 17, "Then the king of Sodom said to Abram, 'Give me the persons, but take the goods for yourself'" (Gen 14:21). In another exchange, Abram gives the booty to Sodom's king, swears to "the LORD, God Most High [Hebrew 'el 'elyon], maker of heaven and earth," and assures the king that he will "not take a thread or a sandal-thong or anything that is yours, so that you might not say, 'I have made Abram rich'" (Gen 14:22–23). The fact that the Melchizedek story can be removed from Genesis without creating any narrative gaps adds to the suggestion that it is a secondary addition.[11]

Problems continue with the translation of Melchizedek's name. The Hebrew offers *malki-zedek*, a Hebrew name similar to that of Adoni-zedek, king of Jerusalem (Josh 10:1, 3). The Septuagint reads a single word, *Melchisedek*, as does the (Aramaic) Genesis Apocryphon (1QapGen) from Qumran. As one word, Melchisedek must be a personal name, but as two words, *malki* plus *zedek*, we may have a noun followed by another noun that functions adjectivally. For a modern analogy, Greenstreet is a personal name, but the name can be written as two words, the adjective "green" and the noun "street." Further increasing the mystery, the meaning of both Hebrew words is insecure.[12] The first element, *malki*, may mean either "my king" or "king" (with a following vowel [-*i*] that is not translated);[13] the second, *zedek*, may be a common noun meaning "justice," and thus the name might mean "my/the king is just." If so, the Hebrew name Malkizedek is identical in meaning to the name of the Mesopotamian king Sargon, which derives from *shar* ("king") and *kenu* ("just"). The name, indicating legitimacy,[14] is used in cases of debated succession. Alternately, *zedek* may refer to the West Semitic deity of justice, Zedek,[15] and thus the name may mean "my/the (divine) king is (the divinity) Zedek." That name is known in reverse order in Phoenician.[16]

Melchizedek is open to yet another interpretation. Hebrew does not capitalize personal names, and even today, the Hebrew alphabet, as we have seen, does not have lowercase and uppercase letters. It is thus possible that the Hebrew *malki-zedek* in some of its occurrences is a noun phrase, and not a personal name; if so, it should be translated "(O) (my) righteous king!"[17] This is unlikely for Genesis 14 but possible for Psalm 110:4, which we discuss below.

Not only are the form and meaning of the name open to multiple interpretations, so is this king's location. According to Genesis 14:18, Melchizedek is king of Salem, Hebrew *shalem*. Along with speculation that "Salem" originally read "Sodom," we find that according to Psalm 76:2 (76:3 Heb.), *shalem* is another name for Zion (or Jerusalem): "His abode has been established in Salem [Hebrew *shalem*], / his dwelling place in Zion." Josephus's *Antiquities of the Jews* (1.181) and the Genesis Apocryphon (22:13) similarly suggest that Salem is a shortened form of Jerusalem.[18] If the chapter, or even this section within it, is a late supplement, its author, aware that the Torah does not elsewhere mention Jerusalem, may have avoided an explicit mention.[19]

Still other interpretations of the name, and identifications of the city, are possible. The church father Jerome, following Samaritan tradition (e.g., Pseudo-Eupolemus), identifies the Salem of Abraham's encounter with Melchizedek as a location in Samaria, near Scythopolis, a possible reading given the city of Salim or Salem, mentioned in Judith 4:4 and the Septuagint of Genesis 33:18, "And Jacob came to Salem a city of Secima." But it is not certain that Genesis 33:18 mentions Salem (Hebrew *shalem*); that verse could also be translated, "And Jacob arrived safely or peacefully [*shalem* functioning adverbially] at the town of Shechem."[20]

Problems of interpretation continue in Genesis 14:18, which identifies Melchizedek as a priest of "God Most High," Hebrew *'el 'elyon*, the same expression that Abram shortly will use in speaking with the king of Sodom in 14:22. That Melchizedek would function as both priest and king is not anomalous; most kings in the ancient Near East, including Solomon, served as temple patrons and offered sacrifices. Our question is the identification of this *'el 'elyon*. El, the high god in Canaanite religion, is well attested in numerous circa-thirteenth-century cuneiform tablets excavated at Ugarit, a city on the Syrian coast. These texts are our most important evidence for pre-Israelite Canaanite religion. El's role in creation is debated,[21] though the ninth-century BCE Phoenician Karatepe inscription calls him "El maker of earth," a shorter form of his epithet in Genesis 14:19, "maker of heaven and earth." The epithet *'elyon*, "Most High," is absent in the early Ugaritic material, though it may appear in an eighth-century Aramaic treaty from Sefire, near Aleppo, Syria.[22] This relatively late attestation suggests that the biblical use of this epithet is not from the earliest strata of Israel's scriptures. Genesis 14:22, using the phrase "the LORD [YHWH], God Most High [*'el 'elyon*], maker of heaven and earth," claims these titles for Israel's God; early readers aware of the Canaanite El would recognize, and delight in, the reattribution of the title to Israel's God. A similar borrowing may underlie Psalm 46:4 (Ps 45:5 LXX), which refers to Jerusalem as the "holy habitation of the Most High" (Hebrew *'elyon*). Thus, only the broader biblical context, especially Genesis 14:22, where Abram swears to the LORD (YHWH), God Most High (*'el 'elyon*), tells us that Abram and Melchizedek worship the same God.

Melchizedek the priest does not offer a sacrifice. Instead, he brings Abram the typical hospitality of "bread and wine" (Gen 14:18; see especially Judg 19:19). The Hebrew for "bread," *lechem*, also functions as a generic word for food; telling the same story, the Genesis Apocryphon reads "food [*m'chl*] and drink." Wine was nothing special in the ancient Mediterranean—it was, usually watered down, the drink that accompanied most meals. For Jesus's followers, familiar with Eucharistic practices involving "bread and wine," the story of Melchizedek the priest in Genesis 14 may have had resonances, although the Epistle to the Hebrews does not develop them. Explaining the absence of evidence is always a problem. As R. Williamson wrote back in 1975, "No generally accepted conclusion has yet been reached on the subject of the Eucharist and Hebrews."[23] The only reference to "bread" in Hebrews is in 9:2, a reference to the "bread of the Presence" in the wilderness sanctuary. Hebrews does not mention wine.

The short unit ends with more ambiguity. The NRSV translation of the last clause, "and Abram gave" (Gen 14:20), is a guess. The Hebrew reads, "And he gave him one-tenth of everything," and both the Hebrew and the Greek are ambiguous about who tithed to whom. The NRSV may be correct: since priests collect tithes (*ma'aser*, literally "one-tenth"), it makes sense that Abram would give a tithe to Melchizedek the priest. Had the reverse been true, had Melchizedek given the tithe to Abram, the text should have explicitly said, "And

Melchizedek gave him one-tenth of everything" or "he gave *Abram* one-tenth of everything" to indicate the atypical situation.[24] The next unit makes explicit that Abram gave goods to the king of Sodom in order to preserve his reputation of gaining his wealth independently. Genesis emphasizes the importance of patriarchs' tithing also in 28:22, where Jacob says to God, "of all that you give me I will surely give one-tenth to you."

Despite such ambiguities, the verses have several functions already in Genesis. First, the implied connection between Salem and Jerusalem[25] associates Abram, the first Hebrew, with Judah's capital and so with its Temple.[26] References to Melchizedek's blessing Abram extend a theme introduced in Genesis 12:2–3, which uses the root *b-r-ch* ("to bless") five times; the root appears three times in 14:19–20. Abram is thus blessed both by God and by a significant human priest-king. The verses also bolster the institution of tithing.[27] And they show how El, the ancient Canaanite deity, has been absorbed by YHWH, the Israelite national god.[28] But with the problems in translation and interpretation, the chapter proved irresistible both to the author of Hebrews and to later Jewish writers, who found in it both prophetic implications and polemical arguments.

PSALM 110: AN ENIGMATIC ROYAL PSALM

PSALM 110, consisting of seven verses, not only receives notice in Hebrews but also features prominently elsewhere in the New Testament.[29] These New Testament interpretations, however, are by no means obvious readings of the psalm.

The first reference occurs in the Gospel accounts of Jesus's Temple teaching. After besting his interlocutors in arguments over controversial subjects such as paying taxes to Caesar and the role of marriage in the eschatological age, and after pleasantly surprising a scribe in listing love of God (Deut 6:5) and love of neighbor (Lev 19:18) as the greatest of the Torah's commandments, Jesus issues a challenge of his own. Mark 12:35–36 (cf. Matt 22:42–46; Luke 20:41–44) records Jesus asking,

> "How can the scribes say that the Messiah is the son of David? David himself, by the Holy Spirit, declared,
> > 'The Lord said to my Lord,
> > "Sit at my right hand,
> > > until I put your enemies under your feet."'"

The verse cites Psalm 110:1, which like Psalm 22 is ascribed to King David.

In this psalm, the LORD (Hebrew YHWH) addresses the Davidic

king as "My lord" (Hebrew 'adoni); that is, God (YHWH) is speaking to the king ('adoni). The word 'adon, appearing more than seven hundred times in the scriptures of Israel, means "lord" or "master" or "sir." Sometimes it indicates God, and other times, a person of superior status. For example, when Sarah overhears the news that she, in her postmenopausal state, will become pregnant, she asks herself, "After I have grown old, and my lord ['adoni; the NRSV reads "husband"] is old, shall I have pleasure?" (Gen 18:12). After Jews determined, probably in the first centuries BCE, that the Tetragrammaton, YHWH, was too sacred to pronounce, they usually substituted 'adonai, "my master," a variant of 'adoni. This tradition is reflected in the Septuagint's translation of the Tetragrammaton as kyrios, "master" or "lord," a word also used for human masters, as in the Greek translation of Genesis 18:12—here Sarah calls her husband "lord."

The Greek of Psalm 110 collapses the distinct words for LORD/ YHWH and my lord/'adoni into the single word kyrios. This connection in the Greek allows Jesus to conclude: "David himself calls him Lord [Greek kyrios]; so how can he be his son?" (Mark 12:37). The question presumes, following the superscription, that the speaker is David and not, as is more likely, a Levite, prophet, or courtier. It also presumes that this second "lord" must be the Messiah, for no one else could sit next to God. Jesus asks: How can the Messiah be a "son of David" because David calls him "lord"? The implied answer: the Messiah, the son of David—Jesus—is greater than David. Mark concludes the scene by noting, "And the large crowd was listening to him with delight" (Mark 12:37). Greek speakers (as well as English speakers who hear the repetition of "lord . . . lord") should take delight in the wordplay; those looking at the written Hebrew texts, with the different words for "God" and "lord," might be befuddled.

Peter's speech in Acts 2 finds a different nuance in Psalm 110. Continuing the theme of Jesus's superiority to David, Peter states:

> For David did not ascend into the heavens, but he himself says,
>> "The Lord said to my Lord,
>>> 'Sit at my right hand,
>>>> until I make your enemies your footstool.'" (Acts 2:34–35)

The point here is that Jesus sits enthroned in the heavens. A similar claim of Jesus's heavenly location appears in Acts 7:56 where Stephen testifies, "I see the heavens opened and the Son of Man standing at the right hand of God!"[30]

These New Testament messianic, heaven-focused, and potentially eschatological readings are a move away from the original import of Psalm 110. In its own setting, the psalm has earthly, political implications.

Psalm 110 is a royal psalm.[31] Only a king might be told to sit at God's right (v. 2), and only a king could lead Israel in war (vv. 1–3, 5–7). In vocabulary and structure Psalm 110 is similar to Psalm 2, another royal psalm the New Testament frequently cites. For example, Psalm 2:2 also mentions kings and military concerns, "The kings of the earth set themselves, / and the rulers take counsel together, / against the LORD and his anointed [Hebrew *mashi'ach*, whence "messiah"]." Like Psalm 2, Psalm 110 changes speakers and quotes a divine oracle. Psalm 2:5–6, "Then he will speak to them in his wrath, / and terrify them in his fury, saying . . . ," introduces a quotation ascribed to God, "I have set my king on Zion, my holy hill"; similarly, Psalm 110:4 contains both the introduction to the oracle and the oracle itself, "The LORD has sworn and will not change his mind, / 'You are a priest forever according to the order of Melchizedek.'" Both psalms, using the same term, even speak of the king as the son of God. Psalm 2:7b proclaims, "You are my son; / today I have begotten [Hebrew *yldtyk*] you"; Psalm 110:3b, although the text is very difficult, reads, "From the womb of the morning, / like dew, your youth [Hebrew *yldwtyk*] will come to you." As John J. Collins observes, "The main implication of the declaration is that the king had the promise of divine support, especially in warfare."[32]

Psalm 110 focuses both on the king's role as commander in chief and on his sacerdotal responsibilities. Kings built, renovated, and served as the patrons of the Jerusalem Temple; they offered prayers even as priests and pilgrims offered prayers on their behalf. For example, 1 Kings 8 depicts Solomon offering two prayers at the Temple's dedication (vv. 12–13 and 22–53) and 1 Kings 12:3–33 depicts the northern king Jeroboam sacrificing on a festival that, from the perspective of the Judean author, he invented. These regal connotations suggest three possibilities for the *Sitz im Leben*, the "setting in life," for Psalm 110: the occasion of a military event, part of the divine enthronement festival, or part of a royal coronation. These occasions are not mutually exclusive.

The first option reads part of the psalm as a consultation with a prophet before launching a military campaign. Such consultation is seen, for example, in Judges 20:18: "The Israelites proceeded to go up to Bethel, where they inquired of God, 'Which of us shall go up first to battle against the Benjaminites?' And the LORD answered, 'Judah shall go up first.'" Psalm 2 imagines the same setting: it opens with kings conspiring against the Judean king, and then it poetically predicts their defeat, "You shall break them with a rod of iron, / and dash them in pieces like a potter's vessel" (Ps 2:9). Psalm 110 similarly twice mentions the defeat of enemies: "The LORD sends out from Zion / your mighty scepter. / Rule in the midst of your foes" (v. 2), and

> He will execute judgment among the nations,
>   filling them with corpses;
> he will shatter heads
>   over the wide earth.
> He will drink from the stream by the path;
>   therefore he will lift up his head. (Ps 110:6–7)

The image of drinking from the stream is well-known from Mesopotamian texts, where the victorious king drinks from his enemy's water source.[33] Recounting divine consultation that resulted in victory, the psalms could be reused to foster support for later campaigns.

Alternately, most biblical scholars find a preexilic *Sitz im Leben* for royal psalms in YHWH's enthronement festival, possibly connected with a preexilic new year celebration.[34] Hermann Gunkel suggested that ancient Israel held an annual fall festival marking YHWH's re-enthronement, comparable to the Mesopotamian Akitu festival, which celebrated the kingship of the god Marduk.[35] The king, cast as YHWH's son and perhaps hailed in divine terms, would have played a major role in this celebration, so that we may have in the psalm both a divine enthronement and a coronation or reaffirmation of the king's rule. For example, in Psalm 45:6 (45:7 Heb.), the psalmist says to the king, "Your throne, O God [*'elohim*, i.e., the king], endures forever and ever."[36]

Third, although the scriptures of Israel offer no direct evidence for a divine enthronement festival, Psalms 93 and 95–99 describe YHWH's enthronement in a manner that strongly suggests it. In addition, such a festival helps explain one of the most surprising features of the Jewish new year, Rosh Hashanah: the significance it attributes to the shofar, the ram's horn. As demonstrated by verses such as 1 Kings 1:34, "There let the priest Zadok and the prophet Nathan anoint him [Solomon] king over Israel; then blow the trumpet

[Hebrew *shofar*], and say, 'Long live King Solomon!,'" the shofar was crucial to ancient Israel's coronation ritual. The suggestion that the Rosh Hashanah service preserves elements of an earlier biblical new year festival, celebrating God's kingship—and where the Davidic king may have represented God—explains this usage.[37] Psalm 110 likely functioned as part of this festival, during which YHWH, Judah's national God, was reenthroned.[38]

Whether its original context was divine enthronement, royal coronation, or military consultation, Psalm 110 supposes that a prophet would have been the main speaker. The opening words are his: "The LORD says to my lord," and again in verse 4, "The LORD has sworn and will not change his mind." Biblical scholars call such prophets "cultic prophets" and reconstruct their role based on ancient Near Eastern analogies and the many hints scattered throughout the Hebrew Bible.[39] For example, Lamentations 3:57, "You came near when I called on you; / you said, 'Do not fear!,'" suggests that they who consulted YHWH could receive the answer "Do not fear!"

Complicating the question of its origin, Psalm 110 is difficult to translate. The Hebrew of Psalm 110:3, one of the Bible's most confusing verses, is "notoriously corrupt";[40] a literal translation of the vocalized Hebrew text would be: "Your nation are free-will offerings on the day of your strength; in the splendors of holiness, from the womb from dawn (?), to you is the dew of your childhood." The translation of the Septuagint—"With you is rule on a day of your power among the splendors of the holy ones. From the womb, before Morning-star, I brought you forth"[41]—may be based on a slightly different Hebrew text or at least on a different vocalization of the same consonants.

The Greek translator understood the verse's last word as a verb, "I brought you forth" (*yeladticha*), and as referring to the divine birth of the king, and similar to Psalm 2:7, "You are my son; / today I have begotten you [*yeladticha*]." In contrast, the Hebrew (MT) text has a noun and a pronominal suffix: "(from) your youth [*yaldutecha*]." It is possible that Psalm 110:3 originally read *yeladticha*, "I have begotten you" as well, but later Jewish scribes revocalized it to avoid a Christian reading suggesting the conception of a divine being.[42] The NRSV reads,

> Your people will offer themselves willingly
>> on the day you lead your forces
>> on the holy mountains.
> From the womb of the morning,
>> like dew, your youth will come to you.

The NJPS suggests, "Your people come forward willingly on your day of battle. / In majestic holiness, from the womb, / from the dawn, yours was the dew of youth." Both are viable; both are guesses. John Collins's reconstruction, "In sacred splendor, from the womb, from dawn, you have the dew wherewith I have begotten you," is another plausible understanding.[43]

This impossible verse is followed by another oracle (parallel to v. 1), introduced by "The LORD has sworn and will not change his mind [Hebrew *yinachem*, from the root *n-ch-m*]." God *does* change his mind elsewhere in the Bible; for example, in 1 Samuel 15:11, God states, "I regret [Hebrew *nichamti*, from the same root *n-ch-m*] that I made Saul king, for he has turned back from following me, and has not carried out my commands." Yet several verses later, that same chapter asserts that God *does not* change his mind: "for he is not a mortal, that he should change his mind" (1 Sam 15:29). The concern in Psalm 110 that God will not change his mind evokes God's promise to David: "But I will not take my steadfast love from him, as I took it from Saul, whom I put away from before you. Your house and your kingdom shall be made sure forever before me; your throne shall be established forever" (2 Sam 7:15–16).

So far, we have had textual confusion (Ps 110:3) and theological confusion (110:4a). God's oath to the king in verse 4b, the passage oft-quoted in Hebrews like a refrain, introduces semantic and syntactic confusion. We begin with the transliterated Hebrew and follow with the NRSV's English:

'Atah	kohen	le'olam	'al-divrati	malki-zedek
You [are a]	priest	forever	according to the order [of]	Melchizedek.

Since the word order of the English follows the Hebrew, we have spaced out the words: the English of each word is directly below its Hebrew basis. While the NRSV translation is fine, it covers up three key ambiguities of this verse: the semantic ambiguity of "forever" (*le'olam*) and the semantic *and* syntactic ambiguities of "according to the order of" (*'al-divrati*).

First, the Hebrew expression *le'olam* does not typically mean "forever"; more often it connotes "for a long time" or until the individual dies at a ripe old age. For example, the Hebrew slave who decides to stay with his master after an initial six years of servitude remains *le'olam*, which the NRSV properly translates in Exodus 21:6 (but not Deut 15:17) as "for life." Similarly, the author of Lamentations 3:6 compares his dire situation to those "dead of long ago," again using *'olam*. Psalm 110:4 thus promises that the king will be a priest for a very long time; the verse implies both an ongoing priestly role and his long life, a frequent wish for kings, as in Bathsheba's comment to her aged and infirm husband in 1 Kings 1:31, "May my lord King David live forever [*le'olam*]!" In its original context, the blessing does not suggest personal immortality. Alternatively, Psalm 110:4 may refer not to the king's immortality but to a perpetual line of priests; the same term appears in Exodus 40:15 concerning the descendants of Aaron: "and their anointing shall admit them to a perpetual ['olam] priesthood throughout all generations to come." Yet nowhere else in early Jewish texts do we find such a perpetual order originating with Melchizedek. Not only is he without father, mother, or genealogy; Genesis also mentions no children.

Second, the Hebrew phrase 'al-divrati, which the NRSV translates as "according to the order," is especially problematic. The first part, 'al, is a preposition broadly meaning "on." The second is the problematic word divrah, with the first-person common suffix -i, "my"— the same suffix that ends malki in malki-zedek. The word divrah appears in Aramaic, and it is otherwise found only in late biblical texts. To determine what words mean, whether in the Bible or elsewhere, we look at both their etymologies and their literary contexts. Divrah is a feminine form of the very common masculine Hebrew davar, "thing, matter, utterance"; it is usually translated into Greek as logos. Typically, as in our verse, the feminine form divrah is preceded by the preposition 'al, and the two words together create an idiom. In Ecclesiastes 3:18, the NRSV translates 'al-divrah as "with regard to"; for 'al-divrah in Ecclesiastes 7:14, the NRSV translates "so that" and in 8:2, "because of." 'Al-divrah also appears in Daniel's Aramaic chapters (Dan 2:30 and 4:17 [4:14 Heb.]), where it suggests "in order."[44] Idioms can have different connotations depending on literary context.

Along with the ambiguous semantics of 'al-divrati, the syntax of 'al-divrati malki-zedek creates another problem.[45] It is difficult to determine which of the connotations of 'al-divrati makes the most sense in our verse. Several options are possible depending on whether the phrase is connected with what precedes, concerning priesthood, or with the name Melchizedek that follows. The four most likely possibilities are:

1. "You are a lifetime priest because of what I have said,
   O righteous king," taking *divrah* as a (feminine) variant
   of *davar*;

2. "utterance of," and interpreting the name as a title, "king
   of righteousness";

3. "you are a lifetime priest because of what I have said,
   O Melchizedek"; or

4. "you are a lifetime priest because of/with regard to
   Melchizedek."

This last interpretation is given weight by the Masoretic accents, which divide the phrase between *le'olam* and *'al-divrati*. However, the Masoretic Text comes more than a millennium after the psalm's authorship. The New Testament, following the Septuagint, is closer to the final sense as well. If that is the original sense, as most commentators think, the psalmist is invoking this divine oracle as an archetype for the Davidic kings, who are great priest-kings like Melchizedek.

To summarize: We cannot be sure of either the original context or the original meaning of Psalm 110. Its superscription, "of David," cannot be used to demonstrate Davidic authorship. Psalm 110 was likely part of the preexilic new year festival celebrating God's reenthronement, and at the same time, affirming his earthly representative, the Davidic king. As part of this festival, the prophet promised the Davidic king victory over his enemies and reaffirmed his priestly responsibilities.

Davidic kingship effectively ended after the Babylonian conquest in 586 BCE. It was restored only for a brief period when the Judeans began to return from the Babylonian exile in 538. By the time the Second Temple was completed circa 515 BCE, the enthronement festival no longer existed because the Davidic monarchy had been weakened and then disappeared. Psalm 110, absent the king's participation, became a prime candidate for reinterpretation. Given its enigmatic (possible) reference to Melchizedek, it would become intertwined with Genesis 14:18–20, and these texts, with their multiple ambiguities, would continue to be explained and utilized.

MELCHIZEDEK IN
LATER JEWISH TRADITION

PSALM 110 does not show up explicitly in Second Temple Jewish texts,[46] but Melchizedek does. From Josephus to Philo to the Dead Sea Scrolls and the texts of the Pseudepigrapha, we see various attempts to explain this mysterious priest-king.[47] Here we begin to see speculation on his priestly role, his enigmatic background, and his prophetic potential.

Josephus mentions Melchizedek twice in his retelling of Genesis. *Antiquities of the Jews* explains that his name means "righteous king" and that therefore "he was without dispute, insomuch that, on this account he was made the priest of God" (1.180). That is, his righteousness shows why he was chosen for this role. Josephus also claims that Melchizedek generously equipped Abram's army, a generosity that preceded Abram's tithe of the spoils from the earlier battle. In *Jewish War* 6.438, Josephus adds five details concerning Melchizedek: he was a Canaanite ruler; his name means "righteous king" (Greek *basileus dikaios*); because of his righteousness, he built the first temple in Jerusalem; he renamed Solyma "Jerusalem"; and he was the first priest of God.[48] The additions enhance Josephus's interests in depicting gentiles as welcomed by, and supporting, Jewish traditions.

Philo discusses Melchizedek on several occasions. In *Allegorical Interpretation*, he finds Melchizedek "especially worthy" of his priesthood because of his love of peace and his pursuit of justice. Commenting on his hospitality, Philo notes the offering of "unmixed wine, in order that they may be wholly occupied with a divine intoxication, more sober than sobriety itself." From here, he launches into a poetic discussion of "God most high" (3.79, 82). In *On the Preliminary Studies*, commenting on Jacob's vow of tithing (Gen 28:22), Philo adduces the "self-instructed and self-taught" priest Melchizedek as the model (99).

Jubilees, in its retelling of Genesis 14, may not mention Melchizedek by name,[49] but it does mention the import of tithing.[50] The author may have objected to Melchizedek, who was not a Levite, receiving a tithe and thus omitted this episode. Conversely, 2 (Slavonic) Enoch presents the account of Melchizedek's miraculous conception to the (celibate) Sopanim, Noah's sister-in-law. The prompt may well have been the Greek translation of Psalm 110:3, which we have already seen.

The extent to which Melchizedek is mentioned in the Dead Sea Scrolls remains debated. His name is plausibly, but not certainly, restored in several scrolls.[51] One scroll from Qumran cave 11, preserved in fourteen fragments spread over three columns, mentions Melchizedek often and has even been named 11QMelchizedek. It is likely, but not certain, that its Melchizedek is a personal name rather than a title, "the righteous king."[52] No part of the preserved text, which is full of quotations, cites either Genesis 14 or Psalm 110. The fragments depict this figure not as an earthly messiah[53] but as a heavenly high priest who at the eschaton, that is, the end of time, will defeat evil, facilitate the exiles' return to their true "homeland" (2:6), and "carry out the vengeance of Go[d's] judgments" (2:13a). The text also speaks of the time when "atonement shall be made for all the sons of [light and for] the peopl[e of the] lot of Mel[chi]zedek" (2:7–8).[54] Brendan Byrne summarizes, Melchizedek is "entirely the agent and instrument of the divine reclamation of the world in the final age."[55] The rabbis do not go here; in their view, Melchizedek is more shut down than lifted up.

Let us now turn to postbiblical Jewish commentary. The Hebrew text's use of pronouns leaves the verse ambiguous as to whether Abram is the donor or the recipient of the tithes. Translations sometimes replace such unclear pronouns with nouns; we earlier saw how the NRSV made such a replacement in Genesis 14:20. Thus, on the question "to whom were the tithes paid?" the Septuagint, the Syriac version, Targum Pseudo-Jonathan, and Targum Neofiti repeat the ambiguity. Targum Onkelos indicates that Abram paid, as does Hebrews.

As for Melchizedek's origins, 2 Enoch's notice of a miraculous conception is not the only explanation. Targum Pseudo-Jonathan and Targum Neofiti, alongside some later rabbinic traditions, identify Melchizedek with Shem, the third son (following Cain and Abel) of Adam and Eve.[56] James Kugel has explained this as "domesticat[ing]" Melchizedek—turning him into another clearly human character.[57] This tradition in its many forms also helps to explain why Genesis calls him a priest (kohen), even if he is not from the line of Levi and Aaron—he is from a different, ancient priestly line.[58] The Babylonian Talmud, Nedarim 32b, develops this approach: "Rabbi Zekharya said in the name of Rabbi Yishmael: The Holy One, Blessed be He, wanted the priesthood to emerge from Shem, so that his children would be priests, as it is stated, 'And Melchizedek king of Salem brought forth bread and wine, and he was priest of God the Most High [Genesis 14.18].'"[59] In these readings, we can detect no anti-Christian polemic.

More postbiblical Jewish readings de-emphasize Melchizedek's priesthood, and here there may be implicit polemic. The targum to Psalms translates kohen in Psalm 110:3 not as "priest" but as "leader" or "prince" (Aramaic rb') in the "world to come" (not "forever"). The targum also translates the end of Psalm 110:4 as "because of the merit that you were a righteous king" and thus eliminates any new priestly order.[60] Martin McNamara states, "The targumic renderings seem to exclude any liturgical-sacrificial interpretation of Melchizedek's action."[61] Similarly, Targum Onkelos and Targum Pseudo-Jonathan make no reference to Melchizedek's priesthood; they render instead, "he ministered before God Most High,"[62] in keeping with the use of the term *kohen* only for descendants of Aaron. These targumim describe Melchizedek as the "king of Jerusalem" and thereby "clarify" the meaning of Salem. Other priests, such as Potiphar of Genesis 41 and 46, or Jethro, similarly become "princes" in these translations.

The postbiblical Jewish tradition also explains how Melchizedek loses his priesthood. The passage from b. Nedarim 32b, cited above to show Melchizedek's priestly connection to Shem, continues by quoting Genesis 14:19–20: "As it is stated, 'And he blessed him and said: Blessed be Abram of God Most High, Maker of heaven and earth, and blessed be God the Most High.'"[63] The problem the rabbis find is that Melchizedek blessed God and Abram in the wrong order, and this impropriety leads to the transfer of the priestly line to Abram. Remarkably, the Talmud supports this claim with an appeal to Psalm 110: "Once Melchizedek placed the blessing of Abraham before the blessing of the Omnipresent, He [God] had the priesthood emerge from Abraham in particular, and not from any other descendant of Shem." Because Melchizedek's blessing was incorrect, he is rebuked:

> "And does one place the blessing of the servant before the blessing of his master? You should have blessed God first." Immediately the Holy One, Blessed be He, gave the priesthood to Abraham, as it is stated, "The Lord says to my lord: Sit at My right hand, until I make your enemies your footstool" [Ps 110.1], and afterward it is written: "The Lord has sworn, and will not repent: you shall be a priest forever, because

you are a king of righteousness" ['al-divrati malki-tzedek; Ps 110.4], which is explained homiletically to mean: Due to the improper words [divrati] of Melchizedek, the offspring of Abraham shall be priests of God forever.

The passage continues: "And this is as it is written, 'And he was a priest of God the Most High' [Gen 14.18], which emphasizes that he, Melchizedek, is a priest, but his children will not be priests."[64] Because the priestly line shifts from Melchizedek to Abraham and then delimits to the descendants of Aaron, such rabbinic arguments preclude Jesus from claiming any priestly authority.

Rabbinic commentary offers other treatments of Psalm 110. The targum on Psalms, like the Gospels, understands Psalm 110's "my lord" ('adoni) as referring to David: "By David, a Psalm. The Lord said in his Memra[65] that he would give me the lordship, because I had sat for the instruction of the Law: 'Wait at my right hand, until I make your enemies a stool for your feet.'" Then, as is typical in rabbinic literature, an alternative is provided: "*Another Translation*: The Lord said in his Memra that he would make me lord over Israel. However, he said to me, 'Return and wait for Saul, who is of the tribe of Benjamin, until he dies, for you are not associated with a kingdom that is near [or, "the present kingdom"]; and afterwards I will make your enemies a stool for your feet.'"[66] This translation anchors the psalm to David and so by implication precludes its referring to any other figure—which might be a polemic against Christian interpretation.

Justin Martyr (*Dialogue* 33) notes that some Jews used Psalm 110 in reference to King Hezekiah, though no extant Jewish source says this. Justin may be conflating the psalm with Jewish interpretations of Isaiah 7:14, the passage that he cites, following Matthew's Gospel, in relation to Jesus's conception. For Psalm 110:3, rabbinic tradition does not read with the Septuagint's "I have begotten you" (Ps 109:3 LXX) and so lacks any reference to the birth of the king. Robert Cargill has recently suggested, "The fact that the LXX and the (Christian) Peshitta [the Syriac translation] both preserve the references to birth but that the Psalms Targum and MT both eliminate them, suggest [*sic*] that the changes were in response to the Christian appropriation of Ps. 110, which is demonstrated by the frequency of the NT references to it."[67] Unlike Cargill, we are unsure that the Hebrew of Psalm 110:3 has eliminated a reference to birth—the entire verse is problematic—but we agree that different translations and interpretations can be explained as anti-Christian polemic.

THE PROBLEM OF SUPERSESSIONISM
IN THE EPISTLE TO THE HEBREWS

NOT ALL of Jesus's early followers agreed with Paul that the "gifts and the calling of God are irrevocable" (Rom 11:29). The Epistle to the Hebrews is supersessionist. It sees the scriptures of Israel fulfilled by the Christ and understood fully only in the light of the Christ; the promises given to Israel (i.e., Jews, seen as descendants of Abraham, Isaac, and Jacob) are transferred to the followers of Jesus. These followers, initially both Jews and gentiles, eventually become the gentile church, in which distinct Jewish markers such as circumcision and dietary regulations are no longer observed.[68]

Noting this type of supersessionism is Jonathan Homrighausen's essay describing his visit to the Tabernacle Experience, an interactive reenactment of the wilderness sanctuary traveling around to various evangelical churches. Homrighausen writes: "At one point it described the shift from Temple to Jesus, from old covenant to new, as a shift 'from law to love' and 'from ritual to relationship.' These old canards paint Jews in Jesus's time—and, indirectly, our own time—as mired in law and ritual, and as bereft of love for and relationship with God."[69]

Nevertheless, a number of well-intentioned Christian exegetes argue that Hebrews does not fit the definition of supersessionism as one of "Christians replacing Jews."[70] Their readings are grounded in both the recognition that ethics and exegesis should go hand in hand and a commitment to ending supersessionist Christian theology. While deeply appreciating their concerns, we find the various arguments that Hebrews is not, or not primarily, supersessionist unconvincing. It may be that theologians and ethicists, rather than biblical scholars, are the ones to determine what an "acceptable" reading will be. There are other texts that many today reject, such as "slaves, obey your earthly masters with fear and trembling, in singleness of heart, as you obey Christ" (Eph 6:5), and "women should be silent in the churches. For they are not permitted to speak, but should be subordinate" (1 Cor 14:34). Were we to determine that Hebrews is supersessionist, that does not prevent Christian readers today from seeing Jews as still under covenant with God, for as Paul states, "the gifts and the calling of God are irrevocable" (Rom 11:29). Here are a few of the arguments that deny to Hebrews a supersessionist conclusion, as well as our assessments of them.

First is the claim that the text does not transfer Israel's election to the church; rather, it offers a "new covenantalism"[71] that adopts Israel's legacy while also transforming its identity. It seems to us that the idea that everything in the Hebrew text is at best a shadow, with the true reality revealed in Jesus, is more than a transformation of identity. Calling Hebrews a form of "new covenantalism" sounds like a rhetorical attempt to turn a "problem" into an "opportunity."

Second is the generous assertion that the "sermon is an antidote for a triumphalistic attitude about Christianity because it does not allow its audience to see itself as radically separate from Judaism."[72] Problems here are twofold. First is that pesky term "radical"—any determination of what constitutes a "radical" separation from a less radical one, or at what point radicality is achieved, is arbitrary. We can imagine one early auditor, upon first hearing Hebrews read circa 90 CE, asking, "Do you think we're at the radical separation or just the above-ground distinction level?" Second, we cannot determine what constitutes the "Judaism" from which the sermon is separate. Hebrews is clearly not separate from the scriptures of Israel; to the contrary, it is entirely dependent on them. But "Judaism" is more than its scripture, just as "Christianity" is more than the pages of the New Testament. Hebrews has no connection to the earthly Jerusalem, the people Israel, or the postbiblical Jewish tradition. Most groups that call themselves "Christian" are anchored in the "Old Testament," but such mooring does not make them Jews.

Some interpreters, drawing on Aristotelian rhetorical formulations, claim that Hebrews does not intend "to denigrate Jewish institutions"; rather, "the rhetorical device of *synkrisis* sought to amplify the honor of a person or object by comparing the subject to an object or person whose excellence was conceded by all (*Rhetoric* 1.9.38–39)."[73] But the comparison is more than a matter of honoring the original; in Hebrews, that older model is "wearing out" and soon to be "obsolete." Further, Hebrews 13:10 reads, "We have an altar from which those who officiate in the tent have no right to eat." This is elimination, not *synkrisis*.

Others argue that Hebrews 7:12—"For when there is a change in the priesthood, there is necessarily a change in the law as well"— applies "only to a change in ritual law, not to the entire covenant itself" or that it concerns "restricting the sacrificial cult" and "may not have the entirety of the Sinaitic covenant in view."[74] Hebrews does not mention the Sinaitic covenant; it has no references to the matters that so concerned Paul, such as circumcision or more broadly "works of the law." Nor does it mention Pharisees or Sadducees or even use the term "Jew" (Greek *Ioudaios*). On the other hand, it did not need to do so: absence of evidence is not evidence of absence. It is doubtful that early auditors asked, "Do you think that reference to the law (Greek *nomos*) was *only* about a few verses in Leviticus, or did it mean the whole shebang?"

This minimal reading of supersessionism goes against the entire tenor of Hebrews, in which the issue is not only the sacrificial cult but also the place of the land of Israel, the role of the priesthood, the meaning of the Sabbath, and a number of other Jewish markers. For Hebrews, land is irrelevant since the true home is in heaven; thus, Hebrews strips Jews of their ethnic marker. As Kenneth Schenck states, the author's "interpretation of the earthly setting is intrinsically as a place of alienation . . . we are seeking a heavenly homeland and have no city here on earth that will remain permanently (13:14)."[75] The heroes, and readers, are "strangers and foreigners on the earth" (Heb 11:13), and so landless. Gone also is the Sabbath: "For if Joshua had given them rest, God would not speak later about another day. So then, a sabbath rest still remains for the people of God" (4:8–9). For Hebrews, Sabbath is pushed into the eschatological age.

Those who date Hebrews after 70 CE attempt to read the text "less [as] a polemic against the temple and more of a consolation in its absence"[76] and thus not as supersessionist. Yes, Hebrews does provide an explanation of how, if there is no forgiveness without the shedding of blood, forgiveness remains available via the cross.[77] But we have little evidence to suggest that Jews were worried about lack of forgiveness following the tragic events of 70 CE. Jews had already lost one Temple in 586 BCE, when Nebuchadnezzar ravaged Jerusalem, but they did not think that the loss severed their relationship with God or obviated forgiveness. Nor is it clear that the majority Jewish community, let alone Jesus's gentile followers, felt that the destruction of the Second Temple precluded forgiveness from sin. Jonathan Klawans cogently questions "whether the extant evidence justifies the claim that the destruction of 70 CE brought about a theological crisis at all."[78] And, as Klawans adds, after noting rabbinic approaches to atonement sans Temple, "when the destruction is described in apocalyptic literature, various questions are raised, but the problem of atonement is not among them."[79] The reading of Hebrews as a "consolation" to Jews with the blood of Jesus as the only means for facilitating atonement seems thus to us to be overgenerous.

Other attempts to avoid supersessionist readings are even less convincing. Claims that the author of Hebrews is a Jew and therefore the text cannot be anti-Jewish do not hold:[80] the author is unknown, the target audience appears to be gentile, and a Jew is not incapable of making anti-Jewish or Christian supersessionist comments. Claims that Hebrews is a type of synagogue sermon, to be given on Tisha b'Av (the day commemorating the destruction of the Temple) or Yom Kippur following the Torah and *haftarah* (prophetic) readings, are intriguing[81] but tenuous. The idea that this text would go over well in any group save for a group of Jesus-followers of undetermined and probably irrelevant Jewish or gentile origins strikes us as unlikely.

In short, we find Hebrews to be supersessionist. In effect, Hebrews colonizes the Jewish tradition—taking from it all material it feels is usable and repackaging the tradition in a way its own adherents would not have recognized. And then, as in "mansplaining," it tells the original custodians of the tradition what their system "really" means.

Ironically, rabbinic Judaism is also supersessionist in regard to at least some of the same things as Hebrews: the wilderness sanctuary and any temple with Levitical priests and animal sacrifices. Rabbinic Judaism replaces, in importance, the Temple and the priesthood with prayer, the house of study, and the rabbis; thereby rabbinic Judaism supersedes all other types of Judaism (however defined) that existed during the Second Temple period. Comments about the Temple such as "a woman never miscarried on account of the stench of the meat of Holy Things" (Avot 5.5) are not strong endorsements of the system (although they would make memorable restaurant reviews).

There are different types and extents of supersessionism: When Hebrews says that Christ-believers replace Jews who do not believe in the Christ, it denigrates a group of people still living and who still claim covenantal status; this claim is of a different order than the rabbis' claim that prayer has replaced the now-defunct sacrifices. We should also distinguish between the replacing of one institution by another, and the replacing of one people by another. Finally, as we have seen, the rabbis engaged in anti-Christian polemic with reference to Hebrews 7.[82]

It would be odd, at best, for people in antiquity, and even today, to suggest that mutually exclusive systems built on the same texts have equally valid interpretations. Yet once we are aware that we have chosen one reading over another, we might return to the original text and see how all systems based on it have their own, necessarily limited logic.

One way forward would be to respect the distinct claims each tradition makes regarding atonement. For Christians, Jesus's death is the mechanism for atonement, but that does not eliminate the need for personal repentance. The New Testament signals this importance throughout, but in particular by making it the signature line of Jesus's mission: "Repent, for the kingdom of heaven has come near" (Matt 3:2; 4:17; cf. Mark 1:15). Further, Christians anticipate, to varying degrees depending on the individual and the denomination, that Jesus will return.

For Jews, prayer, good deeds, and charitable giving replace Temple sacrifice. Such a reading is consistent with parts of the Torah that do not find blood the necessary detergent for washing away sin.[83] But these views do not eliminate some yearning in Jewish tradition (again, to varying degrees) for the return of the Temple. Post-70 CE Jewish daily prayers include the petition that God rebuild the Jerusalem Temple. For example, this brief paragraph appears at the conclusion of the Amidah ("the standing [prayer]"), the main Jewish prayer traditionally recited three times a day:

> May it be Your will, LORD our God and God of our ancestors,
> that the Temple be rebuilt speedily in our days,
> and grant us a share in Your Torah.
> And there we will serve You with reverence,
> as in the days of old and as former years.
> Then the offering of Judah and Jerusalem
> will be pleasing to the LORD
> as in the days of old and as in former years.[84]

Any Jew who prays regularly using this liturgical formula thus recalls the importance of the Temple and its sacrifices.

Jews and Christians both participate in unfinished systems; they both recognize, albeit in different ways, the importance of atonement and sacrifice, sin and repentance. There is little reason to claim which system "replaces" the other or which is the "better" path. They both have their own logic, and everyone does well to recognize how each functions. Jews and Christians both have plausible readings of Genesis 14 and Psalm 110, and here we can agree that the scriptures of Israel require interpretation.

Chapter 6

⚘

"An Eye for an Eye" and "Turn the Other Cheek"

ANTITHESES OR EXTENSIONS?

IN THE Sermon on the Mount (Matt 5–7), Jesus instructs his disciples:

> "You have heard that it was said, 'An eye for an eye and a tooth for a tooth.' But I say to you, Do not resist an evildoer. But if anyone strikes you on the right cheek, turn the other also; and if anyone wants to sue you and take your coat, give your cloak as well; and if anyone forces you to go one mile, go also the second mile. Give to everyone who begs from you, and do not refuse anyone who wants to borrow from you." (Matt 5:38–42)

This passage, too often stripped down to "turn the other cheek, give the coat off your back, and go the extra mile," is among the most familiar and highly regarded of the New Testament's writings. It is also among the most likely to be cited, by people unfamiliar with the Hebrew Bible or Judaism, as demonstrating a contrast between the teachings of the "Old Testament," seen as legalistic, and the teachings of the "New Testament," seen as merciful. We have frequently heard that Judaism promotes an "eye for an eye" mentality, a focus on retribution, and a system that would, as Mohandas Gandhi is supposed to have said, "make the whole world blind." We have also heard, although not as often, that Jesus was a pacifist who would reject not only gun ownership but also self-defense. Both views are incorrect.

Jesus's statement is best understood in its literary and historical contexts. Turning the other cheek is, first, to be located in the context of his teachings on murder, adultery, divorce, oath-taking, and love of neighbor. Second, unless we recognize how the antecedent laws in Israel's Torah functioned in their own time and in subsequent generations, we will necessarily misunderstand what Jesus is saying.

The teachings on turning the cheek, giving the shirt, and going the extra mile appear within a collection of sayings that begin with some variant of the formula, "you have heard it said. . . . But I say to you." These are typically called "antitheses"—or oppositions. The label creates an immediate problem, for it suggests Jesus is opposing, or saying the opposite of, what the Torah teaches. That is clearly not the case. An antithesis would be, "You have heard that it was said to those of ancient times, 'You shall not murder'; and 'whoever murders shall be liable to judgment'" (Matt 5:21)—"but I say to you, lock and load!" This incorrect understanding is part of the broader view that Jesus replaces the Old Testament law of vengeance with the New Testament gospel of grace. Jesus is not presenting antitheses, in the sense of rejecting Old Testament law in favor of New Testament grace and mercy. Such interpretations do violence to the Torah, to the Jewish tradition, and to Jesus's own message.

In providing instruction on how to interpret not only "an eye for an eye" but also such commandments as "you shall not murder," "you shall not commit adultery," and "you shall not swear falsely," Jesus is doing two things that Jews have always done: (1) interpreting the text—for the biblical text, as we discussed in Chapter 1, always needs interpretation; and (2) seeking to understand how the Torah functions in their own lives and the lives of their community.

The problems Jesus addresses here are not unique to Jews or Judaism; they are universal: all peoples have had questions about how to respond to violence and to sexual impropriety, about personal honesty, and about dealing with enemies. All cultures have various norms—legal, cultural, familial, religious—that suggest or mandate responses. Yet these norms also require interpretation—they rarely are broad or clear enough to cover every circumstance. Nor do such norms remain static; they necessarily change when circumstances change. Jesus, like other Jews of his day as well as before and since, interprets the Torah. Indeed, for Matthew, Jesus is the preeminent interpreter, as he ascends a mountain like a new Moses.[1] His interpretation is not a replacement of one Torah by another: to the contrary (an antithesis!), he extends rather than abrogates the Torah. He makes the law more rigorous rather than less. Instead of jettisoning the Torah, he seeks to determine how best it might be understood and practiced.

Any sense that Jesus opposes the Torah is precluded by the opening of the Sermon on the Mount where Matthew front-loads both the importance and the permanence of the Torah. Immediately before introducing the "you have heard it said" formula, Jesus insists that he has not "come to abolish the law [Greek *nomos*; the underlying Hebrew would be *torah*, typically translated as *nomos* in the Septuagint] or the prophets [i.e., the Nevi'im]; I have come not to abolish but to fulfill" (Matt 5:17).

Contrary to some speculation, "fulfill" does not mean "take care of what needs to be done so that you do not have to" or more simply, "end."[2] Instead, Jesus proclaims that the Torah and the Prophets, and the practices they teach, will remain for at least the lifetime of anyone hearing his words: "For truly [the Greek here uses the Hebrew *amen*] I tell you, until heaven and earth pass away, not one letter, not one stroke [KJV: "one jot or one tittle"] of a letter, will pass from the law until all is accomplished" (Matt 5:18). "To fulfill" here means "to complete" in the sense of drawing out the full implications of the Torah and the Prophets. "Fulfill" is a Matthean theme, found mostly in relation to Jesus's "fulfilling" what was said by an earlier prophet. We will see this motif in Chapter 8, where we turn to Matthew 1:22, which, in introducing the Greek version of Isaiah 7:14 to explain Jesus's virginal conception, states, "All this took place to fulfill what had been spoken by the Lord through the prophet." According to Matthew, Jesus—not just by his teachings but also by his life—shows the complete meaning of Israel's scriptures.

Jesus also commands his disciples that they must follow his interpretation of the Torah: "Therefore, whoever breaks one of the least of these commandments, and teaches others to do the same, will be called least in the kingdom of heaven; but whoever does them and teaches them will be called great in the kingdom of heaven. For I tell you, unless your righteousness exceeds that of the scribes and Pharisees, you will never enter the kingdom of heaven" (Matt 5:19–20). Despite the popular view that Jesus cares primarily about what one believes, Matthew's Gospel focuses rather on how one acts, on what one does.

When Jesus sets Pharisaic behavior as the minimum, he is not setting a low bar. According to Josephus, Pharisees were popular teachers known for their mutual friendship (*War* 2.166), "conduct of reason," respect for their elders, and belief in free will and therefore that people choose whether or not to follow the path of virtue, as well as their view that people will be judged on their behavior (*Antiquities* 18.12–15). He compares them to the Stoics, a respected philosophical school (*Life* 12). Of direct relevance to the Sermon on the Mount, Josephus suggests that the Pharisees are popular because their traditions of Torah interpretation "alleviated the harsher prescriptions of the Bible in civil and criminal law" (*Antiquities* 13.294).[3] How ironic: Jesus promotes practices that have harsher prescriptions than the Pharisees mandate. Once we realize that Jesus is not abrogating the

Torah or substituting some other code for it, we are in a better position to understand the antitheses or, better, the extensions.

Matthew offers in 5:21–47 six statements that begin with some variant of the formula, "you have heard it said. . . . But I say to you." In a few manuscripts, the first and fourth begin with the longer formula, "You have heard that it was said by people of old." Most quote biblical commandments, and a few paraphrase them. Despite the setting on a mountain and so the evocation of Moses, Jesus is not reading from a text, and Matthew does not imagine Jesus teaching in a schoolhouse, with disciples arguing over words on a scroll. In fact, no source in antiquity presents Pharisees as arguing over a text; that is the role of the later rabbis. The setting for Jesus is one of oral tradition and so of popular belief. Jesus need not quote the Torah word-for-word in order to convey, generally speaking, the text under discussion. The import is in how the teaching is to be interpreted, not the exact words.

Matthew sets a scene of popular expositions, but the evangelist is actually writing with a lovely rhetorical balance: the first three antitheses contain 1,131 letters; the second three, 1,130 letters.[4] The subjects are, in order: (1) murder and by extension anger, (2) adultery and by extension lust, (3) divorce and by extension the breaking of the family, (4) oath-taking (swearing) and by extension personal honesty, (5) proportional justice and by extension retribution, and (6) loving the neighbor and by extension loving the enemy. The first (murder), second (adultery), and fourth (swearing) allude to the "Decalogue" or "Ten Commandments," with swearing relating to the commandment forbidding taking the divine name in vain (Exod 20:7). In number 5, we find Jesus's application of the famous "eye for an eye." The meaning of Jesus's exposition of this law becomes clear only within the unit as a whole.

But I Say to You...

On Murder

THE FIRST extension begins, "You have heard that it was said to those of ancient times" (Matt 5:21). The allusion is to God's revelation to Moses on Mount Sinai. Next, in the same verse, comes the commandment itself, "'You shall not murder'; and 'whoever murders shall be liable to judgment.'" "You shall not murder" is a citation of Exodus 20:13 and Deuteronomy 5:17, part of the Decalogue. Since the Hebrew root *r-tz-ch* refers to intentional killing or what we today would call murder, the well-known King James translation, "thou shalt not kill," is overly broad. The Bible contains laws that mandate capital punishment and allows, even in some cases mandates, killing in war.

The second clause, "whoever murders shall be liable to judgment," is not a quotation but a paraphrase. Apodictic laws, laws that take the form "you shall (not) . . . ," require a practical result: If I do this wrong thing, what are the consequences? "Liable to judgment," a vague but ominous threat, likely refers to the well-known biblical view found in Genesis 9:6, that murder is a capital offense:

Whoever sheds the blood of a human,
by a human shall that person's blood be shed;

186

> for in his own image
> God made humankind.

Although God tells Noah that murder should be punished by death, only five chapters earlier, in Genesis 4, God protected rather than executed Cain, who killed his brother Abel. Similarly, although Moses committed murder (Exod 2:12), he is not executed. As with the present-day legal system, what the law mandates is not necessarily what is carried out in practice.

"Those of ancient times" as well as Jesus's audience would have known the Decalogue along with other passages that unambiguously find intentional homicide to be a capital offense (see especially Num 35:16–18). Jesus the interpreter then asks: Is premeditated murder the only serious offense that the commandment means to cover?

He then offers the extension: "But I say to you that if you are angry with a brother or sister [i.e., any community member], you will be liable to judgment; and if you insult a brother or sister, you will be liable to the council [Greek *sanhedrin*, here meaning the local court; the same usage appears in Matt 10:17]; and if you say, 'You fool,' you will be liable to the hell of fire" (Matt 5:22). These threats may be rhetorical flourish. The communities gathered in Jesus's name had nondeadly procedures for disciplining recalcitrant members; Matthew 18:15–17 prescribes a formal process for reprimand followed, if necessary, by a removal from the fellowship.

Should an earthly court fail to provide appropriate punishment, Jesus assures that the heavenly judge will: hence the reference to "hell" (Greek *gehenna*) in Matthew 5:22.[5] The Talmud offers a similar saying. Rabbi Yehoshua ben Levi proposes that a disciple could be excommunicated for insulting his teacher: "One who speaks disparagingly after the biers of Torah scholars and maligns them after their death will fall into Gehenna, as it is stated, 'But those who turn aside unto their crooked ways, the Lord will lead them away with the workers of iniquity; peace be upon Israel' [Ps 125:5]" (b. Berakhot 19a).[6]

Jesus's extension, meant to convey the seriousness of angry words, does what rabbinic Judaism calls "building a fence about the Torah." The expression comes from the Mishnah. Avot 1:1 reads: "Moses received Torah at Sinai, and handed it on to Joshua, Joshua to the elders, and the elders to the prophets. And prophets handed it on to the men of the Great Assembly. They said three things: Be prudent in judgment, raise up many disciples, make a fence for the Torah." As a fence about a house protects what is inside, so the fence about the Torah protects the commandments by creating the circumstances that make violation more difficult. If one is not angry, one is less likely to commit murder. Some scribes, recognizing that anger is sometimes justified—what we would call "righteous anger"—added to Greek manuscripts of Matthew the exception, "without cause."[7]

On Adultery

FOLLOWING a few examples concerning reconciling with enemies, Jesus moves to the second intensification. Again, the formula alludes to the Torah, "You have heard that it was said . . . ," which is followed by a direct quotation, "You shall not commit adultery" (Matt 5:27). The citation is to Exodus 20:14 and Deuteronomy 5:18; Leviticus 20:10 provides the penalty: "If a man commits adultery with the wife of his neighbor, both the adulterer and the adulteress shall be put to death."

Adultery in this context—in Israelite society men could have more than one wife, but women could have only one husband—means sexual relations between a married or betrothed woman and a man other than her husband or betrothed. Whether Jews in the early or even in the Second Temple period were actually executing people guilty of adultery remains an open question. The scriptures of Israel contain no examples of such execution, although adultery shows up on occasion. David and Bathsheba are the most notable example (2 Sam 11), and neither is executed. However, their son conceived from their adulterous relationship dies (2 Sam 12), so a vicarious capital punishment is carried out by God. Hosea (1:2–9) is married to an adulterous wife, but the relationship prompts reconciliation, not death. Indeed, the prophetic metaphor of Israel as an adulterous spouse does not lead to the death of all Israel, but to shame, repentance, and ultimately reconciliation with God. The story of Susanna, an appendix to the book of Daniel found in the deuterocanonical literature (Protestant Apocrypha), and one of the world's first detective stories, depicts a woman facing execution on the false charge of adultery. She is rescued when Daniel proves that the elders who accused her of improper sexual relations were lying. This fictional account was designed to show Daniel's wisdom, not historical judicial procedure.

The more famous story in John 8 of the "woman taken in adultery" also does not presume an execution. This narrative, which begins to appear in New Testament manuscripts only from the fourth century,[8] depicts no court case, and procedures that do appear are incomplete. For example, the story lacks any reference to, let alone appearance of, the man with whom the accused was said to have committed adultery. A woman cannot commit adultery on her own. Eyewitness testimony is absent; rather, "the scribes and the Pharisees" assert, "this woman was caught in the very act of committing adultery" (John 8:3–4). Further undermining the notion that the scene depicts a trial, the setting is not a court but the Jerusalem Temple.

John's story does not presume that people are executed for adultery. To the contrary, Jesus's opponents are trying to trap him by asking him what should be done with this guilty woman: If he says "execute her," they will accuse him of barbarism or of failing to follow court procedure. If he says "release her," they will condemn him for allowing a transgression of the Torah without warrant. Jesus refuses to play this game. Instead, he traps his opponents by asking them not about the woman's punishment but about their qualifications for implementing it: "Let anyone among you who is without sin be the first to throw a stone at her" (John 8:7). The opponents, self-condemned, leave. They drop no stones; they were not carrying any.

Confirming the lack of capital punishment for adultery at the time of Jesus is Matthew's nativity story. When Joseph learns that his betrothed, Mary, is pregnant, he decides to divorce her quietly (Matt 1:19). Mary is not in danger of stoning, and Matthew makes no mention of any public shaming.

Rabbinic Judaism goes out of its way to make execution, for any reason, impossible. The Talmud devotes to adultery an entire tractate, called "Sotah" in reference to the "test of bitter waters" given to a wife whose husband suspects her of infidelity (Num 5:11–31). The rabbis insist not only that the adulterous act be observed by two witnesses (most adultery, as far as we are aware, is not done in public) but also that the couple be warned in advance that their actions could lead to fatal consequences. Rather than execution, adultery according to rabbinic Judaism could have led to divorce without any monetary compensation to the wife, to public shaming, and to the social detriment of children produced from an adulterous relationship.

It is possible that Jewish courts did carry out the death penalty during the rabbinic period, and the Christian writer Origen suggests that they had such authority (*Letter to Africanus* 20.14). The most we can conclude is that if, at the time of either Jesus or Matthew, adultery was punished by death, the punishment was exceptionally rare.[9] In effect, the rabbis build a fence around the death penalty; they insist on just legal procedures, and then they make the procedures in this case so rigorous that executing the guilty party becomes almost impossible. For example, while Deuteronomy 21:18–21 required that a rebellious son be stoned, the Mishnah (Sanhedrin 8) makes the rules so stringent for stoning that son that it is virtually impossible to fulfill them. Another Mishnah (Makkot 1:10) notes how rare capital punishment was: "A sanhedrin which imposes the death penalty once in seven years is called murderous. R. Eleazar b. Azariah says, 'Once in seventy years.' R. Tarfon and R. Aqiba say, 'If we were on a sanhedrin, no one would ever be put to death.'"[10]

Jesus finds adultery to be a serious problem, and so he addresses its causes. He builds the fence by equating (male) lust with adultery and therefore prohibiting it: "But I say to you that everyone who looks at a woman with lust has already committed adultery with her in his heart" (Matt 5:28). The Greek term for "lust" or "desire" (*epithymeō*) appears elsewhere in the Septuagint's rendition of the Ten Commandments: in forbidding the coveting of the neighbor's house and of his wife (Exod 20:17; Deut 5:21). Jesus then goes further in fence building with the hyperbolic command: "If your right eye causes you to sin, tear it out and throw it away; it is better for you to lose one of your members than for your whole body to be thrown into hell" (Matt 5:29). This verse alerts us that commandments in the form of cause and effect, including this one, may be cautionary laws, more along the lines of parental threats than judicial responses. It also likely put a damper on any lustful feelings that community members might have had.

On Divorce

FOLLOWING discussion of adultery, Matthew addresses a related concern, divorce. The third extension presumes the full formula "you have heard it said" by beginning, "It was also said, 'Whoever divorces his wife, let him give her a certificate of divorce'" (Matt 5:31). The citation alludes to Deuteronomy 24:1: "Suppose a man enters into marriage with a woman, but she does not please him because he finds something objectionable [Hebrew 'ervat davar, a matter of indecency] about her, and so he writes her a certificate of divorce, puts it in her hand, and sends her out of his house." The Hebrew 'ervat davar is vague, as is the English equivalent, "matter of indecency." The term 'ervah (a form of 'ervat) almost always refers to sexual impropriety, although the same phrase, 'ervat davar, appears in Deuteronomy 23:14 [23:15 Heb.] in the nonsexual sense of digging trenches for latrines. The term thus concerns something unpleasant, even disgusting. The divorce law in Deuteronomy 24 adds that if the divorced wife were to marry someone else who then divorced her or died, the first husband is forbidden from remarrying her.

Jesus extends the prohibition against remarrying the first wife by forbidding divorce and remarriage entirely: "But I say to you that anyone who divorces his wife, except on the ground of unchastity [Greek logou porneias; the expression is vague, as is the Hebrew in Deut 24:1], causes her to commit adultery; and whoever marries a divorced woman commits adultery" (Matt 5:32; cf. 19:1–12). This "matter of porneia," whence the English term "pornography," could refer to an incestuous relationship, an illegal one (e.g., the wife was still married to someone else), one that continues following the adulterous relationship, or one in which behavior suggests lewdness. As with the Hebrew, the Greek becomes the subject for later legal minds.

In the earlier Marcan (10:2–12) as well as Lucan (16:18) versions of this extension, no porneia exception appears, although Mark includes the possibility that a woman might want to divorce her husband (Mark 10:12), a possibility available to some Jewish women in the first century.[11] Paul alludes to this possibility for his gentile congregants in Corinth: "To the married I give this command—not I but the Lord—that the wife should not separate from her husband (but if she does separate, let her remain unmarried or else be reconciled to her husband), and that the husband should not divorce his wife" (1 Cor 7:10–11).

Jesus's prohibiting divorce makes him more conservative than the Dead Sea Scrolls. Speaking specifically of the king, the Temple Scroll (11QT^a 57:17–19) reads: "And he may not take any other woman in addition to her, but she alone shall be with him all the days of his life. And if she dies, he shall take for himself another from his father's house, from his clan."[12] It also moves Jesus very far to the right of the later rabbis, for whom divorce was a legal possibility. The rabbis did not debate the legality of divorce; rather, they debated the appropriate grounds:

> The House of Shammai says, "A man should divorce his wife only because he has found grounds for it in unchastity, since it is said, *Because he has found in her indecency in anything* [i.e., something objectionable] (Deut. 24.1)." And the House of Hillel says, "Even if she spoiled his dish, since it is said, *Because he has found in her indecency in anything* [i.e., something objectionable]." R. Aqiba says, "Even if he found someone else prettier than she, since it is said, *And it shall be if she find no favor in his eyes* (Deut. 24.1)." (m. Git. 9.10; cf. Sifre Deut. 269; y. Sota 1:2, 16b; spelling altered for clarity)

The House of Shammai takes the Hebrew *'ervat davar* to refer to adultery (thereby indicating that no one is being stoned for adultery) and makes divorce permissible only on that ground. Conversely, the House of Hillel allows men to divorce their wives for any offense, following a broader understanding of *'ervat davar*. But the House of Hillel still would have demanded that the husband compensate his wife according to the *ketubah,* the marriage contract, so she would not have been thrown out, penniless. Claims that the Hillelite version was designed to *protect* divorced women from charges of adultery (i.e., if she can be divorced for any reason, there is no reason to suggest that she sinned) are modern apologetics for a reading that today sounds harsh.

Contrary to some popular teaching, Jesus's forbidding divorce is not designed to protect women from husbands who issue arbitrary divorce decrees, a point that should be obvious from Mark's forbidding a wife from divorcing her husband (Mark 10:12). Jesus grounds his teaching not in social reform, but in Genesis. He first explains that although Deuteronomy permits divorce, it does so as a concession: "Because of your hardness of heart he wrote this commandment [regarding divorce] for you" (Mark 10:5). He then, in good Jewish fashion, puts Deuteronomy into dialogue with Genesis and concludes that Genesis, the earlier reading, offers the better model: "But from the beginning of creation, 'God made them male and female.' 'For this reason a man shall leave his father and mother and be joined to his wife, and the two shall become one flesh.' So they are no longer two, but one flesh" (Mark 10:6–8). Being taken from the man's body, the woman returns to the man and so completes him (see Chapter 4). Extrapolating from the garden of Eden story, Jesus concludes that any relationship between a husband and a wife is both divinely sanctioned and therefore permanent: "Therefore, what God has joined together, let no one separate" (Mark 10:9).

However, for Jesus, the permanent marital bond does not require husbands and wives to live together. His movement consists of some followers without spousal accompaniment. In Luke 14:26, Jesus advises followers to "hate" family members, including "wife and children" (the injunction presumes that all followers are male), and in Luke 18:29–30, he states, "Truly I tell you, there is no one who has left house or wife or brothers or parents or children, for the sake of the kingdom of God, who will not get back very much more in this age, and in the age to come eternal life." In Jesus's mission, there is no divorce, but there is also no procreation, for creating heirs to inherit property, nor cohabitation. This is because the end of time as we know it is soon approaching.

In anthropological language, there is for Jesus no "pair bonding," for loyalty and love are to be focused on Jesus and then equally distributed among members of the community gathered in his name. The love is spiritual, not carnal. Judaism, which had strains of celibacy in the first century,[13] would go on to reject both apocalyptic thinking and celibacy. But for the Second Temple period, Josephus (*Antiquities* 18.21; *War* 2.120–21) and Philo (*Hypothetica* 11) both describe celibate Essenes. Philo also describes the Therapeutae and Therapeutrides, a utopian community of celibate Jewish men and women (*On the Contemplative Life* 8.68–90).

Jesus's comments forbidding divorce do not fit within other streams of early Judaism, although Matthew's *porneia* clause looks like the teaching of the House of Shammai, who found adultery the only viable reason to end a marriage. His teaching on celibacy, which reappears in Paul (1 Cor 7:7) and Revelation (14:4), became as time went on a distinguishing marker between Christians, who promoted virginity and continence, and the rabbinic tradition, which promoted marriage, marital relations, and children.

On Oath-Taking

THE FOURTH extension concerns oath-taking. Jesus begins, "Again, you have heard that it was said to those of ancient times, 'You shall not swear falsely, but carry out the vows you have made to the Lord'" (Matt 5:33). There is no exact correspondence in the Torah for this wording, in part because the statement concerns two separate issues: false swearing and (positive) vowing. False swearing is insisting on the truth of one's words, even if they are false. Vowing here means making a promise to God. For example, one might take a Nazirite vow to live a life of particular holiness and purity (see Num 6). We see Paul under such a vow in Acts 18:18 and redeeming people at the completion of their Nazirite term in Acts 21:23–26.

The scriptures of Israel advise against vowing. Deuteronomy 23:22 states, "But if you refrain from vowing, you will not incur guilt"; since the vow may not be fulfilled, Deuteronomy suggests avoiding the risk. Ecclesiastes 5:4–5 makes a similar point: since God "has no pleasure in fools," quickly fulfill the vow you take, although "it is better that you should not vow than that you should vow and not fulfill it." While the Torah permits oath-taking, Jesus forbids it: "But I say to you, Do not swear at all, either by heaven, for it is the throne of God, or by the earth, for it is his footstool, or by Jerusalem, for it is the city of the great King" (Matt 5:34–35). Matthew 23:22 picks up the same point, "whoever swears by heaven, swears by the throne of God and by the one who is seated upon it." All such oaths take the name of God in vain; "heaven," "earth," and "Jerusalem" are circumlocutions for God's name, which was at the time considered too holy to pronounce.[14] Underlying Jesus's statement is the Torah's concern for misusing the divine name. Exodus 20:7 reads, "You shall not make wrongful use of the name of the LORD your God, for the LORD will not acquit anyone who misuses his name," translated less accurately in the King James Version, "Thou shalt not take the name of the LORD thy God in vain" (Deut 5:11; see also Lev 19:12, "And you shall not swear falsely by my name, profaning the name of your God: I am the LORD" [NRSV]).

Although Christian scholars occasionally suggest that Jesus was resisting Jewish views of oath-taking, which had devolved into "such casuistry, of which the Mishnah provides numerous examples,"[15] the claim overstates. The Mishnah is speaking of legal liability; we might think of taking the oath for an office in the US government or in a law court or the signing of a business contract. The words one says are formal and binding, and the oath, or the signature to the contract, shows the seriousness of the issue. Furthermore, rather than engaging in "casuistry," Rabbi Meir, like Jesus, notes that it is best not to vow at all, an opinion that other rabbis endorse (b. Nedarim 22a, 77b).

Jesus continues, "And do not swear by your head, for you cannot make one hair white or black" (Matt 5:36): since one cannot change what occurs naturally, the oath is useless. He concludes in the next verse, "Let your word be 'Yes, Yes' or 'No, No'; anything more than this comes from the evil one." The "evil one" is a euphemism for "Satan"; in marvelous irony, this is the same type of euphemism that he condemns in speaking of God by terms such as "heaven" or "Jerusalem."

From forbidding false witness, Jesus mandates honesty at all times. From forbidding oath-taking to ensure that one will carry through a promise, Jesus insists that the promises—even if not accompanied by oaths in God's name—be kept. The point of both extensions is that there is no need for oath-taking or vowing when honesty is the norm.

On Loving Your Neighbor

WE SKIP Jesus's comments on "an eye for an eye" to turn to the final, sixth extension, Matthew 5:43–48. Jesus begins, "You have heard that it was said, 'You shall love your neighbor.'" The citation is a direct quotation of most of the second half of Leviticus 19:18, "You shall not take vengeance or bear a grudge against any of your people, but you shall love your neighbor as yourself; I am the LORD."

The omission of "as yourself" may be designed to create a better rhetorical parallel to what follows concerning enemies.

The Levitical concern regarding bearing a grudge has the same fence-building protection as Jesus's earlier comment, "if you are angry with a brother or sister, you will be liable to judgment" (Matt 5:22). In Leviticus, "neighbor" means a fellow Israelite or Jew, a point made clear by the following injunction in Leviticus 19:34, "The alien who resides with you shall be to you as the citizen among you; you shall love the alien as yourself, for you were aliens in the land of Egypt." The Torah distinguishes between Israelites and strangers (we might think of the distinction between a citizen and a resident alien), but Leviticus insists that both must be loved.

Jesus then follows "You have heard . . . you shall love your neighbor" with "and hate your enemy" (Matt 5:43). The concern for hating the enemy does not appear in the Torah, although it is found in the Dead Sea Scrolls. For example, the Community Rule (1QS 1:3–4) advises, "He is to teach them to love everything (or everyone) He chose and to hate everything (or everyone) He rejected."[16]

Typically cited in terms of "Old Testament" hatred of enemies is the last verse of Psalm 137, perhaps known better for its opening line, "By the rivers of Babylon— / there we sat down and we wept." Psalm 137:9, concerning the Edomites who participated in the Babylonians' destruction of Jerusalem, reads, "Happy shall they be who take your little ones / and dash them against the rock!" The rock (Hebrew *hasala'*) is another name for a city in Edom (2 Kgs 14:7), perhaps where Petra (from the Greek word for "rock") in present-day Jordan was built; the sense of retribution, not uncommon in the Psalms, is a brutally honest emotion. The psalmist is not encouraging the people to kill infants; the retribution, as with Exodus 23:22, belongs to God. For the scriptures of Israel, as God states, "Vengeance is mine" (Deut 32:35), a point echoed by Paul (Rom 12:19) and the author of

Hebrews (10:30). We see this concern for divine justice elsewhere, for example, Exodus 23:22, "But if you listen attentively to his [i.e., the angel of the LORD's] voice and do all that I say, then I will be an enemy to your enemies and a foe to your foes."

Conversely, the scriptures of Israel do have laws to prevent abuse of enemies. For example, Proverbs 24:17 eliminates schadenfreude: "Do not rejoice when your enemies fall, / and do not let your heart be glad when they stumble." The rationale is not to avoid adding insult to injury, but lest "the LORD will see it and be displeased, / and turn away his anger from them" (Prov 24:18). A similar backhanded mandate appears in Proverbs 25:21: "If your enemies are hungry, give them bread to eat; / and if they are thirsty, give them water to drink." The rationale is not to turn enemies into friends but to frustrate them, "for you will heap coals of fire on their heads, / and the LORD will reward you" (Prov 25:22; Paul quotes this couplet in Rom 12:20). The Torah commands that you must help your enemy's ox or donkey: "When you come upon your enemy's ox or donkey going astray, you shall bring it back" (Exod 23:4). Even more positive regarding enemies is Jeremiah's address to the exiled Judeans in Babylon, "But seek the welfare of the city where I have sent you into exile, and pray to the LORD on its behalf, for in its welfare you will find your welfare" (Jer 29:7).

Jesus extends the scriptural injunctions that one must not abuse an enemy and even pray for the welfare of the conquering empire. Not only does he reject the idea of hating enemies, he insists, "Love your enemies and pray for those who persecute you" (Matt 5:44). The rationale is consistent with the theological view that people should act as God acts "so that you may be children of your Father in heaven" who is concerned about the righteous and the unrighteous alike (Matt 5:45). To be children of the Father means acting as that Father would act. We find a similar teaching in rabbinic literature:

"Just as He is compassionate and merciful, so too should you be compassionate and merciful" (b. Shabbat 133b).

The section concludes with the demand, "Be perfect, therefore, as your heavenly Father is perfect" (Matt 5:48). The Greek term for "perfect," *teleios*, does not mean here "never to have sinned" or "made a mistake." Sirach 44:17 states that "Noah was found perfect [*teleios*] and righteous," without implying that Noah was without sin. The Hebrew term *tamim*, sometimes translated "blameless" (e.g., the NRSV to Gen 17:1, in which God tells Abraham, "walk before me, and be blameless"), captures a similar sense.[17] Thus, "perfect" in Matthew 5:48 suggests acting in complete accord with divine will, as Jesus understands it.

The extensions show how the Torah is to be followed by building fences about the law and so extending it: from forbidding murder to forbidding anger; from forbidding adultery to forbidding lust; from forbidding false or violated oaths to forbidding oath-taking; from permission to divorce to forbidding it; from not abusing the enemy and praying for the enemy to loving the enemy. Our final example follows the same format—but in this case with something other than an extension.

On an Eye for an Eye

THE OTHER examples are prophylactic: to avoid murder, avoid anger; to avoid adultery, avoid lust; and so on. With "an eye for an eye," the issue is justice *after* a crime has been committed or an accident has occurred. In Matthew 5:38, Jesus states, "You have heard that it was said, 'An eye for an eye and a tooth for a tooth.'" These words appear three places in the Torah: Exodus 21:23–25, Leviticus 24:19–20, and Deuteronomy 19:21. Each passage spells out, in different ways, compensation for damage to any body part. And many readers invoke this law as indicating the Old Testament's barbarity. The issue is not barbarism but justice in the case of physical injury; the irony is that the Torah is speaking not of actual practice but of legal principle.

The principle was known in Roman law as *lex talionis*, "the law of equals," or more simply as talio or talion.[18] It appears in the classic Roman law code *The Twelve Tables*, table 7, law 2, which stipulates, "If a man broke another's limb, the victim could inflict the same injury upon the wrongdoer [*talio*], but only if no settlement was agreed upon."[19] Jews and gentiles both would have known the law of talion, whether from the Torah or *The Twelve Tables*.

Were Jesus to have extended the law, in line with what we have seen in the surrounding units, he would have demanded greater loss: "You have heard it said, 'an eye for an eye,' but I say to you, 'a head for an eye.'" Nor does he say either, "You lost your eye; don't worry about it," or, "You lost your eye; give to the perpetrator the other." The first approach, demanding more bodily harm, would truly be barbaric; the second approach, ignoring the injury, would be ridiculous.

Rather than countering or extending the law of talion, Jesus changes the subject. The talion speaks of physical mutilation; Jesus speaks about public humiliation: "But I say to you, Do not resist an evildoer. But if anyone strikes you on the right cheek, turn the other also; and if anyone wants to sue you and take your coat, give your cloak as well; and if anyone forces you to go one mile, go also the second mile" (Matt 5:39–41). There is a major difference between losing an eye and getting slapped on the cheek. The three examples Jesus gives, regarding the slap, the suit, and the subjugation, together reveal their import: do not escalate violence; do not give up your agency; shame your attacker and retain your honor. As with the other injunctions in this section, his concern is correct community relations, rejection of violence, honesty to others, and acting mercifully and justly as God would.

These expressions—turn the other cheek, give the coat off your back, go the extra mile—have become so commonplace in the English language that it is difficult to appreciate their original import. "Turn the other cheek" asks more than "ignore the problem"; giving the coat is not about "being generous"; "go the extra mile" demands much more than "make an extra effort." When heard in their first-century context, the three injunctions all serve to prevent the escalation of conflict, which is exactly what the original "eye for an eye" legislation does.

To be struck on the right cheek presumes, if the striker is right-handed, a backhanded slap (you might practice this, carefully, by pretending to slap the right cheek of a brave friend). It is the slap that would be given by a master to a slave, or a soldier to a peasant. A backhanded slap is designed to humiliate, not to injure; it does not do the serious damage a right jab does. The motif appears in Lamentations 3:30, which speaks of giving "one's cheek to the smiter, / and be filled with insults" (the Hebrew for "insults," *cherpah*, connotes reproach, disgrace, scorn, and shame), and in 2 Corinthians 11:20, where Paul speaks about the humiliation of being slapped in the face.[20]

When slapped, the victim has a few options, none of them good. Hitting back escalates the violence, which in situations of social inequality can have deadly consequences. But cowering does not help either; it functions only as short-term self-protection, and it opens the possibility for continued or more extreme violent acts on the part of the perpetrator.

Jesus offers what the biblical scholar Walter Wink called the "third way": rather than escalate violence, and rather than accept the loss of personal dignity, confront the violence.[21] Matthew 5:39 reads, "Do not resist an evildoer. But if anyone strikes you on the right cheek, turn the other also." The situation of humiliation—being slapped, being stripped naked, carrying gear—becomes instead an opportunity of expressing agency. Warren Carter points out that the term translated "resist" (Greek *anthistēmi*) can refer to "armed resistance in military encounters" or "violent struggles."[22] Therefore, the verse concerns the *type* of resistance practiced. By offering the left cheek, the victim resists humiliation by displaying agency and courage. Further, offering the left cheek invites the right jab, the punch of greater violence. It reveals to the perpetrator that a slap is itself a violent act; it shows that a slap of dismissal does not decrease the humanity of the victim.

From physical violence, Jesus turns to judicial violence. The setting is the court: someone "wants to sue you and take your coat." Behind this concern is Exodus 22:26–27: "If you take your neighbor's cloak in pawn, you shall restore it before the sun goes down; for it may be your neighbor's only clothing to use as cover; in what else shall that person sleep? And if your neighbor cries out to me, I will listen, for I am compassionate." Again, the victim has few options, none good. One option is to accept the verdict and freeze that night. Another would be to avoid the court, but that could result in arrest and an even worse situation. The third way, to "give your cloak as well," means to strip off one's other garment in the court and so to lay bare, literally, the injustice of the situation. In this setting, it is the one suing who is shamed.

Finally, the issue of the extra mile concerns military violence, a system of compulsion, or as the NRSV reads, "forces you to go." We see such conscription in Matthew 27:32 and Mark 15:21, where Roman soldiers "compel" (the same Greek term, *aggareuō*) Simon of Cyrene to carry Jesus's crossbeam. To refuse is to risk a beating. To comply is to be humiliated and more, to be turned into a pack animal. The third way is to accept the inevitable, to carry the baggage. Yet at the end of the mile, the victim adds, "I'll go the second." In other words: You sought to treat me as less than human. I refuse to allow you to do this—I will use my own agency to carry it farther.

Matthew ends this section with a potentially impractical injunction, "Give to everyone who begs from you, and do not refuse anyone who wants to borrow from you" (Matt 5:42). The verse could be an intensification of Deuteronomy 15:9, which concerns withholding funds in anticipation of the sabbatical year, when debts are to be forgiven: "Be careful that you do not entertain a mean thought, thinking, 'The seventh year, the year of remission, is near,' and therefore view your needy neighbor with hostility and give nothing; your neighbor might cry to the LORD against you, and you would incur guilt."[23] It is also possible that Jesus is extending the Torah's command in the previous verse to "open your hand, willingly lending enough to meet the need, whatever it may be" (Deut 15:8); the rationale: "Since there will never cease to be some in need on the earth, I therefore command you, 'Open your hand to the poor and needy neighbor in your land'" (Deut 15:11). Or again, he could be using hyperbole, as he elsewhere does in stressing wholehearted commitment to ethical behavior.

More than giving charitably, the Torah's mandate, Jesus demands giving without restraint. The verse matches the call to the man who, although Torah faithful, was still attached to worldly wealth: "Sell all that you own and distribute the money to the poor, and you will have treasure in heaven; then come, follow me" (Luke 18:22; cf. Matt 19:21; Mark 10:21). Such a command works in cases where disciples have no familial responsibilities. The Mishnah states that "the things for which no measure is prescribed" (m. Peah 1:1) include generosity regarding leaving the corners of the field unharvested so that the poor can glean (cf. Lev 19:9; 23:22), offerings such as first fruits, deeds of loving kindness, and the study of the Torah. The Yerushalmi (the Jerusalem Talmud) insists that charity without limit "concerns actions done with one's body (such as visiting the sick or burying the dead)."[24] But total divestment is not permitted, for the Mishnah presupposes its readers have families to support.

With five extensions and one change of subject, the Sermon on the Mount confirms Jesus's initial assertion in Matthew 5:17: "Do not think that I have come to abolish the law or the prophets; I have come not to abolish but to fulfill." No Torah practice is abrogated; instead, Jesus reinforces several. It's time the term "antitheses" for these passages be replaced. Once that is done, we can turn to see how the talion in the Torah initially functioned.

The Hebrew Bible's Context

W<small>E COULD</small> take literally the injunction "an eye for an eye," in the same way that we understand laws such as, "motorists who are caught speeding in school or construction zones face a fine of $250." However, biblical laws are distinguished from modern law codes in several ways.

First, the Torah is not a law code in the sense of a comprehensive set of laws intended for use by the court, and in a number of cases, such as the Decalogue, it is unclear how or by whom they were enforced. Second, it contains several collections of laws[25] that reflect different periods, authors, and audiences. Biblical scholars call the earliest collection, Exodus 20:22–23:33, the Covenant Collection (see Exod 24:7, "the book of the covenant"). It was compiled in Judah during the preexilic period and it was influenced by the eighteenth-century BCE Laws of Hammurabi, king of Babylon. Also during the preexilic period, the authors of the Deuteronomic Law Collection (Deut 12–26) modified and supplemented the Covenant Collection. The Torah's latest law collection is Leviticus 17–26, the Holiness Collection, so named after its injunction "You shall be holy, for I the L<small>ORD</small> your God am holy" (Lev 19:2). Although it has roots in the preexilic period and is related to the Priestly (P) source, its current form is postexilic. Other laws, such as the law of circumcision on the eighth day (Gen 17), are interspersed in the Torah's narratives.

Because the Torah contains these collections and other laws, it is best to speak of biblical laws rather than "the law." It is also helpful to see how they often either contradict each other or contain significant differences. For example, the Covenant Collection and the Deuteronomic Law Collection allow Israelites to be slaves, in normal circumstances, for up to six years (Exod 21:2–6; Deut 15:12–18), while Leviticus 25:39–40 legislates, "If any who are dependent on you become so impoverished that they sell themselves to you, you shall not make them serve as slaves. They shall remain with you as hired or bound laborers. They shall serve with you until the year of the jubilee" instead of at the beginning of the seventh year. Thus, Leviticus abolishes slavery; those who are impoverished have a higher status, like "hired or bound laborers." Deuteronomy 15:13–14 insists that the slave released at the seventh year must not be sent "out empty-handed," but instead the former master must "provide [him] liberally out of your flock, your threshing floor, and your wine press"—legislation lacking in the Covenant Collection.

Several laws are theoretical or ideal; they reflect societal aspirations rather than legal norms.[26] It is unlikely, for example, that Leviticus 25:8–12, which suggests that every fifty years "shall be a jubilee for you: you shall not sow, or reap the aftergrowth, or harvest the unpruned vines . . . you shall eat only what the field itself produces" (vv. 11–12), was ever followed, since that would have meant avoiding agricultural pursuits for two consecutive years—during the sabbatical year (once every seventh year) and the following jubilee year. Indeed, "there is no evidence at all that the jubilee was ever observed."[27] A comparable, earlier example of theoretical legislation is law 218 in the Laws of Hammurabi: "If a physician performs major surgery with a bronze lancet upon an *awīlu* [a free upper-class person] and thus causes the *awīlu*'s death, or opens an *awīlu*'s temple with a bronze lancet and thus blinds the *awīlu*'s eye, they shall cut off his hand."[28] This could not have been a real law—no one would opt to be a physician in such a society. There are, however, no clear criteria for distinguishing between real and ideal laws in the absence of more evidence.

With these considerations in mind, it is now possible to approach the "eye for an eye" formulation to see how it is more humane and sensible than its detractors realize. First, the comparison of the Torah's talion with antecedent texts reveals a change in the formulation. The same concern, albeit with variants, appears in the Laws of Hammurabi:[29]

§196 If an *awīlu* should blind the eye of another *awīlu*, they shall blind his eye.

§197 If he should break the bone of another *awīlu*, they shall break his bone.

§198 If he should blind the eye of a commoner or break the bone of a commoner, he shall weigh and deliver 60 shekels of silver.[30]

§199 If he should blind the eye of an *awīlu*'s slave or break the bone of an *awīlu*'s slave, he shall weigh and deliver one-half of his value (in silver).

§200 If an *awīlu* should knock out the tooth of another *awīlu* of his own rank, they shall knock out his tooth.

§201 If he should knock out the tooth of a commoner, he shall weigh and deliver 20 shekels of silver.[31]

These punishments discriminate among upper-class individuals, commoners, and slaves; commoners are compensated in silver while the talion applies to bodily harm from one *awīlu* to another. The Bible has no such gradations.[32] Equal treatment before the law is explicit in Deuteronomy 1:17: "You must not be partial in judging: hear out the small and the great alike." This abolition of social classes, this equal treatment of people from different classes, perhaps based in the biblical notion that all are created in God's image (so Gen 1),[33] is a parade example of how the Bible improves upon the legal system it inherited.

Second, the Torah's talion contrasts with Genesis 4:24, where the antediluvian figure Lamech insists, "If Cain is avenged sevenfold, / truly Lamech seventy-sevenfold." Therefore, the principle of "an eye for an eye and a tooth for a tooth" represents "a decisive effort to set limits on vengeance: only *one* eye for an eye, only *one* tooth for a tooth."[34]

We can see the idea of talion as a principle in that the listings of body parts are meant to be representative rather than comprehensive. The earliest talion list is Exodus 21:22–25:

> When people who are fighting injure a pregnant woman so that there is a miscarriage [better, "so that she gives birth prematurely"; literally, "so that her child goes out"[35]], and yet no further harm follows, the one responsible shall be fined what the woman's husband demands, paying as much as the judges determine. If any harm follows, then you shall give life for life, eye for eye, tooth for tooth, hand for hand, foot for foot, burn for burn, wound for wound, stripe for stripe.[36]

The same formula appears in Leviticus 24:17–20, where it is appended to the episode describing the stoning of a man for blasphemy: "Anyone who kills[37] a human being shall be put to death. (Anyone who kills an animal shall make restitution for it, life for life.)[38] Anyone who maims another shall suffer the same injury in return: fracture for fracture, eye for eye, tooth for tooth; the injury inflicted is the injury to be suffered." The final time it appears is in Deuteronomy 19:21, immediately following the laws of a false witness: "Show no pity: life for life, eye for eye, tooth for tooth, hand for hand, foot for foot." Exodus gives the longest version, beginning with "life" and then moving from eye to foot, and ending with three types of injury: burns, wounds, and stripes. Deuteronomy reproduces only the first part of Exodus's list, while Leviticus starts with a general "injury" and a short list of body parts: head, eyes, and teeth.

A careful reading of these texts suggests that the list, in various forms, circulated independently of the laws to which it is now attached.[39] They could be attached to other legislation concerning capital punishment, since the list begins, "life for life." It is clearly secondary to the case of the fetus: two fighting men cannot harm the eye—let alone the tooth—of a fetus.[40] Similarly, the law in Leviticus has nothing to do with the unit concerning blasphemy, punishable by death. Furthermore, the list disrupts the continuation of Leviticus 24:16: "One who blasphemes the name of the LORD shall be put to death; the whole congregation shall stone the blasphemer. Aliens as well as citizens, when they blaspheme the Name, shall be put to death." The Leviticus talion list is found in its current place because the list begins with the death penalty, the punishment meted out on the blasphemer.[41] In Deuteronomy's context of the lying witness, this law fits: the witness is punished with the penalty that the witness wanted to inflict on the accused.

Only once in the entire scriptures of Israel is something like the talion carried out. According to the book of Judges, the Israelites entering Canaan caught an enemy king named Adoni-bezek "and cut off his thumbs and big toes" (Judg 1:6). The following verse notes: "Adoni-bezek said, 'Seventy kings with their thumbs and big toes cut off used to pick up scraps under my table; as I have done, so God has paid me back.'" This text presents an exceptional case dealing with a foreign king.

Jewish scholars in particular have emphasized that the law of an eye for an eye was theoretical or ideal. For example, the British historian of ancient law Bernard Jackson suggests: "There was no *lex talionis*, but there was a *ius talionis*,"[42] with *lex* indicating the law as applied, and *ius* signaling a more abstract legal principle. The American scholar of biblical Priestly literature Jacob Milgrom concurs in claiming, "it is hard to believe that strict talion (except for murder) was ever anything but legal theory."[43] "An eye for an eye" thus can be seen to express an ideal—that poking out an eye *should* be punished by poking out an eye, indicating the severity of the offense and serving as a deterrent, at least on the philosophical level.

Other scholars have also argued that *lex talionis* was not meant to be taken literally. David Wright observes that Exodus 21:23 employs the verb *n-t-n*, "to give," to govern talionic punishments, and that elsewhere the Covenant Collection uses the verb for monetary compensation, as in 21:32: "If the ox gores a male or female slave, the owner shall pay [*n-t-n*] to the slaveowner thirty shekels of silver, and the ox shall be stoned."[44] However, although monetary compensation is a possible meaning of *n-t-n*, the Torah typically uses a different expression for "to make restitution for," *sh-l-m . . . tachat*, as in Leviticus 24:18: "Anyone who kills an animal shall make restitution for it, life for life."

It remains possible that gouging out eyes and other forms of talion were meant literally,[45] despite lack of evidence of its being carried out and lack of clarity concerning who would enforce it. Although the principle appears three times in the Torah, we are unsure whether it was ever implemented by a court, taken literally by any of its readers, served as a theoretical or ideal law, or was interpreted in practice as monetary compensation.

THE STRUGGLE BETWEEN
JUSTICE AND MERCY

W E DO NOT know whether *lex talionis* was ever a reality in ancient Israel, but we have ample evidence of postbiblical Jewish interpreters increasingly denying its practice from Hellenistic
times to the present.[46]

The earliest extant interpretation is Jubilees 4:31–32, which indirectly addresses the talion by describing Cain's punishment for killing his brother:

> His house fell on him, and he died inside it and was killed by the stones
> of it; for with a stone he had killed Abel, and by a just retribution he
> was killed by a stone himself. There is a rule about this on the heavenly
> tablets, With the instrument with which one kills another man, with
> the same instrument shall he be killed: if he has done a particular injury
> to another man, the same injury shall be done to him.

This text, however, does not bear on how any court would implement "an eye for an eye." Further, the punishment is exacted by God,
not a human judge.

The Septuagint and Targum Onkelos, the most literal translation,
do not clarify whether the talion is literal or monetary, while Pseudo-
Jonathan and Neofiti, as they often do, expand upon the text, making

it clear that the compensation is monetary.[47] Josephus, writing with an eye to gentile readers, suggests that the physical talion is carried out only if the victim is unwilling to accept monetary compensation: "He that maims anyone, let him undergo the like himself, and be deprived of the same member of which he has deprived the other, unless he that is maimed will accept money instead of it; for the law makes the sufferer the judge of the value of what he has suffered, and permits him to estimate it, unless he will be more severe" (*Antiquities* 4.280).

Philo starts by affirming the talion: "Our law, being the interpreter and teacher of equality, commands that offenders should undergo a punishment similar to the offence which they have committed" whether the injury is to people or property (*Special Laws* 3.182). He then nuances the point by considering extenuating circumstances: whether the victim was a family member or a stranger, a ruler or a citizen, the timing of the offense, and so on. The Torah suggests no such qualifications.

Philo then turns to the particular circumstance of a master injuring a slave, as the Torah does immediately following the talion law (Exod 21:26–27). Whereas Philo promotes the talion in a case where a free man knocks out the eye or tooth of another free man, when a free man injures a slave, he advises that the slave be granted freedom, following Exodus. His rationale is both practical and moral. First, he reasons that should the master be "mutilated in retaliation," he would make the life of the slave unbearable; the slave would be "so oppressed that he will be ready to die" (*Special Laws* 3.195). Second, he finds justice in the manumission of the injured slave, since the master would not only be deprived of the value of his slave and his services but also be "compelled to do good to his enemy in the most important matters, whom very likely he wished to be able to ill-treat forever" (*Special Laws* 3.197). The point is not the same thing as Jesus's "love your enemies," but it does show the practical impact of such a command.

While some evidence may suggest that the Sadducees or a related group understood the law as reflecting bodily talion,[48] almost all rabbinic texts on the subject reflect the "rabbis' unease with talion."[49] The Mishnah (m. Bava Qamma 8:1) presumes that the talion is applied only in a monetary sense: "He who injures his fellow is liable to [compensate] him on five counts: (1) injury, (2) pain, (3) medical costs, (4) loss of income [literally "loss of time"], and (5) indignity."[50] The Mishnah continues by citing the custom of valuing a slave in defining how "injury" should be assessed monetarily: "For injury: How so? [If] one has blinded his eye, cut off his hand, broken his leg, they regard him as a slave up for sale in the market and make an estimate of how much he was worth beforehand [when whole], and how much he is now worth." The Babylonian Talmud (Bava Qamma 84a) does cite, in the name of the late first-century sage Rabbi Eliezer, that "an eye for an eye" "refers to an actual eye,"[51] but his is a minority opinion.

Later midrashim expand on this preference against physical violence by formulating different textual proofs.[52] For example, the Babylonian Talmud (Bava Qamma 83b–84a) opens with the question of whether "an eye for an eye" refers to bodily harm or financial restitution. To answer this question, the sages concoct test cases:

There may be a case where there was a blind person and he blinded another, or there was one with a severed limb and he severed the limb of another, or there was a lame person and he caused another to be lame. In this case, how can I fulfill "an eye for an eye" literally, when he is already lacking the limb that must be injured? If one will suggest that in that case, a monetary penalty will be imposed, that can be refuted: But the Torah stated: "You shall have one manner of law" (Leviticus 24:22), which teaches that the law shall be equal for all of you.[53]

They cannot have one *lex talionis* for a sighted man and another for a blind man. Therefore, the sages reason, the reciprocal punishment must be not bodily harm but financial restitution. On the practical level, financial restitution will help the victim far more than bodily mutilation of the aggressor.

The rabbinic understanding of all talion references in terms of monetary compensation is enshrined in Rashi's gloss to Exodus 21:24: "If one blinded the eye of his fellow-man he has to pay him the value of his eye, i.e., he pays him how much his value would be diminished if he were to be sold as a slave in the market. In the same way all other cases are to be dealt with, but it does not mean the actual cutting off of the offender's limb—just as our Rabbis have explained (Bava Qamma 84a)."

Karaites, Jews who did not accept rabbinic interpretation, were divided on whether these laws refer to monetary compensation or not. Therefore, they developed four different options: talion, monetary compensation, determination of punishment depending on whether the injury was intentional, and leaving the decision of punishment, talion or monetary, to the court.[54]

A small number of medieval scholars recognized that the simple meaning of the text refers to talion. In *The Guide of the Perplexed*, Maimonides observes: "'As he who has deprived someone of a member, shall be deprived of a similar member: As he hath maimed a man, so shall it be rendered unto him' [Lev 24:20]. You should not engage in cogitation concerning the fact that in such a case we punish by imposing a fine. For at present my purpose is to give reason for the [biblical] texts and not for the pronouncements of the legal science" (3.41).[55] Maimonides recognizes that the plain sense of the verse is talion, but he insists, like the other medieval Jewish scholars, that the compensation be monetary.

It is difficult to know whether the medieval Jewish understanding that these verses refer to monetary compensation stems from the rabbinic sources, is based in a polemic against the Karaite interpretation,[56] is a response to anti-Jewish understandings of these verses among some Christians, or is a combination of these factors.

Evaluating talion is not a simple exercise. In fact, the question, "What is more fair: monetary compensation or physical compensation?" is difficult to answer. Monetary compensation favors the rich, who can pay more easily, while physical talion would act to discourage even the very wealthy from harming others.[57] Even were the Torah to favor physical talion, we cannot so easily determine whether such a view is fundamentally unjust.

Beyond these musings, it is crucial to remember that postbiblical Jewish law may never have implemented talion. Christian culture often presumes that it did, and still does. When Jesus advises "turn the other cheek," many readers still conclude that he is rejecting current practice. As literary critic Adam Kirsch summarizes, "To Christianity, 'an eye for an eye' represented everything that was wrong with Judaism, as a religion of law rather than love."[58] And as Kirsch goes on to note, this view receives support from Shakespeare's *The Merchant of Venice*, where the Jew Shylock seeks his "pound of flesh" from the titular merchant, Antonio. It is not uncommon in Christian contexts to hear that by speaking of turning the other cheek rather than promoting physical injury, Jesus's teaching is shocking in its repudiation of the Torah.[59]

Jesus's remarks are not formulated as antitheses, and he does not reject the scriptures of Israel in favor of a new law. He has not come to abolish the Torah, as he himself states according to Matthew's Gospel. Jesus is no more rejecting the Torah than are the rabbis, who insist that "an eye for an eye" is a legal principal, not a juridical mandate. In the case of "an eye for an eye," he changes the subject from bodily harm to humiliation. Therefore, we cannot determine how he would rule regarding actual injury. The irony is that, despite the fre-quent Christian claim that Jews take texts literally whereas Christians understand their spiritual value, here it is Christians who are reading the Torah literally and imposing that literal reading on Judaism.

We think it helpful to address how law—and especially the talion—should be understood today. A 2014 Gallup poll reported, "Ameri-cans who favor the death penalty most often cite 'an eye for an eye' as the reason they hold their position, with 35% mentioning it."[60] Coming in at distant seconds are "save taxpayers money" and "they deserve it." People who use the Bible to support capital punishment might take notice that in Jesus's citation of the talion law, he does not mention "a life for a life." Thus the claim that Jesus himself would approve of capital punishment receives minimal support—and only from what is not said.

The discussion of what to take literally and what to take as hyper-bole applies to the words of Jesus as well. Jesus speaks of nonretal-iation, and yet for many of his followers the expression "praise the Lord and pass the ammunition" still holds a sacred place. It is about such matters as refusing retaliation that Martin Luther King, Jr., cor-rectly stated concerning Jesus's teaching, "He wasn't playing."[61]

We agree. Justice without mercy, reflected in "an eye for an eye" taken literally, is intolerable. Yet mercy without justice—a perma-nent physical injury that receives no compensation at all, or receives unequal compensation based on the economic status of the perpe-trator—to us is equally intolerable. When we put Jesus into his Jew-ish tradition, we see that both concerns, justice and mercy, remain. Great care must be taken in using the Bible as a precedent for judicial issues—especially when the biblical materials are not as clear as we may think.

CHAPTER 7

"Drink My Blood": Sacrifice and Atonement

THE SACRIFICIAL LAMB

CRUCIFIXION kills by asphyxiation, exhaustion, organ failure, exposure, heart attack, or pulmonary embolism—but not, generally, by exsanguination. Yet the New Testament language on the death of Jesus flows with blood. It is, in fact, a blood-soaked text. Jesus gives his disciples a cup of wine and proclaims, "This is my blood of the covenant, which is poured out for many for the forgiveness of sins" (Matt 26:28; cf. Mark 14:24); repeating this Last Supper account, Luke changes the phrasing slightly: "And he did the same with the cup after supper, saying, 'This cup that is poured out for you is the new covenant in my blood'" (Luke 22:20). The Gospel of John makes the commandment to drink blood even more visceral:

> So Jesus said to them, "Very truly [Greek *amen amen*], I tell you, unless you eat the flesh of the Son of Man and drink his blood, you have no life in you. Those who eat my flesh and drink my blood have eternal life, and I will raise them up on the last day; for my flesh is true food and my blood is true drink. Those who eat my flesh and drink my blood abide in me, and I in them." (John 6:53–56)

In Acts 20:28, Paul advises, "Keep watch over yourselves and over all the flock, of which the Holy Spirit has made you overseers, to shepherd the church of God that he obtained with the blood of his own

Son," and in his own letters, he insists that Jesus is the one "whom God put forward as a sacrifice of atonement by his blood, effective through faith" (Rom 3:25). Indeed, he proclaims, "Much more surely then, now that we have been justified by his blood, will we be saved through him from the wrath of God" (Rom 5:9).

Paul also reminds the Corinthians: "The cup of blessing that we bless, is it not a sharing in the blood of Christ? The bread that we break, is it not a sharing in the body of Christ?"—for "in the same way he [Jesus] took the cup also, after supper, saying, 'This cup is the new covenant in my blood. Do this, as often as you drink it, in remembrance of me'" (1 Cor 10:16; 11:25).

The Epistle to the Ephesians, ascribed to Paul but likely written by one of his followers, makes the blood an agent of reconciliation between Jews and gentiles by telling its gentile audience, "But now in Christ Jesus you who once were far off have been brought near by the blood of Christ" (Eph 2:13). Its companion volume Colossians, also ascribed to Paul and with better claims for Pauline authorship, offers that through Jesus "God was pleased to reconcile to himself all things, whether on earth or in heaven, by making peace through the blood of his cross" (Col 1:20).

The Epistle to the Hebrews, as we have seen, insists that blood is required for sealing a covenant (Heb 9:18), that "without the shedding of blood there is no forgiveness of sins" (9:22), and that the only effective blood sacrifice is the one Jesus makes of himself. Jesus's blood, which with his flesh marks him as human (Heb 2:14), is of unique value, for "if the blood of goats and bulls, with the sprinkling of the ashes of a heifer, sanctifies those who have been defiled so that their flesh is purified, how much more will the blood of Christ, who through the eternal Spirit offered himself without blemish to God, purify our conscience from dead works to worship the living God!" (Heb 9:13–14). Evoking similar sacrificial language, the First Epistle of Peter speaks of "the precious blood of Christ, like that of a lamb without defect or blemish" (1 Pet 1:19). The First Epistle of John proclaims that Jesus's blood cleanses from all sin (1 John 1:7; cf. 5:6, 8), and Revelation, also stating "for you were slaughtered and by your blood you ransomed for God" (Rev 5:9; cf. 12:11), even speaks of the cleansing properties of the "blood of the Lamb" (7:14).

These texts do not explain how blood seals a covenant or atones for sin; they do not need to do so. The world of Jesus and his earliest followers was a world in which sacrifice was religious currency; everyone knew of it and everyone recognized its value. Sacrifice was normative not only for Jews but also for pagans, as we see in Paul's concern that followers be careful about eating meat sacrificed to idols (see 1 Cor 8), lest fellow believers think the diner is participating in idolatrous worship. It would have been very strange had Jesus's followers, in light of the cross, not developed the category of sacrifice. And it is entirely understandable that this development depended substantially on the scriptures of Israel.

The Gospels and Paul draw connections between the death of Jesus and one specific sacrifice, the Passover offering. For the Synoptic Gospels, Jesus's Last Supper is a Passover celebration, a meal that developed in postbiblical tradition into the *seder*, a Hebrew term meaning "order." Several elements of this choreographed meal were already in place while the Jerusalem Temple still stood, including eating certain foods, such as matzah (unleavened bread) and bitter herbs.

At the time of Jesus, the dinner also consisted of a lamb, sacrificed in the Temple on the Day of Preparation, with the holiday beginning that evening at sundown. The lamb is to remind the people of how the Israelites in Egypt sacrificed lambs and then painted the doorposts of their houses with the lambs' blood. God instructs, "The blood shall be a sign for you on the houses where you live: when I see the blood, I will pass over you, and no plague shall destroy you when I strike the land of Egypt" (Exod 12:13). The blood served an apotropaic function, that is, it protected the people. Exodus 12:27 describes this offering: "It is the passover [Hebrew *pesach*] sacrifice to the LORD, for he passed over [Hebrew *pasach*, better translated as "protected"] the houses of the Israelites in Egypt, when he struck down the Egyptians but spared our houses."[1] Lambs sacrificed in the Temple and then eaten by Jews in Jerusalem on the first night of Passover recalled the Israelites' freedom from slavery.

In John's Gospel, the Last Supper is not a Passover meal. Rather, Jesus dies the day before, when the priests slaughter the Passover lambs. John 19:14 describes: "Now it was the day of Preparation for the Passover ["the" Passover refers to the paschal offering, the lamb, and by extension to the dinner at which it is eaten]; and it was about noon. [Pilate] said to the Jews, 'Here is your King!'" In John's Gospel, Jesus thus becomes the new "Passover," whose blood will protect his followers from (eternal) death. John enhances this connection between Jesus and the Passover lamb by mentioning that the people standing near the cross as Jesus dies "put a sponge full of the wine on a branch of hyssop and held it to his mouth" (John 19:29). According to Exodus 12:22, the Israelites used hyssop branches to paint the blood on their doorposts.

Writing earlier than John's Gospel, Paul had already connected Jesus to the Passover rituals and the paschal offering: In 1 Corinthians 5:7, he exhorts the assembly, "Clean out the old yeast so that you may be a new batch, as you really are unleavened. For our paschal lamb, Christ, has been sacrificed." As Exodus 12 describes, because the Israelites, fleeing Egypt, did not have the time needed for the dough to rise, they ate unleavened bread. In Paul's day, and to the present day, Jews traditionally eat matzah for the seven- to eight-day Passover celebration.

Eventually, the understanding of Jesus as a sacrificial "lamb" became common vocabulary. In John 1:29 (cf. 1:36), John the Baptist proclaims, "Here is the Lamb of God who takes away the sin of the world!" The sacrificial imagery is implicit: the lamb becomes efficacious only in terms of removing sin when its blood is shed in sacrifice. Jesus becomes, as the Epistle to the Hebrews emphatically insists, the perfect sacrifice, whose blood creates a new covenant, saves from death, and washes away sin. First Peter 1:19 speaks of the "precious blood of Christ, like that of a lamb without defect or blemish," and the book of Revelation consistently refers to the Christ through the symbolism of a slain lamb. This entire program of Jesus as a paschal offering that removes sin is a specific understanding of the Passover offering not found outside of the followers of Jesus.

The Passover offering was not, as we will see, ever regarded by the Jewish community as a sin offering. Josephus reports:

> In the month of Xanthicus, which is by us called Nisan, and is the beginning of our year, on the fourteenth day of the lunar month, when the sun is in Aries for in this month it was that we were delivered from bondage under the Egyptians, and law ordained that we should every year slay that sacrifice which I before told you we slew when we came out of Egypt, and which was called the Passover; and so we do celebrate this Passover in companies, leaving nothing of what we sacrifice till the day following. (*Antiquities* 3.248)

He puts no stress on blood and makes no mention of sin. Philo finds an allegorical meaning rather than an atoning one in the festival celebrations: "The Passover is when the soul is anxious to unlearn its subjection to the irrational passions, and willingly submits itself to a reasonable mastery over them" (*Heir* 192).

In the New Testament, the ancient sacrifices all bleed into one: Jesus is the lamb of God, associated with the paschal offering, which becomes a sin offering. And once Jesus becomes the prime sacrifice, no other offerings were needed. His followers, especially after the destruction of the Temple, justified this rejection of other sacrifices by appealing to prophetic texts that emphasize repentance over sacrifice. For example, in Matthew 9:13 and again in 12:7, Jesus quotes Hosea 6:6a, "For I desire steadfast love [Hebrew *chesed*; Greek *eleos*, "mercy"] and not sacrifice"; the next line repeats the point in poetic parallelism: "the knowledge of God rather than burnt offerings." Isaiah 1:11 similarly asks:

> What to me is the multitude of your sacrifices?
>   says the LORD;
> I have had enough of burnt offerings of rams
>   and the fat of fed beasts;
> I do not delight in the blood of bulls,
>   or of lambs, or of goats.

Such texts, in their historical contexts, do not call for the abolition of sacrifice. This Hebrew poetry establishes not an elimination, but an emphasis, as we see also in 1 Samuel 15:22b, "Surely, to obey is better than sacrifice, / and to heed than the fat of rams." In the following chapter, Samuel invites David's father, Jesse, to a sacrifice. These texts, with their polemical bent, show how entrenched the idea of sacrifice was. The frequent modern depiction of "prophetic religion" as being in favor of ethics and absolutely against sacrifice is incorrect.[2] Ideally, personal ethics and liturgical and cultic activity should be mutually reinforcing. To see how this system works, we turn to the function of sacrifice according to the scriptures of Israel.

Sacrifices in Ancient Israel

S ACRIFICE, in its various forms, was fundamental to ancient Near Eastern life—sacrifices represented a return to God (or gods) of the gifts people thought God (or gods) had given them. Sacrifice also reflected the confidence that God/gods would reward the worshiper with additional animals or produce.

Ancient Israel's sacrificial system—its gifts to God—developed over time and involved offerings of both animals and agricultural products. The J author depicts Abel offering "the firstlings of his flock, their fat portions" (Gen 4:4), while his brother Cain "brought to the LORD an offering of the fruit of the ground" (4:3). The divine preference for Abel's sacrifice over that of his brother may suggest that this author placed greater value on animal sacrifice, although Genesis 4 never specifies the rationale for God's preference. Likely it reflects the greater cost of an animal sacrifice as well as an imagined divine preference for more "tasty" and good-smelling meat, rather than grain or vegetables. Noah builds an altar after the flood (Gen 8:20), and because of the "pleasing odor" of the offering, God promises never again to destroy every living creature by water (8:21).

Moving from the primeval history to the time of the patriarchs, Genesis recounts how Abraham, Isaac, and Jacob all built altars (Gen 12:7; 26:25; 33:20). This altar building shows the centrality of animal offerings: *mizbe'ach*, the Hebrew word for an altar, is derived from the root *z-b-ch*, "to slaughter," and thus means "a slaughter site."

According to Deuteronomy 12:6, later than the Yahwist (J) source, God commands the people of Israel to offer "your burnt offerings and your sacrifices, your tithes and your donations, your votive gifts, your freewill offerings, and the firstlings of your herds and flocks." Deuteronomy offers some details of how different animals should be sacrificed, but only the later initial chapters of Leviticus, from the Priestly (P) source, prescribe specific rituals concerning sacrifices.

The extensive Priestly sacrificial system, the background for New Testament texts that concern sacrifice, blood, and atonement, differentiates among types of sacrifice. The burnt offering (Hebrew *'olah*; Greek *holokautōma*, the origin of the term "holocaust") is fully consumed by God (Lev 1), and the well-being offering (*shelamim*, Lev 3)[3] is shared between the offerer and God, with God receiving the choice parts. This sharing indicates human-divine communion. In these offerings, blood plays no role, other than that the people do not consume it.

In contrast, rituals that involve the manipulation of blood play a central role in what the NRSV and most translations call a "sin offering," Hebrew *chata't*—the offering most relevant for understanding the role of the cross. The word *chata't* is used both for "sin," as in Genesis 4:7 where God tells Cain, "sin [*chata't*] is lurking at the door," and for the sacrifices that counter sins. This offering is not typified by the formula "a pleasing odor to the LORD"[4] because its blood, not its consumption on the altar, was central. For this offering, an animal is almost always used—for animals, not plants, have blood.[5]

Leviticus 4 outlines five different types of *chata't* offerings: ones brought by the high priest (vv. 3–12), by the entire community (vv. 13–21), by the ruler (vv. 22–26), by an individual who brings a female goat (vv. 27–31), and by an individual who brings a sheep (vv. 32–35).

The offerer eats no part of the sacrifice, although some of the meat is given to the priests (Lev 6:26, 29; 6:19, 22 Heb.). The chapter concludes with a note that clarifies the objective of these offerings (Lev 4:35): "Thus the priest shall make atonement [Hebrew *k-p-r*, as in Yom Kippur, the Day of Atonement] on your behalf for the sin that you have committed, and you shall be forgiven." As we shall see, it is specifically the blood that atones.

Each of the offerings in Leviticus 4 involves blood manipulation. For example, in the first offering, the text prescribes:

> The priest shall dip his finger in the blood and sprinkle some of
> the blood seven times before the LORD in front of the curtain of the
> sanctuary. The priest shall put some of the blood on the horns of
> the altar of fragrant incense that is in the tent of meeting before the
> LORD; and the rest of the blood of the bull he shall pour out at the
> base of the altar of burnt offering, which is at the entrance of the tent
> of meeting. (Lev 4:6–7)

Leviticus 4:17–18, 25, 30, and 34 also describe blood rituals. In the first two cases, which concern sins by the high priest or the entire community (vv. 3–21) and which therefore are especially grievous, the priest sprinkles the blood against the curtain that protected the holy of holies from view. Thus, the blood comes as close as possible to the ark and the divine presence imagined residing behind the curtain. In these as well as the other cases, the priest "put[s] [the blood] on the horns of the altar of burnt offering, and he shall pour out the rest of its blood at the base of the altar." These "horns" are quarter-round stone protuberances that have been found in several excavated altars in Israel—they were probably utilitarian, designed to keep the sacrifice on the flat altar. In sum, the *chata't* involved lots of blood.[6]

The Yom Kippur (Day of Atonement) ritual in Leviticus 16 offers the most detailed description of a *chata't*, with its subrituals. The complexity of such practices shows how central the idea of blood as the means of removing sin was to ancient Israel. Leviticus 16:14–20a, describing first the offering that the high priest sacrifices for himself and his family and then the offering for the nation, highlights the centrality of blood; in this long quotation, "blood" (Hebrew *dam*) appears repeatedly:

> He shall take some of the blood of the bull [his *chata't*], and sprinkle it with his finger on the front of the mercy seat [the ark cover; Hebrew *kapporet*; Greek *hilastērion*], and before the mercy seat he shall sprinkle the blood with his finger seven times. He shall slaughter the goat of the sin offering that is for the people and bring its blood inside the curtain, and do with its blood as he did with the blood of the bull, sprinkling it upon the mercy seat and before the mercy seat. . . . Then he shall go out to the altar that is before the LORD and make atonement on its behalf, and shall take some of the blood of the bull and of the blood of the goat, and put it on each of the horns of the altar. He shall sprinkle some of the blood on it with his finger seven times, and cleanse it and hallow it from the uncleannesses of the people of Israel. (Lev 16:14–15, 18–19)

At the beginning of this chapter, we cited Romans 3:25, where Paul speaks of the Christ as "put forward as a sacrifice of atonement by his blood, effective through faith." The Greek term the NRSV translates as "sacrifice of atonement" is *hilastērion*. Paul is referring to Leviticus 16:13–15.

Several subsequent verses in Leviticus clarify the atoning nature of the blood:

> Leviticus 16:30: "For on this day atonement shall be made for you, to cleanse you; from all your sins you shall be clean before the LORD."

Leviticus 16:33: "He shall make atonement for the sanctuary, and he
shall make atonement for the tent of meeting and for the altar, and
he shall make atonement for the priests and for all the people of the
assembly."

As these verses testify, atonement according to Leviticus is not accomplished through prayer, contrition, and fasting but through precisely following rituals of blood manipulation.

Unclear, however, is who (or what) is atoned for (*kiper*-ed)—
the people (v. 30) or various physical spaces, such as the sanctuary
(v. 33a). This crucial question of the object that receives atonement is
intrinsically related to the proper translation of *chata't*, and it therefore has implications for understanding how Jesus served as a *chata't*.

Until 1976, translators typically rendered *chata't* as "sin offering" (so in the NRSV and the original version of the NJPS) and understood the term as indicating a sacrifice for undoing sin and/or
removing the consequences of sin, that is, the punishment of the
sinner. In 1976, Jacob Milgrom published an article titled "Israel's
Sanctuary: The Priestly 'Picture of Dorian Gray.'"[7] In Oscar Wilde's
novel *The Picture of Dorian Gray*, Dorian Gray's portrait absorbs his
misdeeds and becomes hideous, while Dorian himself stays young
and healthy. Milgrom states, "On the analogy of Oscar Wilde's novel,
the priestly writers would claim: sin may not leave its mark on the
face of the sinner, but it is certain to mark the face of the sanctuary [with ritual impurity—NRSV's "uncleanness"], and unless it is
quickly expunged, God's presence will depart."[8] Milgrom observes
that particular sins create impurities that are attracted to particular
parts of the sanctuary; such attraction is due to the "Priestly notion
of impurity as a dynamic force, magnetic and malefic to the sphere
of the sacred, attacking it not just by direct contact but from a distance."[9] This thesis explains the beginning of Leviticus 16:33, cited

above: "He shall make atonement [Hebrew *kiper*] for the sanctuary, and he shall make atonement for the tent of meeting and for the altar"[10]—in other words, the *chata't* cleanses not the sinner but the impurities that various sins created, impurities that now reside at the sanctuary, the tent of meeting, and the altar.

Central to Milgrom's argument is his understanding of the root *k-p-r* as "purge," on the basis of the same root in Akkadian, which connotes "wipe off" or "cleanse."[11] Milgrom translates Leviticus 16:33 as "He shall purge [NRSV: "make atonement for"] the holiest part of the sanctuary, and he shall purge [NRSV: "make atonement for"] the Tent of Meeting and the altar." Such cleansing is needed because impurities may cause the divine presence, which likes to live in a low-sin environment, to flee the sanctuary. The initial chapters of Ezekiel display this concern (e.g., Ezek 3:12, "as the glory of the LORD rose from its place"). Milgrom translates "Yom Kippur," usually known as "the Day of Atonement," as "the Day of Purgation" and so keeps the focus on the blood rituals practiced while the sanctuary still stood.

Milgrom also coined a brilliant term, "ritual detergent," to explain the function of the sacrificial blood of the *chata't*.[12] Just as real detergent cleanses dirt from clothes, so blood—properly applied—cleanses (or purges) sin from the sanctuary. This cleaning can be done any time of the year, as noted in Leviticus 4, and Yom Kippur is a special annual cleansing in the early fall—comparable to weekly housecleaning and a giant, daylong spring cleaning. And this cleansing is effective without any personal repentance.

Some scholars have pushed back against Milgrom's understanding of the root *k-p-r* and the function of the *chata't*. Yitzhaq Feder, noting that "blood is used as a means of expiation, purification, and consecration" in Hittite rituals from the fourteenth to thirteenth centuries BCE (in what is now modern-day Turkey),[13] suggests that the *chata't* cleanses only the sinner, not the tabernacle. He cites Leviticus 16:30, which notes that Yom Kippur "cleanse[s] you; from all your sins you shall be clean before the LORD"; similarly, Leviticus 16:33 states that the high priest "shall make atonement for the priests and for all the people of the assembly." Blood did not serve this purpose in ancient Mesopotamia,[14] so verses concerning cleansing people from sin look all the more striking.

According to Feder, the blood purifies the sinners; conversely, Milgrom suggests that the blood purifies the temple/tabernacle areas that were made ritually impure through people's sins. Each position has some support in parts of Leviticus 16. They may both be right. And according to both interpretations, blood plays a crucial role in this *kiper*-ing, this atoning and/or purging.

Blood elsewhere in the Bible is similarly superpowerful.[15] Leviticus 17:11, forbidding Israelites from consuming any type of blood, explains: "For the life of the flesh is in the blood; and I have given it to you for making atonement [Hebrew *k-p-r*] for your lives on the altar; for, as life, it is the blood that makes atonement [*k-p-r*]." Most likely, this verse indicates that "animal blood is identified with animal life, and the application of animal life to the altar has a positive impact on the life of the offerer: the animal's life, in the animal's blood, functions as a ransom for the life of the offerer."[16] By killing the animal and completing certain blood rituals, sinners may live; their lives are ransomed. We have here the origins of quotations such as Revelation 5:9, "by your blood you ransomed for God." The idea of Jesus's death as a "ransom" appears as well in Matthew 20:28 (cf. Mark 10:45), where Jesus states that "the Son of Man came not to be served but to serve, and to give his life [as] a ransom for many" (see also 1 Tim 2:6; 1 Pet 1:18).[17]

However, the concept of an animal's life replacing a human life appears *only* in Leviticus 17:11,[18] and the precise meaning and translation of the verse are uncertain.[19] In addition, Leviticus 17 is from a later author (or source) than the *chata't* texts from Leviticus 4, 6, and 16, and it may not reflect those texts' notion of how blood works. The ransom thesis, that the animal's life is given so that the human may live, does not appear to hold for the numerous other descriptions of ancient Israelite sacrifice.

The discussion up to now relates to the original Israelite understanding of the *chata't* and its possible roles. The Septuagint translates *chata't* as *harmartia*, "sin," and its readers may well have understood the purgation to apply to people in addition to, if not rather than, the Temple. For Jews during the Hellenistic period and living far away from the Temple, there was greater concern for the person than for the building surfaces.

In some cases, the Septuagint's translation also influences Christian understandings of sacrifice. For example, the Epistle to the Hebrews uses the Greek of Psalm 40:6a (40:7a Heb.; 39:7 LXX) to support its claim of the Christ's superior sacrifice. The Hebrew reads, "Sacrifice [*zevach*] and offering [*minchah*] you do not desire, but you have given me an open ear [literally "ears you have hollowed out or bored" from the Hebrew verb *k-r-h*, "hollow out"]." Several early Septuagint manuscripts (e.g., Vaticanus, Alexandrinus, and Sinaiticus) translate, "Sacrifices and offerings you do not wish, but *a body* you have prepared [Hebrew *b-r-h*] for me." It is possible that the translators misread one letter in Hebrew, such that *barah* ("choose") became *karah* ("hollow out")—in Hebrew script, the letters "k" (כ) and "b" (ב) visually resemble each other. That would explain the distinction between "choose" or "prepare" and "hollow out." How certain Septuagint manuscripts came to read "body" (Greek *sōma*) for "ear" is less clear. It is possible that the scribes who prepared the Septuagint manuscripts read backward from Hebrews to the psalm; it is also possible that there were different versions of the Hebrew original. A third possibility is that the Greek transcribers took "ear" to stand, as a metonymy, for the entire body.[20]

In other cases, the Greek includes new rituals not mentioned in any extant Hebrew sources. Leviticus 24:7, which speaks of the showbread, or "bread of the Presence," reads, "You shall put pure frankincense with each row, to be a token offering for the bread, as an offering by fire to the LORD."[21] To this mixture, the Greek translators add "salt." As with many of the variants, the difference is literally a matter of taste.

PASSOVER

THE PASSION narrative, the story of Jesus's last days in Jerusalem, is deeply connected to Passover and the Passover sacrifice. The initial description of the Passover offering appears in Exodus 12:1–28, although how much of the ritual carried into the Second Temple period is, as with many things, debated. Even if the practices were not carried out as described, Exodus 12 remains the source to which early followers of Jesus turned in order to understand his death.

Exodus 12 describes blood rituals twice, in verses 13 and 22–23, each reflecting a separate source: verses 1–20 are from the Priestly (P) source and 21–27 are from the earlier Northern Israel Elohist (E) source. Verse 13 (P) states, "The blood shall be a sign for you on the houses where you live: when I see the blood, I will pass over you, and no plague shall destroy you when I strike the land of Egypt." Verses 21–23 (E) read:

> Then Moses called all the elders of Israel and said to them, "Go, select lambs for your families, and slaughter the passover lamb. Take a bunch of hyssop [like a paintbrush], dip it in the blood that is in the basin, and touch the lintel and the two doorposts with the blood in the basin. None of you shall go outside the door of your house until morning. For the LORD will pass through to strike down the Egyptians; when he sees

the blood on the lintel and on the two doorposts, the LORD will pass over that door and will not allow the destroyer to enter your houses to strike you down."

The use of the blood here differs significantly from the blood of the *chata't* because the paschal lamb is not a *chata't* offering. Unlike the *chata't*, this lamb is not primarily for God and the priests but is a family offering, eaten by the laity. In both sources, the sacrificial blood of the Passover lamb is "a sign" (so explicitly in Exod 12:13), a way of saying "Israelites inside," so that they are not killed. The blood is apotropaic—that is, it protects rather than atones. Furthermore, this blood ritual is a one-shot deal; blood does not play a significant role in subsequent Passover offerings because only in Egypt did the Israelites need protection from "the destroyer."

Another factor, however, may have connected blood to subsequent paschal lamb offerings. In general, P's "signs," such as the Sabbath and circumcision, are perpetual,[22] and the blood in Exodus 12:13 is also called a "sign." This may have caused some readers to see the blood of the paschal lamb in Egypt as having perpetual significance, even if the ritual was not perpetually practiced. What, however, it "signified," since the Israelites were not annually placing the blood on their lintels, cannot be determined.

For the followers of Jesus, this sign becomes the warding away of death. Jesus, sacrificed as the paschal lamb, protects his followers, through his blood, from eternal death, or damnation.

HUMAN SACRIFICE
IN THE HEBREW BIBLE

THE IDEA of human sacrifice as depicted in the scriptures of Israel also informs the passion narrative. Genesis 22 is called in Jewish tradition "the Akedah," the "binding" of Isaac. God commands Abraham to offer his son as a "burnt offering," and Abraham proceeds to take Isaac to Mount Moriah, tie him securely, and raise the knife; he stops only when "an angel of the LORD" calls to him. Abraham spots a ram caught by its horns in a nearby bush and offers the ram instead. Many readers view this chapter as a polemic against human sacrifice, and later it was taken to be so. Yet for Israel's scriptures, Genesis 22 is not a polemic against human sacrifice.[23] At the end of the chapter, the angel appears to Abraham and repeats the promise of progeny, land, and blessing (vv. 17–18). This angel does *not* say, "Because you have shown your willingness to sacrifice your son, I will now find human sacrifice abhorrent among your descendants (or all peoples)."

A number of texts may suggest that under certain circumstances human sacrifice is expected, and effective. Exodus 22:29–30 (22:28–29 Heb.), in the oldest legal collection in the Bible, contains the following legislation: "You shall not delay to make offerings from the fullness of your harvest and from the outflow of your presses. The firstborn of your sons you shall give to me. You shall do the same with your oxen and with your sheep: seven days it shall remain with its mother; on the eighth day you shall give it to me." The offering from the harvest and presses are given to God, and the oxen and sheep are given, presumably as sacrifices; the command "The first-born of your sons you shall give to me" may be read in the same way. The text may suggest the time when firstborn sons served in priestly capacities, since there is no indication that Exodus expected human sacrifice. Micah 6:7 similarly reads:

> Will the LORD be pleased with thousands of rams,
>> with ten thousands of rivers of oil?
> Shall I give my firstborn for my transgression,
>> the fruit of my body for the sin of my soul?

The quotation suggests that offering the "firstborn," "the fruit of my body," could sometimes happen. This was an offering of something of great value, like "thousands of rams" or "ten thousands of rivers of oil." Alternatively, such verses again may imply that the firstborn was donated to serve at a local temple, as illustrated by Hannah dedicating her son Samuel to the temple at Shiloh (1 Sam 1:24). Eventually these firstborn sons may have been replaced by the Levites.

The scriptures of Israel only rarely depict human sacrifice. According to Judges 11, Jephthah sacrificed his daughter in fulfilling a vow: were God to grant him military victory, he would offer the first to come out of his house (the oft-heard proposal that he was thinking of the family dog is unlikely, as well as itself abhorrent). Unambiguously indicating that human sacrifice both occurred and was seen as efficacious, 2 Kings 3:27 explains how the Moabite king "took his firstborn son who was to succeed him, and offered him as a burnt offering on the wall." The continuation of this verse, written by an Israelite author, is remarkable: "And great wrath came upon Israel, so they [the enemy force] withdrew from him and returned to their own land." In other words, from the author's perspective, the human sacrifice worked. Ezekiel 20:25–26 also refers to child sacrifice: "Moreover I gave them statutes that were not good and ordinances by which they could not live. I defiled them through their very gifts, in their offering up all their firstborn, in order that I might horrify them, so that they might know that I am the LORD."[24]

We are not saying that human sacrifice was widely or even typically practiced in ancient Israel. But the textual evidence suggests that some believed it to be effective either in atoning for sins (Mic 6:7) or in diverting a great disaster (2 Kgs 3:27). None of the Hebrew Bible texts that depict human sacrifice, however, suggests that the blood in particular of the human sacrificial victim has any special role in atoning. In the Hebrew Bible, only the blood of the animal *chata't* offering, not human blood, atones.

Nonsacrificial Atonement

Blood is not the only way ancient Israel effected atonement. The *chata't* texts, emphasizing the tabernacle and so the Temple, all come from the Priestly (P) source. Deuteronomy and related works, emphasizing not sacrifice but "repentance," use the Hebrew root *sh-u-v*, "to turn, return" (in this case, to God).

The first usage of *sh-u-v* in reference to (re)turning to God is Deuteronomy 4:29–30, which addresses Israel in exile. The setting is key, since it presumes that Israel had no access to Jerusalem and so to the Temple: "From there you will seek the LORD your God, and you will find him if you search after him with all your heart and soul. In your distress, when all these things have happened to you in time to come, you will return [Hebrew *sh-u-v*] to the LORD your God and heed him." That root reappears several times to frame Deuteronomy 30:1–10, which speaks about the results of turning away from sin and toward standing in a right relationship with God:

> When all these things have happened to you, the blessings and the curses that I have set before you [as described in Deut 28], if you call them to mind among all the nations where the LORD your God has driven you, and return [*sh-u-v*] to the LORD your God, and you and your children obey him with all your heart and with all your soul, just as I am commanding you today, then the LORD your God will

restore [sh-u-v] your fortunes and have compassion on you, gathering you again from all the peoples among whom the LORD your God has scattered you. . . . For the LORD will again [sh-u-v] take delight in prospering you, just as he delighted in prospering your ancestors, when you obey the LORD your God by observing his commandments and decrees that are written in this book of the law, because you turn [sh-u-v] to the LORD your God with all your heart and with all your soul. (Deut 30:1–3, 9–10)

Sh-u-v, used of both God and Israel in this passage, makes a simple point: if you return (sh-u-v) to God, God will return (sh-u-v) to you. This emphasis on turning is different from the language of forgiveness (Hebrew s-l-ch) effected by sacrifices, which typifies the Priestly source. This returning has nothing to do with animals or blood.

Even in places where we might expect an emphasis on sacrifice, we find the promotion of a change in action. The exilic text 1 Kings 8, affiliated with Deuteronomy, ascribes to Solomon a prayer at the completion of his Temple.[25] The text briefly mentions a huge offering (1 Kgs 8:63), but the chapter focuses instead on the efficacy of prayer in various situations:

If they [the Israelites] sin against you—for there is no one who does not sin—and you are angry with them and give them to an enemy, so that they are carried away captive to the land of the enemy, far off or near; yet if they come to their senses [literally "return," sh-u-v] in the land to which they have been taken captive, and repent [sh-u-v], and plead with you in the land of their captors, saying, "We have sinned, and have done wrong; we have acted wickedly"; if they repent [sh-u-v] with all their heart and soul in the land of their enemies, who took them captive, and pray to you toward their land, which you gave to their ancestors, the city that you have chosen, and the house that I have built for your name; then hear in heaven your dwelling place their prayer and their plea, maintain their cause and forgive your people who have sinned against you, and all their transgressions that they have committed against you; and grant them compassion in the sight of their captors, so that they may have compassion on them. (1 Kgs 8:46–50)

Shuv-ing, not sacrifices or blood, brings about reconciliation. This prayer not only repeats the root but also offers similar sounding roots such as *veshavum shovehem* (from the root *sh-v-h*), "that they are carried away captive" in verse 46, or *nishbu . . . shovehem*, "have been taken captive . . . captors" in the following verse. These word-plays are difficult to reproduce in English.

Shuv-ing, apart from sacrifice, is a core idea of prophetic texts. Jeremiah 4:1 quotes God as saying,

If you return [*sh-u-v*], O Israel,
     says the LORD,
          if you return [*sh-u-v*] to me,
     if you remove your abominations from my presence,
          and do not waver.

Hosea 14:1–2 (14:2–3 Heb.), a passage read on the Sabbath before Yom Kippur, explicitly demands *shuv*-ing with words (namely, prayer) rather than sacrifices:

Return [*sh-u-v*], O Israel, to the LORD your God,
     for you have stumbled because of your iniquity.
Take words with you
     and return [*sh-u-v*] to the LORD;
say to him,

"Forgive all guilt
　　And accept what is good;
　　Instead of bulls we will pay
　　[the offering of] our lips."[26]

Again, no animals, blood, or *chata't* offering is required.

SACRIFICE IN POSTBIBLICAL JUDAISM

THE INSISTENCE that repairing a relationship with God is possible without sacrifice continues after the Temple's destruction in 70 CE. Indeed, *not a single text* in the huge corpus of rabbinic Judaism suggests that after the Temple had been destroyed, atonement is impossible or that blood is essential for atonement. When rabbinic texts speak about the power of blood to effect atonement, they refer to past Temple ritual, not the postdestruction reality.

Several rabbinic texts, imagining that sacrifices were carried out, cite Leviticus 17:11, "For the life of the flesh is in the blood; and I have given it to you for making atonement for your lives on the altar; for, as life, it is the blood that makes atonement," to make the point that sacrificial blood atones. From the Babylonian Talmud, Zevahim 6a begins with Leviticus 1:4, "And he shall place his hand on the head of the burnt offering, and it shall be accepted for him to atone for him," which might suggest that the laying of hands on the sacrificial animal atones for the person offering the sacrifice. The talmudic passage then suggests that only the blood atones: "And does placing hands atone for one's sins? But isn't atonement achieved only by the sprinkling of blood, as it is stated, 'For it is the blood that makes atonement by reason of the life (Leviticus 17:11)'?"[27] Rabbinic authors recognized that, while the Temple stood, blood is the typical ritual detergent, but even there it is not always necessary.[28] And after the Temple was destroyed, alternatives to blood atonement would continue to develop.

In determining that blood sacrifice is not necessary, some rabbinic texts follow a precedent in Priestly literature, which in a single case allows for a flour offering to atone. Leviticus 5:11–13 reads:

> But if you cannot afford two turtledoves or two pigeons, you shall bring as your offering for the sin that you have committed one-tenth of an ephah of choice flour for a sin offering; you shall not put oil on it or lay frankincense on it, for it is a sin offering. You shall bring it to the priest, and the priest shall scoop up a handful of it as its memorial portion, and turn this into smoke on the altar, with the offerings by fire to the LORD; it is a sin offering. Thus the priest shall make atonement on your behalf for whichever of these sins you have committed, and you shall be forgiven.

From a biblical perspective, too much should not be made of this single exception.

The rabbinic tradition regards repentance, apart from blood sacrifice, as fully effective. While the scriptures of Israel speak of *shuv*, turning, in the sense of an action, rabbinic material stresses the efficacy of *teshuvah* in the sense of internal contrition[29] and repentance. As the great scholar of rabbinics Ephraim Urbach summarizes concerning the idea of repentance in the Yerushalmi (the Jerusalem Talmud): "'The Holy One, blessed be He, was asked: "What is the sinner's punishment?" He answered them: "Let him repent and I shall accept him," for it is written "Good and upright is the Lord"' [Ps 25:8]. Obviously, the homilist intended to ascribe to God that the power of repentance was absolute, transcending that of atonement through sacrifices."[30] Some early rabbis claim that the daily prayers along with repentance and charity replace the morning and afternoon Temple offering.[31] The point continues in Jewish liturgy, for example, in the congregational response to the medieval *Unetaneh Tokef* prayer, one of the central prayers recited on Rosh Hashanah and Yom Kippur: "But repentance [Hebrew *teshuvah*], prayer [*tefillah*] and charity (or: "good deeds") [*tzedakah*] cancel the harsh decree."[32] In other classical rabbinic texts, fasting or the study of the Torah makes atonement.[33] And in still other texts, "The death of the righteous atones for sin."[34] In Leviticus Rabbah 20:12, the rabbis backdate this idea to ancient Israel: "Just as the Day of Atonement atones, so does the death of the righteous atone. And where is it shown that . . . the death of the righteous atones? Where it is stated, 'And they buried the bones of Saul.' . . . And God responded to the plea of the land thereafter" (the citation is to 2 Sam 21:14). Here we may see a response to Christian proclamation.

The Blood of Circumcision

ALTHOUGH circumcision is mentioned already in Genesis, its significance develops over time. Among its many interpretations is the postbiblical association of the blood of circumcision with atonement. Though sacrificial blood loses its role in Judaism, blood remains closely aligned with atonement in the *brit* or *bris* (Eastern European pronunciation) *milah,* the circumcision ceremony performed upon eight-day-old Jewish males. Immediately following the physical act of circumcising, as part of the boy's naming ceremony, the person performing the circumcision (the child's father, or more typically the professional circumciser [Hebrew *mohel*]) says:

> Our God and God of our fathers preserved this child to his father and mother, and let his name be called in Israel (*baby's name* son of *father's name*). May the father rejoice in the issue of his body, and the mother be glad with the fruit of her womb, as is written, "May your father and mother rejoice, and she who bore you be glad." [Prov 23:25] And it is said, "Then I passed by you and saw you downtrodden in your blood, and I said to you: Because of your blood live; and I said to you: Because of your blood live."[35]

This last verse is from Ezekiel 16, one of scripture's most problematic, even pornographic, chapters. It describes God's adoption of

248

abandoned (female) Israel, whom he eventually marries and then punishes in lurid terms when she strays. Ezekiel 16:6 describes the newborn baby "befouled and uncared for"[36]—not even cleaned of the blood from birth. Ezekiel's phrase *bedamayich chayi* means "in your blood(y state), live!"—words of encouragement to the abandoned child. But the circumcision prayer understands the preposition *be-* as "because of" (instead of "in," its more typical meaning), another meaning it has in Biblical Hebrew. And thus the prayer states that the blood of circumcision is life-giving.

The idea that the blood of circumcision is life-giving is found only in the rabbinic interpretation of Ezekiel 16, not in Ezekiel itself. However, according to Exodus 4:24–26, set when Moses is returning from Midian to Egypt, the blood of circumcision does preserve life: "On the way, at a place where they spent the night, the LORD met him and tried to kill him. But Zipporah took a flint and cut off her son's foreskin, and touched Moses's feet with it, and said, 'Truly you are a bridegroom of blood to me!' So he let him alone. It was then she said, 'A bridegroom of blood by circumcision.'" The laconic text is "terribly mysterious";[37] it is not even clear from the Hebrew whom God seeks to kill: Moses or the child. The account fits folktale patterns of attacking demons and using blood to ward off evil (apotropaic magic), as we saw also with the blood of the Passover lamb put on the doorposts of the Israelite houses. While the story may have something to do with an early concern that Moses, raised in an Egyptian household, was not circumcised, it has nothing to do with sin and repentance.[38]

Postbiblical Jewish authors likely knew that gentile Christians did not circumcise their sons. In fact, Paul so strongly argues against such a practice in his Epistle to the Galatians that he says of those who preach circumcision to the gentiles, "I wish those who unsettle you would castrate themselves!" (Gal 5:12). For Paul, gentiles should remain gentiles, but they should give up their pagan religious practices, such as sacrificing to the state gods. Jews remain Jews, but they are to welcome gentile Christ-followers as equal members of their messianic community. Thus, for Paul and even more so for Jews who did not follow Jesus, circumcision functioned as an important boundary marker. The act of circumcision came to represent the broader set of Torah laws and rituals; it could thus exemplify, from a Jewish perspective, being put in a right relationship with God through deeds rather than faith.[39]

Pirkei de-Rabbi Eliezer 29, a chapter devoted to circumcision, notes: "Know then that on the Day of Atonement Abraham our father was circumcised. Every year the Holy One, blessed be He, sees the blood of our father Abraham's circumcision, and He forgives all the sins of Israel, as it is said, 'For on this day shall atonement be made for you, to cleanse you' (Lev 16:30)." Not only is atonement, the theme of Yom Kippur, accomplished through the blood of circumcision, the same chapter notes, "everyone who brings his son for circumcision is as though (he were) a high priest bringing his meal offering and his drink offering upon the top of the altar." The verse is a possible polemic against claims that Jesus, in the line of Melchizedek (see Chapter 5), is the only effective high priest. The anti-Christian implication is secured by the next line: "Rabbi [Judah the Prince] said: Isaac circumcised Jacob, and Esau; and Esau despised the covenant of circumcision just as he despised the birthright." This is likely one of many cases in rabbinic literature where "Esau" is code for "Christianity"; Christianity's abandonment of this ritual is projected here, critically, into hoary antiquity.

Pirkei de-Rabbi Eliezer 29 also connects the blood of circumcision to the blood used in the Passover ritual.

The Israelites took the blood of the covenant of circumcision, and they put (it) upon the lintel of their houses, and when the Holy One, blessed be He, passed over to plague the Egyptians, He saw the blood of the covenant of circumcision upon the lintel of their houses and the blood of the Paschal lamb, He was filled with compassion on Israel, as it is said, "And when I passed by thee, and saw thee weltering [lying in blood] in thy (twofold) blood, I said unto thee, In thy (twofold) blood, live; yea, I said unto thee, In thy (twofold) blood, live" (Ezek 16:6).

Here may be a polemic against seeing Jesus as a paschal offering. The basis of its exposition is Ezekiel 16:6, "in your blood(y state), live!"—or "in/because of your blood live."

After clarifying that the double mention of blood refers to the blood of circumcision and the blood of the paschal lamb, the midrash continues:

Rabbi Eliezer said: Why did the text say twice, "I said unto thee, In thy blood, live; yea, I said unto thee, In thy blood, live"? But the Holy One, blessed be He, said: By the merit of the blood of the covenant of circumcision and the blood of the Paschal lamb ye shall be redeemed from Egypt, and by the merit of the covenant of circumcision and by the merit of the covenant of the Passover in the future ye shall be redeemed at the end of the fourth kingdom; therefore it is said, "I said unto thee, In thy blood, live; yea, I said unto thee, In thy blood, live."

This rabbinic connection among circumcision, blood, and Passover again looks like an anti-Christian polemic: it is the blood of Passover and circumcision, not of the Christ, that atones.

THE BLOOD OF THE COVENANT

THE NEW TESTAMENT connects blood, atonement, and covenant. The scriptures of Israel connect blood and covenant explicitly only in two texts.

Exodus 24, a composite chapter put together from several sources, describes the events that occurred after the revelation at Mount Sinai/Horeb. It begins with the Elohist (E) source's description of an unusual ritual that may have some basis in Northern Israelite religion. Speaking of Moses, verses 4b–8 read:

> He rose early in the morning, and built an altar at the foot of the mountain, and set up twelve pillars, corresponding to the twelve tribes of Israel. He sent young men of the people of Israel, who offered burnt offerings and sacrificed oxen as offerings of well-being to the LORD. Moses took half of the blood and put it in basins, and half of the blood he dashed against the altar. Then he took the book of the covenant, and read it in the hearing of the people; and they said, "All that the LORD has spoken we will do, and we will be obedient." Moses took the blood and dashed it on the people, and said, "See the blood of the covenant that the LORD has made with you in accordance with all these words."

Most likely the shared blood "establishes a bond between the two parties"[40] of God and Israel. Alternatively, or in addition, the animal's blood may reflect the "mutilation that will befall whichever party proves faithless."[41]

The only other Hebrew Bible text to associate blood and covenant is the postexilic Zechariah 9:11, which likely refers back to Exodus 24.[42] Thus, blood and covenant are not strongly connected in Israel's scriptures; that connection develops only in postbiblical Jewish thinking concerning the *brit milah*, the covenant of circumcision. This is another case where something peripheral in the ancient texts becomes central in the New Testament and then reappears in Jewish thinking.

Blood remains a powerful image in both biblical testaments. In Christian thought, the Christ's blood atones for sin, and the wine of the Eucharist is, whether literally or metaphorically, his blood. For Jews, male circumcision—and the blood of circumcision—remains a ritual central to Jewish identity.

It is not unusual for Jews to be told by some Christians that they are damned to hell because they do not accept the atoning blood of Jesus to save them from their sins or ransom them from hell. Such comments reflect a lack of knowledge of Jewish views of atonement, including the rabbinic emphasis of repenting and turning (*shuv*-ing) from sin and toward God. At the same time, Jews would do well to understand the *Jewish* background of Christian claims regarding the blood of Jesus. The development of Jewish and Christian rituals, especially absent the animal sacrifice conducted in the Temple, shows how deeply interwoven the two traditions are.

CHAPTER 8

"A Virgin Will Conceive
and Bear a Child"

TO FULFILL WHAT HAD BEEN SPOKEN

Following a genealogy beginning with Abraham and working its way down to "Jacob the father of Joseph" (Matt 1:16), the Gospel of Matthew records that Joseph had discovered his betrothed, Mary, to be pregnant. He knows the child is not his, since he and Mary had not consummated their relationship. Rather than create a scandal, Joseph, whom Matthew calls a "righteous man," resolves to divorce Mary quietly. There is no mention of, or need for, public trial, let alone stoning.

Readers familiar with Israel's scriptures might well anticipate what happens next. The reference to a Joseph, the son of Jacob, would have reminded them of Joseph, son of Jacob, from the book of Genesis. This earlier Joseph, best known today for having an "amazing Technicolor dreamcoat," both dreamed prescient dreams and saved his family from famine by arranging for food to be stored in Egypt (see Gen 37, 39–49).

Matthew's Joseph dreams, and in his dream, an angel tells him:

"Joseph, son of David, do not be afraid to take Mary as your wife, for the child conceived in her is from the Holy Spirit. She will bear a son, and you are to name him Jesus, for he will save his people from their sins." All this took place to fulfill what had been spoken by the Lord through the prophet:

> "Look, the virgin shall conceive and bear a son,
>   and they shall name him Emmanuel,"
> which means, "God is with us." (Matt 1:20–23)[1]

"What had been spoken by the Lord through the prophet" refers to Isaiah 7:14. This is the first of Matthew's numerous "fulfillment citations" (2:15, 17, 23; 4:14; 8:17; 12:17; 13:35; 21:4; 26:56; 27:9; without the "to fulfill" formula: 2:5; 3:3; 13:14).[2] By marking events and sayings with reference to sacred texts, Matthew reinforces Jesus's connection to Abraham and David, Moses and Israel. The first fulfillment citation also provides part of the frame of the Gospel: Matthew's first chapter contains the promise, "they shall name him Emmanuel, which means 'God is *with us*,'" and the Gospel ends with Jesus's promise to his disciples, and so to Matthew's readers, "And remember, I am *with you* always, to the end of the age" (Matt 28:20; emphasis added).

The angel next informs Joseph that Mary "will bear a son, and you are to name him Jesus, for he will save his people from their sins" (Matt 1:21). The connection between the name and the vocation is evident in Hebrew, but not in English or Greek. The name Jesus, from the Hebrew *yeshua'*, comes from the root *y-sh-'*, which means "deliverance" or "salvation" and evokes God's saving powers. "Jesus" is a shortened form of the name Joshua (Hebrew *yehoshua'*) and is related to Hosea (Hebrew *hoshea'*), Isaiah (Hebrew *yesha'ayah[u]*), and the term *hosanna* (Hebrew *hoshi'ah na'*), which means "save!" "Salvation" in Israel's scriptures typically means being saved by God from oppression, war, or enemies. Matthew changes the focus to speak of salvation from sin.

Matthew's Gospel is the only New Testament text to cite Isaiah 7:14 in relation to Jesus or to state explicitly that Mary was a virgin at the time Jesus was conceived. Luke may hint at these concerns when the angel Gabriel tells Mary:

"And now, you will conceive in your womb and bear a son, and you will name him Jesus. He will be great, and will be called the Son of the Most High, and the Lord God will give to him the throne of his ancestor David. He will reign over the house of Jacob forever, and of his kingdom there will be no end." Mary said to the angel, "How can this be, since I am a virgin?" The angel said to her, "The Holy Spirit will come upon you, and the power of the Most High will overshadow you; therefore the child to be born will be holy; he will be called Son of God." (Luke 1:31–35)

While Luke agrees with Matthew that Mary's pregnancy is from the Holy Spirit's activity, it is not clear here that Luke regards Mary as having conceived virginally. She is a virgin at the time of Gabriel's annunciation, but the angel does not tell her that she will be so at the time of Jesus's conception.

Matthew 1:25 states that Joseph "had no marital relations with her [Mary] until she had borne a son; and he named him Jesus," and this verse can suggest that Mary's virginity ended after Jesus was born. The four Gospels and Paul's letters mention that Jesus had siblings (e.g., Matt 12:46; Mark 6:3; Luke 8:19–20; John 2:12; 1 Cor 9:5; Gal 1:19).

Later apocryphal texts extended the citation of Isaiah 7:14 to find notice of Mary's perpetual virginity. According to the early second-century Protevangelium (i.e., "pregospel") of James, ascribed to Jesus's "brother" James (here understood to be Joseph's son from a previous marriage), Mary remains a virgin not only prepartum but also in partu and postpartum. The Protevangelium describes how Salome (a common name for first-century Jewish women) refused to believe that Mary, who had just given birth, could remain a virgin:

And Salome said, "As the Lord my God lives, unless I insert my finger and investigate her, I will not believe that a virgin has given birth." And the midwife went in and said, "Mary, position yourself, for not a small test concerning you is about to take place." When Mary heard these things, she positioned herself. And Salome inserted her finger into her body. And Salome cried out and said, "Woe for my lawlessness and the unbelief that made me test the living God. Look, my hand is falling away from me and being consumed in fire."

An angel then advises Salome to touch the child, and her hand is healed.

For some readers, Matthew records both a fulfillment of prophecy and a miraculous conception. Others, less likely to accept claims of divine activity, suggest that Mary was raped or involved with someone other than Joseph[3] and that Matthew sought to explain Jesus's conception out of wedlock. Still others suggest that Joseph was the father, and the account of a virginal conception developed in competition with stories of Greek and Roman gods fathering children or in concert with other Jewish tales of miraculous conceptions. Jesus's siblings have been variously understood to be Jesus's younger brothers and sisters, the children of Joseph's earlier marriage, or even first cousins, with Joseph himself being a virgin.

Historians cannot determine all the details of Jesus's conception and birth. What we can do is explain how Matthew comes to proclaim a miraculous conception when the scriptures of Israel make no mention of it. Isaiah speaks not about a virgin but about a pregnant young woman.

ISAIAH IN HIS CONTEXT

L IKE MOST prophetic books, Isaiah has a long and complicated history, and none of these books represents an autograph of a prophet's original words. All have gone through some process of editing. Most scholars attribute much, but not all, of Isaiah 1–39 to the prophet mentioned in the superscription, "Isaiah son of Amoz, who prophesied concerning Judah and Jerusalem in the reigns of Uzziah, Jotham, Ahaz, and Hezekiah, kings of Judah." This "First Isaiah" flourished in the second half of the eighth and very early seventh centuries BCE. Isaiah also appears in 2 Kings 19:2–20:19, and a bulla (clay seal impression) that may partially preserve the inscription "Isaiah the prophet" recently was unearthed in Jerusalem.[4]

Isaiah 40–55 (including the references to the famous "suffering servant" we discuss in the next chapter) and 56–66 have different authors and settings. Isaiah 40–55, which scholars call "Second Isaiah," was composed during the Babylonian exile and the early years of the community's restoration to the land of Israel. "Third Isaiah," the designation for chapters 56–66, comes from the next generation following the return from exile.

Narrowing the setting of the prophecy concerning the woman, Isaiah 7:1 sets the prediction in "the days of Ahaz son of Jotham son of Uzziah, king of Judah." The situation is political: "King Rezin of Aram and King Pekah son of Remaliah of Israel went up to attack

Jerusalem, but could not mount an attack against it." This setting is what scholars call "the Syro-Ephraimite war" of 734–732 BCE, when the Northern Kingdom of Israel joined with the Aramaean city-state of Damascus to confront the Assyrian Empire. Israel and Aram ("Damascus") wanted Judah, the Southern Kingdom, to join their coalition, but Judah's king, Ahaz, refused. Believing that the Assyrians, whose territory encompassed much of present-day Iraq and southeastern Turkey, could not be defeated, Ahaz made Judah an Assyrian vassal state.

Isaiah is not pleased. He had earlier counseled the king, "Take heed, be quiet, do not fear, and do not let your heart be faint" (Isa 7:4). The prophet insists that Judah rely on its God rather than on military alliance. Isaiah 1–39 continues the two themes of the importance of trust in God and the inviolability of Jerusalem; because God will protect the city, Judah need not fear defeat.

To convey his message, the prophet seeks out, or waylays, the king. In the first part of chapter 7, God commands Isaiah: "Go out to meet Ahaz, you and your son Shear-jashub, at the end of the conduit of the upper pool on the highway to the Fuller's Field" (Isa 7:3). Shear-jashub means, literally, "a remnant will return [from exile]." Isaiah does not describe how he came to name his son, but the name does anticipate his prophecy about exile and repatriation: "A remnant will return, the remnant of Jacob, to the mighty God. For though your people Israel were like the sand of the sea, only a remnant of them will return" (Isa 10:21–22a). Such symbolic names appear elsewhere in Israel's scriptures. For example, the northern prophet Hosea (Hos 1:4–9) names his children Jezreel ("God will plant"), Lo-ruhamah ("not pardoned"), and Lo-ammi ("not my people").

Instructions continue in 7:4, where God tells Isaiah to say to the king, "Take heed, be quiet, do not fear, and do not let your heart be faint." The prophet's message: don't worry, and don't make any alliances. Yet Isaiah also warns Ahaz, "If you do not stand firm in faith, / you shall not stand at all" (Isa 7:9), in Hebrew an alliterative statement: 'im lo' ta'aminu ki lo' te'amenu. Despite this clever rhetoric, the king remained unconvinced. Isaiah tries again.

God next tells Isaiah to instruct the king, "Ask a sign of the LORD your God; let it be deep as Sheol [the underworld] or high as heaven" (Isa 7:11). In the Bible, "sign" can signal a supernatural occurrence, such as the "signs and wonders" performed by God at the exodus from Egypt (e.g., Exod 7:3), or the "signs" (Greek sēmeia, whence the English "semiotics") in John's Gospel, such as Jesus's turning water into wine (2:6–11) and raising Lazarus from the dead (11:1–44). But not all signs indicate miracles. Circumcision is a "sign" of the covenant (Gen 17:11); Exodus mandates that Israelite men wear a headband (later understood as tefillin) "as a sign upon your hand and as a symbol on your forehead" (Exod 13:16). Biblical signs are also often remarkable, in the sense that people would notice them. In Isaiah 20:3, for example, God states, "my servant Isaiah has walked naked and barefoot for three years as a sign and a portent against Egypt and Ethiopia." As with the Hebrew term 'ot, not every sēmeion in the New Testament is a supernatural event. The child wrapped in swaddling clothes and lying in a manger (Luke 2:12) is a "sign" to the shepherds that the Messiah has been born. The kiss of Judas is a "sign" to the soldiers that Jesus is the man to arrest (Matt 26:48).

Ahaz refuses to ask for a sign: "I will not put the LORD to the test" (Isa 7:12). Isaiah, annoyed at the rejection of God's command, retorts: "Hear then, O house of David! Is it too little for you to weary mortals, that you weary my God also?" (7:13). Whether asking for a sign is appropriate depends on context. Generally, in Israel's scriptures, the request is appropriate. The judge Gideon asks God for several signs, and God complies (Judg 6:36–40); when King Hezekiah asks Isaiah for a sign, the prophet agrees (2 Kgs 20:8–11). The Gospel of Mark, conversely, presents Jesus as refusing to give a sign to people who doubt his authority; Matthew and Luke offer the enigmatic "sign of Jonah" (see Chapter 10).

Although the king will not ask for a sign, Isaiah tells him that the sign will appear nonetheless: "Therefore the Lord himself will give you a sign" (Isa 7:14). The opening Hebrew term, *lachen*, "therefore," appears frequently in biblical prophecy to introduce a response to previous comments. In the majority of cases, *lachen* introduces a punishment, but that is not the case here. *Lachen* is rhetorically effective, since a punishment would have been the expected response to Ahaz's refusal to ask for a sign. Instead of a punishment, Isaiah offers a sign of hope:

> Look [*hineh*], the young woman is with child and shall bear a son, and
> shall name him Immanuel. He shall eat curds and honey by the time
> he knows how to refuse the evil and choose the good. For before the
> child knows how to refuse the evil and choose the good, the land before
> whose two kings you are in dread will be deserted. The LORD will bring
> on you and on your people and on your ancestral house such days as
> have not come since the day that Ephraim departed from Judah—the
> king of Assyria. (Isa 7:14b–17)

The prophecy continues by noting (v. 17—most likely an addition) that Assyria will later be the instrument of punishing Judah for its sins, for in 701 BCE, the Assyrian king Sennacherib ravaged the Judean countryside and besieged Jerusalem.

Isaiah 7:14 in its original context concerns political events in the last third of the eighth century BCE. The short timeframe is standard for biblical prophets. Both Jeremiah and Ezekiel, who began to prophesy shortly before the destruction of Jerusalem in 586, focus on that event. Biblical prophets do not offer predictions concerning the faraway "latter days." When the NRSV reads, for Jeremiah 23:20,

> The anger of the LORD will not turn back
>> until he has executed and accomplished
> the intents of his mind.
> In the latter days [*'acharit hayamim*] you will understand it clearly,

it mistranslates the Hebrew *'acharit hayamim*. The expression simply means "(some time) in the future"—and not an eschatological age. The same point holds for the same expression in Micah 4:1, which the NRSV translates,

> In days to come [*'acharit hayamim*]
>> the mountain of the LORD's house
> shall be established as the highest of the mountains,
>> and shall be raised above the hills.
> Peoples shall stream to it.

A prophecy that states "Unless you show concern for the poor, the widow, the orphan, and the stranger, you will be destroyed in seven hundred years" is not much of a threat. Nor is "in seven hundred years redemption will come" much of a promise to the people of the time.

Isaiah's sign is given "to you"—a plural in Biblical Hebrew. Kings were typically surrounded by their advisors, so Isaiah is addressing Ahaz along with his retinue. But the plural makes it easier to read the sign as addressed not only to the king, but to anyone, from any time.

The word that introduces the sign, *hineh*, is often rendered "Behold" (NRSV: "Look"), although etymologically the Hebrew term has nothing to do with seeing. Appearing more than one thousand times in the Tanakh, *hineh* functions as an attention-getter. The prophet may be directing attention to the young woman's pregnancy, the birth, the naming of the child, or even the child's move toward eating solid food—or perhaps the word draws attention to all these images. At the time, eyes would turn to the young woman.

We now come to the verses that underlie Matthew's citation: "the young woman is with child." The Hebrew words are *ha'almah harah*. *Ha-* is the definite article "the," as we see in *ha'adam*, the earthling. *'Almah* is the feminine form of *'elem*, used twice (1 Sam 17:56; 20:22) to indicate a "young man." In all of its nine occurrences, *'almah* refers to a young woman of marriageable age. These young women may be virgins, but lack of sexual experience is not the noun's main connotation. In Genesis 24:43–44, the word's first appearance, Abraham's servant states, "I am standing here by the spring of water; let the young woman [*'almah*] who comes out to draw, to whom I shall say, 'Please give me a little water from your jar to drink' . . . let her be the woman whom the LORD has appointed for my master's son.'" The woman will be the matriarch, Rebekah. In Exodus 2:8, the word refers to Moses's sister: "the girl [*'almah*] went and called the child's mother." Song of Songs 1:3 (cf. Song 6:8) speaks of lovestruck *'alamot* (NRSV: "maidens"). Finally, Proverbs 30:18–19 announces:

> Three things are too wonderful for me;
>   four I do not understand:
> the way of an eagle in the sky,
>   the way of a snake on a rock,
> the way of a ship on the high seas,
>   and the way of a man with a girl [*'almah*].

The quotation, concerning events for which there is no lasting sign, has sexual connotations, but the details are (appropriately) vague.

The Hebrew word used to indicate a woman who has not engaged in sexual intercourse is *betulah*; for example, Exodus 22:16, which concerns the seduction of a "virgin [*betulah*] who is not engaged to be married."

The following word in the Hebrew *ha'almah harah* is *harah*, an adjective meaning "is pregnant." It cannot be rendered by grammar or context as "shall conceive," which would be expressed with the imperfect (future) form *tehereh*. Thus, Isaiah says, "Look at the pregnant young woman." Had Isaiah wanted to predict a virginal birth, he would have said *habetulah tehereh*. Nothing in the phraseology of the verse suggests a miracle.

Isaiah never identifies this *'almah*, although her identity must have been known to those present at the time of the prophecy. Since Isaiah's wife, who had previously given birth to Shear-jashub, would probably not be seen as still an *'almah*, the most likely candidates are a wife or concubine of Ahaz.[5] Despite the suggestion of several sources from antiquity to the present, the child is not the future King Hezekiah, since at the time of Isaiah's prophecy, Hezekiah had already been born.

A central part of Isaiah 7:14 is the naming of the child "Immanuel." Isaiah displays a fondness for such symbolic names, as indicated by the earlier reference to Shear-jashub, "a remnant will return" (Isa 7:3). In the following chapter, after Isaiah's wife "conceived and bore a son," the prophet states, "Then the LORD said to me, Name him Maher-shalal-hash-baz" (8:3). This compound, meaning "pillage hastens, looting speeds," would have stuck out in Judah, as it does now—four-part compound names are not attested elsewhere in the Bible. The following verse explains that it refers to the Assyrians' impending conquest of Israel and Damascus. Securing the connection: the Assyrians were known as consummate looters.

The next two Hebrew words in Isaiah 7, *veyoledet ben*, a verb followed by a noun, mean "she is giving birth to a son." The first two actions, "to be pregnant and to bear," are commonly linked in the Bible, found first regarding Eve's conceiving and giving birth to Cain (Gen 4:1). The formula is often followed by one of the parents naming the baby. The entire series in Isaiah 7:14—pregnancy, birth, and naming—appears in Genesis 16:11, in the description of Hagar and her son-to-be, Ishmael:

> And the angel of the LORD said to her,
>> "Now you have conceived [or, "are pregnant"; Hebrew *harah*]
>> and shall bear a son;
>>> you shall call him Ishmael,
>>> for the LORD has given heed to your affliction."

Judges 13:3, concerning Samson, uses similar language, and similar phrasing from a pre-Israelite Ugaritic (Syrian) text suggests that it is a well-known formula.

As for who will name the child, the consonants of the MT read *qr't*. The verb can be read as "she will name" or "you will name," depending on what vowels are placed into the consonantal text. Jewish tradition dating back to at least the early Middle Ages reads this verb as *qara't*, "she will name." In the Tanakh, mothers frequently name their children: Leah and Rachel name their sons and the sons of Jacob's secondary wives, and Leah also names her daughter Dinah (as in Gen 29:32–35; 30:6–13, 18–21); in 1 Samuel 1:20, Hannah names her son Samuel. Slightly different vowels (*qara'ta*) yield the meaning "you [masculine singular] name." The Great Isaiah Scroll from the Dead Sea reads *qr'*, "he will name," which may also be understood in the passive voice, as "he will be named."

This verse has no special significance in the Dead Sea Scrolls or in other Second Temple literature. As with the suffering servant from

Isaiah 52:13–53:12 (see Chapter 9), it is only in Christian texts where this prophecy takes on a special meaning—one related to events far past the crisis of Assyrian invasion.

We learn few specifics about this child. Immanuel is a compound name: *immanu* (with us) + *'el* ([is] God). Written as two words in the Masoretic Text, but as a single word in the Great Isaiah Scroll from Qumran, it expresses divine presence. It is similar in meaning to the name *'amadyahu*, "YHWH is standing (with you)," found on a seventh-century BCE ostracon (broken piece of pottery), and the Aramaic name *'amenayah* (Hebrew *'immanuyah*), "Yah [a shortened form of YHWH] is with us," found in a fifth-century BCE papyrus. This same idea of divine presence is found in the famous Psalm 23:4, "I fear no evil; / for you are with me." Yet, the name "God [*'el*] is with us," rather than "YHWH is with us," is surprising, for outside of Isa 7:14 and the related 8:8, Isaiah never calls God *'el*.

The next verse, Isaiah 7:15, continues to offer information about this child: "by the time he knows how to refuse the evil and choose the good" refers to the son's youth, at which point he will "eat curds and honey," most likely a reference to a child old enough to eat solid food.

The sign Isaiah offers is not a miracle but an assurance. When Ahaz and his court would see this pregnant woman, they would be reminded of Isaiah's warnings against international alliances and assurances of divine protection. Once born and named, the child becomes the reminder that God is with the people of Judah and that they should have no fear.

Despite the clarity of the Hebrew, translations prove controversial. Conservative Protestants burned copies of the 1952 Revised Standard Version because it, correctly, translated *'almah* in Isaiah 7:14 as "young woman" rather than "virgin." Some Roman Catholic bishops insisted that for the New American Bible (NAB, 2002), Isaiah 7:14 be translated as "virgin," and it was.[6] For the NAB Revised Edition (promoted with the tagline "love your NABRE"), the verse reads "young woman."[7]

Since Isaiah clearly spoke of a pregnant young woman, and since the sign clearly addressed the looming political crisis, how did the idea of a virginal conception arise? For that, we need to look at the Greek translation of Isaiah 7:14.

From "Young Woman" to "Virgin"

Instead of translating *'almah* as "young woman of marriageable age," with the expected Greek term *neanis*, the Septuagint offers *parthenos*. And with this one word, centuries of Jewish-Christian debate, as well as of internal Christian litmus tests, begin.

Parthenos is the term that underlies the "Parthenon," the Greek temple dedicated to the (virgin) goddess Athena; it also underlies "parthenogenesis," reproduction by way of an unfertilized ovum, that is, conception that does not require (male) sperm.

But not every *parthenos* is a virgin in the sense of a sexually inexperienced person. The term can also mean "young woman," as we see in the story of Dinah, the daughter of Jacob and Leah. In Genesis 34:3, the Hebrew twice describes Dinah, who has just had sexual intercourse, as a *na'arah*, a "young woman," and the Septuagint uses *parthenos* in each case.

A comparison to the English word "maid" demonstrates how *parthenos* takes on different connotations depending on literary and historical contexts. The term "maid" dates to twelfth-century England, where it appears as a contraction of "maiden," that is, either "virgin" or "young and unmarried woman" (at the time, "unmarried woman" and "virgin" were presumed to be synonymous). A maid was a woman with a "maidenhead," that is, a hymen. Thus, bridesmaids were supposed to be virgins, as was Robin Hood's girlfriend, "Maid Marion."

The term "maid" then shifted from referring to a virgin (presumed to be a young woman) to referring to a young woman (presumed to be a virgin), and it begins to appear in compound nouns such as milkmaid and, later, barmaid and meter maid. Eventually, the connotation "virgin" dropped out. We still have "bridesmaids," but their sexual status is, like the sexual status of the bride, not a matter for concern.

It is possible that the scribe who rendered *'almah* as *parthenos* did mean to suggest that the woman in question was a virgin. The next term, in Hebrew the adjective *harah*, "is pregnant," comes into Greek as *en gastri eksei*, literally, "in (her) womb will have." The verb is in the future tense, which indicates that the woman is not yet pregnant. The Greek therefore reads "the virgin will conceive." It does not explicitly propose a miracle, or at least no more of a miracle than any other conception. For the Greek, Isaiah points to a young woman, still a virgin, and predicts that soon, she will become pregnant. For the Greek version of Isaiah, the king has more time to rely on Judah's safety. The woman, not yet pregnant, will first have to conceive the child (and in the process, cease to be a virgin), and then the child, Immanuel, will be born, named, and eventually eat solid food.

Finally, whereas the Hebrew states that *she* will name the child, the Greek has Isaiah telling the king, "*You* [singular] will call his name Immanuel." Matthew then offers one more permutation of this prediction: instead of "she will call his name" (MT) or "you will call his name" (Greek), Matthew has "*they* will call his name" (1:23). Matthew's reference is not to Mary and Joseph, but to Jesus's followers, who will identify him as God. For the Gospel writers, as with some early rabbis, liberty can be taken with textual citation.

Neither the Hebrew nor the Septuagint offers a miraculous sign; neither anticipates the fulfillment of the sign centuries after it was given. Neither, before Matthew, was cited in relation to a messianic figure. Once Jesus's followers began to proclaim that his birth was miraculous, Isaiah 7:14 provided, retrospectively, a suitable prooftext.

Most Jews at the time Matthew was writing, toward the end of the first century CE, would not have been flummoxed to hear of divine beings and humans having sexual relations and producing children. In the diaspora and even the towns of Judea and the Galilee, Jews would be familiar with Greek and Roman accounts of divine births: of Aeneas, the son of the goddess Aphrodite and the human Anchises (Homer, *Iliad* 2.819, 5.247–48; Ovid, *Metamorphoses* 14.581–608), and Hercules, the son of the god Zeus and the human Alcmene (Homer, *Iliad* 14.315–28). They heard that various emperors, philosophers, and military heroes had divine fathers: Alexander the Great was the son of Zeus; Apollo was the father of Asclepius and Augustus.[8] Ascription of divine conception usually worked backward: a person of impressive prowess or intellect had to be the child of a god; nothing else would explain his (always "his") extraordinary accomplishments.

Divine conceptions also appear in Israel's scriptures. Genesis, before detailing the story of Noah, records how the "sons of God" (Hebrew *benei ha'elohim*; Greek *huioi tou theou*), the divine beings of the heavenly court, had intercourse with the "daughters of men," who then gave birth to a race of giants (Gen 6:2–4). This account is developed in the Second Temple texts found among the Dead Sea Scrolls, including 1 Enoch (106–7) and the Genesis Apocryphon. The story of Samson in Judges 13 also intimates, strongly, that Samson's mother, the wife of Manoah, had some angelic help in conceiving her child.[9] A few Second Temple texts speak of the miraculous birth of Melchizedek, the mysterious priest-king in Genesis 14:18–20 (see p. 166). In one account from 2 Enoch, a Jewish text preserved only in Old Church Slavonic, Noah's brother, Nir, a priest, had stopped having sexual relations with his wife, Sopanim, so that he might remain in a state of ritual purity. When Sopanim becomes pregnant,

Nir accuses her of adultery. Shamed by his words but innocent of any extramarital relations, she dies, and while dying gives birth to Melchizedek. George Nickelsburg asks, "Is this story a Christian creation that reflects knowledge of Matthew and Hebrews, or has a Jewish author concerned about priestly succession and authority, who knows the Noachic stories, speculated about the possibility of a divine conception?"[10]

The Jewish philosopher Philo suggests that both Abraham and Isaac had some supernatural aid in conceiving their children.[11] It is possible that Paul alludes to a related tradition in his Epistle to the Galatians, where he contrasts the carnality of Ishmael (and so of gentile followers of Jesus who want to follow Jewish practice, such as circumcision) and the spirituality of Isaac (and so of gentile followers who enter into Abraham's family without practicing distinctive Jewish rituals): "One, the child of the slave [Hagar], was born according to the flesh; the other, the child of the free woman [Sarah], was born through the promise" (Gal 4:23).

What might have surprised Jews was not the claim of Jesus's miraculous conception; it was the citation of Isaiah 7:14 to legitimate the claim. The followers of Jesus read the scriptures of Israel in light of their understanding of him as the Messiah and risen Lord and so found references to him that outsiders would not have recognized. Matthew, who quotes Israel's scriptures (usually in their Septuagintal form) more than sixty times, finds in Isaiah the model for Jesus's birth. For Matthew, Israel's scriptures frequently function as predictions that Jesus fulfills. For other Jews, especially those following the Hebrew rather than the Greek versions, Matthew's claims would be peculiar if not illegitimate. The issue is not one of right reading versus wrong reading; rather, if one begins with the premise that the Christ is predicted by and present in what becomes called the "Old Testament," one will find him there.

FROM PREDICTION TO POLEMIC

ALTHOUGH IN the New Testament only Matthew's Gospel cites Isaiah 7:14, later authors deployed the verse in their arguments against non-Messianic Jews as well as other Jesus-followers whose Christology they found deficient. The next extant textual citation of Isaiah 7:14 in relation to Jesus appears in Justin Martyr's *Dialogue with Trypho* (ca. 160). Justin, who lived circa 100–165, was born in Samaria to pagan parents. He was one of Christianity's foremost apologists, who sought to show the Roman Empire that Christianity was not a subversive or depraved sect but a philosophically logical and ethically moral movement. He gained the title "martyr" when he and his disciples refused to renounce their faith.

In the *Dialogue*, Justin and Trypho discuss what have remained major issues in Jewish-Christian conversation: the ongoing value of the covenant with Moses, supersessionism, the messianic identity of Jesus in relation to Israel's scriptures, the relation of Trinitarian thought to Jewish monotheism, the role of the *Logos*, and the distinctive wordings of the Hebrew scriptures versus their Greek translations. While speculation that the *Dialogue*'s Trypho is based on Rabbi Tarfon, an early second-century companion of the famous Rabbi Akiva, cannot be confirmed, James E. Kiefer aptly observes that the dialogue was "probably a real conversation with a real rabbi (although it may be suspected that Justin in editing it later gave himself a few good lines that he wished he had thought of at the time), whom he met while promenading at Ephesus shortly after the sack of Jerusalem in 135."[12] Given that the emperor Hadrian, by destroying the city, ended hopes that the Temple destroyed by Roman troops in 70 CE would be rebuilt, the followers of Jesus became increasingly convinced that God's covenant had passed from the Jews to them.

In *Dialogue 67*, Trypho and Justin turn to the question of Jesus's conception. Trypho, as expected, states that Isaiah describes not a "virgin" but a "young woman" and adds, "But the whole prophecy refers to Hezekiah and it is proved that it was fulfilled in him, according to the terms of this prophecy."[13] As we have seen, his dating for the birth of Hezekiah is off. Trypho nevertheless quotes the Hebrew correctly.

Trypho goes on to cite some miraculous-birth stories from what we today would call "Greek mythology": "It is written that Perseus was begotten of Danae, who was a virgin; he who was called among them Zeus having descended on her in the form of a golden shower. And you ought to feel ashamed when you make assertions similar to theirs. . . . But do not venture to tell monstrous phenomena, lest you be convicted of talking foolishly like the Greeks." Justin had to guard the front on the pagan side, a front that saw Jesus as just another god, like Hercules or Mithra, Dionysius or Pythagoras. Placing the mythological examples on Trypho's lips, Justin is able to deny the charge that Christians were copying pagan stories. He goes on to insist rather that all the competing accounts of miraculous births were the work of Satan.

Then Justin, on the offensive, moves to the Greek of Isaiah 7:14. He accuses the Jew, "Here too you dare to distort the translation of this passage made by your elders at the court of Ptolemy, the king of Egypt, asserting that the real meaning of the Scripture is not as they translated it, but should read, 'Behold, a young woman will conceive.'" He goes on to assert that a woman pregnant by normal means cannot be a sign, since a sign has to have a supernatural import. But, as we have seen, that definition of "sign" does not hold even in the New Testament alone.

Trypho, not finding Justin's initial salvo convincing, pushes his Christian interlocutor: "Please show us how that passage [Isaiah 7:14] refers to your Christ and not to Hezekiah, as we Jews believe" (*Dialogue* 77). Justin responds by quoting other verses from the Septuagint, in which he makes subtle changes to support his claim. For example, he cites Isaiah 8:4, "for before the child knows how to call 'My father' or 'My mother,' the wealth of Damascus and the spoil of Samaria will be carried away by the king of Assyria," and concludes, "You cannot prove that this ever happened to any of you Jews, but we Christians can show that it did happen to our Christ" (*Dialogue* 77). His prooftext: the gifts of the Magi described in Matthew 2. That the Magi are Chaldean (Babylonian) astrologers rather than from Damascus in Syria or Samaria is irrelevant to Justin. Trypho responds, "The words of God are indeed holy, but your interpretations are artificial" (*Dialogue* 79). The *Dialogue* ends as the two men part on remarkably civil terms. Trypho states:

> You see that it was not by design that we fell into a discussion over these matters. And I acknowledge that I have been extraordinarily charmed with our intercourse, and I think that these are of like opinion with myself. For we have found more than we expected, or than it was even possible for us to expect. And if we could do this more frequently we should receive more benefit, while we examine the very words [of Scripture] themselves. (*Dialogue* 142)

Following Justin, the North African church father Tertullian similarly realizes that the proper text of Isaiah 7:14 is a fundamental dividing point between Jews and Christians: as long as the Jews have a

Hebrew text that mentions not a virgin but a young woman, and as long as they can explain Isaiah's prophecy as having been fulfilled by the birth of King Hezekiah, they can call the Christian project illegitimate. Tertullian writes, "Accordingly, the Jews say: 'Let us challenge the predictions of Isaiah, and let us institute a comparison whether, in the case of the Christ who is already come, there be applicable to Him, firstly, the name which Isaiah foretold, and (secondly) the signs of which he announced of Him'" (*In Answer to the Jews* 9).

By the time we get to Jerome's Latin translation at the beginning of the fifth century, Isaiah's "young woman" has become a "virgin": *ecce virgo concipient*. Despite living in the land of Israel and claiming that he is translating his text from the Hebrew, Jerome doubles down on Matthew's text: for Jerome, Isaiah's young woman is not only a virgin, she is a cloistered one. He makes his case by suggesting that the Hebrew term *'almah* comes from a Hebrew root, *'-l-m*, which means to "hide." Therefore the correct reading of Isaiah 7:14 concerns an *abscondita* (Latin for "hidden"), a woman hidden away from men, or "cloistered," ensuring the woman's virginity.[14] This wordplay would be familiar to his rabbinic counterparts, who also connected *'almah*, "young woman," to *'elem*, "hidden," although not in the context of sexuality. (In Hebrew, the root *'-l-m* is homonymic, meaning both a "young person" and "hidden.") In explaining why Exodus 2:8 refers to Moses's sister, who approaches Pharaoh's daughter with an offer to provide a Hebrew midwife, as an *'almah*, Rabbi Samuel offers, "because she concealed her words [i.e., her identity and intention]."[15]

Isaiah 7:14 plays no significant role in Judaism. It does not appear in the liturgy, nor is it ever chanted as a *haftarah* (prophetic reading). It primarily appears in anti-Christian polemics.[16] Such polemic may be reflected as early as the mid-second-century CE Greek versions of the Tanakh by Theodotion and Aquila, who translate *'almah* into Greek as *neanis*, "young woman." The Greek translation ascribed to

Symmachus, whom the church father Eusebius (*Demonstration of the Gospel* 7.1, ca. 320) identified as an Ebionite (a member of a Christian group who adhered to Jewish customs or, as Eusebius puts it, "a heresy of some so-called Jews who claim to believe in Christ"), similarly reads *neanis* for '*almah*. The same Greek term appears in the Septuagint's description of the Levite's concubine (who is manifestly not a virgin) in Judges 19; it describes the widow Ruth, who is also not a virgin, in Ruth 2:5.

Classical rabbinic literature rarely refers to Isaiah 7:14, and its few citations have no messianic import. Just the opposite: Although classical and medieval Jewish readings often take prophetic passages as referring to the distant future, Isaiah 7:14 is read in its historical context. Exodus Rabbah 18:5, unaware of the chronological problems it is creating, suggests that Immanuel is Ahaz's son Hezekiah, under whom the Assyrians failed to conquer Jerusalem, since the Chronicler (2 Chr 32:8) states that "with him [i.e., Sennacherib, the king of Assyria] is an arm of flesh; but with us [Hebrew '*immanu*—part of the name Immanuel] is the LORD our God."

In the Middle Ages, as Jews in Europe became aware of claims concerning Mary's perpetual virginity, either explicitly or implicitly they began to polemicize against the Christian interpretation of Isaiah 7:14. The medieval French exegete Rashi claimed that Immanuel's mother was the prophet Isaiah's wife and that this prophecy was meant to be fulfilled in the short term (in Rashi's words, "this very year"). For Rashi, Hezekiah could not be the son, since he was born before Ahaz gained the throne (see 2 Kgs 16:2; 18:2). Given Rashi's status among many European Jews, this interpretation became well-known and accepted.

Some Messianic Jews have insisted that Rashi recognized that Isaiah was actually talking about a virgin. The Messianic Jewish *Complete Jewish Study Bible* asserts regarding Isaiah 7:14: "Even Rashi is quoted in *Mikraoth Gedaloth* [The Rabbinic Bible] on this passage: 'Behold the *'almah* shall conceive and have a son and shall call his name Immanuel. This means that our Creator will be with us. And this is the sign: the one who will conceive is a girl *who never in her life had intercourse with any man*. Upon this one shall the Holy Spirit have power" (emphasis added).[17] These authors, however, misquote Rashi. Rashi has no "virginal" conception.

Abraham ibn Ezra (1089–1167), a Jewish commentator and poet born in Muslim Spain but who later traveled in Christian Europe, explains in greater polemical detail why Isaiah cannot be referring to Jesus:

> It is to me a matter of surprise that there are those who say the prophet here refers to Jesus, since the sign was given to Ahaz, and Jesus was born many years afterwards; besides, the prophet says, "For before the child shall know to refuse the evil and choose the good, the land shall be forsaken"; but the countries of Ephraim and Syria were wasted in the sixth year of Hezekiah, and it is distinctly said "of those two kings" etc. . . . We know that a male child is called *na'ar*, a female child *na'arah* or *'almah*—the feminine of *'elem*—whether she be a virgin or not; for *'almah* signifies a person of a certain age, like the masculine *'elem*; and in *derekh gever be'almah* "the way of a man with a young woman" (Prov. 30: 19), *'almah* is certainly not a virgin; because at the beginning of the passage it is said, "which I know not" (v. 18).[18]

Although ibn Ezra does not refer to the Septuagint—he did not know Greek—he is clearly polemicizing against its rendition of *'almah* as *parthenos*.

This strong anti-Christian polemic spills over to Mary, as some early Jewish commentators countered claims of her virginity with claims of her promiscuity. For example, the Tosefta (ca. 250 CE) suggests she had a sexual liaison with a Roman soldier named Ben Pan-thera (t. Hullin 2.22–24); the same story circulated in pagan circles, as we find it in Origen's *Contra Celsum* 1.69. The name Ben Panthera ("Son of Panthera") may be a play on the term *parthenos*.[19]

On the other hand, not all Jewish readings of Isaiah 7:14 are po-lemical. A late addition to the Zohar (2:212b), the central thirteenth-century mystical work, understands Isaiah's prophecy as referring, allegorically, to divine assistance to Israel in exile. Some medieval Jews, especially in Italy, named their children "Immanuel"; the most famous is the scholar and poet Immanuel of Rome (1261–1328).

By the time the author of Matthew was writing circa 90 CE, more than seven centuries after the time of Isaiah, Isaiah 7:14 had become reinter-preted and recontextualized. Later readers of Isaiah, including those from the Dead Sea Scroll community and the early Christ-believing community, knew and cared little about the Syro-Ephraimite war. They also regarded their scripture as a divinely inspired work with wisdom for future generations. It was thus natural for them to see Isa-iah's ancient prophecy as relevant to their own communities.

Christian readers today, aware of the lack of a virginal conception in the Hebrew of Isaiah 7:14, will sometimes argue that while Isaiah *in his own time* referred to the birth of Hezekiah or some other indi-vidual, *he also* was referring to Jesus. This argument generally hangs on the reference to the plural "you" in Isaiah 7:14 ("the Lord himself will give you [pl.] a sign"), which is understood not as referring to Ahaz and his court but to Ahaz and unspecified people in the fu-ture. Such a reading is consistent with what the Catholic Church calls the *sensus plenior*, the "fuller sense." Jesuit scholar Daniel Har-rington in *The Bible and the Believer* describes this process in relation to Isaiah 7:14:

This is the deeper meaning of a text that was intended by God but not consciously or clearly expressed by the biblical author. . . . Whereas Isaiah and his audience at the royal court in Jerusalem might have assumed that he was talking about a male child (perhaps Hezekiah) to be born from one of King Ahaz's wives, in the fuller sense, the Holy Spirit, speaking through the prophet, was really looking forward centuries later to the virginal conception of Jesus by Mary who was a *parthenos* according to the Greek in Matthew 1:18–25. This sense is obviously a theological accommodation.[20]

Other scholars begin with the premise that the virginal conception was a historical event reported by Mary. Methodist scholar Ben Witherington offers the following retrospective explication:

Since Isaiah 7:14 in the Hebrew or even in the LXX does not necessarily imply a miraculous conception, it must have been the actual miraculous conception in the life of Mary that prompted the rereading of the OT text in this way. In other words, this is not an example of a fictional story about Mary generated by a previous prophecy about a miracle. To the contrary, it is a reinterpretation of a multivalent prophecy in light of what actually happened to Mary.[21]

Witherington's view raises the question of how we do history. For him and many others, that God would contravene the laws of nature and so create not simply a "sign" but a miracle is historical fact. We read history differently: we seek interpretations that would make sense to believers—Christian, Jewish, Muslim, whoever—as well as to people who have no belief in a supernatural divine figure.

Like almost all biblical texts, Isaiah's prophecy opens to multiple interpretations, and we would do well to realize how different readings, translations, and historical contexts have led to these differences, and to appreciate that our personal preference should not determine how others, from different religious communities, must read the text. Nor should the Jewish community cede certain scripture to Christianity. Rather than engage in another *Dialogue with Trypho* and run through the potential problems with the various readings, we think it more prudent to talk about what we might do with Isaiah 7:14 today. What pregnant questions might it pose?

Too often today blind faith is emphasized. Yet all readings of this text suggest that it is not only proper but on occasion crucial to doubt, to ask God to provide signs about future events. Isaiah speaks of a sign given to Ahaz, a king who refuses to believe the prophet's original message and refused to look for a sign: What are the signs given to people who refuse to believe the signs of the times?

We should also attend to what the sign of a pregnant woman might be today. Look, a woman is pregnant: What will happen before her child is old enough to eat solid food? Will there be food for him to eat, or healthcare for her to thrive?

The history of interpretation of this chapter should also teach us some humility. At one time or another we might claim certainty about what a text means. The different interpretations of Isaiah 7:14 by different religious groups over time should warn us against any narrow or restricted meaning.

Finally, the fact that such a central notion in Christianity as the virginal conception is mentioned explicitly only once in the New Testament offers a central lesson as to how all scriptural religions develop over time: Sometimes a notion barely attested in scripture becomes significant at a later period, and sometimes an idea that a scripture emphasizes time and time again becomes less important, or even falls by the wayside. Thus the history of interpretation of the sign of Immanuel teaches us much about how all religions have, and can, change over time.

CHAPTER 9

✤

Isaiah's Suffering Servant

By His Bruises We Are Healed

In the previous chapter, we discussed the role of Isaiah 7:14 in Christian understandings of Mary's virginity. A much longer passage in Isaiah, with many more citations and allusions in the New Testament, comes from Second Isaiah, writing during the Babylonian exile.[1] Explicitly citing sections of Isaiah 52:13–53:12 seven times (Matt 8:17; Luke 22:37; John 12:38; Acts 8:32–33; Rom 10:16; 15:21; and 1 Pet 2:22), the New Testament finds in this passage confirmation that Jesus's suffering and death on behalf of humanity, followed by his exaltation and his universal acclamation, were part of God's redemptive plan. This unit, the fourth of what are known as four Servant Songs in the book of Isaiah, is a parade example of how a passage from the Hebrew Bible can take on different meanings in different historical and religious contexts.

Part of the reason that Isaiah 52:13–53:12 can take on different interpretations is because it is such a difficult text. The poetry of Isaiah 40–55, in which it is embedded, is among the most complex and multilayered in the Bible, and the meaning of almost every verse differs, sometimes significantly, among various translations. We illustrate this by comparing two verses in the NRSV and the NJPS translations. Each translates a slightly different text, and each understands words and grammatical forms in different ways. While many of the differences seem small, cumulatively, these translations offer quite different images of the servant. The first is Isaiah 53:8:

NRSV	NJPS
By a perversion of justice he was taken away.	By oppressive judgment he was taken away,
Who could have imagined his future?	Who could describe his abode?
For he was cut off from the land of the living, stricken for the transgression of my people.	For he was cut off from the land of the living [t]hrough the sin of my people, who deserved the punishment.

The difference between "his future" (NRSV) and "his abode" (NJPS) depends on the meaning of the homonymic Hebrew word *dor*. These versions also translate the last phrase differently because of differences among the standard Hebrew text (MT), the Dead Sea Scrolls, and the Septuagint. The last word of Isaiah 53:8 in the Masoretic Text and in three Dead Sea Scrolls is *lmw*, "to him," but the Septuagint translates this "to death":

> In his humiliation his judgment was taken away.
>   Who will describe his generation?
> Because his life is being taken from the earth,
>   he was led to death on account of the acts of lawlessness of
>   my people.

The Septuagint presumes a Hebrew text of *lmwt*—different by just a single letter. But the difference between "(to) him" (which NJPS paraphrases as "who deserved") and "death" (NRSV: "stricken") is substantial—the NRSV emphasizes the death of the servant, so central to the Christian interpretation, but the Dead Sea Scrolls and the Masoretic Text do not.

Another example is 53:11:

NRSV	NJPS
Out of his anguish he shall see light;	Out of his anguish he shall see it;
he shall find satisfaction through his knowledge.	He shall enjoy it to the full through his devotion.
The righteous one, my servant, shall make many righteous,	"My righteous servant makes the many righteous,
and he shall bear their iniquities.	It is their punishment that he bears."

The third word in the standard Hebrew text (MT) is *yr'h*, "he will see," and the NJPS translates "he shall see it," which, as a note explicates, the editors understand as "the arm of the Lord"; three Dead Sea Scroll manuscripts follow *yr'h* with the word *'wr*, "light," which is lacking in the Masoretic Text. (These two words look and sound similar in Hebrew, so it is easy to see how *'wr* might have gotten lost in the process of textual transmission.) The Septuagint also has the extra word "light," and the NRSV follows this reading with "Out of his anguish he shall see light."[2]

Depending on the text and the translation, the servant sees either God's power or God's light. Several unresolvable grammatical problems account for other differences between the two translations. Ancient Hebrew has no quotation marks, so each translator must determine whether and where they should be inserted; the NJPS understands the last part as God speaking (through the end of v. 12) and thus inserts quotation marks while the NRSV does not.[3] Finally, the English tense into which these final verbs should be translated is uncertain, with the NJPS rendering them as present tenses, "makes, bears," and the NRSV as future tenses, "shall make, shall bear," lending more readily to a christological interpretation. Such textual and grammatical problems typify every verse of Isaiah 52:13–53:12.

For Christians, the central suffering servant verse is Isaiah 53:5:

> But he was wounded for our transgressions,
> crushed for our iniquities;
> upon him was the punishment that made us whole,
> and by his bruises we are healed.

This verse summarizes the major christological claim regarding Jesus's salvific suffering. Read in light of the cross, Isaiah's suffering servant could be none other than Jesus of Nazareth. Indeed, Jesus may have seen himself in the role of this servant.

Suffering servant imagery pervades the New Testament. When Paul states in 1 Corinthians 15:3, "I handed on to you as of first importance what I in turn had received: that Christ died for our sins in accordance with the scriptures," Isaiah 52:13–53:12 is in the background. Paul's proclamation that Jesus "was handed over to death for our trespasses and was raised for our justification" (Rom 4:25) follows from Isaiah 53:12:

> because he poured out himself to death,
> and was numbered with the transgressors;
> yet he bore the sin of many,
> and made intercession for the transgressors.

The Synoptic passion predictions, with their notices that "the Son of Man must undergo great suffering, and be rejected by the elders . . .

and be killed, and after three days rise again" (Mark 8:31; cf. Matt 16:21; Luke 9:22), reflect knowledge of Isaiah's servant, who suffers, is rejected, is (understood to be) killed, and is (understood to be) resurrected.

The early followers of Jesus consistently identified the servant in Isaiah 52:13–53:12 as their Lord, the one who suffered and died, but they did not limit themselves to this focus. Here are five other ways they understood this suffering servant, saw Jesus as fulfilling the passage, and understood themselves in its light.

First, Matthew appeals to Isaiah 52:13–53:12 in the context of a healing. After noting that Jesus "cast out the spirits with a word, and cured all who were sick" (Matt 8:16), Matthew adds, "This was to fulfill what had been spoken through the prophet Isaiah, 'He took our infirmities and bore our diseases'" (8:17). Matthew is citing the first half of Isaiah 53:4: "Surely he has borne our infirmities / and carried our diseases." Surprisingly, Matthew follows the Hebrew reading of "our infirmities" or "our weaknesses" (*cholayenu*), rather than the Septuagint, which reads *tas hamartias hemōn pherei*, "he bore our sins." It is possible that Matthew expected readers, familiar with the Greek translation, to understand "bore our infirmities" as synonymous with "bore our sins."[4]

Second, several New Testament texts apply this Servant Song both to the refusal of most Jews to accept Jesus as Lord and to his acceptance by gentiles. Following the notice that the crowds did not believe in Jesus despite his many signs (John 12:37), John quotes Isaiah 53:1: "This was to fulfill the word spoken by the prophet Isaiah: 'Lord, who has believed our message, / and to whom has the arm of the Lord been revealed?'" (12:38). John 12:40 paraphrases Isaiah 6:10 on how the people will look but not see. John thus emphasizes the crowds' failure to see how their own scriptures point to Jesus. Similarly, concerned that most of his fellow Jews have not responded to his proclamation of Jesus, Paul cites the same verse: "But not all have obeyed the good news; for Isaiah says, 'Lord, who has believed our message?'" (Rom 10:16). Also in Romans, Paul speaks of Isaiah's suffering servant in relation to his own mission of bringing the message of Jesus to gentiles: "As it is written, 'Those who have never been told of him shall see, / and those who have never heard of him shall understand'" (15:21). The underlying text is Isaiah 52:15b: "for that which had not been told them they shall see, / and that which they had not heard they shall contemplate."

Third, Jesus's suffering becomes for his followers, and especially slaves, a paradigm to be followed. The First Epistle of Peter addresses slaves directly:

> For to this you have been called, because Christ also suffered for you, leaving you an example, so that you should follow in his steps.
> "He committed no sin,
>   and no deceit was found in his mouth."
> When he was abused, he did not return abuse; when he suffered, he did not threaten; but he entrusted himself to the one who judges justly. He himself bore our sins in his body on the cross, so that, free from sins, we might live for righteousness; by his wounds you have been healed. For you were going astray like sheep, but now you have returned to the shepherd and guardian of your souls. (1 Pet 2:21–25)

Verse 22 is a quotation of Isaiah 53:9b. The author focuses not on Jesus's salvific death but on the example he provides by silently suffering: *actual slaves* are to accept abusive treatment because Jesus, the "slave of God," so suffered.

Fourth, New Testament authors are aware that the servant requires interpretation. Acts 8:32–33 describes an Ethiopian court official, a eunuch, who is reading Isaiah 53:7–8:

Now the passage of the scripture that he was reading was this:
"Like a sheep he was led to the slaughter,
    and like a lamb silent before its shearer,
        so he does not open his mouth.
In his humiliation justice was denied him.
    Who can describe his generation?
        For his life is taken away from the earth."

The official asks Philip, "About whom . . . does the prophet say this, about himself or about someone else?" (Acts 8:34), and Philip responds with instructions about Jesus. Luke's focus on the servant's humiliation may be of specific relevance to the eunuch,[5] given Isaiah's prediction nearby:

For thus says the LORD:
To the eunuchs who keep my sabbaths,
    who choose the things that please me
    and hold fast my covenant,
I will give, in my house and within my walls,
    a monument and a name. (Isa 56:4–5)

Fifth, Luke cites Isaiah 53 as a prooftext predicting Jesus's arrest. Jesus tells his disciples, "the one who has no sword must sell his cloak and buy one" and then quotes Isaiah 53:12: "For I tell you, this scripture must be fulfilled in me, 'And he was counted among the lawless'; and indeed what is written about me is being fulfilled" (Luke 22:36–37). The prediction is fulfilled not only in Luke 23:32–33, when Jesus is crucified between two evildoers, but also at Jesus's arrest, when he is "counted" among sword-carrying and so rebellious disciples.[6]

Isaiah's Servant Song of 52:13–53:12 is so embedded in the New Testament that Ben Witherington III titles his first chapter of *Isa-*

iah Old and New: Exegesis, Intertextuality, and Hermeneutics "Isa-ianic Fingerprints Everywhere."[7] Richard Hays finds Romans to be "salted with numerous quotations of and allusions to Isaiah 40–55, including several passages that seem to echo the suffering servant motif of Isaiah 53 (e.g., Rom. 4:24–25, 5:15–19, 10:16, 15:21)."[8] Dale Allison summarizes, "The Synoptic passion narratives otherwise implicitly equate Jesus with Isaiah's Suffering Servant," and points to several examples in all four Gospels, including the "blood poured out for many," the "silence before accusers," Jesus/the servant being slapped and spit upon, the "amazement of Gentile ruler," the theme of "criminal saved/innocent killed," "association with criminals in death," "burial by a rich man," "fate shared with transgressors," and "scourging."[9]

Christian readers consistently identified the servant in Isaiah 52:13–53:12 as Jesus, who healed, who suffered and died, and who was rejected by "the Jews." They also indicated that Isaiah's servant required interpretation: he could not be identified apart from Christian instruction, both because his identity is not self-evident and because there are other candidates for the role.

These views and others then receive reinforcement from the church fathers. For 1 Clement 16:1–14 (ca. 90 CE), the servant serves to encourage humility among Jesus's followers; for the contemporaneous Epistle of Barnabas 5:2, Isaiah 53:5 and 53:7 prove both that Jesus is Lord and that his blood redeems from sin.

We shall spare our readers additional lists. Instead, we focus on how Isaiah's servant would have been understood in the context of the Babylonian exile, and then how the Jewish community has understood the servant over time.

THE "SUFFERING SERVANT"
IN HIS HISTORICAL CONTEXT

THE SUFFERING SERVANT is found only in the book of Isaiah, and within that book, only in chapters 40–55, most likely written during the Babylonian exile (597/586–538 BCE) or shortly thereafter. Scholars have debated, and continue to debate, his status, his death, and even how to identify him.

The term "suffering servant," though widely used, is never found in the Bible. It is a modern construct, introduced into biblical studies in 1892 by a German Lutheran scholar, Bernhard L. Duhm (1847–1928), to label four separate passages: Isaiah 42:1–4; 49:1–6; 50:4–11; and 52:13–53:12. Each mentions a "servant" (Hebrew 'eved) and several verses depict his suffering and faith, such as those that follow:

Isaiah 42:2   He will not cry or lift up his voice,
                or make it heard in the street;

Isaiah 50:6   I gave my back to those who struck me,
                and my cheeks to those who pulled out the beard;
              I did not hide my face
                from insult and spitting.

The rubric "Servant Songs" connects these four passages into a single picture or individual.

The rubric, however, can be misleading. Tryggve N. D. Mettinger suggests that scholars "excise Duhm's theory from the arsenal of acceptable exegetical tools and instead relegate it to the curio shelf for obsolete hypotheses."[10] Yet the label "suffering servant" persists, in part because once in place it is difficult to eliminate a technical term and, we suspect, in part because the term resonates with christological claims. Rather than looking at all four songs together, our focus here is on Isaiah 52:13–53:12, the longest of the Servant Songs, and the one the New Testament explicitly cites.

But who is the servant? Some scholars suggest that the servant represents the community of Israel; they note that Isaiah 40–55 several times calls the community of Israel God's 'eved or servant. For example, Isaiah 44:1–2 reads:

> But now hear, O Jacob my servant,
>   Israel whom I have chosen! . . .
> Do not fear, O Jacob my servant,
>   Jeshurun whom I have chosen.

The antimissionary movement Jews for Judaism (opposite to "Jews for Jesus") both proposes that the servant is Israel and supports this claim by suggesting that the narrator takes the role of the gentile nations who witness the servant's (i.e., Israel's) exilic suffering and glorious return: "52:15 tells us explicitly that it is the nations of the world, the gentiles, who are speaking in Isaiah 53. See, also, Micah 7:12–17, which recounts the nations' astonishment when the Jewish people again blossom in the Messianic age."[11] A similar position is found in the medieval Jewish commentator Abraham ibn Ezra to Isaiah 53:11. The redemption or healing of the nations occurs when they recognize the power of Israel's God. Indeed, in this reading, Isaiah 53:6b, "the LORD has laid on him / the iniquity of us all," means that Israel's suffering is on behalf of the gentile nations. The antimissionary movement similarly insists that the servant always refers to Israel.[12]

This reading is possible; the text is sufficiently difficult to preclude it. Arguing against it: The gentiles are not present elsewhere in the Servant Songs, and these songs, and their broader context, do not suggest that the gentiles need to recognize God's power or that Israel is suffering on their behalf. In fact, this idea is never found in Israel's scriptures.

Isaiah 40–55 uses "servant" in reference to several different people or groups. For example, in Isaiah 49:3, God calls the prophet "my servant."[13] "My servant" in 52:13–53:12 similarly refers to an individual—though not necessarily the prophet. Isaiah 53:6b, in which the people of Israel are speaking, reads, "the LORD has laid on him / the iniquity of us all." Interpreted collectively, as all Israel, the verse would mean that the servant Israel is being punished for the sins of Israel ("all of us"), which makes no sense. Thus, evidence internal to 52:13–53:12, which should be the primary determinant for identifying the servant, suggests that this figure was an individual. His disabilities, caused by Israel's sin, allow forgiveness to a group referred to in the first-person plural, "us," that is, Israel. The application of the servant to Jesus is consistent with this understanding of the servant as an individual.

The Hebrew term 'eved, usually translated "servant," used twice in this song in the form 'avdi, "my 'eved" (52:13; 53:11), merits its own discussion. Depending on context, the noun is translated "slave, servant, subject, official, vassal, or 'servant' or follower of a particular god."[14] The pronominal suffix -i ("my") in 'avdi refers to God, so the word here means "my servant." The designation appears elsewhere in the Bible: Moses (Josh 1:2; cf. Exod 4:10), Caleb (Num 14:24), Job (Job 1:8), David (1 Kgs 11:32–38; cf. 1 Sam 23:10), and others. Nine biblical individuals including a minor prophet are named Obadiah, "the servant of Yah(weh)"; the name Abdiel, "the servant of God," has the same meaning. That same identification of "servant" or "slave" appears in the New Testament in reference to Mary the mother of Jesus (Luke 1:48, *doulē*), Paul (Rom 1:1, *doulos*), and Jesus (Phil 2:7).

For Isaiah 52:13–53:12, we choose to translate both the Greek and the Hebrew with "servant" rather than "slave." Isaiah is not describing a chattel slave of the sort described in Exodus 21:2–6 ("When you buy a male Hebrew slave, he shall serve six years, but in the seventh he shall go out a free person, without debt," v. 2) or Deuteronomy 15:15–17 ("Remember that you were a slave in the land of Egypt," v. 15). When used with the personal pronoun "my" in reference to God in Isaiah 52:13 and 53:11, *'eved* conveys the individual's close relationship with, and dependence on, God. The servant belongs to God.

This central figure is never called a "messiah" (Hebrew *mashiach*), a term for an eschatological savior that became popular after the turn of the eras. Within Second Isaiah (Isa 40–55), where all four songs occur, only Cyrus is called the LORD's "messiah," meaning, most basically, "anointed" (Isa 45:1). Isaiah 40–55 lacks the notion of an ideal Davidic king; instead, Isaiah 55:3b–5 suggests that the covenant promising eternal kingship to David's household is about to be transferred to all Israel. Thus, within Second Isaiah, the servant is not a messianic figure—and cannot be one.

Nor does the servant die on behalf of others. The song's death language is figurative, since the passage clearly states that the servant remains alive throughout (see below). Isaiah 53:7 notes that the servant is "like a lamb that is led to the slaughter," but this simile does not suggest his actual death. Being led to the slaughter conveys images from innocence to fear to resignation, but the text does not say that the lamb died. Verses 8–9, which speak of the servant being "taken away" and "cut off from the land of the living," and which observe, "they made his grave with the wicked / and his tomb with the rich," are metaphorical as well.

The same figurative use of death for grave illness is found in verse

12, "poured out himself [or "emptied himself"] to death." Elsewhere the Hebrew Bible uses "death" imagery to represent grave danger. For example, Jonah 2:6 (2:7 Heb.) reads: "I went down to the land / whose bars closed upon me forever; / yet you [YHWH] brought up my life from the Pit [Hebrew *shachat*, a synonym for *Sheol*, the underworld]." Similarly, in Psalm 86:13, a quite living psalmist says: "For great is your steadfast love toward me; / you have delivered my soul from the depths of Sheol."

Such verses in Isaiah, Jonah, or Psalms do not refer to death and resurrection: with very few exceptions, and all later than Second Isaiah, the Tanakh neither addresses the concept of resurrection nor promotes a beatific afterlife. The closest that biblical literature contemporaneous with Isaiah 40–55 comes to the idea of resurrection appears in Ezekiel 37. Ezekiel depicts exilic Israel as a valley "full of bones" (37:1) that miraculously become enfleshed, living bodies, but that chapter points to national revival rather than individual resurrection. Isaiah 52:13–53:12 is therefore better understood as suggesting a horrific ordeal experienced by one individual, who survives.

Rather than dying, the servant will not only live; he will be "exalted and lifted up, / and shall be very high" (Isa 52:13). Isaiah 53:10b notes, "he shall see his offspring, and shall prolong his days." God promises, "I will allot him a portion with the great, / and he shall divide the spoil with the strong" (53:12). These verses confirm that the various references to death throughout are metaphorical.

Since he is not killed, the servant does not have a sacrificial role, despite this popular interpretation. The NRSV's rendering of 53:10a, "Yet it was the will of the LORD to crush him with pain / When you make his life an offering for sin," is a possible translation but, given the context of the chapter, an unlikely one. The Hebrew underlying "offering for sin" is *'asham*, which can, especially in Leviticus, refer to a sacrificial offering. But neither this passage nor Isaiah 40–55 as a whole is permeated with priestly language: the texts do not use other sacrificial terms such as "altar" or "blood." As Jeremy Schipper correctly observes, "comparisons between the servant and an unblemished animal that dies a sacrificial death work only if one ignores or downplays the repeated images of disease or sickness throughout Isaiah 53."[15] Thus, 'asham here is better understood in terms of its other common meaning of "guilt" or "compensation from guilt." These meanings are well-attested; for example, the first use of this word in the Bible is in Genesis 26:10, when Abimelech chastises Abraham, who had tried to pass off his wife as his sister: "What is this you have done to us? One of the people might easily have lain with your wife, and you would have brought guilt ['asham] upon us." In Isaiah 53, the servant is sick as a result of other people's guilt, but this sickness is not depicted as a sacrifice.

The central figure is not described as the messiah, is not dead, and is not offered as a sacrifice. Nevertheless, we can make some definite observations about him. First, the servant suffers terrible physical disabilities that have social repercussions: "marred was his appearance, beyond human semblance, / and his form beyond that of mortals" (Isa 52:14); this translation may suggest that the servant is superhuman, "beyond . . . mortals," but the Hebrew means simply that this appearance is much worse than that of the average Joe. In addition, he had "no form or majesty that we should look at him, / nothing in his appearance that we should desire him" (53:2); he was "despised and rejected by others; / a man of suffering [KJV: "man of sorrows"] and acquainted with infirmity; / and as one from whom others hide their faces" (v. 3), "wounded" and "crushed" (v. 5), "oppressed" and "afflicted" (v. 7), "crush[ed] . . . with pain" (v. 10). The servant is so severely disabled, in such dreadful condition, that people do not want to look at him. We should linger at these descriptions, since they force us to look at what we do not want to see. In attending to the details, which the prophet forces upon us, we are brought into his suffering rather than becoming inured to it.

Moreover, the prophet believes that this servant suffers unjustly. Isaiah 53:8 describes his affliction as "a perversion of justice"; 53:9 claims that "he had done no violence, / and there was no deceit in his mouth." The verse undermines the common view that ancient Israel both understood all suffering as connected to sin and saw health along with wealth as a sign of righteousness. The book of Job similarly undermines this view.

This suffering has positive vicarious effects: the servant was "stricken for the transgression of my people," namely Israel (Isa 53:8); and

> he was wounded [Hebrew *chalal*, can also translate "pierced";
> Greek *traumatizō*, whence "trauma"] for [Hebrew *min*; Greek
> *dia*, "on account of"] our transgressions,
>> crushed for our iniquities;
> upon him was the punishment that made us whole,
>> and by his bruises we are healed. (53:5a)

We note here the importance of the prepositions *min* (Hebrew) and *dia* (Greek). In Isaiah's Hebrew, the servant is wounded *for* the transgressions of the people but not *on account of* them. The sins of Israel cause the servant to be wounded, but this phrase does not state that the wounding is designed to atone. It is a symptom, not a salvation. The vicarious nature of his punishment is also reinforced toward this prophecy's end: "The righteous one, my [YHWH's] servant, shall make many righteous, / and he shall bear their iniquities" (53:11).

The idea of vicarious punishment is found elsewhere in the Hebrew Bible, but it is rare.[16] The Decalogue stipulates that when God punishes those who worship other deities, he also "punish[es] chil-

dren for the iniquity of parents, to the third and the fourth generation of those who reject me" (Exod 20:5; Deut 5:9; cf. Exod 34:7).
Second Samuel 12:13 describes the aftermath of David's adulterous
affair with Bathsheba: "Nathan said to David, 'Now the LORD has
transferred your sin; you shall not die'" (authors' translation)—and
indeed, a few verses later, the innocent child born of adultery dies.
Isaiah 53 is unique in the Hebrew Bible in suggesting that a single
individual absorbs the sin of many people.

It is easy to imagine how the community, exiled from its homeland, without Temple and king, would feel excessive guilt. Unwilling
to believe that its God was unjust, possessing both a law collection
that mandated righteous behavior and a prophetic history that
warned against injustice, the exiled community logically blamed itself for its losses.

And then they concluded that they had paid the penalty for their
sins—and perhaps even overpaid. Isaiah 40:2 claims that Israel "has
received from the LORD's hand / double for all her sins." At this turn,
the exiles express their feelings of abandonment; the exilic poet of
Lamentations 5:20 cries out to God: "Why have you forgotten us
completely? / Why have you forsaken us these many days?" The following verse shows that the poet is convinced that the repentance of
the people is insufficient, that God must take the first step to restore
Israel: "Restore us to yourself, O LORD, that we may be restored; /
renew our days as of old." Only after such extraordinary means may
Israel be restored.

This is the milieu of the anonymous prophet whose words were
collected in Isaiah 40–55. Mired in exile, and absent the Temple—a
significant locus of expiation until it was destroyed in 586 BCE—the
community needed to find new ways to feel that it was deserving of
forgiveness. The suffering servant of Isaiah 52:13–53:12 fills this need.

We would love to know who the servant was—if indeed the

prophet intended it to be a single individual. Identifying this person, and even determining whether the servant is identical in all of its uses in Isaiah 40–55, is impossible. Tryggve N. D. Mettinger recapitulates a typical list of potential candidates, including Isaiah himself, Moses (b. Sotah 14a), Jeremiah (Saadia Gaon and Ibn Ezra; cf. Jer 10:18–24; 11:19), Hezekiah, the Davidic king in exile or Zerubbabel, the people Israel (b. Sanhedrin 98a; Numbers Rabbah 13.2), the righteous in every generation (b. Berakhot 5a), Cyrus, the messiah (b. Sanhedrin 98b; Ruth Rabbah 5.6; cf. Isa 45:1), the faithful remnant mentioned by Isaiah 10:20–22 (David Kimchi), the high priest Onias, and others. Mettinger finds that these various suggestions "resemble the contents of a successful big-game hunt on the exegetical savannah."[17]

Isaiah 52:13–53:12 originally referred to one of the prophet's exilic contemporaries, whom he viewed as vicariously atoning for the guilt-ridden exilic (or early postexilic) community. We know neither this individual's name nor anything about him beyond what this difficult passage says. Or perhaps he is a figure imagined by the prophet. Yet given the vividness of this individual, and his unusual description, it is easy to see why even the earliest readers of this passage sought to identify the servant.

THE SERVANT'S HISTORY IN LATER
JEWISH AND CHRISTIAN TRADITIONS

WHILE Second Temple writers did not engage the Servant Song of Isaiah 52:13–53:12 often, the interpretations we do have are diverse. The earliest extant allusion to and identification of the servant is in Daniel 12:3, a text written in the mid-second century BCE, at the time of the oppression of Antiochus IV Epiphanes, which included his laws against Jewish practice. The author states, in reference to the faithful, "Those who are wise shall shine like the brightness of the sky, and those who lead *many* to *righteousness*, like the stars forever and ever" (emphasis added), that is, they will live forever. Daniel 12 here repurposes Isaiah 53:11b, "The righteous one, my servant, shall make *many righteous*" (emphasis added).

Isaiah 53:11b also likely underlies Daniel 11:33: "The wise among the people shall give understanding to *many*; for some days, however, they shall fall by sword and flame, and suffer captivity and plunder" (emphasis added); and additional verses in Daniel may also allude to Isaiah 52:13–53:12 in describing settings of persecution. The author understands the servant to represent a collective of righteous individuals who resisted the decrees of Antiochus IV, such as banning Jews from observing the Sabbath and circumcising infant boys (see 1 Macc 1:44–50 and Chapter 12, below). Daniel does not, however, reuse all the elements of Isaiah 52:13–53:12, nor should we expect him to; for example, nowhere is vicarious punishment explicitly mentioned.

Other Second Temple authors, including the central figure in Qumran's *Hodayot* or Thanksgiving Scroll, show some interest in our song, and it is possible that the Teacher of Righteousness self-identified with the despised but vindicated "servant."[18] However, contrary to some popular press, no Dead Sea Scroll, based on Isaiah 52:13–53:12, refers to a suffering and dying "messiah."[19] Of Sefer Hamilḥamah (4Q285), so often cited as proof of a suffering and dying messiah in the Dead Sea Scrolls, the eminent scrolls scholar James VanderKam writes, "The fourth line—the controversial one—should be translated: 'and the prince of the congregation [another title for the Davidic messiah] . . . will kill [or: killed] him'" and concludes that the verse refers to Isaiah 11:4, which describes how David's son "shall kill the wicked."[20] As James Charlesworth writes, "The Qumran community did not develop the concept of a servant-messiah who would vicariously suffer for the many and save them."[21]

We start to find more Jewish interest in this servant in the second century CE, mainly in opposition to Christian claims. The initial sources for this interest are Christians. In his *Dialogue with Trypho* (ca. 160),[22] Justin Martyr adduces Isaiah's suffering servant to show how Jesus improves upon Jewish ritual. For example, after quoting all of Isaiah 52:10–54:6 (LXX) in *Dialogue* 13.2–5 (cf. 40.1), Justin contrasts Jewish ritual immersion with cleansing in the blood of the Christ, the "lamb that is led to the slaughter" (Isa 53:7). Discussion then turns more polemical when Justin concludes that the Jews deliberately tortured this innocent lamb (*Dialogue* 72.1), whom Isaiah proclaims "sinless" because "he committed no iniquity" (Isa 53:9). To Trypho's resistance to the idea of a crucified Messiah, Justin cites, among other things, Isaiah 53:3 on the "man of suffering." As for Isaiah's question, "Who has believed what we have heard?" (Isa 53:1),

Justin answers: the gentile church (*Dialogue* 89.3; 118.3). As Jeffrey Bingham puts it, "These connections may be seen as incredible by those outside the community, but they form the warp and woof of Christian faith."[23]

Origen records another debate:

> Now I remember that, on one occasion, at a disputation held with certain Jews, who were considered wise men, I quoted these prophecies, to which my Jewish opponent replied that these predictions bore reference to the whole people, regarded as one individual, and as being in a state of dispersion and suffering, in order that many proselytes might be gained among them, on account of the dispersion of the Jews among numerous heathen nations.[24]

While the church fathers were insisting on Jesus as the only possible reading of Isaiah's servant, postbiblical Jews promulgated the communal interpretation. But this particular Jewish view was only one of several options available.

Despite what Origen suggests, most of the early Jewish interpretations of the servant in Isaiah 52:13–53:12 suggest that he is an individual; for example, Targum Jonathan to Isaiah 52:13–53:12, likely composed some point before the Jewish Bar Kochba revolt (132–135 CE), reads the Hebrew of 52:13, "Behold, my servant," as "Behold, my servant, the Messiah."[25] This figure then serves as an intercessor for Israel. We cannot determine whether this reference is a response to Christian reading, though it is the earliest reference where non-Christ-believing Jews understand the servant as the Messiah.

Early rabbinic texts also generally understood the servant as an individual rather than as collective Israel.[26] Some agree with Targum Jonathan that these verses refer to the messiah—who is, of course, in their view, definitely not Jesus of Nazareth. For example, b. Sanhedrin 98b records: "The Messiah, what is his name? The Rabbis say, 'the scholar with leprosy,' as it is said, 'surely he has borne our griefs and carried our sorrows; yet we did esteem him a leper, smitten of God and afflicted.'" The passage follows a discussion in which the prophet Elijah informs Rabbi Joshua ben Levi that the messiah "sits bandaging his leprous sores one at a time, unlike the rest of the sufferers, who bandage them all at once. Why? Because he might be needed at any time and would not want to be delayed." The passage can be an anti-Christian polemic: had the messiah come, it suggests, no one would be suffering griefs and sorrows. At the same time, the rabbis responsible for this passage stress that the messiah is not a military figure or an angel, but a scholar who suffers a debilitating disease. Finally, the passage can be read as saying that the messiah may be found among the ones who suffer.

Another rabbinic image of a suffering messiah, although not based on Isaiah 52:13–53:12, appears in Pesiqta Rabbati, whose core is likely from the fifth to sixth centuries. In traditions that it utilizes, which likely date two or three centuries earlier, this text discusses the Messiah ben Ephraim.[27] This figure, who appears in a number of early and medieval Jewish sources, is typically depicted as a warrior who precedes the arrival of the "Messiah ben David," the Davidic messiah, and who sometimes dies in battle.[28] In what looks like a response to Christian claims, Pesiqta Rabbati records the willing, vicarious suffering, though not the death, of the Messiah ben Ephraim:

> [The Holy One, blessed be He,] began to talk about the terms with him [Messiah Ephraim], saying to him: In the future the sins of those that have been hidden with you {Messiah Ephraim} will bring you under an iron yoke. They will make you like a calf whose eyes grow dim; and they will choke your spirit with

[your] yoke; and because of their sins your tongue will stick to the roof of your mouth (Ps 22:16). Are you willing [to endure] this?

The Messiah said in [God's] Presence: Will this suffering [last] for many years?

The Holy One said to him: By your life and the life of My head! I have decreed for you a week [seven years]. If your soul is saddened, I will immediately banish them [the sinful souls hidden with you under the Throne of God].

[The Messiah] said in His presence: Master of the universe, I will take this upon myself with a joyful soul and a glad heart, provided that not one [person] in Israel perish; not only those who are alive should be saved in my days, but also those who are dead, who have died since [the days] of the first human being up until now should be saved [at the time of salvation] in my days {ed. pr.: but also the aborted ones}; [including] those whom You thought to create, but who were not yet created. Such [are the things] I desire, and for this I am ready to take [all this] upon myself. (36)

The prooftext for this midrash is Isaiah 60:1, "Arise, shine; for your light has come, / and the glory of the LORD has risen upon you," one of the *haftarot* (prophetic texts) of comfort read in the weeks following the ninth of Av, the day on which Jews mourn the destruction of the First and Second Temples in Jerusalem. The Messiah ben Ephraim who suffers in this Jewish text is not Jesus, the suffering is not crucifixion, and this messiah does not die. His suffering is not even based on the suffering servant passages from Isaiah.

Other Jewish texts focus on the suffering of the messiah in Isaiah 52:13–53:12. A talmudic passage (b. Sukkah 52a) specifically notes that the Messiah son of Joseph is pierced; although it quotes Zechariah

12:10, "when they look on the one whom they have pierced," it likely also alludes to Isaiah 53:5, which could be translated not, as in the NRSV, "he was wounded for our transgressions," but, following the Hebrew, "he was pierced."[29] Explicating Ruth 2:14, "Come here, and eat some of this bread, and dip your morsel in the sour wine [or "vinegar"]," the midrash Ruth Rabbah 5:6 also interprets Isaiah 53:5 messianically: "He is speaking of the king Messiah: 'Come hither,' draw near to the throne; 'and eat of thy bread,' that is the bread of the kingdom; 'and dip thy morsel in vinegar,' this refers to chastisements, as it is said, 'But he was wounded for our transgression, bruised for our iniquities.'" These interpretations show that some Jews understood this servant to be the messiah, although that messiah is for them not Jesus.

Other talmudic texts, difficult to date, understand the servant as an individual other than the messiah (b. Berakhot 5a), even as Moses (b. Sotah 14a). B. Berakhot alludes to Isaiah 53:10:

> Yet it was the will of the LORD to crush him with pain.
> When you make his life an offering for sin,
>   he shall see his offspring, and shall prolong his days;
> through him the will of the LORD shall prosper.

In doing so, the talmudist states that God may afflict with disease anyone "in whom the Lord delights." The claim does not glorify suffering. Rather, it suggests that suffering is not arbitrary, that suffering may reflect divine love (see already Prov 3:12), is to be accepted with love for God, and that rabbis too suffer.

Most medieval Jewish interpreters, well acquainted with the use of the servant passages in reference to Jesus, understand the servant as representing all Israel. For Rashi, the servant explained the Jews' persecution in the face of the First Crusade's devastation of the Rhineland Jewish communities in 1096–1099 and promised them a reward for their fidelity. As Joel Rembaum states, "It is precisely because the idea of an innocent human sacrifice affording universal atonement and reconciliation of humanity with God became so prominent in early twelfth-century France that Rashi was moved to incorporate it into his Isaiah 53 exegesis."[30]

Rashi's commentaries became standard within Jewish communities, and most writers followed him in understanding the servant as Israel punished in exile and to be restored to the land. Many of these commentators are explicitly polemical. Ibn Ezra, for example, notes, "Our opponents say that it refers to their God . . . this, however, is not possible," because a dead person cannot "see his offspring" (Isa 53:10). Emphasis on the collective interpretation also responded to anti-Jewish Christian claims that Israel's exile is a sign of divine abandonment. Jews counterclaimed that Israel's diminished status actually reflected its role—and not the role of the church that claimed to be a new Israel—as God's chosen servant.

Nevertheless, personal and even messianic interpretations of Isaiah 52:13–53:12 continued, albeit weakly, in the Middle Ages. They are found, for example, in Karaite (nonrabbinic) commentaries, including in the most important Karaite commentator, Yefet son of Eli (tenth-century Iraq and Israel), who, citing the early Karaite Benjamin ben Moses Nahawandi, claims this passage "is being said about the messiah."

Modern Jewish interpreters, following Rashi, usually understand the servant as Israel, or at least as a nonmessianic figure. Yet most Jews today, unless they have encountered Christian missionaries or studied the "man of sorrows" in art history, are unlikely to be familiar with Isaiah 52:13–53:12, since it is absent from Jewish liturgy. Perhaps the verses dropped out of Jewish liturgical readings under Christian pressure; perhaps they were never included. In contrast, Christians who follow a lectionary will hear of Isaiah's servant frequently, both implicitly and, twice, explicitly. In the *Revised Common Lectionary*, Isaiah 52:13–53:12 is proclaimed, annually, on Good Friday, the date commemorating Jesus's crucifixion. It is paired with Psalm 22, a psalm frequently interpreted christologically and quoted by Jesus on the cross (see Chapter 11); with the discussion in Hebrews 10:16–25 of Jesus as the high priest of the new covenant (see Chapter 5); and with a portion of John's passion narrative (John 18:1–19:42). Isaiah 53:4–12 is read on the twenty-second Sunday after Pentecost in Cycle B, paired with Hebrews 5:1–10 on Jesus as high priest, and Mark 10:35–45 in which Jesus tells his disciples that "the Son of Man came not to be served but to serve, and to give his life a ransom for many" (Mark 10:45).[31]

Isaiah 52:13–53:12 has yielded numerous readings, some prompted by Hebrew and Greek nuances, some polemical, and others pastoral. This diversity of interpretations warns us against reading the text in only one way or at the expense of someone else. Perhaps Jews, who have denied that Jesus is Isaiah's servant, can come to appreciate how Christians, reading typologically, adopted this interpretation. Perhaps Christians might come to appreciate that Jews have their own understandings and therefore might not read this passage only as the suffering of the servant, but as his exaltation, offering hope for those who suffer everywhere.

This passage forces Jews to wrestle with notions of vicarious atonement, especially when used to explain or justify horrific events that are void of meaning. It is inappropriate to suggest, for example, that the Shoah (Holocaust) was ultimately a good thing since it contributed to the existence of the modern State of Israel. The end does not justify the means.

Conversely, we must appreciate that some who live under oppressive circumstances believe the assurance that God understands their suffering, and therefore that their suffering has some value, some meaning. Nor should we too quickly dismiss the fact that the word translated as "servant" in both Greek and Hebrew can also mean "slave"; we see how this translation leads to 1 Peter's exhortation that slaves suffer as Jesus did, a passage with a sordid past in the United States' justification for enslavement of Africans and their descendants. All texts take on new meanings over time, and in light of our knowledge of slavery in our more recent past as well as the ongoing problem of human trafficking, we must ensure that biblical texts not be used to support oppressive practices. For some readers, any approval of "slave language" is anathema. For others, the title "slave of God" indicates that since God is the true and only master to whom loyalty is due, no human beings may ultimately own others.

We might also use the suffering servant to rally Jews and Christians together to endorse new readings of Isaiah. In 1978, the Jesuit priest Ignacio Ellacuría, rector of the Universidad Centroamericana (UCA) in El Salvador, argued that the traditional reading of the slave as a "prefiguration" of Jesus's passion "should [not] close our eyes" to the power of the words as "a real description of . . . the vast majority of humanity" today. For him, the suffering servant today "'is anyone who discharges the mission described in the Songs—anyone unjustly crucified for the sins of human beings' whose suffering produces a kind of 'expiation' through its demand for a 'public' and 'historical' return to righteousness and justice."[32] Sister Mary Francis Reis similarly asks: "Where is the suffering servant to be found today? In Flint, Michigan? In African American teens fearing to be shot by the police? In refugees in search of home? In immigrants living in fear of deportation? In the homeless and the hungry?"[33] We can all, whatever our religious affiliation, share these pointed questions prompted by Isaiah.

CHAPTER 10

❦

The Sign of Jonah

Jesus and the Sign of Jonah

THE BOOK OF Jonah is difficult to find in the Hebrew Bible. It is buried within the collection known as the twelve Minor Prophets—a group of short (only in that sense "minor") books that in antiquity were copied on a single scroll, hence the designation "Book of the Twelve." In most orders, Jonah is the fifth book there, after Obadiah, the Hebrew Bible's shortest book, and before Micah.[1]

Among the prophets, Jonah is also anomalous. Although a Hebrew prophet, Jonah is commissioned to preach to gentiles; moreover, his story is the only prophetic book *about* a prophet rather than containing words *attributed to* the prophet. Nor is the word "prophet" (Hebrew *navi'*) ever used in the work. Whereas prophets, both those depicted in 1 and 2 Kings like Elijah and Elisha and those whose words are preserved in the books that bear their names, typically find that their messages go unheeded, Jonah's brief announcement prompts immediate and complete repentance—clearly a fiction. Additionally, the book of Jonah not only offers a profound message about repentance, it is also a rollickingly funny story.[2] The same cannot be said about Jeremiah or Amos.

The book of Jonah is popularly known as "Jonah and the Whale"—but this is inaccurate. The Hebrew mentions a big fish but never a whale. Since chapter 2 finds our prophet praying from the belly of the fish, the book is often treated as a children's story, a biblical version of Pinocchio. Children can understand Jonah, but to regard Jonah as a book written only for children is a confusion of genre. It is also a confusion of genre to regard the book as history. In some circles, the story of Jonah has been a testing point regarding biblical fidelity: because "the Bible tells them so," some people believe the story must be factual. Others, including the two of us, find that despite the popular reference to the whale, Ira Gershwin's evaluation of the historical veracity of the story in his song from *Porgy and Bess* is spot-on: despite the story's insistence that Jonah "made his home in / dat fish's abdomen," Gershwin's Sportin' Life proves the good exegete with, "It ain't necessarily so."

Although the historicity of the story "ain't necessarily so," its literary value is superb and its ethical lessons essential. Like the fables of Aesop and many of the parables of Jesus, the story of Jonah gives us a lesson that we do not want to hear, but need to hear. The book of Jonah is a moral tale: provocative, entertaining, and open to several interpretations, most of which interrogate our sense of justice, remind us of the importance of repentance, proclaim the graciousness of God, affirm the potential morality of sinners, and promote the value of empathy. It comes to mean, especially in Christian contexts, an assurance of resurrection and final judgment and a foreshadowing of the mission to the gentiles. Given today's world where stereotyping, nationalism, threats of violent destruction, and a decided lack of humor mark our culture, is it especially important to read Jonah and find what meanings it still has.

To leave Jonah to children is a loss; to read Jonah only as would a child is a greater loss. The genre, whether fiction or fact, should matter little for Jews or Christians. Fiction, in short stories, in parables, or in midrashim, is often a better teacher than nonfiction.

For many Christian readers, from antiquity to the present, the book's primary meaning concerns the burial and then resurrection of Jesus. We find the first reference to, and explanation of, the "sign of Jonah" in Matthew 12:38–40. When approached by some scribes and Pharisees who ask him, "Teacher, we wish to see a sign from you," Jesus responds, "An evil and adulterous generation asks for a sign, but no sign will be given to it except the sign of the prophet Jonah. For just as Jonah was three days and three nights in the belly of the sea monster, so for three days and three nights the Son of Man will be in the heart of the earth." This quotation alludes to Jonah 1:17 (2:1 Heb.), "But the LORD provided a large fish to swallow up Jonah; and Jonah was in the belly of the fish three days and three nights." Among the earliest examples we have of Christian art are third-century sarcophagi that depict Jonah, read in this light, as a symbol of resurrection and of rest in paradise.[3]

The following verses in Matthew and Luke hint at two other interpretations of the sign of Jonah: the conversion of the gentiles and the final judgment where Jews who do not follow Jesus are condemned by representatives of the gentile world. Here is Luke's version (11:29–32; see also Matt 12:38–42):

> When the crowds were increasing, [Jesus] began to say, "This generation is an evil generation; it asks for a sign, but no sign will be given to it except the sign of Jonah. For just as Jonah became a sign to the people of Nineveh, so the Son of Man will be to this generation. The queen of the South will rise at the judgment with the people of this generation and condemn them, because she came from the ends of the earth to listen to the wisdom of Solomon, and see, something greater than Solomon is here! The people of Nineveh will rise up at the judgment with this generation and condemn it, because they repented at the proclamation of Jonah, and see, something greater than Jonah is here!"

The "queen of the South" is the queen of Sheba, who according to 1 Kings 10 marveled at King Solomon's wisdom. The people of Nineveh repent at Jonah's five-word warning. These gentiles yield, respectively, to Israel's king (Solomon) and prophet (Jonah). The Gospel writer thus conveys the message: anyone listening should submit to Jesus, for he is both the heir of King David and greater than a prophet.

It is possible that Jesus spoke, enigmatically, about the sign of Jonah, without any explication concerning either his fate or the gentile mission. According to the Gospel of Mark, which makes no mention of Jonah, Jesus's contemporaries ask him for a sign: they want some sort of proof that he is the Messiah. Healings, resuscitations, and nature miracles do not prove messianic status, for ancient prophets such as Elijah and Elisha, and contemporary Jewish charismatic figures such as Haninah ben Dosa and Honi the Circle Drawer, do the same. Wise teaching does not prove messianic status, as the stories of Solomon and biblical wisdom literature show. How can one "prove" messianic status? The people were expecting universal changes: a general resurrection from the dead where everyone returns to life, a final judgment, and peace on earth. The request is understandable: assertion needs to be backed up with action.

To this request for a sign, Jesus, according to Mark, "sighed deeply in his spirit and said, 'Why does this generation ask for a sign? Truly I tell you, no sign will be given to this generation'" (Mark 8:12). Mark has Jesus say "no sign"; Matthew and Luke offer a sign with multiple interpretations. These later two Gospels may be reflecting on and interpreting Mark's brief, more original comment. In light of their proclamation of the resurrection of Jesus and their promotion of the gentile mission, Jesus's followers reread their scriptures. They began to see new things, and to interpret in new ways the texts they held sacred—some form of what became for them the "Old Testament." In Jonah, they found confirmation of their beliefs and experiences.

But the sign of Jonah, and the book, should not be limited to interpretations in the Gospels. The book still has much to teach us. We explore in this chapter what the book meant in its ancient Hebrew context, how its images become reused in later scripture, and how Jews and Christians across the centuries have understood these four short chapters.

The Story of Jonah in Its Earliest Historical Context

JONAH'S FIRST READERS, likely living in the aftermath of the Babylonian exile and the repatriation of many Judeans back to their homeland in the sixth century BCE, would find in these forty-eight verses messages about divine compassion, the nature of prophecy, God's universality, the importance of repentance, and the need to recognize their own calling. The book, like the comparable four-chapter book of Ruth, responds to some of the more nationalistic voices that sought to preserve the repatriated community's identity by keeping a distance from outsiders. We note this concern for universalism since we have heard from our Christian students that Judaism (by which they mean the "Old Testament") is xenophobic and that Jesus, in turn, invents universalism. To the contrary, for the Tanakh, the God of Israel is the God of the world, and people are judged not according to ethnicity but by ethics.[4] Jonah is in the same universalistic tradition as the first chapter of Genesis, which proclaims that all people are created in the divine image. It follows Deuteronomy 10:19, which commands, "You shall also love the stranger, for you were strangers in the land of Egypt." The book of Ruth depicts the welcome of the Moabite Ruth into the Israelite community, and she becomes the great-grandmother of King David. It anticipates the Jerusalem Temple and the synagogues of antiquity through today, where gentiles were, and are, also welcome.

The book begins with God commanding Jonah to speak against the "great city" of Nineveh, the seventh-century Assyrian capital. Jonah, with good prophetic antecedents, is not eager to take on the task. Prophets generally do not want to be prophets; most resist their calls. Moses attempts to beg off the commission to set his people free from Egyptian slavery by complaining about his lack of eloquence (Exod 4:10). Jeremiah insists, "Ah, Lord GOD! Truly I do not know how to speak, for I am only a boy" (Jer 1:6). Prophets tell us what we do not want to hear; who wants that job? Earlier prophets sought to talk their way out of their commissions; Jonah, in an extreme move, flees.

Instead of heading northeastward to Nineveh, Jonah attempts "to flee to Tarshish from the presence of the LORD" (1:3). Tarshish is often viewed as a city in Spain. The similar sounding "Tarshish" and "Tarsus," the home of Paul, will be one of various connectors of the prophet to the apostle, but we are not there yet.

Alternatively, Jonah may know from the beginning that the God of Israel is also the God of the world. What then is he fleeing? The book of Jonah can be understood to convey "the theme of an individual running away from his mission, from his destiny, even from himself (Jonah 1:1–3)."[5] His charge is to bring the Ninevites to repentance, and it is not a charge he wants because he knows that, if the Ninevites repent, God will have mercy on them. As he states in 4:2, in explaining his own concerns, "That is why I fled to Tarshish at the beginning; for I knew that you are a gracious God and merciful." Jonah does not want the brutal Assyrians, Israel's archenemy, to be rescued; he wants them obliterated.

To persuade Jonah that he has no choice in the matter of his commission, God raises up a "big storm" (NRSV: "mighty storm"). Everything in Jonah is "big": the Hebrew term *gadol* (big, mighty, great) appears fourteen times in these four chapters: big city (1:2; 3:2, 3; 4:11), big wind (1:4), big fear (1:10, 16), big storm (1:12), big fish (1:17

[2:1 Heb.]), big (great, i.e., noble) people (3:5, 7), big (i.e., great) evil (4:1, indicating Jonah's anger), big joy (4:6), and even big growth of a plant (4:10). It is an overblown, clearly fictional, story. The word "big" is so big in this story that we can imagine the (largely illiterate) people filling in the word "big," when prompted by the storyteller, at the appropriate locations.

The sailors, despite their maritime prowess, panic. Chapter 1 plays upon the Hebrew root y-r-', which means both "to fear" and "to revere": In 1:5, as a result of the storm, "the mariners were afraid"; in 1:10 they become "even more afraid"; and in 1:16, "the men feared the LORD even more [literally "they had a big fear"]"—the phrases get longer and longer and so reflect a growing fear. The same root y-r-', "to fear," describes Jonah in 1:9, when he tells the mariners, "I fear [most translations replace "fear" with "worship"] the LORD, the God of heaven."

Despite this perfect storm, Jonah does not panic. To the contrary, he falls asleep in the hold of the ship (the Septuagint adds that he snores).

The Gospel authors parody the parody (Mark 4:35–41; Matt 8:23–27; Luke 8:22–25). In a scene known as the "stilling of the storm," Mark recounts, "A great windstorm arose, and the waves beat into the boat, so that the boat was already being swamped," but Jesus "was in the stern, asleep on the cushion" (Mark 4:37–38). The disciples, some of whom are fishermen and therefore should know their way around a boat, take the role of the sailors: they fear drowning and realize that the sleeping Jesus is the key to their rescue. Jesus calms the water and the wind. He then rebukes his disciples for their lack of faith. Later, Jesus will walk on water (Matt 14:26; Mark 6:48–49; John 6:19) rather than sink, like Jonah, to the depths.[6] The more one knows of Israel's scripture, the more meaningful the New Testament becomes.

Awakened by the sailors, who learn from casting lots that Jonah is the cause of the storm, Jonah identifies himself: "I am a Hebrew" (1:9; the Hebrew term is 'ivri). The Septuagint reads, "I am a servant of the LORD."[7] It is easy to explain how the divergence occurred. The Hebrew word for "servant" is 'eved, the same term used for Isaiah's "suffering servant." While 'ivri and 'eved look completely different in English, in Hebrew the letter "r" (ר) is very similar to the letter "d" (ד), as we noted on page 19. Next, the term translated as "LORD" is, in Hebrew, the famous four-letter name of God, rendered into English as YHWH. The first letter of this divine name, the Y, which looks in Hebrew like an apostrophe, is also an abbreviation for YHWH.[8] The Greek translators read an "r" as a "d," took the "y" as an abbreviation, and logically came up with "servant of the LORD."

עברי   עבדי = עבד יהוה

Hebrew   Servant of the LORD

Both readings are correct, and each enhances the other. For Jewish readers, "Hebrew" makes an ethnic connection; for Christian readers, Jonah's evocation of the "servant" in the Greek version makes a closer connection to Jesus. This is the sort of textual problem that brings a big smile to biblical scholars.

After identifying himself, Jonah continues, "I fear [NRSV: "worship"] the LORD, the God of heaven, who made the sea and the dry land" (1:9). The comment drips with irony: this very God is, as far as the sailors are concerned, the one about to drown them. And the scene is even more ironic given the fact that just as Jonah claims to be a true worshiper, he is in the process of fleeing his divine commission. The gentile sailors, it will turn out, prove the more faithful—they fear, worship, and understand God better than Jonah—and so they anticipate the repentance of the Ninevites.

When the sailors, aware that Jonah is the cause of the big storm, ask him what they should do, the ever-helpful prophet urges these pious sailors to throw him overboard. Jonah, the epitome of a passive-aggressive personality, knows that he has caused the problem, but he refuses to take responsibility for fixing it. He prefers to have the sailors kill him rather than to jump in the sea on his own volition. Only after expending every effort to save themselves and their passenger, only when they are convinced that they are about to drown, do the sailors acquiesce. They toss the prophet overboard.

When the sea then calms, "the men feared the LORD even more, and they offered a sacrifice to the LORD and made vows" (1:16). The sailors do the right thing. Since the sailors, recognizing divine power, turn to proper worship, there is a chance for Nineveh as well. And perhaps even Jonah will learn from them.

And yet, the story, still in chapter 1, raises essential moral questions. It asks: Do we kill one person for the good of the many? In the Gospel of John, Caiaphas the high priest, in explaining why it is necessary to deliver Jesus to the Romans, insists, "it is better for you to have one man die for the people than to have the whole nation destroyed" (John 11:50). Or, do we take the chance that working together we might all survive? More, it asks to what extent we control our fate and to what extent there are here what we call accidents of nature. Sixteen verses, filled with major questions. And all our culture gives us is "It's about a guy in a whale"!

Jonah, cast out of the boat, is swallowed by a big fish, in Hebrew, *dag gadol*. The Greek translation has *kētos megas* (the technical term cetology, from the Greek, means the study of whales and other large sea mammals). *Kētos* appears in the Greek translation of Job 3:8 where the Hebrew reads "leviathan." The "whale" comes from William Tyndale's 1534 translation of Matthew 12:40, followed by the King James Version. For Jonah 1:17 (2:1 Heb.), Tyndale has "greate fyshe" and King James, "great fish."

After three days in the fish (Geppetto, Pinocchio's maker and father, spent a good two years in a similar situation), *then* Jonah offers a prayer (Jonah 2). Not only is his timing a bit late, the prayer itself is a mash-up of the Psalms and the Prophets. It may well be an earlier composition repurposed by the author; as we'll see in our discussion of the Psalms, a number were generic prayers available for worshipers to apply to their own situations. Although the psalm (metaphorically) mentions the deep and waters, it is not the type of prayer we would expect from a person trapped in the belly of a big fish and threatened with either digestion or drowning.

Jonah, who is among the Bible's whinier characters, blames God for his own predicament. He prays, "You cast me into the deep" (2:3 [2:4 Heb.]); to the contrary, Jonah landed in the water only after the desperate sailors did all they could to protect him. Jonah continues, "I am driven away from your sight" (2:4 [2:5 Heb.]); to the contrary, it was Jonah who attempted to run. Jonah condemns pagans by noting, "Those who worship vain idols / forsake their true loyalty" (2:8 [2:9 Heb.]). To the contrary, those gentile sailors acted rightly, and it will be the idolatrous Ninevites who demonstrate repentance. Once again, still within a comedic setting but with an ethical sting, the story poses broad ethical questions: Have self-serving prayers any value? Is it ever appropriate to cast aspersions on others? Do we make ourselves look good by making others look bad, and if we must resort to this type of self-affirmation, how pathetic are we?

The scene also raises questions of what it means to live. Jonah asserts that God can hear him from the "belly of Sheol" (2:2 [2:3 Heb.]), that is, the underworld. By speaking of Sheol, Jonah understands his situation in terms of what we might call a "near-death experience." He then sees himself as having been restored to life: as he puts it, God "brought up my life from the Pit" (2:6 [2:7 Heb.]; here, "Pit" is a synonym for Sheol). He gets a second chance, just as will the people of Nineveh. With these references to rescue from Sheol, the book of Jonah prompts readers to think about what it means to be alive to the world, its possibilities and promises. The common cliché about behaving like an ostrich with its head in the sand speaks to the same concern. While some later readers will see an allusion here to resurrection, the story of Jonah first demands that its readers ask a question about *this life*: What is my role in life? If I get a second chance, can I do what I should have done the first time?

After "three days and three nights" (1:17 [2:1 Heb.]), on the fourth day the fish vomits up Jonah (2:10 [2:11 Heb.]). Those early readers of the book, upon hearing the reference to three days, already anticipated something momentous on day four. This three-four pattern, common in the Tanakh, is most explicit in Amos 1–2, which contains eight units beginning "For three transgressions of X [the name of a city-state], and for four, I will not revoke the punishment." The climactic fourth sin is the one that dooms the state. The same refrain accompanies Elijah's confrontation with the prophets of Baal in 1 Kings 18:33–34. The narrator sets up Elijah's climactic action by noting, "He said, 'Fill four jars with water and pour it on the burnt offering and on the wood.' Then he said, 'Do it a second time'; and they did it a second time. Again he said, 'Do it a third time'; and they did it a third time"—after this cycle of three, the wood on the altar miraculously ignites. Sometimes this pattern is implicit: Judah, Jacob's most important son from whom the Davidic dynasty derives, is born fourth, after Reuben, Simeon, and Levi.[9] Jonah's original audience, hearing of "three days," would have expected the climax on the fourth day. The story of Jesus, which consistently evokes the scriptures of Israel, plays upon this pattern by presenting his resurrection not after three days, but on the third day. He thus, as often happens, evokes the convention only to break it.

Following Jonah's prayer, God speaks to the fish, which then disgorges its passenger, whole-bodied and unharmed, onto dry land. Oddly, in the Hebrew, the fish is grammatically male in Jonah 1:17 (2:1 Heb.) (twice) and in 2:10 (2:11 Heb.), but female in 2:1 (2:2 Heb.). This might be a case of stylistic variation, especially since the fish's sex is irrelevant to the story. But as we shall see, some rabbinic sources, who read biblical texts closely, have explanations.

The first and third chapters open with the same command from God that Jonah "go to Nineveh, that great city"; Jonah gets a do-over. He finally reaches Nineveh, "an exceedingly large [i.e., "very big"] city, a three days' walk across" (3:3). Nineveh, although capital of the Assyrian Empire, was not that large—the story, again, exaggerates. Then Jonah issues his prediction. A marvel of brevity, the prophecy consists of five (Hebrew) words, which translate to: "Forty days more, and Nineveh shall be overthrown!" (3:4). (The Septuagint offers only "three days," perhaps to match the time Jonah spent in the fish; Justin Martyr's *Dialogue with Trypho* offers both versions [*Dialogue* 107].) The Hebrew root for "overthrown" (3:4), *h-p-ch*, literally means to "turn" or to "reverse," and thus Jonah ironically predicts the fulfillment of his prophecy when the Ninevites "turn" from evil to good.[10]

Upon hearing the prophecy, the people show their repentance by putting on sackcloth and then proclaiming a fast. When "the news reached the king of Nineveh" (3:6), whether news of Jonah's proclamation or the people's reaction, he too dons sackcloth. There was in fact no "king of Nineveh." A comparable error would be the "king of London" or the "president of Washington, DC." This king decrees, "No human being or animal, no herd or flock, shall taste anything. They shall not feed, nor shall they drink water. Human beings and animals shall be covered with sackcloth, and they shall cry mightily to God. All shall turn from their evil ways and from the violence that is in their hands" (3:7–8). That is, he goes one step further than the people: from no food to no water. He can be read as the model of righteousness; in our more cynical moments, he reminds us of politicians who want to do what the polls suggest. The result is what both king and city wished: they are not destroyed.

Nineveh may be modeled after the Sodom of Genesis 18:20–21, which was also overturned (*h-p-ch*); its evil also ascends to God ("for their wickedness has come up before me," Jonah 1:2). Yet, unlike Sodom's population, the Ninevites immediately "turn from their evil ways and from the violence that is in their hands" (3:8). They do so while aware that repentance does not guarantee forgiveness. As the king says, "Who knows? God may relent and change his mind; he may turn from his fierce anger, so that we do not perish" (3:9). The Assyrians, infamous for cruelly treating enemies, conquering Israel, and exiling large populations (this is the origin of the legend of the "Ten Lost Tribes"), repent. If *they* can repent and be forgiven, the book intimates, anyone can!

Jonah himself is "displeased with big displeasure and angry" (4:1, authors' translation) at this result. He was hoping to experience schadenfreude. He wanted the evil people to be punished rather than given a second chance. He obviously did not learn his lesson from his time in the big fish.

Once again, Jonah prays, "O LORD! Is not this what I said while I was still in my own country? That is why I fled to Tarshish at the beginning; for I knew that you are a gracious God and merciful, slow to anger, and abounding in steadfast love, and ready to relent from punishing" (4:2). Jonah's theology is a shortened form of the attributes of God known from the Decalogue (Exod 20:5–6; Deut 5:9–10) and especially Exodus 34:6–7:

> The LORD, the LORD,
> a God merciful and gracious,
> slow to anger,

and abounding in steadfast love and faithfulness,

keeping steadfast love for the thousandth generation,

forgiving iniquity and transgression and sin,

yet by no means clearing the guilty,

but visiting the iniquity of the parents

upon the children

and the children's children,

to the third and the fourth generation.

Yet Jonah, like other texts (see Deut 7:9–10), cites only part of this formula; he omits "yet by no means clearing the guilty, but visiting the iniquity of the parents upon the children." This omission, which would have been obvious to the book's original audience, allows even Jonah to stress God's compassionate nature. Indeed, the last line of the text concerns this divine care: "And should I not be concerned about Nineveh?" (Jonah 4:11).

Jonah does not want a merciful God who offers second chances; he wants a God who will destroy Nineveh for its current great wickedness and so confirm the prophecy. The book thus prompts us to ask what sort of God we want: the one who forgives or the one who destroys? It asks what we want our enemy's fate to be: to be erased from the earth, or allowed to work toward reconciliation? As we saw with our discussion of the Sermon on the Mount and the question of what to do in cases of physical injury, mercy without justice is intolerable, but so, the book of Jonah insists, is justice without mercy.

God spares the Ninevites, but in the next generation, those same Ninevites would not spare Israel. Here we have another brilliant irony. Although fictional, the book of Jonah draws upon the historical figure Jonah ben Amittai. According to 2 Kings 14:25, this Jonah was a nationalistic prophet who lived in the Northern Kingdom of Israel during the reign of King Jeroboam II (d. ca. 742 BCE); he was active at the same time as the prophets Amos and Hosea. The same verse in 2 Kings that identifies Jonah indicates that, at Jonah's message, Jeroboam had "restored the border of Israel from Lebo-hamath as far as the Sea of the Arabah," that is, Jeroboam extended the borders to where they were according to 1 Kings 8:65 at the idealized time of King Solomon. The next verse indicates, "For the Lord saw that the distress of Israel was very bitter; there was no one left, bond or free, and no one to help Israel" (2 Kgs 14:26). The original Jonah spoke about territorial advancement, not about care for the poor. Jonah is thus the perfect protagonist for our story: the prophet who promoted Israel's expansion becomes the one to promote, instead, Nineveh's repentance.

Even more ironic, had the Ninevites not repented, God would have destroyed their city. Had God destroyed their city, they would not, in the next generation, have destroyed Israel. The repentant one day may be the sinful the next; we all have the potential both to repent and to ravage.

At this point, ethical questions abound: Is a preemptive strike ever appropriate? Do we destroy a country that, within a generation, may destroy us? Do we assess groups by what they have done in the past, by how they act in the present, or by what it is feared they will do in the future? Is it our responsibility to rebuke our enemies—should we tell foreign nations how to behave? Like any good biblical text from either testament, the book of Jonah helps us ask the right questions.

Distressed with the repentance of the Ninevites, the prophet decamps to a place outside the city, builds a small booth as a shelter from the sun, and waits to see what happens. God arranges for a bush or gourd (the Septuagint proffers a giant pumpkin) to grow up over Jonah to protect him from the heat. Jonah is finally "very happy"; literally, he has "big joy" (4:6). But then God causes a worm to attack the bush and the east wind and hot sun to distress the prophet. Again, Jonah complains, "It is better for me to die than to live" (4:8). This portrayal parodies Elijah, who "came and sat down under a solitary broom tree. He asked that he might die: 'It is enough; now, O LORD, take away my life, for I am no better than my ancestors'" (1 Kgs 19:4). Elijah, persecuted by King Ahab, had good reason to be distressed; but Jonah? Not so much.

God condemns Jonah for being angry about the bush, "for which you did not labor and which you did not grow" (Jonah 4:10). Then, likely with exasperation, God continues, "Should I not be concerned about Nineveh, that great [or big] city, in which there are more than a hundred and twenty thousand persons . . . and also many animals?" (4:11). Floods and droughts, dirty bombs and chemical warfare, but we focus only on our own comfort: the air-conditioning is not working; the garden needs weeding. Remarkably, in the Hebrew of 4:9 the author uses the same number of words when God speaks ("Is it right for you to be angry about the bush?") and when Jonah speaks ("Yes, angry enough to die"), creating a symmetry between God and prophet. Missing, however, is the symmetry in values. God has the last word.

God's mercy is not limited to humanity. The last verse reinforces the story's concern for the animals, already introduced if not by the great fish than by the picture of hungry and thirsty sheep and cows covered with sackcloth, and shows that divine care extends beyond humanity. Not only is the book replete with references to animals, the Hebrew word "Jonah" means "dove" and Nineveh means "the city of the fish." The book ends with God's question to the prophet about divine compassion not only for the people, but "also many animals." The book thus insists that we attend to animals, but that we not *act like them.*

This question about compassion ends the book, but it does not end discussion of it.

JONAH IN CHRISTIAN EYES

For the New Testament, Jesus is not the only figure identified with Jonah. The ancient prophet also finds symbolic descendants in both Peter and Paul.

Peter's nickname comes from the Greek *petros*, "rock" (hence "petrified"). In Matthew 16:18a, Jesus says to him, "you are Peter [*petros* (the masculine form)], and on this rock [*petra* (the feminine)] I will build my church." However, Peter's given name is Simon bar (*bar* is Aramaic for "son of") Jonah. Peter enacts his role as "son of Jonah" by bringing the message of repentance to gentiles (so Matt 28:19), echoed further in postbiblical legends of Peter's journey to Rome.

Indeed, Peter's reluctance to visit the gentile centurion Cornelius, even after commanded by God (see Acts 10), evokes Jonah's earlier reluctance to preach to Nineveh.[11] Peter states, "You yourselves know that it is unlawful for a Jew to associate with or to visit a Gentile" (Acts 10:28). The problem here is that Peter is, simply, incorrect. There is no such law. Jonah seeks to run away from God rather than visit gentiles, and he resents divine mercy when the gentiles receive it. Jonah attempts to run away from his commission; Peter goes a step further by inventing a law in order to get out of visiting a gentile.[12] Both Jonah and Peter have something to learn.

We can also draw connections between the ancient prophet and Paul, the New Testament's primary evangelist to the gentiles. The book of Acts mentions that Paul is from Tarsus (e.g., Acts 9:11; 21:39; 22:3; Paul, in his letters, never mentions his city of origin), which was early on associated with Tarshish. Tarsus is in Turkey; we do not know where Jonah's "Tarshish" was located, but it has the connotation of "far away." Isaiah 66:19, speaking in God's voice, mentions Tarshish as among the "coastlands far away that have not heard of my fame or seen my glory" and then avows, "they shall declare my glory among the nations." The connection to Paul is made by the similar sounds of the city names and the idea of the gentiles coming to worship Israel's God. But that is not the only prompt connecting Paul to Jonah.

Like Jonah, Paul becomes an "apostle" (from the Greek meaning "one sent") to the gentiles. And like Jonah, Paul takes sea voyages and faces shipwreck. Paul tells us in his own words, "Three times I was shipwrecked; for a night and a day I was adrift at sea" (2 Cor 11:25). The book of Acts develops the stories of Paul onboard and overboard in humorous ways that recall Jonah: trial by ordeal; the possible death and miraculous rescue of the protagonist; conversion of the gentiles; even an animal, a viper, whose threat is defused, or defanged. The sailors in Jonah's story were convinced that Jonah's God had power, since after they pitched the prophet overboard, the storm subsided. In Acts, a miracle of nature—Paul does not die from the viper's bite—prompts the gentiles to regard him as a god (Acts 28:4–6). The author of Acts, like the author of Jonah, knew how to tell a good story.

Early Christian art also draws a connection between prophet and apostle. Both Jonah and Paul typically appear as bald. Visually the two figures—each requiring a direct prod from the deity, each with a message to the gentiles, each associated with maritime dangers—look alike. To explain Jonah's lack of hair, one tradition suggests it was burned off by the heat of the fish's insides.[13]

Beyond the New Testament, the church fathers, never shy to develop allegorical readings, found an ocean of meanings in this short book. Jerome, the great Christian translator of the Vulgate, which became the standard Bible for Western Christendom for more than a millennium, found a connection between Jonah and the passion narrative. Jonah tells the sailors to toss him overboard, and then these sailors pray to Jonah's God, "Please, O LORD, we pray, do not let us perish on account of this man's life. Do not make us guilty of innocent blood; for you, O LORD, have done as it pleased you" (Jonah 1:14). Jerome cites Matthew 27:4, which records that Judas, like Jonah, said to the high priest, "I have sinned by betraying innocent blood"; in Matthew 27:24, Matthew writes, "So when Pilate saw that he could do nothing, but rather that a riot was beginning, he took some water and washed his hands before the crowd, saying, 'I am innocent of this man's blood; see to it yourselves.'" Thus, according to Jerome's *Commentary on Matthew*, the story of Jonah anticipates both Judas Iscariot and Pontius Pilate.

In his *Commentary on Jonah*, Jerome also saw the prophet as prefiguring Jesus: they each leave their home of safety and descend into the world of sin. Yvonne Sherwood notes several additional allegorical readings offered by church fathers, including the view that Jonah asleep in the boat is "the Christ-foetus curled in the womb of the virgin,"[14] and the "sleeping Jonah as a laid-out Christ-corpse, a sign of Jesus in a death-stupor in the tomb."[15] The abbot Columba (ca. 610), whose name in Latin means "dove," identified with Jonah: he was exiled from his home in Burgundy (France), and so he saw himself as "cast into the sea" like the prophet. Images of the prophet entering the fish with his clothes and hair and emerging not only bald but also naked came to symbolize rebirth through baptism.[16] Once the door is open to allegorical interpretations, they will be as numerous as the drops of water in the ocean.

We also need to determine whether an interpretation is moral or not. Reading Jonah as promoting God's universal concern and compassion, the giving of second chances, care for the animal world, and the importance of repenting—all good. Seeing a prediction of resurrection and of final judgment by righteous gentiles? Plausible. But some readings are not only less convincing, they are dangerous—and, we suggest, theologically toxic.

Martin Luther started well: He saw Jonah, whose name means "dove," as the prototype of the Holy Spirit. Correctly, he notes that the Holy Spirit descends on Jesus at his baptism like a "dove" (so Mark 1:10). Yet Luther, whose antipathy toward Judaism is well known, also saw the book of Jonah as representing "Judaism's envy and jealousy." He regarded the book as designed to teach the hopelessness of anyone who relies on the Jewish law rather than on God's grace. In Luther's works and many others, Jonah is a representative *both* of the Christ *and* of the faults and fall of the Jews and Judaism: he is Jewish nationalism versus Christian universalism; he understands a (Jewish) God of wrath rather than a (Christian) God of love. Jonah is, as Sherwood quotes Luther, "the first to make Judaism contemptible and superfluous."[17]

During the Enlightenment, at the rise of academic biblical criticism, some German professors followed in Luther's wake. Janet Howe Gaines summarizes their views: "Jonah typifies the pejorative view of Jews as stingy, heartless, vengeful, unforgiving, and wrongheaded, while Nineveh is seen to characterize the loving, compassionate, superior morality of Christians beloved to God."[18] This interpretation focuses on Jonah's behavior only and not on the way the book as a whole criticizes him. It ignores its significant universalistic message even as it proclaims an anti-Jewish one. And it misses the point of the book: Jonah is an antihero who represents what we *should not do*.

Correctly, the evangelical *New Application Bible* warns against such readings:

Within the last hundred years [the author omits centuries of prior commentary] some Christian interpreters have controverted and flattened the message of the book of Jonah in an irresponsible and anti-Semitic explanation of its meaning. Jonah has been called "a salutary lesson to the Jews . . . renowned for their stubbornness and lack of faith"[19] and seen to be "a type of the narrow, blind, prejudiced, and fanatic Jews."[20]

There are many readings of the book of Jonah within the Christian tradition. Not all are commendable.

Jonah in Jewish Eyes

Jewish interpretation of Jonah during the Hellenistic period is most easily located in the book of Tobit. Written a century or two before the New Testament, Tobit parodies a parody. In Tobit, a giant fish leaps onto the land and attempts to swallow Tobias (Tobit's son), the story's romantic lead. Tobias is then rescued by an angel in disguise. The humorous reuse of the humorous Jonah is an important reminder that the Bible contains funny stories.

Ironically, whereas the book of Jonah speaks to the righteousness of gentiles, be they the pious sailors or the repentant Ninevites, the book of Tobit speaks against the Ninevites. Tobit and his family, from the tribe of Naphtali, are part of the "Ten Lost Tribes" taken into exile when Assyria conquered the Northern Kingdom of Israel. The book ends with the line, "Before he [Tobit] died he heard of the destruction of Nineveh.... Tobias praised God for all he had done to the people of Nineveh and Assyria; before he died he rejoiced over Nineveh, and he blessed the Lord God forever and ever. Amen" (Tob 14:15). Tobias and Tobit see what Jonah wanted to see but did not: the destruction of Nineveh. The rejoicing is both understandable and, from our twenty-first-century perspective, troubling.

In later periods, Jonah is especially well known in the Jewish tradition because it serves as the *haftarah*, or prophetic reading, for the most sacred of Jewish days, Yom Kippur, the Day of Atonement.[21]

During the afternoon service, congregations hear the entire book chanted in Hebrew, and congregants can also follow along in the vernacular. The custom of reading Jonah on Yom Kippur is first attested in the Babylonian Talmud (Megillah 31a); although completed around the seventh century CE, the Talmud incorporates earlier traditions. The connection of Jonah to Yom Kippur is the book's concern for repentance: even the most wicked, if they sincerely repent, will be forgiven. This theme is highlighted by the custom in most synagogues of reading Micah 7:18–20 immediately upon the completion of the book:

> Who is a God like you, pardoning iniquity
> and passing over the transgression
> of the remnant of your possession?
> He does not retain his anger forever,
> because he delights in showing clemency.
> He will again have compassion upon us;
> he will tread our iniquities under foot.
> You will cast all our sins
> into the depths of the sea.
> You will show faithfulness to Jacob
> and unswerving loyalty to Abraham,
> as you have sworn to our ancestors
> from the days of old.

Jonah especially captured the attention of classical rabbinic and medieval Jewish interpreters. The Babylonian Talmud (Sanhedrin 89b) takes up the question of whether Jonah's prophecy failed: it suggests that the prophecy was never revoked but simply was fulfilled after the prophet's lifetime.[22]

The Talmud also addresses the question of divine mercy via a manipulative appeal to the animals: the Ninevites "then said before God, Master of the Universe, if You do not have mercy on us, we will not have mercy on these animals. Even if we are not worthy of Your mercy, these animals have not sinned" (b. Ta'anit 16a).[23] This idea shows remarkable continuity with one of the themes we outlined above—the divine care extending to the animal kingdom.

Pirkei de-Rabbi Eliezer, a text from late antiquity, identifies in chapter 33 Jonah's mother as the widow from Zarephath (1 Kgs 17:8–24) and thus Jonah as the child whom Elijah resurrected from the dead; this is especially appropriate since as we note above, Jonah, like Elijah, asked God to take his life. Readers familiar with the Gospel of Luke will recall that Jesus invokes this widow's story in the sermon he gives in the Nazareth synagogue (Luke 4:25–26); there the widow and her son represent a focus not only on Jesus's miraculous abilities but also on the gentile mission.

Pirkei de-Rabbi Eliezer 10 may also use Jonah to engage in anti-Christian polemic. It presents the sailors as converting to Judaism through circumcision, and it notes that their blood of circumcision (rather than the Christ's blood) "is like the blood of sacrifice."[24] Elsewhere, it claims that the repentance of the Ninevites was insincere, and thereby it undercuts Matthew's claim that the Ninevites will judge the Jews of Jesus's time.[25]

Jews, reading Jonah, not only promoted the theme of repentance, but they developed it in creative ways. Likely, they recognized the fanciful nature of the text and its exaggerated rhetoric, and so, like the author of Tobit, also parodied the parody. For example, b. Ta'anit 16a cites Rabbi Shmuel as describing the king of Nineveh's proclamation, "Even if one stole a beam and built it into his building, he must tear down the entire building and return the beam to its owner."[26] The medieval midrashic compilation Yalqut Shimoni then proposes that the Ninevites, "on the third day,"

all repented from their evil ways, and returned to their owners even
lost objects found in fields, vineyards, market places, or streets. And
when they found stolen bricks in the royal palace—they tore down
the royal palace and returned the bricks to their rightful owners. And
any vineyard that had two stolen seedlings or two stolen trees—
they uprooted them and returned them to the owner. If a garment
contained two strands of stolen thread—they unraveled it and returned
the threads to their owner. . . . [In the case of property found in an
abandoned building] [t]he judge would search for the deed of that
building, and find one stretching back 35 generations [i.e., back to
the time of Noah!], and find a descendent of that person who hid the
property and return it to its owners.[27]

This is one of many instances where the rabbis are being playful.

Jewish commentators, who typically fill in missing details, also
offer numerous suggestions for why Jonah initially fled. The text becomes the object of serious playfulness. One early rabbi suggests that
Jonah knew God would relent and therefore that Jonah would look like
a false prophet; others propose that Jonah feared that the Ninevites,
by repenting, would show up the Jews, who did not repent. A third
reading has Jonah knowing, since he is a prophet, that the Assyrians
would destroy Israel; by attempting to escape his commission, Jonah
was also attempting to ensure Nineveh's destruction. His situation is
comparable to that of Elisha, whom God commands to commission
Hazael of Syria to stage a coup (2 Kgs 8). Elisha weeps, "Because I
know the evil that you will do to the people of Israel" (8:12).

Medieval Jewish commentators go out of their way to celebrate
the righteousness of the sailors—a far cry from Luther's perception
that the book is narrowly nationalistic. They imagine a dialogue in
which the sailors beg Jonah to tell them what he had done.[28] Rashi
has them ask, "Perhaps you have been remiss in the performance

of your occupation, and this calamity is your punishment?" David Kimchi speculates, "Perhaps you engaged in an immoral or criminal occupation as a result of which you are guilty?" Ibn Ezra proposes that the sailors, witnessing the calming of the sea at the moment Jonah left the ship, went directly to Nineveh to announce the miracle. Thus, they serve as an advance party that prepared the way for Jonah's proclamation of repentance. A similar approach surfaces in Herman Melville's *Moby-Dick*, which itself evokes the book of Jonah. Melville composes a sermon, preached by Father Mapple in the Seamen's Bethel in New Bedford (the pulpit is shaped like the prow of a ship); this sermon could have come directly from rabbinic sources. In it, the sailors speculate as to what Jonah had done to bring about the storm. "Jack, he's robbed a widow"; or, "Joe, do you mark him; he's a bigamist"; or, "Harry lad, I guess he's the adulterer that broke jail in old Gomorrah, or belike, one of the missing murderers from Sodom."

The Christian reading of Jonah in terms of resurrection also finds its way into Jewish thought. This is not surprising—Jewish and Christian thinkers often influenced one another. By the early rabbinic period, many Jews believed in the future resurrection of the dead. We can already see this idea taking root in the Gospels, which are early witnesses to first-century Jewish belief. Echoing Pharisaic teaching, Jesus's friend Martha expresses her surety that she will see her dead brother, Lazarus, again: she tells Jesus, "I know that he will rise again in the resurrection on the last day" (John 11:24). The medieval book of Jewish mysticism, the Zohar, finds Jonah to be about resurrection (2.199ab): it reads the book allegorically as "a parable of human experience from the soul's entering the body until God's awakening the dead when death will be no more."[29]

As for the problem of the fish: Despite the attempts by readers from John Calvin to biblical literalists today to *prove* that a fish could swallow a human being and that the human could live, no such fish existed then, or now. Some later rabbinic commentators, noting that the fish changed genders between the end of chapter 1 and the beginning of chapter 2 (see above), propose that a male fish swallowed Jonah and that Jonah was relatively comfortable. Therefore, God arranged for a different female fish to claim the prophet; the female, pregnant with 365,000 little fishies, offered less hospitable accommodations. Jonah then decides to pray his way out of the cramped quarters (Midrash Jonah 1:7). The fifth-century CE mosaic recently unearthed at the Huqoq synagogue in the Galilee offers a different solution to the threefold mention of fish of different genders: it depicts Jonah being swallowed by three fish, each swallowing one another![30]

Jonah's use in the New Testament has made it important for the Christian community, as has its use during Yom Kippur for the Jewish community. It is among the best-known biblical stories, though as we have noted, only small parts of the book, focused on the "whale," are typically remembered. The sign of Jonah has been interpreted as a call to repentance, an assertion of divine mercy, a prediction of both Jesus's resurrection and the general resurrection of the dead, an anti-nationalist manifesto, and an anti-Jewish screed. Perhaps it functions best as we suspect Jesus used it: as an open sign for each listener to fill in. We must not only learn what the book might have meant to its original audience but also appreciate how it has been interpreted over time, for different times call for different emphases.

But the sign of Jonah should not be open to free play. The rest of the biblical text helps us to control against incorrect interpretations. The worst way of reading the book is to see Jonah as a role model, since the biblical text suggests that Jonah is, rather, a negative example: he is the one who wants destruction rather than redemption; he wants justice without mercy; he is concerned about himself, not about others. He's also whiny. If we read Jonah as a hero rather than an antihero—that is, if we miss the textual clues that throughout lead us to disagree with Jonah—then we will wind up with Luther's anti-Jewish reading.[31]

Jonah is also a warning. In attempting to flee from his calling, he shirks his responsibilities not only to others but to himself. He runs from his fate rather than toward it. Jonah asks us all: What are we called to do, and how do we follow difficult callings, even those that call on us to engage positively with our enemies?

The book of Jonah next insists that life has meaning. Jonah, the antihero, twice seeks his own demise at the hand of another: "He said to them [the sailors], 'Pick me up and throw me into the sea; then the sea will quiet down'" (1:12); "And now, O LORD, please take my life from me, for it is better for me to die than to live" (4:3). To wish death is not the right response. The book then extends this concern for life to the world of nature: of winds and rain, oceans and hills, giant fish and giant gourds, hungry worms and repenting animals. They are not incidental to the plot. The book insists that our actions have consequences for nature, and that nature impinges on our lives, for good or for ill. But in either case, it insists: pay attention to the natural world.

Jonah, with its universal import, could have served as a book to unite all people who hold it sacred. On July 24, 2014, the Islamic State (ISIS) bombed what according to tradition was the tomb of Jonah in Mosul, Iraq, a site revered by many Jews, Christians, and Muslims. This destroyed the physical sign of Jonah, but the literary sign of Jonah remains as a legacy of interfaith cooperation and a portent of what happens when intolerance, fundamentalism, and fanaticism reign.

CHAPTER 11

✺

"My God, My God, Why Have You Forsaken Me?"

Jesus and Psalm 22

At three o'clock Jesus cried out with a loud voice, "Eloi, Eloi, lema sabachthani?" which means, "My God, my God, why have you forsaken me?" (Mark 15:34)

THIS "cry of dereliction" is the opening verse of Psalm 22, a psalm that underlies the entire depiction of Jesus's death on the cross.[1] Psalm 22, a lament psalm, speaks not only of despair but also, ultimately, of hope. It also grounds the passion narrative. The extent to which the Gospels describe what actually happened, and the extent to which the passion accounts are meditations, or midrashim, on the psalm, will remain debated in biblical scholarship. Before turning to the psalm in its original context and then in later Jewish interpretation, we begin with how it and other psalms function in the Gospel accounts. (We use English verse numbers only for Psalm 22; the Hebrew counts as verse 1 the superscription, which in English is verse 0, and thus the Hebrew verse numbers are all greater by one than those found in the English.)

Alluding to Psalm 22:18, "they divide my clothes among themselves, / and for my clothing they cast lots," all four Gospels depict the Roman soldiers casting lots for Jesus's clothing. As Mark 15:24 states, "And they crucified him, and divided his clothes among them, casting lots to decide what each should take" (also Matt 27:35; Luke

23:34; John 19:23–24). John 19:23–24 introduces a separate item of clothing:

> They took his clothes [plural] and divided them into four parts, one for each soldier. They also took his tunic [singular]; now the tunic was seamless, woven in one piece from the top. So they said to one another, "Let us not tear it, but cast lots for it to see who will get it." This was to fulfill what the scripture says,
>
> > "They divided my clothes among themselves,
> >
> > and for my clothing they cast lots."[2]

The last citation is a direct quotation of Psalm 22:18 from the Septuagint.

In Psalm 22:7, the psalmist describes how "All who see me mock at me; / they make mouths at me, they shake their heads"; in verse 8 the afflicted hears his enemies state, "Commit your cause to the LORD; let him deliver— / let him rescue the one in whom he delights!" Similarly, Mark 15:29 (cf. Matt 27:39–40) reports, "Those who passed by derided him, shaking their heads and saying, 'Aha! You who would destroy the temple and build it in three days.'" Continuing to list Jesus's enemies, Mark 15:31–32a (cf. Matt 27:41–42) adds, "In the same way the chief priests, along with the scribes, were also mocking him among themselves and saying, 'He saved others; he cannot save himself. Let the Messiah, the King of Israel, come down from the cross now, so that we may see and believe.'" Joel Marcus points out that "unlike the mockers in the psalm, though, who call on *God* to save the innocent Sufferer, those in Mark call on *Jesus* to save *himself.*"[3] There may be Marcan irony here: the taunters place Jesus in the role of God.

Matthew develops Mark's narrative by depicting Jesus's enemies as taunting him, "He trusts in God; let God deliver him now, if he wants to; for he said, 'I am God's Son'" (Matt 27:43). The verse adverts to Psalm 22:4–5:

> In you our ancestors trusted;
>> they trusted, and you delivered them.
> To you they cried, and were saved;
>> in you they trusted, and were not put to shame.

Luke elaborates by depicting the two other crucified men, with one condemning the other for his taunting of Jesus. The "good thief" then implores, "Jesus, remember me when you come into your kingdom." Jesus replies, "Truly I tell you, today you will be with me in Paradise" (Luke 23:42–43). Behind both Matthew and Luke, as in Mark, there may lie an echo of Psalm 22:8. Here the speaker is changed; the verse is not a taunt from Jesus's opponents but a plea from a man who will die alongside him. And here, the "Lord" in question is Jesus.

Luke and John omit the cry. Luke, who tends to omit Aramaic words, has much else going on at the cross, including the two thieves and the famous "Father, forgive them; for they do not know what they are doing" (Luke 23:34).[4] The cry would be inconsistent with the Christology of the Gospel of John; the Johannine Jesus is never abandoned or forsaken by God. To the contrary, he states, "The Father and I are one" (John 10:30) and "I am not alone because the Father is with me" (16:32). John offers no agony in Gethsemane; to the contrary, John depicts a serene, stoic Christ who even controls the moment of his death: in John, Jesus's last words are "It is finished" (19:30). The evangelist then recounts, "He bowed his head and gave up his spirit" (19:30; the KJV translates, "gave up the ghost").[5]

But John adds other allusions to Psalm 22. John records that when Jesus "knew that all was now finished, he said (in order to fulfill the scripture), 'I am thirsty'" (John 19:28). Given the echoes of Psalm

22 throughout the scene, John is likely thinking of Psalm 22:15: "my mouth is dried up like a potsherd, / and my tongue sticks to my jaws; / you lay me in the dust of death." John is also alluding to Jesus's conversation with the Samaritan woman, which begins with his saying to her, "Give me a drink" (John 4:7). The allusion suggests his desire for communion with his followers. Second, in 19:31–37, John offers a number of fulfillment citations. For example, John notes that because "the Jews did not want the bodies left on the cross during the sabbath" (v. 31), they requested that Pilate order the legs of the victims to be broken. Without using their legs to push up their bodies to get air into their lungs, victims would die quickly of asphyxiation. But the soldiers discovered that Jesus was already dead. Rather than break Jesus's legs, a soldier pierces his side with a sword. John explains, "These things occurred so that the scripture might be fulfilled, 'None of his bones shall be broken'" and "'They will look on the one whom they have pierced'" (vv. 36, 37). The primary reference here is to the eschatological prophecy in Zechariah 12:10: "And I will pour out a spirit of compassion and supplication on the house of David and the inhabitants of Jerusalem, so that, when they look on the one whom they have pierced, they shall mourn for him, as one mourns for an only child, and weep bitterly over him, as one weeps over a firstborn." This reference to piercing is also at home in Psalm 22, where verses 16–17 can be translated, "They have *pierced* my hands and feet—I can count all my bones." The connection between these verses and the wounds of the cross, perhaps hinted at in Luke 24:39, where the resurrected Jesus tells his disciples "Look at my hands and my feet; see that it is I myself," becomes an explicit prooftext in the writings of the early church fathers.[6]

Psalm 22 also informs other early Christian writings. Hebrews 2:11b–12 uses Psalm 22 as a prooftext to talk about relationships within the community: here, Jesus rather than the supplicant of the original psalm says, "I will proclaim your name to my brothers and sisters, / in the midst of the congregation I will praise you" (v. 12). The author is quoting Psalm 22:22, "I will tell of your name to my brothers and sisters; / in the midst of the congregation I will praise you." Jerome (*Commentary on Matthew* 4.196) repurposes the same verse by remarking on the connection between Jesus's urging the women at his tomb, "go and tell my brothers to go to Galilee; there they will see me" (Matt 28:10), and Psalm 22:22a, where the supplicant affirms, "I will tell of your name to my brothers and sisters."[7] By late antiquity, "Every verse [of the Psalm] was associated with Jesus."[8] At least one writer, Theodore of Mopsuestia (350–428 CE), claimed that the psalm should not be read as prophecy, but an ecumenical council at Constantinople in 553 condemned him.

Supplemented with a few other allusions to the Psalms, the entire crucifixion narrative could be reconstructed from Psalm 22 (with additions from Psalm 69, which we discuss below). Why Psalm 22 in particular? Several answers are possible.

One option is that everything the Gospels report actually happened, from Jesus's thirst, to the casting of lots for the garments, to the taunters who wag their heads, to those who tell him to trust in the Lord, to the cry of dereliction. Conservative commentators advocate this conclusion. More liberal ones—especially those who note the time between when the events narrated in the Gospels happened and when their authors wrote about them, differences among the Gospels, the variability of eyewitness testimonies, and the tendency of the Gospel writers to use the "Old Testament" as a template for telling the story of Jesus—offer other explanations.

A second possibility is that Jesus called out simply "My God" (Hebrew *'eli*) or "God," and his followers filled in the rest of Psalm 22. Perhaps he had the rest of the psalm in mind but in his agony lacked the strength to recite its entirety.

As a third possibility, perhaps Jesus called for the prophet Elijah, whose name in Hebrew (*'Eliya* or *'Eliyahu*) is very similar to *'eli*, "my God."[9] This suggestion has support from Matthew and Mark. Mark 15:35 (cf. Matt 27:47) states, "When some of the bystanders heard it [the cry], they said, 'Listen, he is calling for Elijah.'" This interpretation is possible, since many Jews expected that the prophet Elijah, bodily assumed into heaven (2 Kgs 2:11; so the song "Swing Low, Sweet Chariot"), would return to inaugurate the messianic age. The book of Malachi, the last book of the prophetic corpus (the Nevi'im) and the last book in the Old Testament (i.e., the Christian canon), ends with the prediction, "Lo, I will send you the prophet Elijah before the great and terrible day of the LORD comes. He will turn the hearts of parents to their children and the hearts of children to their parents, so that I will not come and strike the land with a curse" (Mal 4:5–6; 3:23–24 Heb.). The tradition of Elijah as the precursor of the Messiah appears when the disciples ask Jesus, "Why do the scribes say that Elijah must come first?" (Mark 9:11; cf. Matt 17:10), and when Herod Antipas and others inquire as to whether Jesus is Elijah returned (Mark 6:15). The New Testament here rereads Malachi's prophecy: instead of having Elijah announce the coming of the Day of the LORD, understood as the *messianic age*, Elijah—in the role of John the Baptist—announces the coming of the *Messiah*.

A fourth suggestion is that Mark, the earliest Gospel writer, placed the words on Jesus's lips. Mark emphasizes the necessity of Jesus's suffering and death (e.g., 8:31–32), and Mark's initial audience may have seen themselves as suffering along with him. The psalm assures them that neither Jesus nor they are rejected or abandoned.[10] Mark, like all the evangelists, was a composer and not merely a recorder, and so he could have imagined what Jesus would have said on various occasions. Moreover, Mark and Mark's readers would know that this psalm ends with the universal proclamation of divine favor. Just as the Gospel ends with an empty tomb but anticipates that readers know the rest of the story, so Mark gives the first verse of the psalm, leads readers through other citations, and allows those readers to fill in the glorious ending themselves.

Did Jesus issue an inarticulate cry, a call for God, a call to Elijah, the first verse of Psalm 22? Did Mark, inspired by Psalm 22, compose the scene on the basis of piety rather than history? We have no secure way of answering these questions. We can, however, understand how the psalm originally functioned, explain how and why the New Testament readings change the original meanings, and see how the psalm served as both parable and polemic in the postbiblical period.

AN ASIDE: OTHER PSALMS
IN THE NEW TESTAMENT

ALTHOUGH the focus of this chapter is on Psalm 22, it is not the only psalm the New Testament writers cite to connect Jesus and Israel's scriptures. We have already seen how Psalm 110, with its reference to Melchizedek, appears in Hebrews and elsewhere (see Chapter 5). We note here two other psalms of importance to the early Christ-believing communities: Psalms 69 and 118.

Psalm 69 is a lament, like Psalm 22. Mark alludes to the lines from Psalm 69:21 (69:22 Heb.), "They gave me poison for food, / and for my thirst they gave me vinegar to drink," in describing how, after the people at the cross heard Jesus call for Elijah, "someone ran, filled a sponge with sour wine, put it on a stick, and gave it to him to drink" (Mark 15:36a, with variants in Matt 27:34; Luke 23:36; John 19:28–29). The Gospel writers do not need to provide the citation; readers familiar with the psalms would recognize it.

John offers two additional references to Psalm 69. First, in describing the disruption of Temple activities, John makes several changes to the Synoptic accounts. Whereas in the Synoptic Gospels the Temple incident begins the passion narrative, it occurs for John in chapter 2, early in Jesus's public career. In the Synoptics, Jesus states, "Is it not written, 'My house shall be called a house of prayer for all nations'? / But you have made it a den of robbers" (Mark 11:17, with variations in

Matt 21:13 and Luke 19:46; the allusions are to Isa 56:7 and Jer 7:11). There is nothing about a house of prayer or a den of robbers in John's account. Rather, Jesus tells the vendors, "Take these things out of here! Stop making my Father's house a marketplace!" (John 2:16). Then John glosses this injunction, "His disciples remembered that it was written, 'Zeal for your house will consume me'" (John 2:17), a reference to Psalm 69:9 (69:10 Heb.), "It is zeal for your house that has consumed me; / the insults of those who insult you have fallen on me."

John later uses Psalm 69 to detail how Jesus's own people, "the Jews," generally rejected him. We have already seen this motif in John's citation of Isaiah 53:1 and 6:10. Continuing this motif, John has Jesus state, "But now they have seen and hated both me and my Father. It was to fulfill the word that is written in their law, 'They hated me without a cause'" (John 15:24b–25). The allusion is not to the Torah, the "law," but to Psalm 69:4a (69:5a Heb.):

> More in number than the hairs of my head
> > are those who hate me without cause;
> many are those who would destroy me,
> > my enemies who accuse me falsely.

Here "Torah" refers to the entirety of Israel's scriptures.

Psalm 69 appears once in the book of Acts and twice in Romans. Acts takes the psalm as prophetic—and about Judas. Describing Judas's death, "he burst open in the middle and his bowels gushed out" in a field that became known as "the Field of Blood" (Acts 1:18–19), Luke writes, "For it is written in the book of Psalms, 'Let his homestead become desolate, / and let there be no one to live in it'" (Acts 1:20). The allusion is to Psalm 69:25 (69:26 Heb.), "May their camp be a desolation; / let no one live in their tents."

For Paul, the psalm has additional christological relevance. Romans 15:3 understands Psalm 69:6 (69:7 Heb.) prophetically when it says, "For Christ did not please himself; but, as it is written, 'The insults of those who insult you have fallen on me.'" The citation is to the second half of Psalm 69:9 (69:10 Heb.), the same verse John cites in relation to the Temple incident. After "zeal for your house that has consumed me," the psalmist laments, "the insults of those who insult you have fallen on me" (Ps 69:9 [69:10 Heb.]). Paul's quotation of Psalm 69:22–23 (69:23–24 Heb.) in Romans 11:9–10 understands the psalm prophetically in a different way, as referring to current non-Messianic Jews rather than to Jesus. Paul says:

> And David says,
>> "Let their table become a snare and a trap,
>>> a stumbling block and a retribution for them;
>> let their eyes be darkened so that they cannot see,
>>> and keep their backs forever bent."

Here Paul picks up on the imprecation of the enemies in Psalm 69—a typical element of laments of the individual that was missing in Psalm 22.

Psalms of rejoicing spoke to the followers of Jesus and influenced how they told his story. Psalm 118 accompanies Jesus's entry into Jerusalem. In later Jewish tradition, Psalms 113–118 are called the Hallel ("praise") collection and are recited on Jewish festivals, including Passover, but it is uncertain whether this custom dates to the late Second Temple period.[11] Mark 11:9–10 (cf. Matt 21:9; Luke 19:38; John 12:13) records:

> Then those who went ahead and those who followed were shouting,
>> "Hosanna!

> Blessed is the one who comes in the name of the Lord!
> Blessed is the coming kingdom of our ancestor David!
> Hosanna in the highest heaven!"

The citation is Psalm 118:26, "Blessed is the one who comes in the name of the LORD." "Hosanna" is a transliteration of the Hebrew *hoshi'ah na'*, "save!" Psalm 118:22–23 becomes a prediction of the general rejection of Jesus by his fellow Jews; in Mark 12:10–11 (cf. Matt 21:42; Luke 20:17), Jesus asks in an almost exact citation of the psalm:

> Have you not read this scripture:
> > "The stone that the builders rejected
> >   has become the cornerstone;
> > this was the Lord's doing,
> >   and it is amazing in our eyes"?

This same psalm, having the same function, appears also in Acts 4:11 and 1 Peter 2:4, 6–7.

Like the writers of the Dead Sea Scrolls and the rabbinic texts, Jesus and his disciples found their story in ancient scripture and in turn interpreted that scripture in light of their own experiences. Where they see Jesus throughout, the Jewish community interpreted the same psalms in quite diverse ways.

PSALM 22 IN THE SCRIPTURES OF ISRAEL

BOTH Jewish and Christian traditions attribute most or all of the psalms to King David, whom the King James Version of 2 Samuel 23:1 calls "the sweet psalmist of Israel," but the Hebrew of the psalms is much later than early tenth-century Hebrew, the period when David lived. The book of Psalms is rather a compilation of liturgical poetry from many periods and by many authors,[12] and initial verses that attribute Davidic authorship are likely secondary additions to what were originally anonymous poems.[13] Thus, while the superscription of Psalm 22 (v. 0) reads "A Psalm of David," Davidic authorship should not be assumed. The book of Psalms came together gradually: the verse "the prayers of David son of Jesse are ended" appears halfway through the Psalter (72:20).

Although attributed to David, we cannot know who wrote Psalm 22; we can, however, estimate its date. Based on linguistic analysis of its Hebrew and its placement toward the beginning of the Psalter, it likely derives from the preexilic period, before the Jerusalem Temple's destruction in 586 BCE.

Few psalms provide internal evidence of how they were used, and their superscriptions, which may preserve such evidence, contain much obscure technical terminology. Psalm 22's superscription, "To the leader: according to The Deer of the Dawn," may suggest that the psalm was chanted to the tune of the well-known song "The Deer of the Dawn," just as many Christian hymnals use the same tune for several different texts.

We can also posit how some psalms were used from 1 Samuel 1–2, where Hannah prays twice. Her first prayer is in prose, is a vow, and is directly relevant to her yearning for a child. First Samuel 1:11 records, "She made this vow: 'O LORD of hosts, if only you will look on the misery of your servant, and remember me, and not forget your servant, but will give to your servant a male child, then I will set him before you as a nazirite until the day of his death. He shall drink neither wine nor intoxicants, and no razor shall touch his head.'" Her second prayer, offered after the child, Samuel, has been born, is in poetry. We might have expected this prayer to thank God for opening her womb, but this is not the case. Instead, what follows is a royal psalm—a psalm related to or recited by the Davidic king—that concludes, "he will give strength to his king, / and exalt the power of his anointed" (1 Sam 2:10). This psalm addresses Hannah's situation only tangentially, when she notes, "The barren has borne seven, / but she who has many children is forlorn" (v. 5). Why then attribute this psalm to Hannah?

It is probable that 1 Samuel 2 represents how psalms were used. In some cases, people composed their own prayers. These were typically in prose, and they reflected the individual's specific situation. For example, when Miriam is afflicted with a serious skin disease (often mistranslated as "leprosy"), Moses prays briefly, in prose (Num 12:13), "O God, please heal her." However, ancient Israelites believed that extreme situations, whether dire or thankful, necessitated more formal poetic prayers. In such cases, the individual would go to a shrine, or to the Jerusalem Temple, and would ask for an official, time-tested psalm. It is likely that a Levite recited such a psalm, and the (probably illiterate) worshiper would recite the words after him.[14]

The Levites had ready-made psalms for many different situations of need and appreciation, but not every situation had an ideal psalm. This lack of direct relationship explains the partial fit between Hannah's situation and her psalm—at least her psalm mentions childlessness, and its themes of competition and of victory over enemies are relevant to her rivalry with her co-wife, Peninnah. We might imagine a person in a situation like Hannah's to be moved by some verses in this psalm but not by others—this is true for most people even today who recite formal prayers. We may recite the familiar Psalm 23, "The LORD is my shepherd," and completely relate to "Even though I walk through the darkest valley" (or "the shadow of death") but find ourselves less drawn to "You prepare a table before me / in the presence of my enemies." Perhaps someone could, for extra payment, request a Levite to compose a new psalm tailored for the situation. Such psalms might then become part of the Levite's repertoire and could then be reused, perhaps with modifications, by other worshipers.

These psalms would have fit into different categories, just as we categorize songs today: love songs, patriotic songs, camp songs, and so on. Biblical scholars have a method for helping us understand how to categorize the psalms, and so we can better determine how they were used. The German scholar Hermann Gunkel (1862–1932) shaped the way we now understand Psalms through what is called the form-critical approach. Form criticism explores the formal structure of biblical writings as well as the social and institutional settings (German *Sitz im Leben*, literally "situation in life") of these structures. To use a modern analogy: We know by structure and other formal features that a song beginning with "one hundred bottles of beer on the wall" and having ninety-nine more verses that all say the same thing will have a different setting and purpose than a song beginning with "Amazing grace, how great thou art." Gunkel used this insight to divide the Psalter into different genres based on formal structures as well as on vocabulary. Under his influence, two of the first questions scholars ask of any psalm are, "What is the psalm's genre?" and "What is its *Sitz im Leben* or social setting?"[15] Gunkel characterized most of the psalms according to genre: hymns, songs about God's enthronement, communal complaint psalms, royal psalms, individual complaint songs, and individual thanksgiving psalms.[16] We have already seen a "royal psalm" placed on Hannah's lips. More recent studies have refined and renamed some of these categories; for example, individual complaint songs are now more commonly called laments of the individual.

Of these genres, Psalm 22 fits the "individual complaint song" or lament, which, according to Gunkel, "form[s] the *basic material of the psalter*."[17] Psalm 22 has many elements that characterize such laments of individuals: it opens with an invocation, offers numerous specific complaints, calls on God for help (using the imperative), offers God a motivation to hear the pleas, and concludes with certainty that the plea has been heard.[18] Thus, while we often read Psalm 22 as a unique work, it is very conventional.

The invocation is found at the beginning of verse 1, "My God, my God"; the repetition reflects the supplicant's great need to get God's attention by insisting twice that God is "my God." The individual focus then appears, forcefully, in the first two verses (emphasis added):

> My God, my God, why have you forsaken *me*?
>> Why are you so far from helping *me*, from the words of *my* groaning?
> O my God, *I* cry by day, but you do not answer;
>> and by night, but find no rest.

Such individual focus typifies these laments. The God of the individual lament psalms is a personal God, one the psalmist understands as responding to human need.

The complaints or laments are interspersed in the first two-thirds of the psalm. They include "But I am a worm, and not human; / scorned by others, and despised by the people" (v. 6) and "All who see me mock at me; / they make mouths at me, they shake their heads" (v. 7). The laments continue in verses 16 and 17: "For dogs are all around me; / a company of evildoers encircles me. / My hands and feet have shriveled; / I can count all my bones. / They stare and gloat over me." As is typical of such laments, no precise diagnosis of the sufferer can be determined; because of this lack of precision, the psalms can serve many situations, including Jesus suffering on the cross.

Although visceral, the laments are also poetic. For example, "they divide my clothes among themselves, / and for my clothing they cast lots" (22:18) is typical "synonymous parallelism," where the second couplet restates the first in a slightly different form. Here, the first part of the couplet, part A, in the Hebrew mentions "garments," which are grammatically plural, while the term of "clothing" in part B is grammatically singular. However, the singular term "clothing" is a collective and so indicates more than one clothing item, as in Psalm 45:13b: "The princess is decked in her chamber with gold-woven clothing" (authors' translation). The Septuagint maintains this plural-singular distinction by translating the Hebrew for both "garments" and "clothing" with the same word, the first in the plural and the second in the singular.

The Synoptic Gospels appreciate that the singular "clothing" of part B is a poetic restatement of part A and thus have the soldiers dividing Jesus's clothing only once, via lots. John, finding a distinction between the "garments" in part A and the singular "clothing" in part B, suggests that Jesus's singular tunic was not divided but taken by one of the soldiers.

The psalmist's complaints are not limited to the actions of his enemies. The opening verse is a complaint against God: "why have you forsaken me? / Why are you so far from helping me, from the words of my groaning?" This image of divine abandonment is frequent in the Psalter. Elsewhere in the Tanakh, discussion of divine abandonment is related to sin, as in Deuteronomy 31:17a, where God says: "My anger will be kindled against them in that day. I will forsake them and hide my face from them." In Psalms, individuals who feel abandoned believe that they are guiltless. Thus, the question "Why have you forsaken me?" is not merely rhetorical.[19] The psalmist is reminding God of his or her distress (Hebrew does not distinguish between masculine and feminine for the first person, and 1 Samuel 1–2 shows that women as well as men prayed); the approach is calling God to account. Because many of the psalmists of lament are convinced of their own innocence, their psalms can be understood as protest literature that addresses the problem of theodicy, the justice of God.

The rest of Psalm 22 contains many more calls for divine assistance, often in the imperative: "But you, O LORD, do not be far away! / O my help, come quickly to my aid!" (v. 19) and "Deliver my soul from the sword, / my life from the power of the dog!" (v. 20). Although present-day worshipers might consider it impolite to issue commands to God, ancient Israel did not; such imperatives are common in psalms, especially in laments of the individual. We can see similar commands in Jesus's famous "Our Father" prayer: "Give us this day our daily bread" (Matt 6:11; see Luke 11:3) and "deliver us from evil" (Matt 6:13b KJV) are among several invocations in the imperative.

As is typical, this psalmist offers several different reasons why God should listen. For example, descriptions of grave illness attempt to elicit divine sympathy. Other verses insist that such aid is part of the divine nature: "Yet you are holy, / enthroned on the praises of Israel" (v. 3). This aid is also consistent with God's past behavior:

> In you our ancestors trusted;
>> they trusted, and you delivered them.
> To you they cried, and were saved;
>> in you they trusted, and were not put to shame. (vv. 4–5)

Further, the speaker has already experienced this divine concern:

> Yet it was you who took me from the womb;
>> you kept me safe on my mother's breast.
> On you I was cast from my birth,
>> and since my mother bore me you have been my God.
>> (vv. 9–10)

By the end of the psalm, the speaker will praise God (v. 22) "in the midst of the congregation" and speak to "all you offspring of Jacob" (v. 23)—that is, the psalmist will make a public proclamation. The psalm's conclusion expands the address: "all the ends of the earth . . . all the families of the nations . . . all who sleep in the earth . . . all who go down to the dust . . . posterity . . . future generations . . . a people yet unborn" (vv. 24–31).

Many images and even phrases of Psalm 22 are conventional, appearing throughout the Psalter. The enemies described in Psalm 22 are described similarly in other laments of an individual, as we have seen in the application of Psalm 69 to the death of Judas.[20] Psalm 35:21, "they open wide their mouths against me," offers a direct parallel to 22:13, "they open wide their mouths at me, / like a ravening and roaring lion." Psalm 22:8 quotes the enemies' mocking taunt, "Commit your cause to the LORD; let him deliver— / let him rescue the one in whom he delights!"; another psalmist quotes enemies saying, "There is no help for you in God" (3:2). The demand in 22:19, "come quickly to my aid!," finds strong parallels in Psalm 38:22 (38:23 Heb.), "Make haste to help me"; in Psalm 40:13 (40:14 Heb.), "O LORD, make haste to help me"; and in Psalm 71:12, "O my God, make haste to help me!" The vow made to God in distress in 22:25, "my vows I will pay before those who fear him," also appears in Psalm 56:12 (56:13 Heb.), "My vows to you I must perform, O God; / I will render thank offerings to you," and in Psalm 66:13, "I will come into your house with burnt offerings; / I will pay you my vows."

Psalm 22 does have a few distinct features.[21] Its piling on of rhetorical arguments is otherwise unattested; these "consist of an extended argument about the speaker's worthiness, with both logical and emotional appeals to God's own past behavior, eye-witness testimony form[ing] the speaker's mocking opponents and reminders to God of having directly observed the speaker's birth."[22] Next, Psalm 22 uses extensive animal metaphors, of both the sufferer and the persecutors; the image of a "worm" (v. 6, "But I am a worm, and not human") effectively suggests dehumanization.[23] Third, unlike many laments, this psalm does not call for vengeance or for a curse against the enemies.[24] This may have been one of several factors commending the psalm to Jesus's followers. The opening of the psalm is also unusual—only here in the Tanakh is the word "my God," Hebrew *'eli*, doubled. The use of *'eli* to address God so directly and personally is found thirteen times in the Tanakh, eleven in Psalms, and three in Psalm 22 (twice in v. 1, and once in v. 10). Again, this detail may have been of particular appeal to Jesus and his followers.

Finally, Psalm 22 is more tightly structured than most psalms. It divides neatly into three sections of nearly equal size: vv. 1–11, 12–21, and 22–31.[25] The first two sections largely mirror one another. The first section is demarcated by an *inclusio*—a repetition that functions to delimit or bookend a section: verse 1 asks, "Why are you so *far* from helping me?" and verse 11 begins, "Do not be *far* from me." The second unit introduces three kinds of animal: bulls (v. 12), a lion

(v. 13), and dogs (v. 16); these are repeated in the same unit in reverse order: dog (v. 20), lion (v. 21), and wild bulls/oxen (v. 21). This elegant structure, frequent in Israel's scriptures, is called a chiasm, or an a-b-c/c-b-a pattern. The final section is less structured, though it too may be chiastic; this chiasm highlights the central verse 28, "For dominion belongs to the LORD, / and he rules over the nations."

We have already seen several elements in Psalm 22 that make it relevant to the Synoptic Gospels' depiction of a suffering Messiah and to John's concern for Jesus's rejection. But there is even more that attracted the evangelists to this psalm. In general, the Septuagint and the few Dead Sea Scroll fragments of Psalm 22 agree with the Masoretic Text. The main exception is a single word, *ka'ari*, in verse 16 (v. 17 Heb.)—and this problematic word, which some have understood as "pierced," stands behind the connection of this psalm to Jesus.[26]

The NRSV translates this verse, "For dogs are all around me; / a company of evildoers encircles me. / My hands and feet have shriveled" (22:16); the NJPS offers, "Dogs surround me; a pack of evil ones closes in on me, like lions [they maul] my hands and feet" (22:17); the English Standard Version, following the King James Version, reads, "For dogs encompass me; / a company of evildoers encircles me; / they have pierced my hands and feet" (22:16). The versions translate (and interpret) the Hebrew word *ka'ari* as "have shriveled," "like lions," or "they have pierced." The NJPS accurately reflects the Masoretic Text, which has the preposition and definite article *ka-*, "like the," followed by the noun *'ari*, "a lion," but it must supply a verb, which it prints in brackets. The reference to lions fits the rest of the psalm, which is replete with animal imagery. The NRSV emends the text slightly, and, based on an Akkadian root, reads the Hebrew word in question as *krw*, "shriveled." Still others read the word as *ka'aru*, and, on the basis of an Arabic cognate, translate "they have bound."

(The final letters representing "y" [י] and "u" [ו] are almost identical, and a Dead Sea Scroll fragment, 5/6ḤeverPs, may read ka'aru—the letter in question is ambiguous.) Another proposal suggests dividing the verse differently and so reading, "Dogs surround me, a pack of wicked ones. Like a lion they circumscribe my hands and feet."[27]

The Septuagint (Ps 21:17 LXX)—the version used by most New Testament authors—translates the word in question as ōruxan, which means "gouged" and, hence, "pierced."[28] This reading most likely reflects a different Hebrew text—not ka'ari, but krw, from the root k-r-h, "to dig." This reading is possible—the two words are graphically similar. However, the Hebrew root k-r-h is never else-where used with reference to people, and never elsewhere does it connote piercing. From "dig," some translators as early as the first century CE began to read "pierced" in the sense of "bore through." Plausibly, they were influenced by Zechariah 12:10, which speaks of a "pierced" figure ("when they look on me, on him whom they have pierced, they shall mourn for him"; see Chapter 9). The two other early Jewish Greek translations, Aquila and Symmachus, both render the Hebrew term as "bound," which fits the word's Arabic cognate. Complicating matters more, an earlier edition of Aquila offered not "bound" but "disfigured."[29] The targum, on the other hand, supplies an extra verb and so reads "they bite my hands and feet like a lion."

It is unlikely that we can ever securely determine what this Hebrew word originally read. Therefore, neither Jewish apologists who ac-cuse Christians of misreading the text, nor Christian commentators, such as John Calvin, with his notice that there are "strong grounds for conjecturing that this passage has been fraudulently corrupted by the Jews . . . in their gross ignorance of history,"[30] should have the last word. Whatever the determination, it should make some sense in terms of the lament of an individual: the psalm should be able to be recited by anyone seeking God's attention.

When Psalms Become Prophecy

TRADITIONAL Christian readings require Psalm 22 to function as prophecy and require viewing King David, the reputed author, as a prophet. Deftly summarizing this view, Mark H. Heinemann concludes that David authored Psalm 22 and that "David was conscious of speaking of the future," for "if David was aware that God had spoken about his descendants in the distant future (2 Sam 7:19; Ps 89:29, 36), and if on at least two other occasions he had knowingly looked into the future of his greatest descendant, the Messiah [Ps 16 and Ps 110:1], then it seems likely that he wrote with awareness in Psalm 22."[31] In this reading, psalms become prophecy.

The problem here is that the Tanakh never explicitly indicates that the psalms are prophetic. Nor does it directly ascribe prophetic ability to David, although a few verses come close. For example, Nehemiah 12:24 calls David "the man of God," a term for a prophet like Elijah or Elisha. The first two verses of 2 Samuel 23, David's deathbed speech, read:

> Now these are the last words of David:
> > The oracle of David, son of Jesse,
> > > the oracle of the man whom God exalted,
> > the anointed of the God of Jacob,
> > > the favorite of the Strong One of Israel:

> The spirit of the LORD speaks through me,
>> his word is upon my tongue. (2 Sam 23:1–2)

But nothing following indicates David as a prophet predicting the future, and "the spirit," which in some biblical texts refers to prophetic ability (see especially Num 11:25–26), here more likely refers to God's musical inspiration.

But the idea that the book of Psalms is prophetic is probably not a New Testament innovation. This idea first appears in the Qumran Psalms Scroll, which we can date by handwriting (paleography) to the early first century CE. The scroll contains several psalms found in the scriptures of Israel as well as others from the Septuagint and the Peshitta (the Syriac translation), a few previously unknown poems, and a list categorizing David's musical output of 446 psalms. The author then notes (11Q5 27:11), "All these he composed through prophecy given him by the Most High." That David composed "through prophecy" can, but need not, suggest that the psalms are to be interpreted *as* prophecies.

The idea that the psalms themselves are prophetic is expressed in the Qumran pesher literature on Psalms. For example, 4QPesherPs[a] interprets Psalm 37:23–24:

> Our steps are made firm by the LORD,
>> when he delights in our way;
> though we stumble, we shall not fall headlong,
>> for the LORD holds us by the hand,

as a reference to "the Priest, the [Righteous] Teacher, [whom] God [ch]ose as the pillar."[32] The dominant Qumran use is consistent with the psalm's original purpose: it can be recited by anyone feeling divine abandonment.

By the Middle Ages, many Jews regarded David as divinely in-spired. Abraham ibn Ezra says, "But I tend to agree with the Sages, their memory for a blessing, that this entire book [the Psalter] is di-vinely inspired."[33] However, divine inspiration is not the same thing as prophetic ability—and it is unclear whether viewing the psalms as prophetic was widely believed at the time of Jesus.

The Talmud never, to the best of our knowledge (despite Ibn Ez-ra's statement), claims that the Psalter is a prophetic book. The clos-est it comes to this idea is in a discussion in b. Pesachim 117a of why some psalms begin "A psalm of David" while others begin "Of David a psalm." This discussion suggests that if a psalm begins "Of David a psalm," it "teaches that the Divine Presence [Shechinah] rested upon him first and afterward he recited the song. However, if a psalm opens with 'A psalm of David,' this teaches that he first recited the song, and afterward the Divine Presence rested upon him."[34]

We have seen several claims such as, "It is hardly controversial, then, that at least portions of individual psalms were regarded as 'prophecy' or 'prophetic texts' at Qumran and in Second Temple Ju-daism more generally."[35] This assertion, however, goes well beyond the evidence. Only a small number of Jewish sources consider indi-vidual psalms, or the book as a whole, to be David's inspired words, and in no extant case before the Jesus movement do we find Psalm 22 read as prophecy. Jews had multiple other ways of understanding the psalm, including, in the Middle Ages, as prophetic. But the prophe-cies applied to Esther, to a messianic figure other than Jesus, and to the Jewish people as a whole.

Psalm 22 in Jewish Sources

THE EARLIEST rabbinic sources rarely cite Psalm 22; perhaps the rabbis ignored it because it was so significant to early Christians.[36] The first evidence we have for what might be rabbinic interpretation comes not from the rabbis but from Justin Martyr. Justin's *Dialogue with Trypho* 98 begins by quoting Psalm 22 "in order that you may hear His [Jesus's] reverence to the Father"—and on he goes. In chapter 115, Justin recounts, "As Trypho was about to reply and contradict me," but he withholds Trypho's remarks. It is Justin's book, and he will have the last word:

David in the twenty-first Psalm [i.e., Psalm 22 in the Hebrew enumeration] thus refers to the suffering and to the cross in a parable of mystery: "They pierced my hands and my feet; they counted all my bones. They considered and gazed on me; they parted my garments among themselves, and cast lots upon my vesture." For when they crucified Him, driving in the nails, they pierced His hands and feet; and those who crucified Him parted His garments among themselves, each casting lots for what he chose to have, and receiving according to the decision of the lot. And this very Psalm you maintain does not refer to Christ; for you are in all respects blind, and do not understand that no one in your nation who has been called King or Christ has ever had his hands or feet pierced while alive, or has died in this mysterious fashion—to wit, by the cross—save this Jesus alone. (*Dialogue* 97)

Justin indicates that Trypho, along with other Jews, refuses to see Jesus in the psalm. He is correct. When Jews begin to interpret this psalm, they do so in three main ways: as an explanation of events related to Queen Esther, in reference to King David, and in reference to a messiah other than Jesus. A small number of midrashim apply Psalm 22 to other biblical figures.[37]

Rabbinic connection of Esther to Psalm 22 has good precedents. The Septuagint version of Esther, which is longer than the Hebrew version, contains several "additions" that may have been influenced by Psalm 22. In addition C, Esther prays using language likely taken from Psalm 22.[38] For example, in verse 3 of that addition, Esther prays, "My Lord, you alone are our King. Help me, who am alone and have no help but you"; this verse sounds like Psalm 22:11: "Do not be far from me, / for trouble is near / and there is no one to help." Verse 5 speaks of God's previous action: "From birth, I have heard among my people that you, Lord, chose Israel from among all nations, and our ancestors from among all their forebears, as a lasting inheritance, and that you fulfilled all your promises to them"; this verse echoes Psalm 22:4–5:

> In you our ancestors trusted;
>> they trusted, and you delivered them.
> To you they cried, and were saved;
>> in you they trusted, and were not put to shame.

Both this addition to Esther (vv. 3, 5) and Psalm 22 (v. 21) speak of being saved from "the mouth of the lion." In addition C verse 19, Esther pleads, "O God, whose power is over all, hear the voice of those in despair. Save us from the power of the wicked, and deliver me from my fear." She is paraphrasing Psalm 22.

The most common understanding of Psalm 22, found in several places in the Babylonian Talmud and developed in later texts, concerns Queen Esther.[39] This most theological of psalms, opening with its surprising double reference to "my God," nicely supplements the Hebrew version of Esther's story, which never explicitly presents the name of God and, unlike the Greek version with the additions, does not include Esther's prayers. The Babylonian Talmud reads:

> The verse states with regard to Esther: "And she stood in the inner court of the king's house" (Esther 5:1). Rabbi Levi said: Once she reached the chamber of the idols, which was in the inner court, the Divine Presence [Shechinah] left her. She immediately said: "My God, my God, why have You forsaken me?" (Psalm 22:2). Perhaps it is because You judge an unintentional sin as one performed intentionally, and an action done due to circumstances beyond one's control as one done willingly.
>
> Or perhaps You have left me because in my prayers I called Haman a dog, as it is stated: "Deliver my soul from the sword; my only one from the hand of the dog" (Psalm 22:21). She at once retracted and called him in her prayers a lion, as it is stated in the following verse: "Save me from the lion's mouth" (Psalm 22:22). (Megillah 15b)

Midrash Psalms develops this interpretation: "when David saw through the holy spirit that 'my Strength' was the wording that [Esther] would [use to] call upon the Holy One, blessed be He, he composed this psalm concerning her, To the Director, Concerning the 'Strength of the Dawn.'"[40] In this work, the dogs (plural) of verse 16's "dogs are all around me; a company of evildoers encircles me" are understood as "Haman's sons."[41] The midrash elaborates on verse 19, "But you, O LORD, do not be far away! / O my help, come quickly to my aid!," by having Esther say, "'O Lord, pity me, have compassion for me.' . . . In that instant, an angel came down from heaven and struck Ahasuerus in the face, saying: 'Wicked one, thy lady stands outside, while thou art seated here inside.'" This connection between Psalm 22 and Esther became so strong that in the Middle Ages the tradition developed of reciting the psalm on Purim, the joyous festival that commemorates the Jewish victory over the murderous Haman; the scroll of Esther is read during the holiday.

It is likely that such association of Psalm 22 with Esther reflects an anti-Christian polemic: the psalm is about the queen in her distress and not about Jesus on the cross.[42] Conversely, in 398 CE, Jerome insisted that this psalm should *not* be understood in reference to Mordecai and Esther.[43] He knew what his Jewish neighbors were doing. To this day, ironically, while the book of Esther is read in its entirety on Purim, it plays at best a minor role in Christian lectionaries.

Some rabbinic traditions, following the mention of David in the superscription, assume that Psalm 22 refers to David's life. For example, Midrash Psalms, most of which was likely composed before the eighth century, reads (22:28):[44]

> While David was tending sheep, he came upon the *re'em* [in rabbinic literature, a mythological gigantic bull-like figure; we might think of an enormous unicorn] asleep in the wilderness, and thinking it was a mountain, climbed upon it and continued to tend his sheep. The *re'em* waking up, arose, and David, astride of its horns, was lifted up as high as the heavens. At that moment David said: Master of the universe if Thou bringest me down from the horns of the *re'em*, I shall build Thee a Temple. . . . What did the Holy One, blessed be He, do for David? He caused a lion to come towards the *re'em*, and when the *re'em* saw

the lion he was afraid and cringed before it. . . . When David saw the lion, he also was afraid of it. Thereupon the Holy One, blessed be He, caused a gazelle to come along, and as the lion sprang away after it, David descended and went his way.[45]

The midrash is based on Psalm 22:21, which states at the end, "Save me from the mouth of the lion! / From the horns of the wild oxen [Hebrew re'em] you have rescued me," and offers a wonderful example of the close, vivid, and imaginative ways that the rabbis read biblical texts.

The main Jewish source for a messianic reading of Psalm 22 is Pesiqta Rabbati, a midrash containing material as early as the first century CE.[46] It was lost in the Middle Ages and was not very influential, though sections of it were preserved through quotations in other works. Its main claim in the section concerning Psalm 22 is that the "I" who laments is the Messiah ben Ephraim, sometimes called Messiah Ephraim, a messianic figure who precedes the main Davidic messiah and, according to a few rabbinic texts, dies a martyr.[47] Applying this psalm to him is an attempt to show that it could not refer to Jesus; strikingly, the midrash also cites Zechariah 9:9:

> Rejoice greatly, O daughter Zion!
>> Shout aloud, O daughter Jerusalem!
> Lo, your king comes to you;
>> triumphant and victorious is he,
> humble and riding on a donkey,
>> on a colt, the foal of a donkey.

This verse, applied by the midrash to the Messiah Ephraim, is used by the Gospel writers in reference to Jesus (Matt 21:5; John 12:15).

Continuing discussion of the Messiah Ephraim, Pesiqta Rabbati 36:6 also cites Psalm 22:

During the week [seven-year period] when [the Messiah Ephraim] comes, they will bring iron beams and they will put them on his neck until the Messiah's body is bent. He will scream and weep and his voice will rise up to the height [of heaven]. He will say in His presence: Master of the universe, how much can my limbs endure? How much my spirit? Am I not but flesh and blood? It was this moment that David lamented, saying: *My strength is dried up like a potsherd* (Ps. 22:16 [22:15 NRSV]).[48]

Pesiqta Rabbati 37:2 then strings together several verses from Psalm 22 and also from other biblical texts in relation to this messiah:

In the future, in the month of Nisan, the Fathers of the World [Patriarchs] will arise and say to him: Ephraim, our righteous [true] Messiah, even though we are your fathers, you are greater than we are, because you suffered [for] the iniquities of our children and terrible ordeals came upon you, such as did not come upon earlier [generations] or later ones. For the sake of Israel you [experienced] anguish, derision, and mockery among the nations of the world [Ps. 22:7–8 (22:6–7 NRSV)]. *You sat in darkness* (Micah 7:8) and gloominess, and your eyes saw not light, and your skin cleaved to your bones [Ps. 22:18 (22:17 NRSV)], and . . . *your strength is dried up like a potsherd* (Ps. 22:16 [22:15 NRSV]).[49]

This midrash creates a rabbinic narrative about a messiah that parallels the passion narrative even as it presents "an ideological inversion of Jesus."[50] While it is possible that the Jewish messianic reading of Psalm 22 arose independently of Christian claims, we find the view that it served to counter Christian readings more convincing.

Many medieval Jewish interpreters largely follow the outlines of the Talmud and midrashim, though some engage more clearly with the Christian readings of Psalm 22. Rashi's glosses may be seen as implicitly anti-Christian.[51] He interprets the psalm communally, about all of Israel, first by asserting that the superscription, "The Deer of the Dawn," refers to "the congregation of Israel, who is 'a loving doe' (Proverbs 5:19), 'that shines through like the dawn' (Song of Songs 6:10)"; at the same time, he observes, "Our rabbis interpreted it as a reference to Esther."[52] Rashi notes that David wrote, "why have you forsaken me?" "in reference to the future exile"; his comment on Psalm 22:13, where he equates a "roaring lion" with King Nebuchadnezzar, makes it clear that he is referring to the exile of 586 BCE. Well aware that the psalm speaks in the singular, Rashi claims that "the worm" in 22:6 refers to "Israel metaphorically as one person." This same interpretation of Psalm 22 in reference to the exile is found in the tenth-century Karaite commentary of Yefet son of Eli.[53] Similarly Menachem Meiri glosses the superscription: "It was said prophetically about the long exile [after the destruction of the Second Temple]. And he [David] said it in the singular, concerning the nation, which was unified in exile." Thus, the Jewish tradition *does* have some prophetic understandings of Psalm 22 as referring to future events, but they are much less emphasized than in Christian understanding.

David Kimchi also sees the suffering narrator of Psalm 22 as Israel. He glosses the first verse, where the speaker is singular, grammatically: "it is in the singular concerning the entire nation of Israel together, for they are like one person in exile, with one heart" (authors' translation from the Rabbinic Bible). For him, the notion that God is far (see v. 11) implies that the nation is away from the land of Israel. In explaining verse 17, he suggests that the lion (in the MT) is like exile—lions encircle their prey so that they cannot escape, just as Israel is encircled in exile. The animals of 22:20–21 refer to various nations, while the "brothers" of verse 22 refer to the Edomites or the ten tribes, who were in exile with Judah. For Kimchi, verse 27,

> All the ends of the earth shall remember
>   and turn to the LORD;
>   and all the families of the nations
>   shall worship before him,

refers to nations recognizing Israel when Israel is brought out of exile. This corporate understanding of the psalm removes it far away from the christological interpretation of the New Testament.

In her perceptive study of how Psalm 22 has been understood over time, Esther M. Menn writes, "The Psalms appear to be incapable of entirely surrendering themselves to the extraordinary figures associated with them in the history of biblical interpretation; rather, these poems continue to engage ordinary believers, albeit in more complex ways, because of their secondary associations with exemplary individuals."[54] A psalm that could have been prayed by anyone, perhaps a supplicant aided by a Levite, becomes a psalm of David. Then it becomes a prediction referring, for Christians, to the passion of Jesus and, for Jews, to the sufferings of Queen Esther, to a mysterious Messiah Ephraim, or to the state of the Jewish community in exile. In the words of Abraham Jacob Berkovitz, "Psalm 22 provided a colorful palate [sic] with which ancient Jews and early Christians painted."[55]

The multiple early uses of Psalm 22 that could be sung by, and for, anyone, coupled with its diverse readings in Jewish and Christian contexts, should help us today to once again extend the psalm's meaning. People today may believe that their suffering is not deserved and so call upon God for salvation. Or, they can identify with Jesus's citation of the psalm and its connection to the events at his death: he tells his followers that they too are to take up their crosses;

they too will find themselves, if they truly live the Gospel, mocked by others; and they too can anticipate God's ultimate victory. And Jews, recognizing the repurposing of the psalm in the book of Esther, can approach the holiday of Purim (which celebrates how Queen Esther saved her people from genocide)—and the anti-Judaism the book and the holiday overcome—with a sense of confidence that their prayers will be heard.

We can do even more. On the lips of Jesus, the psalm recollects all those who are put to death by the state. Less well-known: On the lips of Esther, the psalm concerns those who are sexually trafficked. In Midrash Psalms, Esther prays, "My God . . . Why should the order of the world, even the story of the matriarchs, turn out differently for me?"[56] While God rescued Sarah from Pharaoh's harem (Gen 12:17), no one, yet, had rescued Esther from Ahasuerus's bed. Psalm 22 becomes the lament of the victim of rape, and the forceful voice of the survivor.

Today, Psalm 22 is heard in Christian churches on Good Friday. It is still heard in some synagogues in connection with the holiday of Purim. The psalm speaks to horror and danger, but it speaks to more than that. It allows us to express the feeling that many of us have had—that God has abandoned us. At the same time, it ironically insists that we have not abandoned that relationship. A lament psalm is a poem of raw honesty and fidelity. It is appropriate on the lips of Jesus the Jew, and anyone who feels abandoned by God.

CHAPTER 12

❦

Son of Man

Human and/or Divine

THE PHRASE "son of man" (Greek *hious tou anthrōpou*), which appears eighty-five times in the New Testament, eighty-one of those on the lips of Jesus, is an idiom—"a group of words in a fixed order that have a particular meaning that is different from the meanings of each word on its own."[1] Depending on the context, it indicates an apocalyptic figure who gathers his elect, a homeless person, the preeminent interpreter of the Torah, the "Messiah, the son of the Blessed," the one uniquely authorized to interpret the Torah, a human being who gives his body and blood to his disciples to eat and drink, or a tortured man who dies on a Roman cross. In Galilean Aramaic, the expression "son of man" (*bar 'enosh*) can simply mean "I."[2] Jesus could have simply referred to himself as "I" (Greek *egō*), as he does in the Gospel of John, with comments such as "I am the bread of life" (6:48) and "I am the true vine" (15:1). Therefore, when Jesus instead uses "son of man" or his followers use it to refer to him, the term demands attention. It requires his hearers, then and now, to answer the question he posed to his disciples, "Who do you say that I am?" (Matt 16:15; cf. Mark 8:29; Luke 9:20).

In this chapter, we are not going to resolve the questions that plague scholars of the historical Jesus: Did Jesus use the term every time it is attributed to him, or did the evangelists add it? Did he use the term only to refer to himself as one human being among many, and only his followers associated him with a heavenly figure who comes on the clouds? When he spoke of the son of man coming on the clouds to gather his elect, did he speak of himself or someone else? Did he use the term in different ways? There is no end to discussions of the New Testament term, and here we can only begin to sketch how it functioned in its several appearances in the scriptures of Israel, both before and after the time of Jesus. The results will provide some help in determining how those who heard Jesus use the term might have responded, or how people might respond today, to its use.[3]

The meaning of the idiom "Son of Man" or "son of man" (remember, there is no distinction between uppercase and lowercase in ancient Greek and Hebrew) eternally vexes New Testament scholars. The earliest Gospel, Mark, depicts the terrestrial and celestial calamities that will accompany the end of the world. After the sun is darkened and the moon ceases to provide light, the eschatological age is inaugurated by the appearance of a figure called "the Son of Man": "Then they will see 'the Son of Man coming in clouds' with great power and glory. Then he will send out the angels, and gather his elect from the four winds, from the ends of the earth to the ends of heaven" (Mark 13:26–27). This "Son of Man" is no normal son of man in the sense of "human being" or "a fellow like the rest of us."

According to Matthew and Luke, Jesus announces, "Foxes have holes, and birds of the air have nests; but the Son of Man has nowhere to lay his head" (Matt 8:20; Luke 9:58). The statement could apply to any homeless person, then or now. If the statement goes back to Jesus, he could have been saying, "But I have no place to lay [my] head" because my hometown has rejected me: "Prophets are not without honor, except in their hometown, and among their own kin, and in their own house" (Mark 6:4; cf. Matt 13:57; John 4:44).

The Gospels also suggest that a particular Son of Man with unique authority is present in the person of Jesus. Affirming that his disciples did not violate the Sabbath by plucking heads of grain, Jesus announces, "The sabbath was made for humankind [Greek *anthrōpoi*, i.e., all people], and not humankind for the sabbath; so the Son of Man [Greek *huios tou anthrōpou*; the same term, *anthrōpos*, as used for "humankind"] is lord even of the sabbath" (Mark 2:27–28). The saying resembles a comment from the Babylonian Talmud (Yoma 85b): "The Sabbath is given for you, not you to the Sabbath"; so Jesus could have been making a comment about how individuals should determine their own way of celebrating the Sabbath—which would be a very Jewish thing to do. However, in Mark's Gospel, "Son of Man" is a technical term referring to Jesus as having divine authority.

When predicting his suffering and death, Jesus describes himself, again in the third person, with this enigmatic expression. Mark records that Jesus begins "to teach them [his disciples] that the Son of Man must undergo great suffering, and be rejected by the elders, the chief priests, and the scribes, and be killed, and after three days rise again" (Mark 8:31). Since Jesus simply could have said "I," the title must hold additional import.

In John 6:53, Jesus tells "the Jews" that "unless you eat the flesh of the Son of Man and drink his blood, you have no life in you." The injunction causes no small consternation. His followers state, "This teaching is difficult; who can accept it?" (John 6:60). Later, in John 12:34, the crowd says to Jesus, "We have heard from the law that the Messiah remains forever. How can you say that the Son of Man must be lifted up? Who is this Son of Man?" That is, indeed, the question—he is clearly not an ordinary person. He looks to these Jews like the Messiah, but he does not fulfill their messianic expectations. They do not expect a messiah to die, let alone to die on a cross and then to be lifted into the heavens. The general expectation of the time is that the messiah will bring about the messianic age, including the resurrection of the dead, a final judgment, and peace on earth. John notes such expectations in Jesus's conversation with his friend Martha. When Jesus tells her that her brother, Lazarus, who has died, "will rise again" Martha responds, "I know that he will rise again in the resurrection on the last day" (John 11:23–24).

The Gospels associate the designation "Son of Man" with other titles: "Messiah" (Greek *christos*; English "Christ"), "Son of God," and "Son of David." For example, when Caiaphas the high priest asks Jesus, "Are you the Messiah, the Son of the Blessed One?," Jesus responds, "I am, and 'you will see the Son of Man / seated at the right hand of the Power,' / and 'coming with the clouds of heaven'" (Mark 14:61–62). While some scholars suggest that Jesus, when he made this statement, was talking about someone else, this Son of Man is, for the Gospels, none other than Jesus of Nazareth.

"Son of Man" is the perfect self-designation for a man who teaches in parables, as well as for a Jew, familiar with the scriptures of Israel and the various uses of the term there, to invoke. It is, according to the Gospels, Jesus's favorite self-designation.

But "Son of Man" quickly drops out of the vocabulary of Jesus's followers. The term is a Jewish or at least a Semitic one; it does not appear in Greek contemporaneous extracanonical writings. Outside the Gospels, it is all but absent, and it drops out of patristic sources. For the followers of Jesus who did not speak Hebrew or Aramaic, and did not hear their scriptures proclaimed in those languages, the idiom would not have made sense. Idioms do not translate well, as any American who speaks of "rooting" for a sports team in Australia quickly learns. Nor does the Semitic idiom "son of man" have the cache that "son of God" had among the gentiles. While Jesus is acclaimed "son of God," no one ever acclaims him "Son of Man." To understand the meaning of this Jewish, Semitic idiom in the New Testament, we must turn to the Jewish texts of Jesus's day.

In Search of the Son of Man

A S WE HAVE SEEN, the phrase "son of man" is an idiom. Often a phrase can function both literally and idiomatically. "Stop pulling my leg" is something we might say to a toddler who is trying to get our attention, and here the words have a literal meaning; but we might use the same expression with a student who offers a preposterous story about why a paper is late—in that case, we are not referring to any actual pulling or actual legs. If a phrase does not make sense in its usual meaning, we may surmise that it is being used idiomatically. The Bible is replete with idiomatic expressions, from "suck the milk of nations" (Isa 60:16) for gaining wealth from foreign nations, to "remove the foreskin of your hearts" (Jer 4:4), indicating dedication toward perfect faithfulness. The expression "son of man" can mean the male offspring of some fellow, but it also functions as an idiom with various connotations.

The Hebrew typically translated "son of man" is *ben 'adam. Ben,* "son," followed by a noun often means "son of" in a literal, familial sense; for example, Ben-Hur (1 Kgs 4:8, as well as the famous novel by Lew Wallace and the 1959 film) means, literally, "Hur's son." In theory, *ben 'adam* could mean Adam's son (Cain, Abel, or Seth), but in the Bible, it is never used that way. Instead, *ben* with *'adam* refers to a member of a particular class, a "human." We see similar usage with the cognate English term "son of a . . ." (fill in the blank, kindly). Human beings are defined by the fact that they are children of other human beings: they do not drop in from the heavens; they are not created from the earth. This common use of *ben* to describe a class is found in expressions such as "sons of the prophets," in Hebrew *benei* (plural of *ben* + of) *hanevi'im* (the prophets), a member of a prophetic group or guild (see especially 2 Kgs 2:3, 5, 7, 15), or *ben baqar*, literally "son of (the) herd," namely, a large domestic animal (e.g., Gen 18:7, or "calf" in the NRSV). More familiar is the expression *benei* (plural of *ben*) *Yisra'el*, literally "children of Israel" but in the NRSV almost always translated as "Israelites." The translation eliminates the force of the idiom, which suggests both ethnicity and genealogy, a familial affiliation.

Ben 'adam often appears in parallel with other words for humanity. For example, it functions as a poetic synonym for the standard term "man" (*'ish*) four times in Jeremiah, as in "no one [*'ish*] shall live there, nor shall anyone [*ben 'adam*] settle in it" (49:18, 33; 50:40; 51:43—with variants). *Ben 'adam* similarly appears in poetic parallel to the Hebrew term *'enosh*, "humanity." Isaiah 51:12 reads, "I, I am he who comforts you; / why then are you afraid of a mere *mortal* [*'enosh*] who must die, / a *human being* [*ben 'adam*] who fades like grass?" In Job 16:21, *ben 'adam* parallels *gever*, "hegemonic male" or, more colloquially, "manly man": "that he would maintain the right of *a mortal* [*gever*] with God, / as *one* [*ben 'adam*] does for a neighbor." This text emphasizes that the "son" in "son of man" is a male son. While the Hebrew *ben* could be translated "child" (as the plural, *benei Yisra'el*, typically means "children of Israel"), the gender determination of the singular cannot be ignored.

The term "son of man" is never, to our knowledge, used for women. While "human one" is a viable synonym that has become popular among those attuned to gender inclusivity, a concern we appreciate, that alternative loses both the term's masculine implication and its generative as well as familial focus that the word "son" conveys. Already the translation "man" loses its possible connection to the garden of Eden story, since the Hebrew word *'adam* may bring Adam to mind.

Ben 'adam is also sometimes used in a negative sense to indicate a fragile human contrasted to a powerful God. As we saw in our discussion of the garden of Eden (Gen 2–3, Chapter 4), humans are to be distinguished from the divine. Numbers 23:19, the first use of *ben 'adam* in the scriptures of Israel, illustrates this well. The context is the story of the non-Israelite prophet Balaam, who today may be better known for having a talking donkey than for his prophetic message. Balaam had been hired by Balak, the king of Moab, to curse the Israelites on their way from slavery in Egypt to the land of Canaan. The prophet-for-hire agrees, but he is preempted from carrying out his commission by God, who insists, "You shall not curse the people, for they are blessed" (Num 22:12). Balaam, playing the odds, decides to follow Balak's instructions. At this point, an angel blocks the path, and the donkey cannot move. Unable to see the angel, Balaam starts to beat the animal. "Then the LORD opened the mouth of the donkey, and it said to Balaam, 'What have I done to you, that you have struck me these three times?'" (Num 22:28). Balaam comes to learn that Israel's God is to be taken seriously.

When the king again attempts to get his curses pronounced, Balaam states, "God is not a human being [*'ish*], that he should lie, / or a mortal [*ben 'adam*], that he should change his mind" (Num 23:19). The original meaning of "son of man" is exactly that, a human being, the son of a human being. Here the phrase has a pejorative sense—a lying and wishy-washy human in contrast to an honest and consistent deity.

Other uses of the term stress the ephemerality of mortal life. For example, Joel 1:12 reads:

The vine withers,
     the fig tree droops.
Pomegranate, palm, and apple—
     all the trees of the field are dried up;
surely, joy withers away
     among the people [*benei 'adam*].

Several psalms depict God literally looking down from the heavens on human beings, *benei 'adam*, usually in search of a wise person (Ps 11:4; 14:2; 53:2). Job's friend Bildad asks:

How then can a mortal [*'enosh*] be righteous before God?
     How can one born of woman be pure? . . .
how much less a mortal [*'enosh*], who is a maggot,
     and a human being [*ben 'adam*], who is a worm!
     (Job 25:4–6)

This same negative undertone should be heard when God calls the prophet Ezekiel *ben 'adam* ninety-three times in the book that bears his name. (The plural *benei 'adam* is used once, for "people," in Ezek 31:14.) Here *ben 'adam* emphasizes the vast difference between humanity and the divine. Splendid as human beings may be, we are not divine: we lack God's knowledge, power, and eternity. Biblical scholar Moshe Greenberg observes, concerning Ezekiel's first use of the term—"He said to me: O mortal [*ben 'adam*], stand up on your feet, and I will speak with you" (Ezek 2:1)—that it emphasizes the prophet's "mortal nature."[4]

The Dead Sea Scrolls continue this usage. Several dozen times the scrolls use the term *ben 'adam*, "son of man," in both the singular and the plural, always in the sense of "a person."[5] Often, the term highlights people's sinfulness or distance from God; for example, one

Qumran prayer reads, "I know that man ['enosh] has no righteousness, nor does the son of man [ben 'adam] walk in the perfect."[6] This
refers to the depiction of humans found in an extracanonical psalm
in the large Psalms Scroll that begins, "Indeed, no worm gives You
thanks, nor any weevil recounts Your loving-kindness" (11QPs[a] 19:1).

Yet, other uses of the expression build upon a positive view of human beings and their abilities. Psalm 115:16 proclaims, "The heavens
are the LORD's heavens, / but the earth he has given to human beings [benei 'adam]." The phrase, like in Genesis 1, suggests a steward-
ship roll for the descendants of that original creation. An even more
positive view of humanity marks the famous Psalm 8:4, where the
poet asks, "what are human beings ['enosh] that you are mindful of
them, / mortals [ben 'adam] that you care for them?" The response
is the joyous,

> Yet you have made them a little lower than God,
>   and crowned them with glory and honor.
> You have given them dominion over the works of your hands;
>   you have put all things under their feet,
> all sheep and oxen,
>   and also the beasts of the field,
> the birds of the air, and the fish of the sea,
>   whatever passes along the paths of the seas. (Ps 8:5–8)

It is this psalm that the Epistle to the Hebrews quotes with a vague
attribution: "But someone has testified somewhere, 'What are human beings [Greek anthrōpos] that you are mindful of them, / or
mortals [Greek huios anthrōpou, literally "son of man"], that you care
for them?" (Heb 2:6). Hebrews then applies the psalm to Jesus: since
"we do not yet see everything in subjection to them, but we do see
Jesus, who for a little while was made lower than the angels, now

crowned with glory and honor" (2:8–9). The point here is that Jesus took on human form and, like a human being, died.

Finally, the scriptures of Israel do, on occasion, refer to individuals, rather than to all of humanity, as "son of man." The prophet Ezekiel is the preeminent example. Psalm 80:17 (80:18 Heb.) calls the Davidic king a *ben 'adam*, although English readers would miss the usage. The NRSV translates, "But let your hand be upon the one [*'ish*, literally "man"] at your right hand, / the one [*ben 'adam*] whom you made strong for yourself." A royal psalm, yes, but not a messianic prediction; here the term is used of the human, current king from David's line.

In sum, whether used in the singular *ben 'adam* or the plural *benei 'adam*, the phrase "son of man" emphasizes a person's or people's humanity. It may have neutral, negative, or positive connotations. A similar phrase appears in Ugaritic, Aramaic, and Phoenician—Semitic languages closely related to Hebrew.[7] In none of these cases do the Hebrew scriptures or ancient Near Eastern literature regard a *ben 'adam* as having supernatural ability, messianic status, or an eschatological role.

"Son of Man":
From Human to Superhuman

To understand the New Testament usage, we must move to a new use of the expression found in the book of Daniel. In this late biblical text, the expression "son of man" shifts from a figure completely other than God, and even from a figure a little lower than the angels, to one who is superior to the angels in every way.

The scribes who composed Daniel used a variety of rhetorical techniques to create resistance literature as they responded to the cultural pressures that came with Seleucid colonial rule and to the threat of the erasure of Jewish culture. This complex book combines different genres, from heroic court tales to apocalyptic visions combining Aramaic (Dan 2:4–7:28) and Hebrew (Dan 1:1–2:3; 8:1–12:13).[8] For the author of the visions in chapters 7–12, the redemption of God's faithful people, some of whom were being martyred for adhering to their traditions, was at hand. But this redemption, they believed, would not be accomplished by the militarism of the Maccabees. Daniel anticipates redemption by God, and God's agents, including, "one like a son of man" (Dan 7:13). Since the "one like a son of man" is a description, not a title,[9] the connections among Jesus's "son of man," references to the various uses of "son of man" in the earlier texts, and Daniel's "one like a son of man" become matters of interpretation.

This transformation of an idiom meaning "human being" to a phrase meaning something much more occurs as the book of Daniel moves from the court tales in chapters 1–6 to the apocalyptic visions in 7–12. Daniel 1–6 employs the equivalent Aramaic term for "son of man" in 2:38 and 5:21; the NRSV translates the phrase as, respectively, "human beings" and "human society." The first use is satiric. Daniel tells Nebuchadnezzar, the Babylonian king, that although he thinks he has authority to rule, he ultimately has none at all, because God rules the world: "You, O king, the king of kings—to whom the God of heaven has given the kingdom, the power, the might, and the glory, into whose hand he has given human beings [Aramaic *benei 'anasha'*], wherever they live, the wild animals of the field, and the birds of the air, and whom he has established as ruler over them all" (Dan 2:37–38). The following verse proclaims that Nebuchadnezzar's rule will not last.

Daniel 5:21, the next verse to use the expression, reinforces divine sovereignty: "[Nebuchadnezzar] was driven from human society [Aramaic *benei 'anasha'*], and his mind was made like that of an animal. His dwelling was with the wild asses, he was fed grass like oxen, and his body was bathed with the dew of heaven, until he learned that the Most High God has sovereignty over the kingdom of mortals [Aramaic *'anasha'*], and sets over it whomever he will." These usages follow the Hebrew *ben 'adam* for "human" or "humanity" in the Hebrew sections of Israel's scriptures.

The idiom's meaning begins to change in Daniel's Hebrew apocalyptic section. Here Daniel uses *ben 'adam* twice. The first appearance, in Daniel 8:17, is similar to that found in Ezekiel, and the author probably had Ezekiel's rhetoric in mind in composing the verses: "So he [an angel] came near where I stood; and when he came, I became frightened and fell prostrate. But he said to me, 'Understand, O mortal [Hebrew *ben 'adam*], that the vision is for the time of the end.'"

Daniel is the human being who lacks angelic knowledge; *ben 'adam* marks his lower status.

In the second use, in Daniel 10:16, *ben 'adam* changes in import—here it denotes a being who *looks* human: "Then one in human form [Hebrew *kidmut benei 'adam*, literally, "in the likeness of a son of man"] touched my lips, and I opened my mouth to speak, and said to the one who stood before me, 'My lord, because of the vision such pains have come upon me that I retain no strength.'" This supernatural creature *looks like* a human, but he is something more—a heavenly messenger or an angel; these intermediaries become major figures in apocalyptic literature.

The description of this *ben 'adam* echoes depictions in older Hebrew texts of divine messengers (angels; Hebrew *mal'achim*, singular *mal'ach*). We find one such description in Judges 13, of an angel who announces to the wife of Manoah that she is pregnant and will bear a son (who turns out to be Samson). Mrs. Manoah describes this being to her husband: "A man of God came to me, and his appearance was like that of an angel of God, most awe-inspiring" (Judg 13:6). A similar angelic appearance occurs in Genesis 18, where Abraham sees three men (Hebrew *'anashim*, the plural of *'ish*) and invites them to lunch. It is from them that the patriarch receives the prediction that his postmenopausal wife will have a son. And it is to this passage that Hebrews 13:2 alludes when it exhorts, "Do not neglect to show hospitality to strangers, for by doing that some have entertained angels without knowing it." Angels look like people, and they can even disguise themselves as human beings, as the angel Raphael does in the book of Tobit, but they are more than mortal.

In chapter 7, Daniel's last Aramaic chapter, Daniel brings his vision to a climax. He describes a dream in which four frightening beasts arise from the sea. Then, in 7:13–14, he records:

As I watched in the night visions,

> I saw one like a human being [Aramaic *kebar 'enash*, "the one
> like a son of man"]
>> coming with the clouds of heaven.
> And he came to the Ancient One [Aramaic *'atiq yomaya'*,
> literally "ancient of days," i.e., God]
>> and was presented before him.
> To him [*kebar 'enash*] was given dominion
>> and glory and kingship,
> that all peoples, nations, and languages
>> should serve him.
> His dominion is an everlasting dominion
>> that shall not pass away,
> and his kingship is one
>> that shall never be destroyed.

We have already heard something resembling this description. Nebuchadnezzar had been given the "kingdom, the power, the might, and the glory" (Dan 2:37), but all this was taken from him. He is the negative exemplar of this supernatural one "like a son of man [*kebar 'enash*]." In the connection between a king who acts like, and looks like, an animal and this supernatural figure who looks like a human being, but is more, we see the distinction between earthly and heavenly concerns.

Although this individual in Daniel 7 is "one like a son of man" or "one like a human being" (v. 13), the description of the dominion he receives indicates that he is by no means a typical human. He stands in the direct presence of God, his kingdom is eternal, and he receives universal acclamation. He is "like a" son of man in that he appears human, as do angels, but he is not a son of man in that he is *not human*. This one "like a son of man" will later become *the* Son of Man.

"Like a son of man" is a description; "Son of Man" in the Gospels is Jesus's self-designation and functions as a title.

Scholars have long pondered the identity of Daniel's "one like a son of man." Any conclusion is complicated by continuing debates concerning Daniel 7's structure, unity, and history of composition. Early modern biblical scholarship identified the chapter's "one like a son of man" with a wide range of suggestions, from the Messiah to Judah Maccabee, the leader of the revolt against Antiochus and the hero of the Hanukkah story told in the deuterocanonical Maccabees 1–2. However, nothing else either in Daniel 7 or in the rest of the book of Daniel supports any of these identifications. Daniel's only use of the term "messiah" or "anointed one" (Hebrew *mashi'ach*) appears in 9:25–26, where the figure refers not to the redeemer of Israel but to a royal figure ("anointed one") who falls in battle:

> Know therefore and understand: from the time that the word went out to restore and rebuild Jerusalem until the time of an anointed prince, there shall be seven weeks; and for sixty-two weeks it shall be built again with streets and moat, but in a troubled time. After the sixty-two weeks, an anointed one shall be cut off and shall have nothing, and the troops of the prince who is to come shall destroy the city and the sanctuary. Its end shall come with a flood, and to the end there shall be war. Desolations are decreed.

As for Judah Maccabee, the book of Daniel rejects his militarism in favor of God's direct intervention into history.

Others interpret Daniel's "one like a son of man" collectively, as representing the Jewish people; in this reading, the single individual stands for the community, as for example "Uncle Sam" represents the United States. We saw a similar approach in some interpretations of Isaiah's suffering servant or the psalmist of Psalm 22 as the people of Israel.

This communal reading of Daniel's son of man follows from the immediate context of Daniel 7:13. Daniel, who in the earlier chapters of his book emerged as the preeminent interpreter of dreams, here finds himself disturbed by a dream and asks a nearby angel for its interpretation. The angel begins by explaining that the four beasts are "four kings [that] shall arise out of the earth" (Dan 7:17) and then indicates that the fourth beast is the "fourth kingdom on earth" (7:23). If the beasts therefore represent kingdoms, understood to be Babylon, Persia, Greece, and the Seleucid Empire, then the one like a son of man also represents a kingdom—and that kingdom must be Israel. Also supporting this collective identification of the "one like a son of man" is the angel's assurance:

> The kingship and dominion
>> and the greatness of the kingdoms under the whole heaven
>> shall be given to the people of the holy ones of the Most
>> High;
> their kingdom shall be an everlasting kingdom,
>> and all dominions shall serve and obey them. (Dan 7:27)

The "one like a son of man" who is given all authority plays the same role as the "people of the holy ones of the Most High," that is, the people Israel.

The prevailing academic position, however, takes Daniel's "one like a son of man" to be an angelic figure, and most likely to be identified with the archangel Michael, mentioned elsewhere in Daniel (10:13, 21; 12:1). In 12:1, he is called "the great prince."[10] That Daniel 10:16 uses the expression "one in human form [*kidmut benei 'adam*, literally "in the likeness of a son of man"]" to refer to an angel supports the identification of "one like a son of man" in Daniel 7:13 with Michael. Daniel thus builds upon the importance of Michael (and angels in general) during the Hellenistic period.[11]

Daniel's confusing, disturbing vision of "one like a son of man" who receives power *can be* understood to refer to a supernatural being, like an angel, and it *can be* understood to refer to Israel, the "holy nation" (cf. Exod 19:6). For followers of Jesus, familiar with Jesus's use of the term "son of man" or aware of his prediction, "Then they will see 'the Son of Man coming in clouds' with great power and glory" (Mark 13:26), the reference could be to none other than Jesus. Daniel's angelic being, who looks "like a son of man" (i.e., like a human being), becomes for the Gospels an actual human being, Jesus the Son of Man. He is *the* Son of Man, who gains the authority promised to the one "like a son of man" in Daniel.

The title has gone, from Hebrew to Aramaic to Greek, from indicating a human (Psalms, Ezekiel), to one like a human such as an angel (Daniel), to a human (the suffering servant, a Davidic heir) who is divine. Daniel R. Schwartz writes, "What made Christianity succeed was its ability to transform the belief that a 'Son of David' would restore the Kingdom of Israel into the belief that a 'Son of Man' had inaugurated the Kingdom of God."[12] In this single sentence, he encapsulates the complex process by which Daniel's "one like a Son of Man" who receives dominion on earth becomes *the* Son of Man (now a title, rather than a description) who redeems from sin and death.

Like any good apocalyptic symbol, Daniel's "one like a son of man" remains open. And like any good apocalyptic text, Daniel provides a vision of hope that can be applied to any situation. No matter how powerful the emperor might be, no matter how much he threatens to destroy culture and community, divine protection will come. And this heavenly protector will look like one of us (i.e., a human male) but be something more—a supernatural being whose rule is both just and eternal.

Although Daniel is among the latest compositions incorporated in the scriptures of Israel, it was the ancient equivalent of an instant bestseller, attested in eight copies among the Dead Sea Scrolls. Some of the composers of the scrolls may have recognized the special nature of the figure in Daniel 7, but the texts do not adopt the language of "son of man" for their eschatological visions.

The transition from Daniel's "one like a son of man" to the "Son of Man" may appear in a few pseudepigraphal writings. Even when we can date their final form, it is difficult to date the traditions they preserve. Some New Testament authors reflect knowledge of select pseudepigrapha, especially of 1 Enoch, a text ascribed to the obscure figure seven generations down from Adam. And it is from 1 Enoch that the main pseudepigraphal references to the "Son of Man" appear.[13]

According to Genesis 5:24, "Enoch walked with God; then he was no more, because God took him." Although the phrasing is simply a poetic way of stating that Enoch died, later readers concluded that Enoch did not die but, like Elijah, was assumed bodily into heaven. An entire mythology then develops about Enoch, who is regarded as a witness both to earthly events, such as Noah's flood, and to heavenly mysteries, such as the final judgment. He is therefore an appropriate figure to be identified as the Son of Man in an apocalyptic sense: human by birth and in form but possessing eternal existence and special knowledge.

First Enoch is a composite work containing materials that date as early as the third century BCE and as late as the first century CE. Although several fragments have been found among the Dead Sea Scrolls, in its current form, 1 Enoch is best-preserved in Ge'ez, an ancient dialect of Ethiopic, and the Ethiopic Church regards the

book as part of its Old Testament. The text is early, but the manuscripts, themselves translations, date to the tenth century CE,
a millennium after the time of Jesus. Chapters 37–71, known as
the "Parables of Enoch" or "Similitudes of Enoch," do not appear
among the Dead Sea Scrolls, but it is in these chapters (46, 48, 62,
69–70, and especially 71) where the enigmatic "son of man" language appears. Thus, any use of this material for understanding the
New Testament must remain tentative.[14] While 1 Enoch 37–71 may
shed light on the use of the term "Son of Man" in the New Testament, it is also possible that the connection of Enoch to the Son
of Man may be a secondary, perhaps even anti-Christian, addition
designed to ensure that readers will not appropriate the book in
service to Christology.[15]

In 1 Enoch, the Son of Man describes a superhuman character. In
46:1, 1 Enoch alludes to Daniel 7 in describing his own vision of the
Son of Man: "In that place, I saw the One to whom belongs the time
before time. And his head was white like wool, and there was with
him another individual, whose face was like that of a human being."
When Enoch asks an angel about this second figure, he receives the
answer: "This is the Son of Man who is born unto righteousness, And
righteousness abides over him, And the righteousness of the Head
of Days forsakes him not" (1 En 46:3). The expression need not be a
title; it could simply note that this figure is a human being who has a
special role to play.[16] His responsibility according to the angel is:

> "He shall proclaim peace to you in the name of the world that is to
> become. For from here proceeds peace since the creation of the world,
> and so it shall be unto you forever and ever and ever. Everyone that will
> come to exist and walk shall (follow) your path, since righteousness
> never forsakes you. Together with you shall be their dwelling places;
> and together with you shall be their portion. They shall not be

separated from you forever and ever and ever." So there shall be length
of days with that Son of Man, and peace to the righteous ones; his
path is upright for the righteous, in the name of the Lord of the Spirits
forever and ever. (71:15–17)

At the end of the Similitudes, Enoch identifies this Son of Man:
Enoch himself (71:14).

For 1 Enoch, references to this "Son of Man" are subordinate to
other references to this figure, including God's "Anointed One" (1 En
48:10; 52:4) and the "chosen one" (49:2, 4; 53:6). First Enoch 48:3
reads, "Even before the creation of the sun and the moon, before the
creation of the stars, he was given a name in the presence of the Lord
of the Spirits." Created at the dawn of time—and so having some
relation to the Johannine *Logos* and the figure of Wisdom—this Son
of Man remains hidden save to those whom God chose to reveal him
(62:7). His task is to "remove the kings and the mighty ones from
their comfortable seats and the strong ones from their thrones"
(46:4). The language is conventional, but its reference is elsewhere
to God, as in Mary's Magnificat, "He has brought down the powerful
from their thrones, / and lifted up the lowly" (Luke 1:52), and, much
earlier, 1 Samuel 2, the Song of Hannah. As much as the Son of Man
is exalted in 1 Enoch 37–71, however, nothing here suggests that this
figure, however named, was understood to be worshiped, or invoked
in prayer, or substituted for God.

A second pseudepigraphic work, 4 Ezra (also known as 2 Esdras),
perhaps alludes to Daniel 7:13, though both textual and translational
issues make this uncertain. The book in its current form survives
mainly in Christian manuscripts in Armenian and several other languages, but these later versions reflect a translation of a lost Greek
version, itself translated from a Hebrew or Aramaic original written
at the end of the first century CE.[17] In the thirteenth chapter, a Chris-

tian addition to an earlier Jewish text, 4 Ezra refers to "something like the figure of a man" (13:3), language derived from Daniel 7:13. The figure functions as a messianic warrior, much like we find in the book of Revelation.[18]

In the summation of one scholar, "son of man" was just not as emphasized in Second Temple Judaism as in early Christian literature: "The expression 'son of man' does not seem to have existed as a widely recognized title in early first-century Judaism, although a number of scholars do think that a pre-Christian 'son of man' *concept* existed, with Dan 7:13 providing a model and material for Jewish speculation on both earthly and heavenly redeemer figures associated with messianic aspects."[19] This increasingly divine Son of Man, who becomes the focal point for divine justice, speaks to both the human yearning for a savior and the despair that no one on earth has the power or authority to change the present state of the world. At the same time, it opens the door for anyone who has the charisma, the force, and the talent to take on this role.

THE SON OF MAN ELSEWHERE
IN THE NEW TESTAMENT

IN THE GOSPELS, "Son of Man" is Jesus's self-designation, and only he uses the term. Outside of the Gospels, the title "Son of Man" is rare in the New Testament, but it always refers to Jesus.

The term appears once in the book of Acts, likely an early second-century text. Acts records the martyrdom of Stephen, who according to the New Testament is the first person to die for his proclamation of Jesus; he is stoned to death by a mob consisting of the high priest and his associates. Acts recounts a defiant predeath speech: "But filled with the Holy Spirit, he [Stephen] gazed into heaven and saw the glory of God and Jesus standing at the right hand of God. 'Look,' he said, 'I see the heavens opened and the Son of Man standing at the right hand of God!'" (Acts 7:55–56). The historicity of Stephen's speech, and of Stephen himself, is open to debate. The early church fathers, generally happy to mention martyrs, do not mention him.[20] But the speech does neatly fit Luke's rhetorical purposes. It echoes Jesus's self-identification, and it confirms Jesus's prediction in Luke 22:69 that "from now on the Son of Man will be seated at the right hand of the power of God."

The only other New Testament appearances of the expression are in Revelation 1:13 and 14:14. The author of Revelation, who identifies himself as "John," comes from either an Aramaic- or a Hebrew-speaking background. While John never directly quotes any text from the scriptures of Israel, allusions abound. Revelation 1:13–18 has Daniel 7:9–13 in the background:

> and in the midst of the lampstands I saw one like a Son of Man, clothed with a long robe and with a golden sash across his chest. His head and his hair were white as white wool, white as snow; his eyes were like a flame of fire, his feet were like burnished bronze, refined as in a furnace, and his voice was like the sound of many waters. In his right hand he held seven stars, and from his mouth came a sharp, two-edged sword, and his face was like the sun shining with full force.
>
> When I saw him, I fell at his feet as though dead. But he placed his right hand on me, saying, "Do not be afraid; I am the first and the last, and the living one. I was dead, and see, I am alive forever and ever; and I have the keys of Death and of Hades." (authors' translation)

"One like a Son of Man" means here, as it does in earlier Hebrew and Aramaic texts, one in human form. Unlike many of Revelation's other figures, which are bestial (e.g., the famous beast whose number is 666; Rev 13:18) and so resemble the beasts Daniel describes as having power before one like a Son of Man dethrones them, the Jesus whom John sees in his vision resembles a person. His white head and hair likely allude to Daniel 7:9, the description of God as the "Ancient of Days," whose "clothing was white as snow, / and the hair of his head like pure wool." Revelation's "one like a Son of Man" thus *combines* the portraits of Daniel's separate "one like a Son of Man" and the "Ancient of Days."

A Son of Man reappears in Revelation 14:14, this time accompanied by the Danielic cloud setting: "Then I looked, and there was a white cloud, and seated on the cloud was one like a Son of Man, with a golden crown on his head, and a sharp sickle in his hand!" (authors' translation). The cloud becomes an identity marker that connects Jesus the Son of Man with the Danielic "one like" a Son of Man. Yet even here, "like a Son of Man" is an idiom, not a title: the figure *looks* human. The crown indicates royalty; it may refer to connections between Jesus and David, though it might derive simply from Daniel's description of the one like a Son of Man who receives "dominion and glory and kingship." The sickle signifies eschatological judgment, based on Joel 3:13, which describes the events that immediately precede the Day of the LORD:

> Put in the sickle,
>> for the harvest is ripe.
> Go in, tread,
>> for the wine press is full.
> The vats overflow,
>> for their wickedness is great.

Although no messianic figure is found in Joel, by the first century CE the Day of the LORD, a significant theme in Joel, was associated with the arrival of the messiah. We can see this connection in Acts 2, the famous "Pentecost" scene, where the Holy Spirit descends on the followers of Jesus, they begin to proclaim the Gospel in foreign languages, and Peter explains these phenomena by quoting from Joel:

> This is what was spoken through the prophet Joel:
>> "In the last days it will be, God declares,
>> that I will pour out my Spirit upon all flesh,
>>> and your sons and your daughters shall prophesy,
>> and your young men shall see visions,
>>> and your old men shall dream dreams.
>> Even upon my slaves, both men and women,

in those days I will pour out my Spirit;
and they shall prophesy.
... before the coming of the Lord's great and glorious day.
Then everyone who calls on the name of the Lord shall be
saved." (Acts 2:16–21, authors' translation)

The scene, however, makes no mention of a son of man, or one like a son of man, or even a messiah. The end of the age will be marked, here, by the outpouring of the Spirit on everyone.

The Postbiblical Future
of the Son of Man

IN PART BECAUSE "son of man" appears in the New Testament in relation to Jesus, it either drops out of rabbinic teaching or is used in a polemical fashion to indicate that the son of man is not Jesus alone but all of humanity, as the idiom functions in the earlier Hebrew and Aramaic texts. Thus, Daniel 7:13–14 is not as well-represented in the Jewish interpretive tradition as many of the other passages that we discuss.[21]

The Jerusalem Talmud (y. Ta'anit 65b) quotes Rabbi Abahu as stating, "If a man says to you 'I am a god,' he is a liar; if he says, 'I am the son of man,' he will regret it; 'I will go up to heaven,' he says, but he will not do it."[22] That this tradition is recorded in the name of Rabbi Abahu, a sage living in the land of Israel, underscores its polemical import, as Rabbi Abahu would have come into contact with followers of Jesus.

The targum of Ezekiel, redacted in the fourth–fifth century CE, takes the prophet's identification of *ben 'adam* as "son of Adam," that is, as in Adam and Eve.[23] Alinda Damsma suggests that this unexpected translation can also be regarded as a rejection of Paul's claim that Jesus is a second Adam, as in 1 Corinthians 15:45, "The first man, Adam, became a living being; the last Adam became a life-giving spirit."[24]

Less polemical is the targum to the Psalms, which understands the "son of man" as both messianic and fully human. The Masoretic Text of Psalm 80:17 (80:18 Heb.) states, "Let your hand be upon the man ['ish; NRSV: "one"] at your right hand, upon the son of man [ben 'adam; NRSV: "the one"] whom you made strong for yourself." The targum translates this as, "Upon the King Messiah whom you made strong for yourself." As Damsma notes, "it is the only instance in Targumic exegesis where ben (son) has been associated with the Messiah."[25] In general, rabbinic literature shies away from understanding biblical references to "son of man" (bar 'enosh) as the messiah.

Still, a small number of rabbinic texts do understand Daniel's son of man as the messiah. For example, in explicating Daniel 7:9a—"As I watched, / thrones were set in place, / and an Ancient One took his throne"—Rabbi Akiva, martyred in the Bar Kochba revolt of 132–135 CE, interprets the plural "thrones" as thrones for God and for David, suggesting that he understood the son of man as the Davidic messiah (b. Hagigah 14a). Other rabbis object to Akiva's view, since it smacks of binitarianism. Rabbi Yosi the Galilean responds, "Until when will you make the Shekinah [the divine presence] profane?"[26]

In another instance, Rabbi Alexandri says in the name of Rabbi Yehoshua the son of Levi, "It is written [Dan 7:13], 'and behold with the clouds of heaven there came one like a human being,' and it is written [Zech 9:9], 'poor and riding on a donkey!' If they are righteous, with the clouds of heaven; if they are not righteous, poor and riding on a donkey" (b. Sanhedrin 98a).[27] Echoes of both Jesus as Son of Man and his entry into Jerusalem on a donkey are present, but this rabbinic text insists that the messiah himself has not yet come. Jesus's actions are thus, by implication, not indicative of any fulfillment of prophecy.

The targum to Chronicles, in a somewhat clunky literal reading, gives the son of man a name. It begins by observing that in the list of the sons of Elioenai, 1 Chronicles 3:24 speaks of a fellow named Anani. The name resembles the Hebrew word for "cloud" (*'anan*) and so suggests Daniel 7:13, "one like the Son of man came with the clouds of heaven" (KJV). Therefore, the author proposes that Anani is the *name* of the messiah: "and Anani who is the King Messiah who is destined to be revealed."[28] This idea gets little traction in later tradition.

Rashi interprets Daniel 7:13 "like a son of man" as "the king, the messiah." Although he elsewhere polemicizes against Christian interpretations of the Hebrew Bible, Rashi here is pointing to Israel's eschatological vindication, with the (human) messiah, rather than Jesus, serving as its king. Abraham ibn Ezra favors a collective interpretation, although he mentions the plausibility of an individual, messianic figure.[29] The anonymous *Nitzachon Yashan* (*Old Book of Polemic*; see p. 58), a thirteenth-century work, shows awareness of the Christian use of Psalm 8:1 to reference Jesus: "O LORD, our Sovereign, / how majestic is your name in all the earth!" The text then claims that verse 4 would be the better application: "What are human beings that you are mindful of them, / mortals that you care for them?" His explanation for this application is that Christians "say that Jesus was a man; indeed throughout the Gospels he is called son of man, *fili homini*."[30]

Finally, David Kimchi, in speaking about Ezekiel, provides his own interpretation of *ben 'adam*:

> The commentators have explained accordingly that he [God] called him *ben 'adam* so that he would not become haughty and think of himself as one of the angels because he had seen this great vision. In my eyes it seems correct that, because he saw the face of a man in the Merkabah [the divine chariot], he [God] made known to him that he

is upright and good in his eyes and that he is a son of man, not the son of a lion, nor the son of an ox, nor the son of an eagle in the manner in which we have explained.[31]

Thus the "Son of Man" or "son of man" is once again a human being.

The term "son of man" had already lost its popularity with the close of the New Testament canon. The idiom did not transfer well to Greek speakers, and therefore it did not gain broad popularity in the gentile world. While the idiom "son of man" can sound odd, and while it lacks gender inclusivity, it may be worth retaining; in fact, its very peculiarity can be a starting point for talking about Christology, for like the parables and many other of Jesus's teachings, the title requires interpretation.

The term finds a more recent use in the phrase "son of Adam" found in C. S. Lewis's *The Chronicles of Narnia*; here it refers to human males, in distinction to both supernatural creatures and nonhuman animals. In Narnia, human females are "daughters of Eve." If we do think of "son of man" (*ben 'adam*) as related to Adam, what might that connection say about our human interrelationships, and what might it say about our being in the image of the divine? The Gospel of Luke offers a genealogy that backtracks from Jesus and ends "son of Enos, son of Seth, son of Adam, son of God" (Luke 3:38). We are all in this sense "children of God."

For readers concerned about gender inclusivity, both the term "son" and the term "man" are stumbling blocks. Inclusive Bible translations, seeking to avoid the masculine connotations of the two terms, prefer the alternatives "human one" or "child of humanity." The benefit of the gender-inclusive translation is that it fits the connotations that "son of man" has in the Psalms and Ezekiel; the problem is that it lacks the supernatural sense that we find in Daniel and 1 Enoch. Here we have an opportunity to discuss the art of the translator, and particular problems that arise when we try to make the Bible contemporary. The original term is male, as are the various terms for the God of Israel and, in Latin, for the Holy Spirit. What do we change, and what do we keep?

Other readers may find another stumbling block with the Gospel's son of man imagery: the (one like a) son of man is violent, destructive, scary, and even weird. Reflecting on viewing the movie *Monty Python's Life of Brian* in 1979, Bart Ehrman remarks that the scene "where we find a group of apocalyptic preachers of doom in the midst of Jerusalem . . . was the most subversive scene of them all. . . . It made [Jesus], by implication, a complete crazy like these other apocalyptic wackos."[32] For many readers, the pedagogical Jesus of the Sermon on the Mount of Matthew 5–7 is more palatable than the apocalyptic Jesus of Mark 13 or Revelation.

If readers had a better sense of the historical setting of the book of Daniel and of the role of apocalyptic imagery and literature in providing comfort and hope to people who find themselves powerless in the face of an oppressive system, the apocalyptic eschatological Son of Man may continue to speak today. The Son of Man, from Daniel and 1 Enoch through the Gospel tradition, speaks to the righteousness of God who has the power to enact justice. This reading precludes rather than promotes violence on the part of his followers.

Daniel dreams a dream of "one like a son of man" who is to be given "dominion and glory"; "all peoples, nations, and languages should serve him" for "his dominion is an everlasting dominion that shall not pass away." Daniel's vision is an eschatological one. No matter whether we read Daniel's imagery as referring to an angel, the people Israel, the ancient worthy Enoch, or Jesus of Nazareth, the prophecy has yet to be fulfilled.

CHAPTER 13

✿

Conclusion:
From Polemic to Possibility

The New Covenant:
"'At That Time,' Says the Lord . . ."

JEREMIAH WRITES to warn his contemporaries in Judah against the impending Babylonian conquest, the destruction of the Temple, and the exile; thus the term a "jeremiad" means "a prolonged lamentation or complaint."[1] Yet small portions of the book, mostly in chapters 30–31, claim that both Israel, conquered by the Assyrians in 722 BCE, and Judah, conquered by Babylon in the early sixth century, will be restored. This new time will see the ingathering of the people, even those dispersed more than a century before Jeremiah's time: "See, I am going to bring them from the land of the north, / and gather them from the farthest parts of the earth." Included will be those whose ability to travel would be limited: "among them the blind and the lame, / those with child and those in labor" (Jer 31:8). It is this return of the exiles that God promised Rachel, who wept for her children exiled from their homeland in the Northern Kingdom of Israel (31:15–16). But these prophecies, like many prophecies of consolation, gave no specific date for the restoration.

Jeremiah predicted a new covenant as part of this restoration: "The days are surely coming," God proclaims, "when I will make a new covenant with the house of Israel and the house of Judah" (Jer 31:31). The new covenant "will not be like the covenant that I made with their ancestors when I took them by the hand to bring them out of the land of Egypt" (31:32). That covenant Israel broke. The new covenant, made with the "house of Israel" (31:33), will take the form not of a legal document that one chooses to follow; it is inscribed not on stone or papyrus but will be inscribed internally, such that following it would be as natural as breathing: "I will put my law [Hebrew *torah*] within them, and I will write it on their hearts" (31:33). Because Israel will obey *torah* naturally, there will be no more need for instruction: "No longer shall they teach one another, or say to each other, 'Know the LORD,' for they shall all know me, from the least of them to the greatest, says the LORD; for I will forgive their iniquity, and remember their sin no more" (31:34).

The content of this "new covenant"—a phrase that appears only here in the scriptures of Israel—is not stated, and it is ambiguous whether its newness lies in a new set of obligations and/or that Israel will now be preprogrammed to follow it.[2] The idea that Israel will automatically follow God's will, and thus lack free choice, is unusual but not unique: a similar idea is expressed through the idiom "new heart" found in the writings of Jeremiah's contemporary Ezekiel (18:31; 36:26; cf. 11:19; and using the idiom "circumcise your heart," Deut 30:6). Jewish interpreters understand the newness not in the content of the covenant but in its nature—that Israel must follow it. In an explicit polemic against "the uncircumcised ones who err," namely Christians, the medieval commentator David Kimchi states, "its newness is that it will be (automatically) fulfilled, and will not be breached as the covenant which God made with Israel on Mount Sinai that was breached."[3] But this is not the only possible interpretation of this passage.

For the early church, Jeremiah's statements were read as prophecy for the far future and as fulfilled by Jesus, as we have seen with Matthew's nativity story.

Similarly, Jeremiah's "new covenant" is seen as enacted by Jesus's suffering and death and connected to the gift of setting humanity free from Satan and sin. Jesus states in Luke 22:20, "This cup that is poured out for you is the new covenant in my blood." For the church, this new covenant is the one Jeremiah predicted, a covenant not marked in the body by the sign of circumcision (Gen 17:10–11, 14) but marked in the heart of those who accept Jesus as Lord and savior.

Paul affirms this new covenant language in a text written earlier than Luke's Gospel. In 1 Corinthians 11:25, he repeats the tradition he received: that Jesus "took the cup also, after supper, saying, 'This cup is the new covenant in my blood. Do this, as often as you drink it, in remembrance of me.'" This new covenant for Paul is "not of letter but of spirit; for the letter kills, but the Spirit gives life" (2 Cor 3:6). The move of those following the new covenant, the gentiles in Corinth to whom Paul writes, should not be toward obedience to the Torah; such obedience was never meant for gentiles. The move is rather away from anything that might be seen as pagan practice, be it worship of Rome's gods or participation in local cultic activity, and toward Jesus.

Finally, the Epistle to the Hebrews evokes Jeremiah's new covenant language in its understanding of Jesus. According to Hebrews 9:15, Jesus "is the mediator of a new covenant" and so the fulfillment of Jeremiah's prophecy. It is through his self-sacrifice that "those who are called [i.e., his followers, determined not by ethnicity but by belief] may receive the promised eternal inheritance, because a death has occurred that redeems them from the transgressions under the first covenant," that is, the Torah mediated by Moses (Heb 9:15). It is Jesus, "the mediator of a new covenant" (12:24), to which all must turn.

Hebrews 8:8 quotes Jeremiah directly: "The days are surely coming, says the Lord, / when I will establish a new covenant with the house of Israel / and with the house of Judah." Then the author of Hebrews draws one possible conclusion, that "in speaking of 'a new covenant,' he has made the first one obsolete. And what is obsolete and growing old will soon disappear" (8:13). A covenant written on the heart requires no physical markers, and it also requires no teachers.

Read through Christian eyes, Jeremiah's prediction of the new covenant that redeems from sin is fulfilled in Jesus. However, this is only one of several possible interpretations of Jeremiah, and even if one claims that the new covenant is fulfilled in Jesus, the fulfillment is only partial. The return of the people of Israel and Judah to the land of Israel has not yet fully taken place, despite the foundation of the State of Israel in 1948. Neither Christians nor Jews, nor anyone else, has God's instructions written on their hearts; if they did, there would be little need for ongoing Bible study or sermons, since we would be living in that perfect eschatological age, with the wolf living beside the lamb (Isa 11:6).

Indeed, both Judaism and Christianity are unfinished projects awaiting the messiah, though they differ in beliefs about this messiah's identity and job description. For the church, the fulfillment of any new covenant requires Jesus's second coming, sometimes called the "parousia," the Greek term for "appearance" that signals the entry of the conquering hero into his newly gained city. Traditional Judaism still anticipates not only the coming of the messiah and the ingathering of the exiles but also the rebuilding of the Temple in Jerusalem. At the moment, the project is on hold, not least because there is currently a mosque, the Dome of the Rock, on the site of that ancient Temple. Both Judaism and Christianity claim the promises of Jeremiah, and the rest of the scriptures of Israel accompanying those promises. Both await fulfillment—each in its own way.

In the Interim

I N THE PAST, Jews and Christians fought over the legacy of Israel's scriptures: each claimed not only to be the true Israel, possessing the true interpretation, but also that the other's interpretation was wrong. Yet even in polemical contexts, such as Justin's *Dialogue with Trypho*, glimmers of a more irenic approach can be seen; as Justin states, "For we have found more than we expected, or than it was even possible for us to expect. And if we could do this more frequently we should receive more benefit, while we examine the very words [of Scripture] themselves" (*Dialogue* 142). Recently, however, Jewish-Christian dialogue has opened multiple possibilities that do not require a zero-sum conclusion. Leading the way in this conversation is the Roman Catholic Church. Since the 1965 Vatican II document *Nostra Aetate* (*In Our Time*) emphasized that all Jews of all times should *not* be held responsible for the death of Jesus, the merging of ethics with exegesis has become paramount. *Nostra Aetate* 4 reads:

> True, the Jewish authorities and those who followed their lead pressed for the death of Christ; still, what happened in His passion cannot be charged against all the Jews, without distinction, then alive, nor against the Jews of today. Although the Church is the new people of God, the Jews should not be presented as rejected or accursed by

God, as if this followed from the Holy Scriptures. All should see to it, then, that in catechetical work or in the preaching of the word of God they do not teach anything that does not conform to the truth of the Gospel and the spirit of Christ.

This document, as has been widely acknowledged, produced a major change in Jewish-Catholic relations. Several Protestant groups have produced similar statements.[4]

The Catholic Church did not have to make this affirmation. It could have understood the Gospels as condemning all Jews of all times, as many Christians before and some after 1965 had done. Matthew's Gospel states that when Pontius Pilate declared Jesus to be innocent of all accusations against him, the crowd of "all the people" (Greek *pas ho laos*; the NRSV's "the people as a whole" is a paraphrase) shouted, "His blood be on us and on our children!" (Matt 27:25). This infamous blood cry served for centuries as the source for the view that all Jews, from that first generation to the present, bear particular responsibility for the death of Jesus. For centuries, and in some cases still today, Christians have read this verse as damning all Jews as Christ-killers.

From a historical perspective, it is unlikely Matthew was thinking that all Jews of all times bear this guilt. "All the people" in Matthew's Gospel would have meant all the people living in the 30s CE in Jerusalem, people who had been agitated about Jesus since his birth. Matthew's second chapter states that upon hearing the Magi's report of a newborn "king of the Jews," not only was King Herod frightened, so was "all Jerusalem with him" (Matt 2:3). While Matthew does recognize Jerusalem as the "holy city" (4:5; 27:53), the Gospel's depiction of the city's inhabitants is less positive: Matthew regards the people of Jerusalem as having rejected Jesus, and because of this rejection, their children, the people who were alive in 70 CE, saw the destruction of their city. The "our children" of Matthew 27:25 were specifically the children of the people in Jerusalem at the time of Jesus's death.

In this case, historical analysis and ethical reflection combine to help readers avoid an anti-Jewish and anti-Semitic interpretation. The Vatican Council chose how to read its Gospels, just as the followers of Jesus in the first and second centuries chose how to read the scriptures of Israel. We always make choices in our readings— and we must choose wisely.

When the followers of Jesus read what became their Old Testament, they made choices on which translations to use, what to highlight, how to understand prophecy, and where allegorical interpretations might be employed. The Jewish tradition, reading what became their Tanakh, did the same. As we have stated, the process need not imply that one religion wins and the other loses; in literary understanding, a single text necessarily gives rise to multiple interpretations. If it did not, all English teachers would be out of a job, since all students would understand the precise single meaning of every assigned text.

Since *Nostra Aetate*, Vatican groups as well as several national Bishops' Conferences have produced additional documents concerning better relations with the Jewish community. In 2015, the Vatican's Commission for Religious Relations with the Jews released "'The Gifts and the Calling of God Are Irrevocable' (Rom 11:29): A Reflection on the Theological Questions Pertaining to Catholic-Jewish Relations." This twenty-five-page text, produced with the participation of two Jewish consultors (a process showing the impetus to move from polemic to possibility), reaffirms the point: "One cannot understand Jesus's teaching or that of his disciples without situating it within the Jewish horizon in the context of the living tradition of Israel; one would understand his teachings even less so if they were seen in opposition to this tradition."[5] That Jewish context includes, as paramount, the scriptures of Israel.

Jews too, although lacking the hierarchical structure of the Catholic Church, have produced their own texts regarding the relationship between the two traditions. The most recent, also in 2015, is "To Do the Will of Our Father in Heaven: Toward a Partnership Between Jews and Christians." Signed initially by twenty-five Orthodox rabbis and twice that number subsequently, the statement recognizes that Christianity should not be seen as being at odds with Judaism: "As did Maimonides and Yehudah Halevi [two great medieval Jewish thinkers], we acknowledge that the emergence of Christianity in human history is neither an accident nor an error, but the willed divine outcome and gift to the nations." It also reflects the change in Catholic exegesis begun with *Nostra Aetate:* "Now that the Catholic Church has acknowledged the eternal Covenant between God and Israel, we Jews can acknowledge the ongoing constructive validity of Christianity as our partner in world redemption, without any fear that this will be exploited for missionary purposes."[6]

In the twenty-first century, we are finally at the point where Jews and Christians can read their shared texts differently and learn from each other. We all can, and must, even read those texts unique to the other's tradition. Jews do well to read the New Testament and then to share these readings with Christians, and Christians do well to look at nonbiblical Jewish sources and then share them with Jews. We are finally at the point where we can interpret the Bible, whatever its content, not as a zero-sum problem but as an opportunity to correct certain older readings based in polemic, creating newer ones based on the possibility of mutual respect if not in complete agreement.[7]

WHAT WE LEARN

As HISTORIANS, we appreciate what texts meant to their original audiences, and we also think that in many cases we can also
determine what authors intended to say. At the same time, we recognize that texts will always be read outside of their original contexts.
People will, and we think should, bring their own concerns to a text,
especially if the text is one they consider sacred.

When a text is detached from its historical and even contextual
mooring, whether by allegory or by prooftext, the threat of idiosyn-
cratic reading is increased. A few mechanisms can serve to help interpreters from going off the hermeneutical deep end and into the
depths of solipsism.

The first is at least an understanding of how the text may have
been interpreted in its original context and how it has been understood over time. To begin by asking, "What does this text mean to
me?" is a fine start, but it should not be enough. We can learn from
engaging with what others, both from within and outside our particular traditions, have seen.

The second is to look at original languages, such as Hebrew and
Greek. For those who lack such skills—that is, for most people—all
is not lost. Several websites give various versions so that we can see
how, and often why, those who do have the language skills arrive at

their own translations.[8] Many commentaries discuss the nuances of Hebrew and Greek in any given passage.

The third is to raise the question of ethics, since all interpretations have the potential to affect behaviors. We have seen how both Jews and Christians have ways of summarizing their traditions, or of finding touchstones in the text that guide other interpretations. Leviticus 19:18b, on "love of neighbor," which Jesus cites as part of the Great Commandment (Matt 22:39; Mark 12:31), which Paul sees as a summary of the law (Rom 13:9; Gal 5:14), which the Epistle of James (2:8) calls the "royal law," and which Rabbi Akiva notes "is a general principle of the Bible" (y. Nedarim 9:4 and parallels), provides one good example of a touchstone shared by both religions.

Connected with the ethical duty of interpretation is the concern for multiple voices. Jews from Iran or Ethiopia may see things in the Tanakh that Jews from Ukraine or Spain may not; Christians of color may offer different emphases than Christians with European origins. Men and women may note different aspects in a text. At the same time, we return to history, for if we are to support multicultural readings, or readings from a person's particular subject position, we should also respect the fact that the author and the text have their own cultural embeddedness. To ignore that historical connection threatens to colonize the text; it is to impose one culturally determined interpretation upon the original, culturally embedded text.

In looking at the diverse readings of the same text, we have come more deeply to appreciate, broadly, what the Bible means both with and without Jesus in terms of what the Bible means and what it meant. We have shown how a single verse takes on different meanings, depending on our location, and thus the presuppositions we bring to it and the questions we ask of it. The Old Testament, the Tanakh, the Hebrew Bible—whatever we call it—is too complex to hold only one meaning and too theologically relevant to both Jews and Christians to be the property of only one community.

We have seen, for example, how the garden of Eden story gives rise to multiple interpretations, from the Jewish original opportunity to the Christian original sin. If we see the problem addressed in the story of Adam and Eve as one of misguided actions, then we require a code of conduct, and so we have the Jewish Torah, which helps to harness the evil inclination. If we opt for a narrative of a fall, then we require a narrative of a redemption, and so we have the Christian story with Jesus as the second Adam, and for some, Mary as the new Eve.

We have seen over the centuries how different laws have been understood, and we recognize therefore how difficult it is, today, to try to implement what many have called "biblical values": for instance, Jews and Christians disagree among themselves, and with each other, on how to understand Exodus 20:13; should it be rendered "You shall not murder" (so NRSV and NJPS) or "Thou shalt not kill" (KJV), and how should it be implemented?

We saw how complex it is to interpret prophetic texts in their contexts, and even to decide which verses should be considered prophetic, since texts that were not originally prophecies came to be seen as such, as readers in the first century CE and beyond saw ancient texts as being fulfilled in their own time. Added to this complexity is the intermingling of grammatical and theological questions. How we translate a text can influence our theology, and our theology can in turn influence our choice of translation. Yet the contested interpretations of these texts should not obscure the fact that the texts continue to hold meaning. The Bible was not meant to be a source of hidden predictions, with God as the trickster who tells us what is going to happen only after the fact. The Bible is *torah*, "instruction." Yet we must constantly reassess how we teach and live this instruction, for what is appropriate in one period or for one person may not be in another setting or for a different audience.

We have accentuated how Christians might increase their appreciation of the "Old Testament" texts cited in the New Testament, as well as how those texts have ongoing meaning in the Jewish tradition. We have also encouraged Jewish readers to look at texts in the Tanakh, such as Isaiah 7 on the sign of the conception and birth of a child, Isaiah 53 on the suffering servant, and Isaiah 61 on the messianic age, which frequently get downplayed in synagogal contexts. We also want to encourage our Jewish readers to see how the various quotations from their own scriptures are used in the New Testament, for several of the New Testament writers, especially Paul, are reading and writing from within their own Jewish tradition.

And we have seen communities wrestling with theological matters: with the role of sacrifice in relation to atonement, with the urge to codify scriptural readings in liturgy, with determining canons within canons, with how to relate to strangers. We are stronger when we wrestle, and when we read together. And we can, in agreeing to disagree with one reading or another, still ask, "Give me another interpretation," for that supply is inexhaustible.

ACKNOWLEDGMENTS

As we noted in our dedication, "The Sages taught: There are three partners in the creation of all people: The Holy One, their father, and their mother" (b. Niddah 31a). We had many more than three partners in producing this book. We thank Mickey Maudlin, executive editor and senior vice president at HarperOne, for encouraging and nurturing this project and shepherding it so skillfully from idea to published book; Roger Freet from Folio; and the whole Harper team who helped along the way: Anna Paustenbach, Aidan Mahony, Chantal Tom, Suzanne Quist, Makenna Holford, Melinda Mullin, Laina Adler, and all the people behind the scenes.

Our family also served as our partner, and we thank Tova Hartman, Talya Brettler, Immanuel Buder, Ezra Brettler and Jay Geller, Sarah Elizabeth Geller, and Alexander Geller for their love and support. Eliana Sidney Brettler Buder brought much joy and helpful distraction in the final stages of this project. Many colleagues and friends, including Herb Basser, Abraham Berkovitz, Robert Cargill, Esther Chazon, Cody David, Yedida Eisenstadt, Mark Goodacre, Lenn Goodman, Ed Greenstein, Steven Kepnes, Reuven Kimelman, James Kugel, Joseph Lam, Martin Lockshin, Paul Mandel, Joel Marcus, Craig Morrison, Mark Smith, Emanuel Tov, and Shani Tzoref answered queries and offered assistance and encouragement at one time or another. Jonathan Homrighausen of Duke University reviewed the manuscript several times and offered many helpful suggestions; Alexander Geller helped in preparing the final draft for clarity and consistency; and William Brown proofread the manuscript, providing thorough feedback and thoughtful recommendations. The librarians of Duke University, Vanderbilt University, the National Library of Israel, and the Pontifical Biblical Institute assisted us through their excellent collections. We apologize to those we neglected to thank and note that ultimate responsibility for mistakes lies with us alone. We hope that our readers will be generous, applying to us the wish of the psalmist (Ps 19:12 [19:13 Heb.], slightly reworked): "But who can detect (all) errors? Clear us from inadvertent faults."

NOTES

Chapter 1: On Bibles and Their Interpreters

1 Neither finding the definitive context for interpretation nor translating from one context to another is a simple process; see Ben-Ami Scharfstein, *The Dilemma of Context* (New York: New York Univ. Press, 1989). Concerning the Bible, see Ed Greenstein, "Peshat, Derash, and the Question of Context" [in Hebrew], *Ressling* 5 (1998): 31–34.

2 We use the neutral terms BCE (before the common era) and CE (common era) instead of BC ("before Christ") and AD (Anno Domini, Latin for "the year of our Lord"). An alternative Jewish form of dating starts with creation, as determined through counting beginning with Genesis 1. According to this *anno mundi* (Latin for "years of the world" and abbreviated as AM) system, the year 2020 CE = 5780 AM.

3 See Amy-Jill Levine, *The Misunderstood Jew: The Church and the Scandal of the Jewish Jesus* (San Francisco: HarperOne, 2007), 193–99; Lee Martin McDonald, *The Formation of the Biblical Canon*, vol. 1, *The Old Testament: Its Authority and Canonicity* (London: T&T Clark, 2017). See also the summary by Amy-Jill Levine, "What Is the Difference Between the Old Testament, the Tanakh, and the Hebrew Bible?," *Bible Odyssey*, https://www.bibleodyssey.org/en/tools /bible-basics/what-is-the-difference-between-the-old-testament-the-tanakh -and-the-hebrew-bible.

4 McDonald, *Formation of the Biblical Canon.*

5 For the rabbinic terms for the Bible and its parts, see Sid Z. Leiman, *The Canonization of Hebrew Scripture: The Talmudic and Midrashic Evidence* (Hamden, CT: Archon Books, 1976), 56–58.

6 McDonald, *Formation of the Biblical Canon*, 1:33.

7 See, e.g., John Goldingay, *The First Testament: A New Translation* (Downers Grove, IL: InterVarsity, 2018).

8 *Tanakh: The Holy Scriptures; The New JPS Translation According to the Traditional Hebrew Text* (Philadelphia: Jewish Publication Society, 1985), the product of a three-decade collaboration by Jewish scholars. Although classical rabbinic texts use the terms Torah, Nevi'im, and Ketuvim to refer to parts of the Bible, the

acronym Tanakh and its equivalent Aramaic *'anakh* derive from the Masoretes; see Marc Zvi Brettler, "The Canonization of the Bible," in *JSB*, 2153–56; Israel Yeivin, *Introduction to the Tiberian Masorah*, trans. E. J. Revell (Missoula, MT: Scholars Press, 1980), 84, 119.

9 Elvira Martín Contreras, "Medieval Masoretic Text," in *Textual History of the Bible: The Hebrew Bible*, vol. 1A, *Overview Articles*, ed. Armin Lange and Emanuel Tov (Leiden: Brill, 2016), 420–29.

10 Michael L. Satlow, *How the Bible Became Holy* (New Haven: Yale Univ. Press, 2014).

11 For a more positive view of canonization in the first century, see Stephen B. Chapman, "Second Temple Hermeneutics: How Canon Is Not an Anachronism," in *Invention, Rewriting, Usurpation: Discursive Fights over Religious Traditions in Antiquity*, ed. Jörg Ulrich, Anders-Christian Jacobsen, and David Brakke (Frankfurt: Peter Lang, 2012), 281–96.

12 Abraham Wasserstein and David J. Wasserstein, *The Legend of the Septuagint: From Classical Antiquity to Today* (Cambridge: Cambridge Univ. Press, 2006).

13 Leonard Greenspoon, "The Septuagint," in *JANT*, 703–7.

14 Example from R. L. Trask, *Language and Linguistics: The Key Concepts*, ed. Peter Stockwell, 2nd ed. (New York: Routledge, 2007), 14.

15 Ben Witherington, "Hermeneutics—A Guide for Perplexed Bible Readers," *Ben Witherington* (blog), August 21, 2007, http://benwitherington.blogspot.com /2007/08/hermeneutics-guide-for-perplexed-bible.html.

16 See Bart D. Ehrman, *The Orthodox Corruption of Scripture: The Effect of Early Christological Controversies on the Text of the New Testament*, rev. ed. (New York: Oxford Univ. Press, 2011); and Ehrman's popular version of this study, *Misquoting Jesus: The Story Behind Who Changed the Bible and Why* (San Francisco: HarperOne, 2007).

17 See "Second Amendment," Legal Information Institute, Cornell Law School, https://www.law.cornell.edu/wex/second_amendment.

18 Frank H. Easterbrook, "Originalism and Pragmatism: Pragmatism's Role in Interpretation," *Harvard Journal of Law and Public Policy* 901 (2008): 901–6.

19 Alex P. Jassen, *Mediating the Divine: Prophecy and Revelation in the Dead Sea Scrolls and Second Temple Judaism*, Studies on the Texts of the Desert of Judah 68 (Leiden: Brill, 2007).

20 Jubilees 1:27–29. See James C. VanderKam, "The Angel of Presence in the Book of Jubilees," *Dead Sea Discoveries* 7 (2000): 378–93.

21 James C. VanderKam, *Jubilees*, 2 vols., Hermeneia (Minneapolis: Fortress, 2018), 1:79.

22 James L. Kugel, "Jubilees," in *OTB*, 1:289–90.

23 Geza Vermes, *The Complete Dead Sea Scrolls in English* (New York: Penguin, 1997), 478–85.

24 Shani L. Berrin, "Pesharim," in *EDSS*, 2:644–47. See also George J. Brooke, "Prophecy and Prophets in the Dead Sea Scrolls: Looking Backwards and Forwards," in *Prophets, Prophecy, and Prophetic Texts in Second Temple Judaism*, ed. Michael H. Floyd and Robert D. Haak (New York: T&T Clark, 2006), 151–65.

25 Joseph A. Fitzmyer, "The Use of Explicit Old Testament Quotations in Qumran Literature and in the New Testament," in *The Semitic Background of the New Testament* (Grand Rapids: Eerdmans, 1997), 3–58; Geza Vermes, "Biblical Proof-texts in Qumran Literature," *Journal of Semitic Studies* 34 (1989): 493–508.

See also Moshe J. Bernstein, "Introductory Formulas for Citation and Re-Citations of Bible Verses in the Qumran Pesharim: Observations on a Pesher Technique," *Dead Sea Discoveries* 1 (1994): 30–70; Alex P. Jassen, *Scripture and Law in the Dead Sea Scrolls* (Cambridge: Cambridge Univ. Press, 2014).

26 On the distinction between what a text meant and what it means, see Krister Stendahl, "Biblical Theology, Contemporary," in *Meanings: The Bible as Document and as Guide* (Philadelphia: Fortress, 1984), 11–44, esp. 14–15.

27 John Barton, *The Nature of Biblical Criticism* (Louisville: Westminster John Knox, 2007); and also his *Reading the Old Testament: Method in Biblical Study*, rev. ed. (Louisville: Westminster John Knox, 1996); John F. A. Sawyer, "The Bible in Future Jewish-Christian Relations," in *Challenges in Jewish-Christian Relations*, ed. James K. Aitken and Edward Kessler (New York: Paulist, 2006), 39–50, esp. 44–45.

28 Isaak Heinemann, *The Methods of Aggadah* [in Hebrew] (Jerusalem: Magnes, 1954), 4–7.

29 See James L. Kugel, *The Bible as It Was* (Cambridge, MA: Harvard Univ. Press, 1997), 17–23.

30 An excellent summary of Jewish biblical interpretation is Paul Mandel, "Jewish Hermeneutics," in *Religion in Europa heute: Sozialwissenschaftliche, rechtswissenschaftliche und hermeneutisch-religionsphilosophische Perspektiven*, ed. Kurt Appel (Göttingen: Vandenhoeck und Ruprecht, 2012), 210–31. For more detailed description, see the section "Jewish Interpretation of the Bible" in *JSB*, 1835–977, and the essays on Judaism in James Carlton Paget et al., eds., *The New Cambridge History of the Bible*, 4 vols. (Cambridge: Cambridge Univ. Press, 2012–2016); Magne Sæbø, ed., *Hebrew Bible/Old Testament: The History of Its Interpretation*, 5 vols. (Göttingen: Vandenhoeck und Ruprecht, 1996–2014); Benjamin D. Sommer, ed., *Jewish Concepts of Scripture: A Comparative Introduction* (New York: New York Univ. Press, 2012).

31 See David Stern, "Midrash and Jewish Exegesis," in *JSB*, 1879–90, esp. the illustration of a Rabbinic Bible on 1890.

32 Kugel's term is developed in Yaakov Elman, "'It Is No Empty Thing': Nahmanides and the Search for Omnisignificance," *Torah U-Madda Journal* 4 (1993): 1–83; Elman, "The Rebirth of Omnisignificant Biblical Exegesis in the Nineteenth and Twentieth Centuries," *Jewish Studies: An Internet Journal* 2 (2003): 199–249. See also Paul D. Mandel, *The Origins of Midrash: From Teaching to Text*, Supplements to the Journal for the Study of Judaism 180 (Leiden: Brill, 2017), 299–303.

33 First attested in the midrash Numbers Rabbah 13:15–16, https://www.sefaria .org/Bamidbar_Rabbah.13.15?lang=bi&with=all&lang2=en.

34 See discussion by Daniel Boyarin, "Shattering the Logos: Hermeneutics Between a Hammer and a Hard Place," in *The Blackwell Companion to Postmodern Theology*, ed. Graham Ward (Malden, MA: Blackwell, 2001), 315–18.

35 "Bereishit Rabbah 1:10," Sefaria, https://www.sefaria.org.il/Bereishit_Rabbah .1.10?lang=en&with=all&lang2=en.

36 Moshe Idel, "Kabbalistic Exegesis," in Sæbø, *Hebrew Bible/Old Testament*, vol. 1/2, 457–58.

37 Michael Fishbane, *Song of Songs*, JPS Bible Commentary (Philadelphia: Jewish Publication Society, 2015), 26–28.

38 Fishbane, *Song of Songs*, liii.

39 See, e.g., Gary A. Anderson, *Christian Doctrine and the Old Testament: Theology in the Service of Biblical Exegesis* (Grand Rapids: Baker Academic, 2017); G. K. Beale, *Handbook on the New Testament Use of the Old Testament* (Grand Rapids: Baker Academic, 2012); John Goldingay, *Reading Jesus' Bible: How the New Testament Helps Us Understand the Old Testament* (Grand Rapids: Eerdmans, 2017); Richard B. Hays, *Echoes of Scripture in the Letters of Paul* (New Haven: Yale Univ. Press, 1989); Roy E. Gane, *Old Testament Law for Christians: Original Context and Enduring Application* (Grand Rapids: Baker Academic, 2017); Douglas S. Earl, *Reading Old Testament Narrative as Christian Scripture*, Journal of Theological Interpretation Supplement 17 (Winona Lake, IN: Eisenbrauns, 2017); Ben Witherington III, *Isaiah Old and New: Exegesis, Intertextuality, and Hermeneutics* (Minneapolis: Fortress, 2017); Witherington III, *Psalms Old and New: Exegesis, Intertextuality, and Hermeneutics* (Minneapolis: Fortress, 2017); Witherington III, *Torah Old and New: Exegesis, Intertextuality, and Hermeneutics* (Minneapolis: Fortress, 2018). Many of these studies take a conservative, Christian approach.

40 See Shaye J. D. Cohen, "Judaism and Jewishness," in *JANT*, 592–96.

41 Menachem Kellner, *Must a Jew Believe Anything?*, 2nd ed. (London: Littman Library of Jewish Civilization, 2006).

42 Klyne Snodgrass, "*Anaideia* and the Friend at Midnight (Luke 11:8)," *Journal of Biblical Literature* 116 (1997): 505–13; Alan F. Johnson, "Assurance for Man: The Fallacy of Translating *Anaideia* by 'Persistence,'" *Journal of Evangelical Theology* 22 (1979): 123–31.

43 Deeana Klepper, "Theories of Interpretation: The Quadriga and Its Successors," in *The New Cambridge History of the Bible*, vol. 3, *From 1450 to 1750*, ed. Euan Cameron (Cambridge: Cambridge Univ. Press, 2016), 418–38. These senses are still significant in contemporary Christian interpretation; see Pontifical Biblical Commission, "The Interpretation of the Bible in the Church," 1993, section II, "Hermeneutical Questions," https://catholic-resources.org/ChurchDocs/PBC_Interp-FullText.htm.

Chapter 2: The Problem and Promise of Prophecy

1 Martti Nissinen, *Ancient Prophecy: Near Eastern, Biblical, and Greek Perspectives* (Oxford: Oxford Univ. Press, 2017); Nissinen, "Prophetic Intermediation in the Ancient Near East," in *The Oxford Handbook of the Prophets*, ed. Carolyn J. Sharp (Oxford: Oxford Univ. Press, 2016), 5–22. See also Marc Zvi Brettler, *How to Read the Jewish Bible* (New York: Oxford Univ. Press, 2007), 137–47; Reinhard G. Kratz, *The Prophets of Israel*, trans. Anselm C. Hagedorn and Nathan MacDonald (Winona Lake, IN: Eisenbrauns, 2015).

2 See Carol L. Meyers and Eric M. Meyers, *Zechariah 9–14*, Anchor Yale Bible 25C (New Haven: Yale Univ. Press, 1993), 489–92.

3 Moshe J. Bernstein, "Pesher Habakkuk," *EDSS*, 2:647–50.

4 See y. Ta'anit 68d. Aharon Oppenheimer, "Bar Kokhba, Shim'on," *EDSS*, 1:78–80; John J. Collins, *The Scepter and the Star: Messianism in Light of the Dead Sea Scrolls*, 2nd ed. (Grand Rapids: Eerdmans, 2010), chap. 9.

5 Maimonides, *Mishneh Torah*, Kings and Wars 11:1, https://www.sefaria.org

/Mishneh_Torah%2C_Kings_and_Wars.11.1?ven=Laws_of_Kings_and_Wars
._trans._Reuven_Brauner,_2012&lang=bi.

6   Michael Drosnin, *The Bible Code* (New York: Touchstone Books, 1997), and
    several sequels. Biblical scholar Jeffrey Tigay notes, "the entire enterprise of the
    'Bible codes' is specious. It is undercut by what we know about the history of the
    biblical text, by flaws in the 'famous sages' experiment, and by the arbitrariness
    of the methods by which the decoders identify which letters belong to the
    alleged patterns and messages and then proceed to interpret them." See his
    "The Bible 'Codes': A Textual Perspective" (lecture, Princeton Univ., October 13,
    1999), https://www.sas.upenn.edu/~jtigay/codetext.html.

7   Ruth Sheridan, "Scripture Fulfillment," in *JANT*, 727–30.

8   Daniel J. Treier, "Proof Text," in *Dictionary for Theological Interpretation of the
    Bible*, ed. Kevin J. Vanhoozer (Grand Rapids: Baker Academic, 2005), 622–24
    (622).

9   Zack Hunt, "Why Proof-Texting Is Not Like Other Sins," *The Semi-Official Blog
    of Zack Hunt* (blog), Patheos, April 23, 2015, https://www.patheos.com/blogs
    /zackhunt/2015/04/proof-texting-not-like-sins/.

10 James M. Reese, "Pitfalls of Proof-texting," *Biblical Theology Bulletin* 13 (1983):
    121–23 (121).

11 R. Michael Allen and Scott R. Swain, "In Defense of Proof-Texting," *Journal of
    the Evangelical Theological Society* 54 (2011): 589–606.

12 In a conversation with Marc Brettler on May 16, 2019, James Kugel said that he
    would consider prooftexting to be a fifth principle.

13 "Berakhot 48b," Sefaria, https://www.sefaria.org.il/Berakhot.48b?lang=bi.

14 See p. 27.

15 Mekilta, Shirta I; translation and discussion in Jon D. Levenson, *Resurrection and
    the Restoration of Israel: The Ultimate Victory of the God of Life* (New Haven: Yale
    Univ. Press, 2006), 26–27; on p. 33, Levenson acknowledges the "forced nature of
    the exegesis in question."

16 There are also few citations of biblical texts in the Apocrypha; see Andrew
    Chilton, "Citing the Old Testament," in *It Is Written: Scripture Citing Scripture;
    Essays in Honour of Barnabas Lindars, SSF*, ed. D. A. Carson and H. G. M.
    Williamson (Cambridge: Cambridge Univ. Press, 1988), 141–69 (150–64).

17 Kevin L. Spawn, *"As It Is Written" and Other Citation Formulae in the Old
    Testament: Their Use, Development, Syntax and Significance*, Beihefte zur
    Zeitschrift für die alttestamentliche Wissenschaft 311 (Berlin: de Gruyter, 2002).

18 See also Jer 26:18, which cites Mic 3:12.

19 Michael Marmur, "Why Jews Quote," *Oral Tradition* 29 (2014): 5–46 (13, 15, 22).

20 Quoting is also valued among many contemporary cultures; see the first section,
    "Everyone Quotes," of Marmur's essay "Why Jews Quote," with literature cited
    there.

21 *Oxford English Dictionary*, 2nd ed. (1989), s.v. "polemic."

22 Robert L. Wilken, *John Chrysostom and the Jews: Rhetoric and Reality in the Late
    4th Century* (Berkeley: Univ. of California Press, 1983).

23 Yairah Amit, *Hidden Polemics in Biblical Narrative*, trans. Jonathan Chipman,
    Biblical Interpretation 25 (Leiden: Brill, 2000).

24 Tamara Cohn Eskenazi and Tikva Frymer-Kensky, *Ruth*, JPS Bible Commentary
    (Philadelphia: Jewish Publication Society, 2011), viii–xix.

25 See Harvey Sicherman and Gilad J. Gevaryahu, "Rashi and the First Crusade:
    Commentary, Liturgy, Legend," *Judaism* 48 (1999): 181–97 (183–84). See also
    Rashi's Commentary on Psalms, ed. Mayer I. Gruber, Brill Reference Library
    of Judaism 18 (Leiden: Brill, 2004), 130–31. Michael A. Signer surmises that
    "many passages in Rashi's commentaries respond to Christian readings without
    any specific mention of Christian interpretation"; Signer, "Consolation and
    Confrontation: Jewish and Christian Interpretation of the Prophetic Books,"
    in *Scripture and Pluralism: Reading the Bible in the Religiously Plural Worlds
    of the Middle Ages and Renaissance*, ed. Thomas J. Heffernan and Thomas E.
    Burman, Studies in the History of Christian Traditions 123 (Leiden: Brill,
    2005), 77–94 (91). See also Avraham Grossman, "Rashi's Position on Prophecy
    Among the Nations and the Jewish-Christian Polemic," in *New Perspectives on
    Jewish-Christian Relations in Honor of David Berger*, ed. Elisheva Carlebach and
    Jacob J. Schacter, Brill Reference Library of Judaism 33 (Leiden: Brill, 2012),
    399–417.
26 "Rashi on Genesis 1:1:2," Sefaria, https://www.sefaria.org.il/Rashi_on_Genesis
    .1.1.2?lang=en&with=all&lang2=en.
27 Paula Fredriksen and Oded Irshai, "Christian Anti-Judaism: Polemics and
    Policies," in *The Cambridge History of Judaism*, ed. Steven T. Katz (Cambridge:
    Cambridge Univ. Press, 2006), 4:977–1034.
28 See Joshua Ezra Burns, *The Christian Schism in Jewish History and Jewish Memory*
    (Cambridge: Cambridge Univ. Press, 2016), esp. 159–208.
29 For suggested anti-Christian polemics in the Babylonian Talmud, see Moshe
    Benovitz, *BT Sukkah Chapter IV and Chapter V* [in Hebrew], Talmud Ha-Igud
    (Jerusalem: Society for the Interpretation of the Talmud, 2013), 560n10.
30 Steven T. Katz, "The Rabbinic Response to Christianity," in Katz, *Cambridge
    History of Judaism*, 4:259–98. Maximizing the polemic is Israel Jacob Yuval, *Two
    Nations in Your Womb: Perceptions of Jews and Christians in Late Antiquity and the
    Middle Ages*, trans. Barbara Harshav and Jonathan Chipman (Berkeley: Univ. of
    California Press, 2008). For a more nuanced perspective, see Marc Hirshman,
    A Rivalry of Genius: Jewish and Christian Interpretation in Late Antiquity, trans.
    Batya Stein (Albany: State Univ. of New York Press, 1996), esp. 121.
31 Robert Chazan, *Fashioning Jewish Identity in Medieval Western Christendom*
    (Cambridge: Cambridge Univ. Press, 2004); Alon Goshen-Gottstein, "Jewish-
    Christian Relations and Rabbinic Literature—Shifting Scholarly and Relational
    Paradigms: The Case of Two Powers," in *Interaction Between Judaism and
    Christianity in History, Religion, Art and Literature*, ed. Marcel Poorhuis, Joshua
    Schwartz, and Joseph Turner, Jewish and Christian Perspectives 17 (Leiden:
    Brill, 2009), 15–43 (23–25).
32 For examples and discussion, see Peter Schäfer, *Jesus in the Talmud* (Princeton:
    Princeton Univ. Press, 2009).
33 Martin Lockshin, "Jesus in Medieval Jewish Tradition," in *JANT*, 735–36; Peter
    Schäfer, Michael Meerson, and Yaacov Deutsch, eds., *Toledot Yeshu ("The Life
    Story of Jesus") Revisited* (Tübingen: Mohr Siebeck, 2011).
34 See the excellent summary in Robert Chazan, "Disputations, Jewish-Christian,"
    EBR, 6:927–35. For primary texts, see Frank Ephraim Talmage, ed., *Disputation
    and Dialogue: Readings in Jewish-Christian Encounter* (New York: Ktav and
    Anti-Defamation League of B'nai B'rith, 1975).

35 Nina Caputo and Liz Clarke, *Debating Truth: The Barcelona Disputation of 1263;
    A Graphic History* (Oxford: Oxford Univ. Press, 2017).

36 Joseph Kimchi, *The Book of the Covenant*, trans. Frank Talmage (Toronto:
    Pontifical Institute of Mediaeval Studies, 1972).

37 David Berger, ed., *The Jewish-Christian Debate in the High Middle Ages: A Critical
    Edition of the Nizzahon Vetus with an Introduction, Translation, and Commentary*
    (Philadelphia: Jewish Publication Society, 1979), 3.

38 Michel Foucault, "Polemics, Politics and Problematizations: An Interview
    Conducted by Paul Rabinow in May 1984," Michel Foucault, Info (website),
    https://foucault.info/documents/foucault.interview/.

39 Schäfer, *Jesus in the Talmud.*

40 Wilken, *John Chrysostom and the Jews*; the quotations are from pp. 118 and 126.
    On Chrysostom, the Pontifical Biblical Commission comments: "But it must
    be admitted that many of these passages are capable of providing a pretext for
    anti-Jewish sentiment and have in fact been used in this way. To avoid mistakes
    of this kind, it must be kept in mind that the New Testament polemical texts,
    even those expressed in general terms, have to do with concrete historical
    contexts and are never meant to be applied to Jews of all times and places merely
    because they are Jews." "The Jewish People and Their Sacred Scriptures in the
    Christian Bible," February 12, 2002, http://www.vatican.va/roman_curia
    /congregations/cfaith/pcb_documents/rc_con_cfaith_doc_20020212_popolo
    -ebraico_en.html.

41 See also Edward Kessler, *An Introduction to Jewish-Christian Relations*
    (Cambridge: Cambridge Univ. Press, 2010), 34–36.

42 James Parkes, *Prelude to Dialogue: Jewish-Christian Relationships* (New York:
    Schocken Books, 1969), 153. See also Wendy Mayer, "Preaching Hatred? John
    Chrysostom, Neuroscience, and the Jews," in *(Re)Visioning John Chrysostom:
    New Theories and Approaches*, ed. Chris L. De Wet and Wendy Mayer, Critical
    Approaches to Early Christianity 1 (Leiden: Brill, 2019), 58–136.

43 See, e.g., Jonathan Crewe, "Can Polemic Be Ethical: A Response to Michel
    Foucault," in *Polemic: Critical or Uncritical*, ed. Jane Gallop (New York:
    Routledge, 2004), 135–52; Paul J. Griffiths, *An Apology for Apologetics: A Study in
    the Logic of Interreligious Dialogue* (Maryknoll, NY: Orbis Books, 2007).

44 Averil Cameron, "Texts as Weapons: Polemic in the Byzantine Dark Ages," in
    Literacy and Power in the Ancient World, ed. Alan K. Bowman and Greg Woolf
    (Cambridge: Cambridge Univ. Press, 1997), 198–215.

45 Marcelo Dascal, "Types of Polemics and Types of Polemical Moves," in *Dialogue
    Analysis VI*, ed. S. Cmejrkova, J. Hoffmannova, O. Mullerova, and J. Svetla, vol. 1
    (Tübingen: Max Niemeyer, 1998), 15–33, https://m.tau.ac.il/humanities/philos
    /dascal/papers/pregue.htm.

46 The claim that Jews must better appreciate the New Testament was made in the
    nineteenth-century work by Elijah Zvi Soloveitchik, *The Bible, the Talmud, and
    the New Testament: Elijah Zvi Soloveitchik's Commentary to the Gospels*, ed. Shaul
    Magid (Philadelphia: Univ. of Pennsylvania Press, 2019), but was, and still
    remains, highly unusual.

47 Jacob Neusner, *A Rabbi Talks with Jesus, Revised Edition* (Montreal & Kingston:
    McGill-Queen's Univ. Press, 2007), 5.

48 Quoted in Moshe Halbertal, "'Ones Possessed of Religion': Religious Tolerance

in the Teachings of the Me'iri," *Edah Journal* 1 (2000): 1–24 (24), http://www
.edah.org/backend/JournalArticle/halbertal.pdf.

49 Hananel Mack, "The Bifurcated Legacy of Rabbi Moses Hadarshan and the Rise
of Peshat Exegesis in Medieval Europe," in *Regional Identities and Cultures of
Medieval Jews*, ed. Javier Castaño, Talya Fishman, and Ephraim Kanarfogel
(Oxford: Littman Library, 2018), 73–91. Further discussion and the *derashot*
(sermons) are in Mack, *The Mystery of Rabbi Moshe Hadarshan* [in Hebrew]
(Jerusalem: Bialik, 2010).

50 Pope Paul VI, *Nostra Aetate* (1965), http://www.vatican.va/archive/hist
_councils/ii_vatican_council/documents/vat-ii_decl_19651028_nostra-aetate
_en.html; Pontifical Biblical Commission, "The Interpretation of the Bible in
the Church," 1993, https://www.bc.edu/content/dam/files/research_sites/cjl
/texts/cjrelations/resources/documents/catholic/pbcinterpretation.htm;
Pontifical Biblical Commission, "The Jewish People and Their Sacred Scriptures
in the Christian Bible," 2001, http://www.vatican.va/roman_curia/congregations
/cfaith/pcb_documents/rc_con_cfaith_doc_20020212_popolo-ebraico_en
.html; Commission of the Holy See for Religious Relations with the Jews, "'The
Gifts and the Calling of God Are Irrevocable' (Rom 11:29): A Reflection on
Theological Questions Pertaining to Catholic-Jewish Relations," 2015, http://
www.vatican.va/roman_curia/pontifical_councils/chrstuni/relations-jews
-docs/rc_pc_chrstuni_doc_20151210_ebraismo-nostra-aetate_en.html. For
commentary on these, see Joseph A. Fitzmyer, *The Biblical Commission's
Document "The Interpretation of the Bible in the Church": Text and Commentary*,
Subsidia Biblica 18 (Rome: Pontifical Biblical Institute, 1995); Philip A.
Cunningham, *Seeking Shalom: The Journey to Right Relationship Between
Catholics and Jews* (Grand Rapids: Eerdmans, 2015).

51 Pontifical Biblical Commission, "Interpretation of the Bible."

52 Pontifical Biblical Commission, "Jewish People and Their Sacred Scriptures."

53 Adam J. Silverstein, Guy G. Stroumsa, and Moshe Blidstein, "Introduction,"
in *The Oxford Handbook of the Abrahamic Religions*, ed. Adam J. Silverstein,
Guy G. Stroumsa, and Moshe Blidstein (Oxford: Oxford Univ. Press, 2015), xv.

54 Goshen-Gottstein, "Jewish-Christian Relations and Rabbinic Literature,"
esp. 26–29 (28).

55 See the Scriptural Reasoning project website at http://www.scripturalreasoning
.org/, as well as C. C. Pecknold and David F. Ford, eds., "The Promise of
Scriptural Reasoning," special issue, *Modern Theology* 22 (2006); especially the
article by Stephen Kepnes, "A Handbook for Scriptural Reasoning."

56 General Convention of the Episcopal Church, "Guidelines for Christian-Jewish
Relations: For Use in the Episcopal Church," July 1988, https://www.bc.edu
/content/dam/files/research_sites/cjl/texts/cjrelations/resources/documents
/protestant/Episcopal_Guidelines.htm.

57 Amy-Jill Levine and Marc Zvi Brettler, eds., *The Jewish Annotated New Testament*,
2nd ed. (New York: Oxford Univ. Press, 2017); see also Marc Zvi Brettler and
Amy-Jill Levine, "The Jewish Annotated New Testament: Retrospect and
Prospects," *Melilah: Manchester Journal of Jewish Studies* 11 (2014): 1–7.

58 "Dabru Emet: A Jewish Statement on Christians and Christianity," ICJS, 2000,
https://www.bc.edu/content/dam/files/research_sites/cjl/texts/cjrelations
/resources/documents/jewish/dabru_emet.htm; see also Tikva Frymer-Kensky,

Peter W. Ochs, David Novak, David Sandmel, and Michael Singer, *Christianity in Jewish Terms* (Boulder, CO: Basic Books, 2000). For a critique, Jon Levenson, "Podcast: Jon Levenson on the Danger and Opportunity of Jewish-Christian Dialogue," Digital Library, Tikvah, January 16, 2018, https://tikvahfund.org/library/jon-levenson-danger-opportunity-jewish-christian-dialogue/; and earlier at Levenson, "How Not to Conduct Jewish-Christian Dialogue," *Commentary*, December 2001, https://www.commentarymagazine.com/articles/jon-levenson-2/how-not-to-conduct-jewish-christian-dialogue/; Levenson, "The Agenda of Dabru Emet," *Review of Rabbinic Judaism* 7 (2004): 1–26. Note other Orthodox responses: David Berger, "Statement by Dr. David Berger Regarding the New York Times Ad by Dabru Emet," Orthodox Union Advocacy Center, September 14, 2000, https://advocacy.ou.org/statement_by_dr_david_berger_regarding_the_new_york_times_ad_by_dabru_emet/. For a full statement from prominent Orthodox rabbis, see *To Do the Will of Our Father in Heaven: Toward a Partnership Between Jews and Christians*, CJCUC, December 3, 2015, http://cjcuc.org/2015/12/03/orthodox-rabbinic-statement-on-christianity/. We will return to this discussion in our Conclusion.

59 James K. Aitken, "What Does Christianity in Jewish Terms Mean?," in *Challenges in Jewish-Christian Relations*, ed. James K. Aitken and Edward Kessler (New York: Paulist, 2006), 203–17, esp. 211–13.

60 Critiqued half a century ago in Arthur Cohen, *The Myth of the Judeo-Christian Tradition* (New York: Harper & Row, 1969). See also Jacob Neusner and Bruce Chilton, *Jewish-Christian Debates: God, Kingdom, Messiah* (Minneapolis: Fortress, 1998), 3. A more recent and nuanced discussion appears in Emmanuel Nathan and Anya Topolski, eds., *Is There a Judeo-Christian Tradition? A European Perspective* (Berlin: de Gruyter, 2016).

61 George Lindbeck, "Postmodern Hermeneutics and Jewish-Christian Dialogue: A Case Study," in Frymer-Kensky et al., *Christianity in Jewish Terms*, 106–13 (112).

62 The term "canon within a canon" was developed by James A. Sanders, *Torah and Canon* (Philadelphia: Fortress, 1972).

63 Jonathan Sacks, "Opening Address at Interfaith Gathering for Papal Visit," September 17, 2010, http://rabbisacks.org/opening-address-at-interfaith-gathering-for-papal-visit/.

Chapter 3: The Creation of the World

1 Daniel Boyarin, *Border Lines: The Partition of Judaeo-Christianity* (Philadelphia: Univ. of Pennsylvania Press, 2004), 96; see the discussion below; see also Boyarin, "Logos, a Jewish Word: John's Prologue as Midrash," in *JANT*, 688–91.

2 In Jubilees 2:2, God creates the angels on the first day of creation; for other opinions in ancient Jewish literature on their creation, see Jacques van Ruiten, "Angels and Demons in the Book of *Jubilees*," in *Angels: The Concept of Celestial Beings; Origins, Development and Reception*, ed. Friedrich V. Reiterer, Tobias Nicklas, and Karin Schopflin, Deuterocanonical and Cognate Literature Yearbook 2007 (Berlin: de Gruyter, 2007), 588n14; and in rabbinic sources, Bill Rebiger, "Angels in Rabbinic Literature," in Reiterer, Nicklas, and Schopflin, eds., *Angels*, 631.

3 See Bart Ehrman, *How Jesus Became God: The Exaltation of a Jewish Preacher from Galilee* (San Francisco: HarperOne, 2014), 252–53.

4 Tertullian, *Against Praxeas* 12, in *ANF*, 3:356–58.

5 See Gerhard F. Hasel, "The Meaning of 'Let Us' in Gn 1:26," *Andrews Univ. Seminary Studies* 13 (1975): 58–66 (58–59), for discussion of various options.

6 *The Orthodox Study Bible* (Nashville: Thomas Nelson, 2008), 4.

7 For more on these chapters, see Marc Zvi Brettler, *How to Read the Jewish Bible* (New York: Oxford Univ. Press), 29–47; Douglas Knight and Amy-Jill Levine, *The Meaning of the Bible: What the Jewish Scriptures and the Christian Old Testament Can Teach Us* (New York: HarperCollins, 2011), 195–215.

8 Richard Elliott Friedman, *Who Wrote the Bible?* (San Francisco: HarperOne, 1997), offers a popular introduction to the composition of the Pentateuch.

9 On the links between the two stories, see Eckhart Frahm, "Creation and the Divine Spirit in Bible and Babel: Reflections on *mummu* in *Enuma eliš* I 4 and *rûaḥ* in Genesis 1:2," in *Literature as Politics, Politics as Literature: Essays on the Ancient Near East in Honor of Peter Machinist*, ed. David S. Vanderhooft and Abraham Winitzer (Winona Lake, IN: Eisenbrauns, 2013), 97–117. See esp. pp. 97–103 on the debate concerning generic versus genetic similarities.

10 Enuma Elish 6.8, trans. in Stephanie Dalley, *Myths from Mesopotamia: Creation, the Flood, Gilgamesh, and Others*, rev. ed. (Oxford: Oxford Univ. Press, 2000), 261.

11 For an alternative view, in which Israel is the "servant" or "slave" of God, see Lev 25:55.

12 See the essays in Gary Anderson and Markus Bockmuehl, eds., *Creation ex nihilo: Origins, Development, Contemporary Challenges* (Notre Dame: Univ. of Notre Dame Press, 2017). For Jewish scholars who understand the beginning of Genesis as implying creation ex nihilo, see Norbert M. Samuelson, *Judaism and the Doctrine of Creation* (Cambridge: Cambridge Univ. Press, 1994), 133–34, 137–38, 226–27.

13 Ellen van Wolde, "Why the Verb *br'* Does Not Mean 'to Create' in Genesis 1.1–2.4a," *Journal for the Study of the Old Testament* 34 (2009): 3–23.

14 On bringing order out of chaos as the main theme of Genesis 1, see, e.g., Gerhard von Rad, *Genesis*, Old Testament Library (Philadelphia: Westminster, 1972), 49–50.

15 The claim that it is a dual rather than a plural is incorrect; see Paul Joüon and T. Muraoka, *A Grammar of Biblical Hebrew* (Rome: Pontifical Biblical Institute, 1991), §91f.

16 Eckhart Frahm, "Creation and the Divine Spirit in Bible and Babel," assuming a close connection between Genesis 1 and the Enuma Elish, sees *ru'ach* as parallel to the obscure Akkadian term *mummu* and referring to God's "creative spirit."

17 For a detailed exploration of *ru'ach*, see S. Tengström, "Ruah," *TDOT*, 13:365–96.

18 We thank Jonathan Homrighausen for this point.

19 Everett Fox, *The Five Books of Moses*, Schocken Bible 1 (New York: Schocken, 1995), 13.

20 For more on this wind, which "preserves an echo of the myths of the primeval wind that were prevalent in the Levant," see Guy Darshan, "*Ruaḥ 'Elohim* in Gen 1:2 in Light of Phoenician Cosmogonies: A Tradition's History," *Journal of Northwest Semitic Languages* 45 (2019): 5–78 (70).

21 See Joüon and Muraoka, *A Grammar of Biblical Hebrew*, §141n.

22 E. A. Speiser, *Genesis*, Anchor Yale Bible 1 (New Haven: Yale Univ. Press, 1964), 3, 5.

23 David T. Runia, "On the Creation of the World," in *OTB*, 1:893.

24 See Bernard Grossfeld, *The Targum Onqelos to Genesis* (Edinburgh: T&T Clark, 1988), 42; Michael Maher, *Targum Pseudo-Jonathan Genesis* (Edinburgh: T&T Clark 1992), 16 (he notes that "a spirit of mercy" is possible); Martin McNamara, *Targum Neofiti 1: Genesis* (Edinburgh: T&T Clark 1992), 52. The translation in Alejandro Díez Macho, *Targum Neophiti 1* (Madrid: Consejo Superior de Investigaciones Científica, 1968), 497, "and a spirit of love from before the Lord," reflects a Christianizing rendition of the targum into English.

25 See Peter Schäfer, *Mirror of His Beauty: Feminine Images of God from the Bible to the Early Kabbalah* (Princeton: Princeton Univ. Press, 2004), 19–57; Simon Gathercole, "Wisdom (Personified)," in *EDEJ*, 1339; Bernhard Lang, *Wisdom and the Book of Proverbs: An Israelite Goddess Redefined* (New York: Pilgrim Press, 1986).

26 See Lang, *Wisdom and the Book of Proverbs*.

27 Roland E. Murphy, "Wisdom and Creation," *Journal of Biblical Literature* 104 (1985): 3–11 (8).

28 See the references in Gerald Friedlander, *Pirke de Rabbi Eliezer* (New York: Hermon, 1965), 12, and Ephraim E. Urbach, *The Sages: Their Concepts and Beliefs*, trans. Israel Abrahams (Jerusalem: Magnes, 1975), 198–99.

29 The identification of Wisdom with Torah is first found in Ben Sira 24:23–24, "All this is the book of the covenant of the Most High God, the law which Moses commanded us as an inheritance for the congregations of Jacob. It fills men with wisdom, like the Pishon, and like the Tigris at the time of the first fruits." See Roland E. Murphy, *The Tree of Life: An Exploration of Biblical Wisdom Literature*, 3rd ed. (Grand Rapids: Eerdmans, 2002), 139–40.

30 Urbach, *The Sages*, 40.

31 Menahem M. Kasher, *Encyclopedia of Biblical Interpretation: A Millennial Anthology*, trans. Harry Freedman (New York: American Biblical Encyclopedia Society, 1953), 21n82.

32 Urbach, *Sages*, 40–61, and more recently, Schäfer, *Mirror of His Beauty*, 1–102.

33 For more on Philo's *Logos*, see Scott D. Mackie, "Seeing God in Philo of Alexandria: The Logos, the Powers, or the Existent One," *Studia Philonica Annual* 21 (2009): 25–47 (29), citing Philo, *Sacrifices* 8.

34 David T. Runia, "Philo of Alexandria and the Beginnings of Christian Thought, Alexandrian and Jew," *Studia Philonica Annual* 7 (1995): 143–60.

35 See Boyarin, *Border Lines*, part 2: "The Crucifixion of the Logos: How Logos Theology Became Christian," 89–147; and Boyarin, "Logos."

36 Cited by Boyarin, "Logos," 690.

37 See, e.g., Targum Neofiti to Genesis 1, which refers throughout to God's *memra*'; see, e.g., 1:3, "Then the Memra of the Lord said, 'Let there be light,' and there was light, according to the decree of His Memra."

38 The exceptions, such as 1 Sam 4:8 and 1 Kgs 19:2, appear most frequently in the mouth of foreigners who do not recognize that *'elohim* refers to the single deity, YHWH.

39 See Thomas A. Keiser, "The Divine Plural: A Literary-Contextual Argument for Plurality in the Godhead," *Journal for the Study of the Old Testament* 34 (2009): 131–46.

40 See Mark S. Smith, *The Origins of Biblical Monotheism: Israel's Polytheistic Background and the Ugaritic Texts* (New York: Oxford Univ. Press, 2001).

41 W. Randall Garr, *In His Own Image and Likeness: Humanity, Divinity, and Monotheism*, Culture and History of the Ancient Near East 15 (Leiden: Brill, 2003), esp. 17–43, 51–83.

42 For "mighty," see, e.g., Joseph H. Hertz, *The Authorised Daily Prayer Book*, rev. ed. (New York: Bloch, 1952), 103; Jonathan Sacks, ed., *The Koren Siddur* (Jerusalem: Koren, 2015), 82; *Siddur Lev Shalem* (New York: Rabbinical Assembly, 2016), 144.

43 So Benjamin Sommer, *The Bodies of God and the World of Ancient Israel* (Cambridge: Cambridge Univ. Press, 2011), 68–70.

44 Victor Hamilton, *The Book of Genesis, Chapters 1–17*, New International Commentary on the Old Testament (Grand Rapids: Eerdmans, 1990), 134; and more tentatively, Keiser, "Divine Plural."

45 Louis H. Feldman, "The Biblical Interpretations of Josephus's Jewish Antiquities," in *OTB*, 2:1144.

46 Feldman in *OTB*, 2:1144–45, note on "He also fashioned humanity."

47 James L. Kugel, *Traditions of the Bible: A Guide to the Bible as It Was at the Start of the Common Era* (Cambridge, MA: Harvard Univ. Press, 1998), 79–80.

48 Kugel, *Traditions of the Bible*, 80, citing Philo, *On the Creation* 72–76.

49 Emanuel Tov, "The Rabbinic Tradition Concerning the 'Alterations' Inserted into the Greek Pentateuch and Their Relation to the Original Text of the LXX," *Journal for the Study of Judaism* 15 (1984): 65–89.

50 Jarl Fossum, "Gen. 1,26 and 2,7 in Judaism, Samaritanism, and Gnosticism," *Journal for the Study of Judaism* 16 (1985): 202–39, provides texts and translations used below. On these two powers, see Alan Segal, *Two Powers in Heaven: Early Rabbinic Reports About Christianity and Gnosticism*, Studies in Judaism in Late Antiquity 25 (Leiden: Brill, 1977); and Daniel Boyarin, *The Jewish Gospels: The Story of the Jewish Christ* (New York: New Press, 2012), who sees a possible binitarian tradition already in the "son of man" in Daniel 7 and in the elevation of the antediluvian figure to a divine status in 1 Enoch.

51 Fossum, "Gen. 1,26 and 2,7," 210, 215.

52 Cited in Hayim Nahman Bialik and Yehoshua Hana Ravnitzky, eds., *The Book of Legends: Sefer Ha-Aggadah*, trans. William G. Braude (New York: Schocken Books, 1992), 12.

53 Pieter W. van der Horst, "Greek Synagogal Prayers," in *OTB*, 2:2120–21.

54 Rachel Adelman, *The Return of the Repressed: Pirqe de-Rabbi Eliezer and the Pseudepigrapha*, Supplements to Journal for the Study of Judaism 140 (Leiden: Brill, 2009).

55 Friedlander, *Pirke de Rabbi Eliezer*, 76; we have updated the English translation.

56 "Rashi on Genesis 1:26," Sefaria, https://www.sefaria.org/Rashi_on_Genesis .1.26?lang=bi.

57 Martin Luther, *Luther's Works*, vol. 1, *Lectures on Genesis: Chapters 1–5*, ed. Jaroslav Jan Pelikan, Hilton C. Oswald, and Helmut T. Lehmann (St. Louis: Concordia, 1999), 57–58. For additional comments, see Bryan Wolfmueller, "Genesis 1:26, 'Let Us Make Man,' Luther's Defence of the Trinitarian Teaching," *World Wide Wolfmueller* (blog), January 11, 2017, http://www.wolfmueller.co /letusmakeman/.

Chapter 4: Adam and Eve

1 See Joseph A. Fitzmyer, *Romans: A New Translation with Introduction and Commentary*, Anchor Yale Bible 33 (New Haven: Yale Univ. Press, 1993), 413–17.

2 A reading of the garden story that is similar to the Christian concept of original sin is found in some Jewish mystical texts; see Menachem Kellner, "Tabernacle, Sacrifices, and Judaism: Maimonides vs. Nahmanides," *TheTorah.com*, March 17, 2020, https://www.thetorah.com/article/tabernacle-sacrifices-and-judaism-maimonides-vs-nahmanides, esp. notes 8 and 9. Some of these texts even refer to *chet' kadmoni*, primordial sin.

3 See Alan Cooper, "A Medieval Jewish Version of Original Sin: R. Ephraim of Luntshitz on Leviticus 12," *Harvard Theological Review* 97 (2004): 445–59, and Dennis Ronald MacDonald, *The Legend and the Apostle: The Battle for Paul in Story and Canon* (Louisville: Westminster John Knox, 1983).

4 On this section, see, for various perspectives, James Barr, *The Garden of Eden and the Hope of Immortality* (Minneapolis: Fortress, 1992); Tryggve N. D. Mettinger, *The Eden Narrative: A Literary and Religio-Historical Study of Genesis 2–3* (Winona Lake, IN: Eisenbrauns, 2007); Ziony Zevit, *What Really Happened in the Garden of Eden?* (New Haven: Yale Univ. Press, 2013); and Mark S. Smith, *The Genesis of Good and Evil: The Fall(out) and Original Sin in the Bible* (Louisville: Westminster John Knox, 2019).

5 On the J source's interest in nature, see Theodore Hiebert, *The Yahwist's Landscape: Nature and Religion in Early Israel* (New York: Oxford Univ. Press, 1996).

6 The Masoretic Text and Septuagint diverge in some verses on whether '*adam* is a personal name or a common noun; see Antti Laato and Lootta Valve, "Understanding the Story of Adam and Eve in the Second Temple Period," in *The Adam and Eve Story in the Hebrew Bible and in Ancient Jewish Writings Including the New Testament*, ed. Antti Laato and Lootta Valve (Winona Lake, IN: Eisenbrauns, 2016), 1–30 (2–3).

7 Mieke Bal, *Lethal Love: Feminist Literary Readings of Biblical Love Stories*, Indiana Studies in Biblical Literature (Bloomington: Indiana Univ. Press, 1987), 113.

8 Richard Bauckham, "Paradise in the *Biblical Antiquities* of Pseudo-Philo," in *Paradise in Antiquity: Jewish and Christian Views*, ed. Markus Bockmuehl and Guy G. Stroumsa (Cambridge: Cambridge Univ. Press, 2010), 43–56. Also, 4 Ezra identifies the garden with paradise and as a place of eschatological reward (8:52).

9 See Stephanie Dalley, *Myths from Mesopotamia: Creation, the Flood, Gilgamesh, and Others*, rev. ed. (Oxford: Oxford Univ. Press, 2000), 1–38. Kenton L. Sparks, *Ancient Texts for the Study of the Hebrew Bible: A Guide to the Background Literature* (Peabody, MA: Hendrickson, 2005), 313–14, observes: "In its basic structure and even in some of its details, Atrahasis is very close to what we have in the primeval history of Gen 1–11 . . . [and] many scholars believe that the Genesis author was familiar with Atrahasis or with a similar text."

10 Scott F. Gilbert and Ziony Zevit, "Congenital Human Baculum Deficiency: The Generative Bone of Genesis 2:21–23," *American Journal of Medical Genetics* 101 (2001): 284–85.

11 The observations below are based on Phyllis Trible, *God and the Rhetoric of Sexuality* (Philadelphia: Fortress, 1978), esp. 72–143; Alice Ogden Bellis,

Helpmates, Harlots, and Heroes: Women's Stories in the Hebrew Bible, 2nd ed. (Louisville: Westminster John Knox, 2007), 37–56; and Carol Meyers, *Rediscovering Eve: Ancient Israelite Women in Context* (Oxford: Oxford Univ. Press, 2012), 73–76.

12 Elizabeth Cady Stanton, *The Women's Bible: A Classic Feminist Perspective* (1895; repr., Mineola, NY: Dover, 2003), 22.

13 See Henry Ansgar Kelly, "Adam Citings Before the Intrusion of Satan: Recontextualizing Paul's Theology of Sin and Death," *Biblical Theology Bulletin* 44 (2014): 13–28 (13).

14 See Jacqueline Tabick, "The Snake in the Grass: The Problems of Interpreting Symbols in the Hebrew Bible and Rabbinic Writings," *Religion* 16 (1986): 155–67; Reuven Kimelman, "The Seduction of Eve and the Exegetical Politics of Gender," *Biblical Interpretation* 4 (1996): 1–39.

15 "Bereishit Rabbah 19:3," Sefaria, https://www.sefaria.org/Bereishit_Rabbah .19.3?lang=bi&with=all&lang2=en.

16 Trible, *God and the Rhetoric*, 110.

17 Trible, *God and the Rhetoric*, 112–13.

18 Meyers, *Rediscovering Eve*, 102.

19 For translations and discussion, see Anders Aschim, "Adam Translated, Transcribed and Recycled: Ben Sira in Hebrew and Greek," in Laato and Valve, eds., *Adam and Eve Story*, 111–42 (129–32). On Sirach's misogyny, see Aschim, "Adam Translated," 129n54, as well as Claudia V. Camp, *Ben Sira and the Men Who Handle Books: Gender and the Rise of Canon-Consciousness* (Sheffield: Sheffield Phoenix, 2013).

20 Meyers, *Rediscovering Eve*, 96–97.

21 Louis Ginzberg, *Legends of the Jews*, trans. Henrietta Szold and Paul Radin (repr., Philadelphia: Jewish Publication Society, 2003), 5:104–5n93.

22 Zevit, *What Really Happened in the Garden of Eden?*, 251–59, lists other texts, some questionable, that may allude to the garden story.

23 Karl William Weyde, "Does Mal 2:15a Refer to Adam and Eve in the Creation Account in Gen 2:4–25?," in Laato and Valve, *Adam and Eve Story*, 73–90, suggests that Mal 2:15 also refers to Adam, though he is not named there.

24 See Ezek 28:13; 31:9, 16, 18, and James Barr, "'Thou Are the Cherub': Ezekiel 28:14 and the Post-Ezekiel Understanding of Genesis 2–3," in *Priests, Prophets and Scribes: Essays on the Formation and Heritage of Second Temple Judaism in Honour of Joseph Blenkinsopp*, ed. Eugene Ulrich, John W. Wright, Robert P. Carroll, and Philip R. Davies, Library of Hebrew Bible/Old Testament Studies 149 (Sheffield: JSOT Press, 1992), 213–23; Edward Noort, "Gan-Eden in the Context of the Mythology of the Hebrew Bible," in *Paradise Interpreted: Representations of Biblical Paradise in Judaism and Christianity*, ed. Gerard P. Luttikhuizen (Leiden: Brill, 1999), 21–36.

25 See Barr, "'Thou Are the Cherub'"; and Noort, "Gan-Eden."

26 See Edward R. Daglish, *Psalm Fifty-One in the Light of Ancient Near Eastern Patternism* (Leiden: Brill, 1962), 120–21.

27 See Matthew Goff, "Fall of Humankind III. Judaism A. Second Temple and Hellenistic Judaism," *EBR*, 8:753–55.

28 Jonathan Sacks, ed., *The Koren Siddur* (Jerusalem: Koren, 2015), 1040.

29 For these translations and discussion, see Aschim, "Adam Translated," 129–32.

On Sirach's misogyny, see 129n54 and Camp, *Ben Sira and the Men Who Handle Books*.

30 John R. Levison, "Is Eve to Blame? A Contextual Analysis of Sir. 25.24," *Catholic Biblical Quarterly* 47 (1985): 617–23. See also Kelly, "Adam Citings," 13, and the critique of Levison's position by Aschim, "Adam Translated," 129–32.

31 See the survey of Florentino García Martínez, "Man and Woman: Halakhah Based upon Eden in the Dead Sea Scrolls," in *Paradise Interpreted: Representations of Biblical Paradise in Judaism and Christianity*, ed. Gerard P. Luttikhuizen, Themes in Biblical Narrative 2 (Leiden: Brill, 1999), 95–115.

32 Christfried Böttrich, "The Figures of Adam and Eve in the Enoch Tradition," in Laato and Valve, eds., *Adam and Eve Story*, 211–25 (235); see Eccl 7:26, cited above.

33 Böttrich, "Figures of Adam and Eve"; and E. J. C. Tigchelaar, "Eden and Paradise: The Garden Motif in Some Early Jewish Texts (1 Enoch and Other Texts Found at Qumran)," in Luttikhuizen, ed., *Paradise Interpreted*, 37–62.

34 "Misfortune" is likely a better translation, although "fall" appears in the Latin; see Michael Edward Stone, *Fourth Ezra*, Hermeneia (Minneapolis: Fortress, 1990), 258–59.

35 John R. Levison, *Portraits of Adam in Early Judaism: From Sirach to 2 Baruch* (London: Bloomsbury Academic, 1988), 130, 135–36.

36 See George W. E. Nickelsburg, "A New Testament Reader's Guide to *2Baruch*: Or a *2Baruch* Reader's Guide to the New Testament," in *Fourth Ezra and Second Baruch: Reconstruction After the Fall*, ed. Matthias Henze and Gabriele Boccaccini, Supplements to the Journal for the Study of Judaism 164 (Leiden: Brill, 2013), 271–93 (280).

37 See Timo Nisula, *Augustine and the Functions of Concupiscence*, Vigiliae Christianae Supplements 116 (Leiden: Brill, 2012).

38 Kris Lindbeck, "Fall of Humankind II. Judaism B. Rabbinic Judaism," *EBR*, 8:755–58, citing Burton L. Visotsky, "Will and Grace: Aspects of Judaising in Pelagianism in Light of Rabbinic and Patristic Exegesis of Genesis," in *The Exegetical Encounter Between Jews and Christians in Late Antiquity*, ed. E. Grypeou and H. Spurling, Jewish and Christian Perspectives 18 (Leiden: Brill, 2009), 53–59.

39 *Midrash Rabbah*, trans. Harry Freeman, ed. Maurice Simon (London: Soncino Press, 1992), 19.7.

40 Joel Kaminsky, "Paradise Regained," in *Jews, Christians, and the Theology of Hebrew Scriptures*, ed. Alice Ogden Bellis and Joel Kaminsky, Semeia Studies (Atlanta: SBL Press, 2000), 15–44.

41 Kaminsky, "Paradise Regained," 22, quoting Exodus Rabbah 32:1.

42 Tanhuma Buber to Genesis 1:18, trans. in John T. Townsend, *Midrash Tanhuma*, vol. 1 (Hoboken, NJ: Ktav, 1989), 21.

43 Ginzberg, *Legends*, 1:99.

44 See Anne Lapidus Lerner, *Eternally Eve: Images of Eve in the Hebrew Bible, Midrash, and Modern Jewish Poetry* (Waltham, MA: Brandeis Univ. Press, 2007); Gary A. Anderson, *The Genesis of Perfection: Adam and Eve in Jewish and Christian Imagination* (Louisville: Westminster John Knox, 2001); Tamar Kadari, "Eve III. Judaism B. Rabbinic to Medieval Judaism," *EBR*, 8:290–93.

45 Lerner, *Eternally Eve*, 57.

46 Lerner, *Eternally Eve*, 68.

47 Lerner, *Eternally Eve*, 101–2.

48 See y. Shabbat 2:6, 5b.

49 Lerner, *Eternally Eve*, 118.

50 For helpful summaries, see Janet Howe Gaines, "Lilith: Seductress, Heroine, or Murderer?," *Bible History Daily* (blog), Biblical Archaeology Society, October 31, 2001, https://www.biblicalarchaeology.org/daily/people-cultures-in-the-bible/people-in-the-bible/lilith/; Beth E. Macdonald, "In Possession of the Night: Lilith as Goddess, Demon, Vampire," in *Sacred Tropes: Tanakh, New Testament, and Qur'an as Literature and Culture*, ed. Roberta Sterman Sabbath, Biblical Interpretation 98 (Leiden: Brill, 2009), 173–82.

Chapter 5: "You Are a Priest Forever"

1 See Eric F. Mason, *"You Are a Priest Forever": Second Temple Jewish Messianism and the Priestly Christology of the Epistle to the Hebrews*, Studies on the Texts of the Desert of Judah 74 (Leiden: Brill, 2008).

2 On the history of the Israelite priesthood, see Mark Leuchter, *The Levites and the Boundaries of Israelite Identity* (Oxford: Oxford Univ. Press, 2017).

3 See comments on human sacrifice, pp. 238–40.

4 See Susan Gillingham, *A Journey of Two Psalms: The Reception of Psalms 1 and 2 in Jewish and Christian Tradition* (Oxford: Oxford Univ. Press, 2013).

5 Lorenzo DiTommaso, "New Jerusalem," in *EDEJ*, 797–99 (798).

6 Kevin B. McCruden summarizes this new reality: "Christ's sacrificial activity proves superior to the sacrificial activity of ordinary priests since it takes place in what Hebrews describes as an authentic tent or sanctuary located in heaven (8.1; 9:11–12), as opposed to an earthly tent or sanctuary (8:5; 9:1, 11)." See his "The Concept of Perfection in the Epistle to the Hebrews," in *Reading the Epistle to the Hebrews: A Resource for Students*, ed. Eric F. Mason and Kevin B. McCruden, Resources for Biblical Study 66 (Atlanta: SBL Press, 2011), 209–30 (224).

7 We return to Jeremiah 31 in our Conclusion.

8 Alan C. Mitchell, "'Sacrifice of Praise': Does Hebrews Promote Supersessionism?," in Mason and McCruden, *Reading the Epistle to the Hebrews*, 251–68 (251).

9 See Gard Granerød, *Abraham and Melchizedek: Scribal Activity of Second Temple Times in Genesis 14 and Psalm 110*, Beihefte zur Zeitschrift für die alttestamentliche Wissenschaft 406 (Berlin: de Gruyter, 2010), esp. 3–4. Emerton dates it to the Davidic period: J. A. Emerton, "The Riddle of Genesis XIV," *Vetus Testamentum* 21 (1971): 403–39 (412–25). For a more likely late date of this material, see Granerød, *Abraham and Melchizedek*, 170.

10 See Yohanan Muffs, "Abraham the Noble Warrior: Patriarchal Politics and Laws of War in Ancient Israel," in *Love and Joy: Law, Language and Religion in Ancient Israel* (New York: Jewish Theological Seminary of America, 1992), 67–95. See also Robert R. Cargill, *Melchizedek, King of Sodom: How Scribes Invented the Biblical Priest-King* (New York: Oxford Univ. Press, 2019), with extensive bibliography. We thank Professor Cargill for sharing the proofs of this book with us. Cargill, reconstructing an earlier version of the chapter, proposes that *shalem* is an alteration of Sodom and that 14:18–20 are original to the chapter.

11 So, e.g., Emerton, "Riddle of Genesis XIV," 407–12; John Van Seters, *Abraham in*

History and Tradition (New Haven: Yale Univ. Press, 1975), 301–2; Granerød, *Abraham and Melchizedek*, 31–33.

12 See Scott C. Layton, *Archaic Features of Canaanite Personal Names in the Hebrew Bible*, Harvard Semitic Monographs 47 (Atlanta: Scholars Press, 1990), 139–40.

13 Robyn C. Vern, "Case: Vestiges of Case Inflections," in *Encyclopedia of Hebrew Language and Linguistics*, ed. Jeffrey Kahn, http://dx.doi.org/10.1163/2212-4241 _ehll_EHLL_COM_00000807, first published online 2013.

14 E. A. Speiser, *Genesis*, Anchor Yale Bible 1 (New Haven: Yale Univ. Press, 1964), 104.

15 Bernard F. Batto, "Zedeq," *DDD*, 929–34.

16 Ludwig Koehler and Walter Baumgartner, *The Hebrew and Aramaic Lexicon of the Old Testament*, ed. M. E. J. Richardson (Leiden: Brill, 2002), s.v. "מַלְכִּי־צֶדֶק."

17 Most recently, see Cargill, *Melchizedek, King of Sodom*, chap. 8.

18 For the most extensive argument that Salem is Jerusalem, see J. Emerton, "The Site of Salem, the City of Melchizedek (Genesis XIV 18)," in *Studies in the Pentateuch*, Supplements to Vetus Testamentum 41 (Leiden: Brill, 1990), 45–72.

19 On the lack of the explicit mention of Jerusalem in the Torah, see Umberto Moses Cassuto, "Jerusalem in the Pentateuch," in *Biblical and Oriental Studies*, 2 vols. (Jerusalem: Magnes, 1973), 1:70–78.

20 The most extensive defense of this position is John G. Gammie, "Loci of the Melchizedek Tradition of Genesis 14:18–20," *Journal of Biblical Literature* 90 (1971): 385–96.

21 W. Hermann, "El," *DDD*, 274–80 (275–76).

22 E. E. Elnes and P. D. Miller, "Elyon," *DDD*, 293–99 (294–95).

23 R. Williamson, "The Eucharist and the Epistle to the Hebrews," *New Testament Studies* 21 (1975): 300–312 (300). James Swetnam, "Christology and the Eucharist in the Epistle to the Hebrews," *Biblica* 70 (1989): 74–95, states, "The subject of the eucharist in the Epistle to the Hebrews is one of the minor points of disagreement in contemporary New Testament studies" (74).

24 Cargill, *Melchizedek, King of Sodom*, argues that in an earlier version of the story, Melchizedek paid tithes to Abram, as does Victor P. Hamilton, *The Book of Genesis: Chapters 1–17*, New International Commentary on the Old Testament (Grand Rapids: Eerdmans, 1990), 412–13.

25 Walter J. Houston, "Between Salem and Mount Gerizim: The Context of the Formation of the Torah Reconsidered," *Journal of Ancient Judaism* 5 (2014): 311–34 (329).

26 Gerhard von Rad, *Genesis: A Commentary*, trans. John H. Marks, Old Testament Library (Philadelphia: Westminster, 1972), 180–81.

27 Cassuto, "Jerusalem in the Pentateuch," 73.

28 Van Seters, *Abraham*, 307–8.

29 Jared Compton, *Psalm 110 and the Logic of Hebrews*, Library of New Testament Studies 537 (London: Bloomsbury T&T Clark, 2015); and, earlier, David M. Hay, *Glory at the Right Hand: Psalm 110 in Early Christianity*, Society of Biblical Literature Monograph Series 18 (Nashville: Abingdon, 1973).

30 See Chapter 13.

31 Hermann Gunkel, *Introduction to Psalms: The Genres of the Religious Lyric of Israel*, trans. James D. Nogalski (Marcon, GA: Mercer Univ. Press, 1998), 99. We discuss the Psalms, with a focus on Psalm 22, in Chapter 11.

32 John J. Collins, "King and Messiah as Son of God," in *Reconsidering the Concept*

of Revolutionary Monotheism, ed. Beate Pongratz-Leisten (Winona Lake, IN: Eisenbrauns, 2011), 291–316 (298).

33 See Mordechai Cogan and Hayim Tadmor, *II Kings: A New Translation*, Anchor Yale Bible 11 (New Haven: Yale Univ. Press, 1988), 236, on 2 Kgs 19:24; and James B. Pritchard, ed., *Ancient Near Eastern Texts Relating to the Old Testament*, 3rd ed. (Princeton: Princeton Univ. Press, 1969), 292.

34 Sigmund Mowinckel, *Psalm Studies*, 2 vols., trans. Mark E. Biddle, History of Biblical Studies 2 (Atlanta: SBL Press, 2014), 2:581–85. Gunkel's suggestion that the Psalm is preexilic (Gunkel, *Introduction to Psalms*, 119) is compelling; see similarly John W. Hilber, *Cultic Prophecy in the Psalms*, Beihefte zur Zeitschrift für die alttestamentliche Wissenschaft 352 (Berlin: de Gruyter, 2005), 76–88. Arguments for a postexilic date for Psalm 110 by Gianni Barbiero, "The Non-violent Messiah of Psalm 110," *Biblische Zeitschrift* 58 (2014): 1–20, esp. 8–9, are not compelling.

35 See Gunkel, *Introduction to Psalms*; see esp. Benjamin Sommer, "The Babylonian Akitu Festival: Rectifying the King or Renewing the Universe," *Journal of the Ancient Near Eastern Society of Columbia Univ.* 27 (2000): 81–95.

36 On this idea, see Collins, "King and Messiah as Son of God"; Antti Laato, *A Star Is Rising: The Historical Development of the Old Testament Royal Ideology and the Rise of the Jewish Messianic Expectations*, Univ. of South Florida International Studies in Formative Christianity and Judaism 5 (Atlanta: Scholars Press, 1997), esp. 92–93.

37 See Marc Zvi Brettler, "God's Coronation on Rosh Hashanah: What Kind of King?," TheTorah.com, September 5, 2014, http://thetorah.com/coronation-on -rosh-hashanah-what-kind-of-king/.

38 Already Gunkel, *Introduction to Psalms*, 102, connected it to that festival. For a recent evaluation of this putative festival, see J. J. M. Roberts, "Mowinckel's Enthronement Festival: A Review," in *The Book of Psalms: Composition and Reception*, ed. Peter W. Flint and Patrick D. Miller, Supplements to Vetus Testamentum 99 (Leiden: Brill, 2005), 97–115.

39 See Hilber, *Cultic Prophecy in the Psalms*; and in relation to Psalm 110, John W. Hilber, "Psalm CX in the Light of Assyrian Prophecies," *Vetus Testamentum* 53 (2003): 353–66.

40 Collins, "King and Messiah as Son of God," 295.

41 Discussion in Loren T. Stuckenbruck, "Melchizedek in Jewish Apocalyptic Literature," *Journal for the Study of the New Testament* 41 (2018): 124–38 (127).

42 Cargill, *Melchizedek, King of Sodom*, chap. 8.

43 Collins, "King and Messiah as Son of God," 296.

44 So, e.g., Mowinckel, *Psalm Studies*, 2:584n139, that the phrase "does not mean 'after the manner of' but always only 'because of, for the sake of.'"

45 A useful survey of this phase is in Granerød, *Abraham and Melchizedek*, 195–214.

46 "There is no known formal quotations of the text in Second Temple writings outside the NT, nor is any part of the text preserved among fragments to the Psalms among the Dead Sea materials." Stuckenbruck, "Melchizedek in Jewish Apocalyptic Literature," 128, cf. 126.

47 See the summary in James Kugel, *The Bible as It Was* (Cambridge, MA: Harvard Univ. Press, 1997), 151–62.

48 See Louis H. Feldman, *Judaism and Hellenism Reconsidered*, Supplements to the Journal for the Study of Judaism 107 (Leiden: Brill, 2006), 352.

49 It is quite possible that the Hebrew version of Jubilees did mention Melchizedek by name; see James C. VanderKam, *Jubilees*, 2 vols., Hermeneia (Minneapolis: Fortress, 2018), 1:481–83.

50 Annette Steudel, "Melchizedek," *EDSS*, 1:535–37 (535).

51 Steudel, "Melchizedek," *EDSS*, 1:535–37.

52 Eric F. Mason, "Melchizedek Scroll (11Q13)," in *EDEJ*, 932–34 (933).

53 Eric F. Mason, "Cosmology, Messianism, and Melchizedek: Apocalyptic Jewish Traditions and Hebrews," in Mason and McCruden, eds., *Reading the Epistle to the Hebrews*, 53–76 (73).

54 Brendan Byrne, "The Qumran Melchizedek Scroll and the Gospel of Mark: Coherence and Contrast in Soteriology," *Pacifia* 27 (2014): 123–48 (129).

55 Bryne, "Qumran Melchizedek Scroll," 131.

56 Martin McNamara, "Melchizedek: Gen 14,17–20 in the Targums, in Rabbinic and Early Christian Literature," *Biblica* 81 (2000): 1–31.

57 James L. Kugel, *Traditions of the Bible: A Guide to the Bible as It Was at the Start of the Common Era* (Cambridge, MA: Harvard Univ. Press, 1998), 284, 289–91; Kugel, *Bible as It Was*, 160–61.

58 Moshe Reiss, "The Melchizedek Traditions," *Scandinavian Journal of the Old Testament* 26 (2012): 259–65 (261–62).

59 "Nedarim 32b:1–9," Sefaria, https://www.sefaria.org/Nedarim.32b.1–9?lang=bi.

60 Cargill, *Melchizedek, King of Sodom*, 92.

61 McNamara, "Melchizedek," 21; text in brackets supplied by McNamara.

62 Bernard Grossfeld, *The Targum Onqelos to Genesis*, Aramaic Bible 6 (Wilmington, DE: Glazier, 1988), 68, 69n17; Michael Maher, *Targum Pseudo-Jonathan: Genesis*, Aramaic Bible 1B (Wilmington, DE: Glazier, 1992).

63 "Nedarim 32b:1–9," Sefaria, https://www.sefaria.org/Nedarim.32b.1–9?lang=bi.

64 "Nedarim 32b:1–9," Sefaria, https://www.sefaria.org/Nedarim.32b.7–8?lang=bi. McNamara provides a slightly different translation of Nedarim 32b.

65 See the discussion of *memra'* in relation to *logos* on pp. 82–87.

66 Translation from McNamara, "Melchizedek," 20.

67 Cargill, *Melchizedek, King of Sodom*, 88.

68 Some material in this section comes from Amy-Jill Levine, "Yet His Shadow Still Looms: Citations from the 'Obsolete Covenant' in the Epistle to the Hebrews," (paper presented at Society of Biblical Literature Annual Meeting, Epistle to the Hebrews section, Denver, CO, November 2018).

69 Jonathan Homrighausen, "The Jewish Jesus in the California Desert: A Report from the Tabernacle Experience," *The Interfaith Observer* (October 2016), http://www.theinterfaithobserver.org/journal-articles/2016/9/23/a-report-from-the-tabernacle-experience.

70 Jesper Svartvik defines the term as "the influential idea that Christians (the people of 'the new covenant') have replaced Jews (the people of 'the old covenant') as the people of God." He cites, as an early example, not Hebrews but the Epistle of Barnabas. Jesper Svartvik, "Supersessionism," Bible Odyssey, http://www.bibleodyssey.org/passages/related-articles/supersessionism.aspx.

71 Richard B. Hays, "'Here We Have No Lasting City': New Covenantalism in Hebrews," in *The Epistle to the Hebrews and Christian Theology*, ed. Richard Bauckham, Daniel R. Driver, Trevor A. Hart, and Nathan MacDonald (Grand Rapids: Eerdmans, 2009), 151–73.

72   Mitchell, "'Sacrifice of Praise,'" 266.

73   McCruden, "Concept of Perfection," 217; see also Mitchell, "'Sacrifice of Praise,'" 256.

74   Hays, "'Here We Have No Lasting City,'" 165, cited in Mitchell, "'Sacrifice of Praise,'" 266; see also Hays, "'Here We Have No Lasting City,'" 154.

75   Kenneth Schenck, "Hebrews as the Re-presentation of a Story," in Mason and McCruden, *Reading the Epistle to the Hebrews*, 171–88 (187); see also James W. Thompson, "What Has Middle Platonism to Do with Hebrews?," in Mason and McCruden, *Reading the Epistle to the Hebrews*, 31–52 (49), who states, "According to Hebrews 11, the knowledge that reality is not in the phenomenal world makes one a stranger to this world."

76   Schenck, "Hebrews as the Re-presentation of a Story," 177.

77   See pp. 228–34 on the role of blood in atonement.

78   See Jonathan Klawans, "Josephus, the Rabbis, and Responses to Catastrophes Ancient and Modern," *Jewish Quarterly Review* 100 (2010): 278–309 (283).

79   Klawans, "Josephus, the Rabbis," 305.

80   As summarized by Jody A. Barnard, "Anti-Jewish Interpretations of Hebrews: Some Neglected Factors," *Melilah* 11 (2014): 25–52 (25).

81   Gabriella Gelardini, "Hebrews, Homiletics, and Liturgical Scripture Interpretation," in Mason and McCruden, *Reading the Epistle to the Hebrews*, 121–44. See also Gelardini, "Hebrews, an Ancient Synagogue Homily for Tisha be-Av: Its Function, Its Basis, Its Theological Interpretation," in *Hebrews: Contemporary Methods, New Insights*, ed. Gabriella Gelardini, Biblical Interpretation 75 (Leiden: Brill, 2005), 107–28. For the argument that the Epistle to the Hebrews is a sermon for Yom Kippur, see, e.g., C. P. März, *Hebräerbrief*, Die Neue Echter Bibel NT 16 (Würzburg: Echter, 1989); Daniel Stökl Ben Ezra, *The Impact of Yom Kippur on Early Christianity: The Day of Atonement from Second Temple Judaism to the Fifth Century*, Wissenschaftliche Untersuchungen zum Neuen Testament 163 (Tübingen: Mohr Siebeck, 2003), 180–87.

82   Including Louis Ginzberg, R. Travers Herford, Paul Billerbeck, and Marcel Simon. See discussion in McNamara, "Melchizedek," 16–17.

83   See pp. 241–44.

84   Jonathan Sacks, *The Koren Siddur for Shabbat and Ḥagim* (Jerusalem: Koren, 2013), 26.

Chapter 6: "An Eye for an Eye" and "Turn the Other Cheek"

1   See, e.g., Dale C. Allison, Jr., *The New Moses: A Matthean Typology* (1993; repr., Cascade: Wipf & Stock, 2013).

2   See discussion in Eric Huntsman, "The Six Antitheses: Attaining the Purpose of the Law Through the Teachings of Jesus," in *The Sermon on the Mount in Latter-day Scripture*, ed. Gaye Strathearn, Thomas A. Wayment, and Daniel L. Belnap (Provo, UT: Religious Studies Center, Brigham Young Univ., 2010), 93–109, also available at https://rsc.byu.edu/sermon-mount-latter-day-scripture/six-antitheses. He notes, "Because the outward, ceremonial aspects of the law of Moses were fulfilled with the sacrificial death of Jesus Christ, Christians—and especially Latter-day Saints—are sometimes predisposed to seeing the term 'fulfill' here as meaning 'bring to an end.'"

3 Steve Mason, "Flavius Josephus and the Pharisees," *The Bible and Interpretation* (April 2003), http://www.bibleinterp.com/articles/Flavius_Josephus.shtml.

4 Ulrich Luz, *Matthew 1–7*, trans. James E. Crouch, Hermeneia (Minneapolis: Fortress, 2007), 274n1.

5 Martha Himmelfarb, "Afterlife and Resurrection," in *JANT*, 691–94, writes, "The Essenes believed that immortal souls would enjoy reward or endure punishment according to their deeds in life without any role for the body (Josephus, *War* 2.154–58; see also Josephus, *Antiquities* 18.18), but the Pharisees held that 'the soul of the good alone passes into another body, while the souls of the wicked suffer eternal punishment'" (Josephus, *War* 2.163; see also Josephus, *Antiquities* 18.14) (691). Himmelfarb goes on to document rabbinic expectations of postmortem rewards and punishments.

6 "Berakhot 19a:9," Sefaria, https://www.sefaria.org/Berakhot.19a.9?lang=bi.

7 It strikes us as more likely that a scribe added "without cause" to allow for righteous anger. See discussion in David Alan Black, "Jesus on Anger: The Text of Matthew 5:22a Revisited," *Novum Testamentum* 30 (1988): 1–8. Black leaves the question of authenticity open.

8 For discussion about the originality of the account to John's Gospel, see David Alan Black and Jacob N. Cerone, eds., *The Pericope of the Adulteress in Contemporary Research*, Library of New Testament Studies 551 (London: T&T Clark, 2018); Jennifer Knust and Tommy Wasserman, *To Cast the First Stone: The Transmission of a Gospel Story* (Princeton: Princeton Univ. Press, 2018).

9 See Beth A. Berkowitz, *Execution and Invention: Death Penalty Discourse in Early Rabbinic and Christian Cultures* (New York: Oxford Univ. Press, 2006); Michael Satlow, *Tasting the Dish: Rabbinic Rhetorics of Sexuality* (Atlanta: Scholars Press, 1995), 173–74.

10 Neusner, *Mishnah*, 612.

11 Josephus (*Antiquities* 15.259–60) suggests that Salome, sister of Herod (the Great), divorced her husband, Costobarus, although that "was not in accordance with Jewish law, for it is (only) the man who is permitted by us to do this." Josephus also insists that divorced women must obtain the former husband's permission to remarry, a law found nowhere else in Jewish sources and likely designed to emphasize Judaism's patriarchal (and so "Roman") practices. Papyrus Se'elim 13 from the Judean desert (early second century) is a scroll sent from "Shelamzion, daughter of Joseph Qebshan of Ein Gedi" to her husband "Eleazar son of Hananiah"; it states, "This is from her to you a bill of divorce and release." See David Instone-Brewer, "Jewish Women Divorcing Their Husbands in Early Judaism: The Background to Papyrus Se'elim 13," *Harvard Theological Review* 92 (1999): 349–57; Tal Ilan, "Notes and Observations on a Newly Published Divorce Bill from the Judean Desert," *Harvard Theological Review* 89 (1996): 195–202; Adiel Schremer, "Divorce in Papyrus Se'elim 13 Once Again: A Reply to Tal Ilan," *Harvard Theological Review* 91 (1998): 193–202.

12 See discussion in Raymond Collins, *Divorce in the New Testament* (Collegeville, MN: Liturgical Press, 1992), 81.

13 See, e.g., Pieter W. van der Horst, "Celibacy in Early Judaism," in *Japheth in the Tents of Shem: Studies on Jewish Hellenism in Antiquity*, Contributions to Biblical Exegesis & Theology 32 (Leuven: Peeters, 2002); Adiel Schremer, "Celibacy in

Second Temple Judaism," in *EDEJ*, 466–67. See also the Cairo Geniza copy of the Damascus Document (CD) 6.11–7.9 and Philo, *On the Contemplative Life* 8.68–90, on the Therapeutae.

14 David L. Turner, *Matthew*, Baker Exegetical Commentary on the New Testament (Grand Rapids: Baker Academic, 2008), 173.

15 R. T. France, *Matthew*, New International Commentary on the New Testament (Grand Rapids: Eerdmans, 2007), citing m. Shevuot 4:13; m. Nedarin 1:3; m. Sanhedrin 3:2. See also Douglas R. A. Hare, *Matthew*, Interpretation (Louisville: Westminster John Knox, 1993), 45, on the "false casuistry that too subtly distinguishes between binding and nonbinding oaths."

16 Accordance Bible Software translation, slightly modified.

17 K. Koch, "תמם," in Ernst Jenni, ed., with assistance from Claus Westermann, *Theological Lexicon of the Old Testament*, trans. Mark E. Biddle, 3 vols. (Peabody, MA: Hendrickson, 1997), 2:1424–28 (1424), explains this use of *tamim* as having "an untroubled human relationship with God."

18 See Trevor W. Thompson, "Punishment and Restitution," in *The Oxford Encyclopedia of Bible and Law*, ed. Brent A. Strawn (Oxford: Oxford Univ. Press, 2015), 2:183–93, esp. 183–84 on *lex talionis*; James F. Davis, *Lex Talionis in Early Judaism and the Exhortation of Jesus in Matthew 5.38–43*, Journal for the Study of the New Testament Supplement Series 281 (London: T&T Clark, 2005); this volume's treatment of the biblical and rabbinic law, however, needs to be used with great caution.

19 See M. Floriana Cursi, "The Scope and Function of Civil Wrongs in Roman Society," in *The Oxford Handbook of Roman Law and Society*, ed. Paul J. du Plessis, Clifford Ando, and Kaius Tuori (Oxford: Oxford Univ. Press, 2016), 596–606 (597–98; the quotation is from 597).

20 See Catherine Hezser, "Paul's 'Fool's Speech' (2 Cor. 11:16–32) in the Context of Ancient Jewish and Graeco-Roman Culture," in *Second Corinthians in the Perspective of Late Second Temple Judaism*, ed. Peter Tomson, Compendia Rerum Iudaicarum ad Novum Testamentum 14 (Leiden: Brill, 2014), 221–44.

21 Walter Wink, *Naming the Powers: The Language of Power in the New Testament* (Minneapolis: Fortress, 1984); Wink, *Engaging the Powers: Discernment and Resistance in a World of Domination* (Minneapolis: Fortress, 1992); and Wink, *Jesus and Nonviolence: A Third Way* (Minneapolis: Fortress, 2003).

22 Warren Carter, "Sanctioned Violence in the New Testament," *Interpretation: A Journal of Bible and Theology* 71 (2017): 284–97 (288–89).

23 See Sharon H. Ringe, *Jesus, Liberation, and the Biblical Jubilee: Images for Ethics and Christology* (Eugene, OR: Wipf & Stock, 2004).

24 See Gary Anderson, *Sin: A History* (New Haven: Yale Univ. Press, 2010), 171–73; Amy-Jill Levine, "'This Poor Widow . . .' (Mark 12:43): From Donation to Diatribe," in *Jews and Christians in the Greco-Roman World: Essays in Honor of Ross Shepard Kraemer*, ed. Susan Ashbrook Harvey, Nathaniel P. DesRosiers, Shira L. Lander, Jacqueline Z. Pastis, and Daniel Ullucci (Providence: Brown Univ. Press, 2015), 183–94.

25 On the use of the term "collections" rather than "codes," see Martha T. Roth, *Law Collections from Mesopotamia and Asia Minor*, 2nd ed., Writings from the Ancient World (Atlanta: SBL Press, 1997).

26 Bruce Wells, "What Is Biblical Law? A Look at Pentateuchal Rules and Near

Eastern Practice," *Catholic Biblical Quarterly* 70 (2008): 223–43. Bernard M. Levinson, *Legal Revision and Religious Renewal in Ancient Israel* (Cambridge: Cambridge Univ. Press, 2008), observes, "Many scholars would consider the laws of the Covenant Code not to have . . . statutory force [enforced as a real statute or law] but rather, on analogy to the literary collections of cuneiform law [e.g., the Laws of Hammurabi], to represent something close to ideal reflections upon social order and ethics" (105).

27 Jacob Milgrom, *Leviticus 23–27*, Anchor Yale Bible 3B (New Haven: Yale Univ. Press, 2001), 247.

28 Martha Roth, "The Laws of Hammurabi," in *The Context of Scripture*, vol. 2, ed. William W. Hallo (Leiden: Brill, 2000), 2.131.

29 David P. Wright, *Inventing God's Law: How the Covenant Code of the Bible Used and Revised the Laws of Hammurabi* (New York: Oxford Univ. Press, 2009), 182. See also Wright, "How Exodus Revises the Laws of Hammurabi," TheTorah .com, February 27, 2019, https://thetorah.com/how-exodus-revises-the-laws-of -hammurabi/.

30 This was a very substantial sum; law 116 suggests that the worth of a slave was 20 shekels of silver.

31 Roth, "Laws of Hammurabi."

32 It distinguishes between slaves and free people in contexts that concern the economic loss to the slave owner; see Exod 21:26–27.

33 So Moshe Greenberg, "Some Postulates of Biblical Criminal Law," in *Studies in Bible and Jewish Religion Dedicated to Yehezkel Kaufman on the Occasion of His Seventieth Birthday*, ed. Menahem Haran (Jerusalem: Magnes, Hebrew Univ. Press, 1960), 5–28.

34 Douglas A. Knight, *Law, Power and Justice in Ancient Israel* (Louisville: Westminster John Knox, 2011), 48.

35 The Hebrew reads a plural, "her children," while the Samaritan and Septuagint have a singular pronoun, "her child."

36 The Hebrew text is not clear as to whether the harm is to the mother, the fetus, or both. The Septuagint reads, "if her child is born imperfectly formed" there is monetary compensation, but if "perfectly formed," talion is imposed. Philo (*Special Laws* 3:108) follows the Septuagint. Josephus reads Exod 21 as speaking of monetary payment in cases of miscarriage caused by injury (*Antiquities* 4.278), but he also considers women who abort their fetuses to be guilty of murder (*Apion* 2.202). The Mishnah (Oholot 7:6) permits the dismemberment of a fetus in the process of being born in order to save the life of the mother, and despite a few minority opinions to the contrary, the Jewish tradition maintains that since the fetus does not have the status of a *nephesh*, a living being, its death is not to be considered murder. See Tirzah Meacham, "Abortion," *Jewish Women: A Comprehensive Historical Encyclopedia*, Jewish Women's Archive, February 27, 2009, https://jwa.org/encyclopedia/article/abortion; Judith R. Baskin, "Abortion: II. Judaism," *EBR*, 1:140–42. For early Christian interpretation prohibiting abortion, see, e.g., Matthew Flannagan, "Feticide, the Masoretic Text and the Septuagint," *Westminster Theological Journal* 74, no. 1 (2012): 59–84.

37 The Masoretic Text reads "hits," which here means "hits to death"; the Septuagint reads "and he dies." The Septuagint is either a clarification or it reflects a word that has fallen out of the Masoretic Text.

38 We have inserted the parentheses; the verse, which switches from people to animals, is intrusive.

39 See, e.g., Sophie Lafont, "Ancient Near Eastern Laws: Continuity and Pluralism," in *Theory and Method in Biblical and Cuneiform Law: Revision, Interpolation and Development*, ed. Bernard M. Levinson, Journal for the Study of the Old Testament Supplement Series 181 (Sheffield: Sheffield Academic Press, 1994), 91–118 (118).

40 For additional arguments that this passage is secondary, see Bernard S. Jackson, *Essays in Jewish and Comparative Legal History*, Studies in Judaism in Late Antiquity 10 (Leiden: Brill, 1975), 74–82, 100–106.

41 See, e.g., Baruch Levine, *Leviticus*, JPS Torah Commentary (Philadelphia: Jewish Publication Society, 1989), 167.

42 Jackson, *Essays in Jewish and Comparative Legal History*, 85.

43 Jacob Milgrom, "Lex Talionis and the Rabbis," *Bible Review* 12, no. 2 (1996): 16, 48 (16).

44 Wright, *Inventing God's Law*, 182. See also Wright, "How Exodus Revises."

45 Sandra Jacobs, *The Body as Property: Physical Disfigurement in Biblical Law*, Library of Hebrew Bible/Old Testament Studies 582 (London: Bloomsbury, 2014), 145.

46 Primary sources, unless indicated otherwise, in this and the following section from Davis, *Lex Talionis*, 55–104.

47 Davis, *Lex Talionis*, 77–81.

48 Davis's discussion (*Lex Talionis*, 86) concerning *Megillat Ta'anit* is incorrect. *Megillat Ta'anit* has no bearing on the issue, but talion is discussed in some versions of the scholion, or commentary text on *Megillat Ta'anit*, which associate literal talion with the Boethusians; see Vered Noam, *Megillat Ta'anit: Versions, Interpretation, History* [in Hebrew] (Jerusalem: Yad Ben-Zvi, 2003), 78–79. For the possible identification of the Boethusians with the Sadducees, see Eyal Regev, "Boethusians," in *EDEJ*, 445–47.

49 Davis, *Lex Talionis*, 16.

50 This and what follows rely on Neusner, *Mishnah*.

51 See "Bava Kamma 84a:19," Sefaria, https://www.sefaria.org/Bava_Kamma.84a .19?lang=bi&with=all&lang2=en.

52 Davis, *Lex Talionis*, 81–86.

53 Davis, *Lex Talionis*, 77–81.

54 David Werner Amram, "Retaliation and Compensation," *Jewish Quarterly Review* 2 (1911–1912), 191–211 (210–11n15). We thank Professor Barry Walfish for this reference.

55 Maimonides, *The Guide of the Perplexed*, trans. Shlomo Pines (Chicago: Univ. of Chicago Press, 1963), 2:558. We thank Professor Marty Lockshin for this reference. For more on this passage in Maimonides, see Mordechai Z. Cohen, "A Talmudist's Halakhic Hermeneutics: A New Understanding of Maimonides' Principle of *Peshat* Primacy," *Jewish Studies: An Internet Journal* 10 (2012): 257–359 (298–99), http://www.biu.ac.il/JS/JSIJ/10-2012/Cohen.pdf.

56 See ben Zita' cited, in dispute with Saadia, in Ibn Ezra's long commentary to Exod 21:24, https://www.sefaria.org/Ibn_Ezra_on_Exodus?lang=bi.

57 William H. C. Propp, *Exodus 19–40*, Anchor Yale Bible 2A (New Haven: Yale Univ. Press, 2006), 229.

58 Adam Kirsch, "Is an 'Eye for an Eye' Really an Eye for an Eye?," *Tablet*,
    August 29, 2016, https://www.tabletmag.com/jewish-life-and-religion/211938
    /daf-yomi-176.

59 See, e.g., Donald Hagner, *Matthew 1–13*, Word Biblical Commentary (Dallas:
    Word Books, 1993), 180. Luz, *Matthew 1–7*, 277–79, provides a brief survey of
    different Christian readings with more nuance.

60 Art Swift, "Americans: 'Eye for an Eye' Top Reason for Death Penalty," Gallup,
    October 23, 2014, https://news.gallup.com/poll/178799/americans-eye-eye-top
    -reason-death-penalty.aspx.

61 Martin Luther King, Jr., "Loving Your Enemies," in *The Papers of Martin Luther
    King Jr.*, vol. 4, *Symbol of the Movement: January 1957–December 1958*, ed.
    Clayborne Carson (Berkeley: Univ. of California Press, 2000), 316; we thank
    Kevin McCruden for this reference.

Chapter 7: "Drink My Blood": Sacrifice and Atonement

1 On "protected" as the likely meaning of the Hebrew root *p-s-ch*, see Barry Dov
   Walfish, "Why 'Passover'? On the True Meaning of Pesaḥ-פסח," TheTorah.com,
   April 20, 2016, https://thetorah.com/why-passover-on-the-true-meaning-of
   -pesah/.

2 See Ziony Zevit, "The Prophet Versus Priest Antagonism Hypothesis: Its
   History and Origin," in *The Priests in the Prophets: The Portrayal of Priests,
   Prophets and Other Religious Specialists in the Latter Prophets*, ed. Lester L. Grabbe
   and Alice Ogden Bellis, Journal for the Study of the Old Testament Supplement
   Series 408 (London: T&T Clark, 2004), 189–217.

3 The precise translation of many of these types of sacrifices is debated; we will
   touch on this debate below, when it is relevant to our main claims. Otherwise,
   we retain the NRSV translation.

4 See Naphtali Meshel, "Which Sacrificial Offerings Require Libations?,"
   TheTorah.com, July 5, 2018, https://thetorah.com/which-sacrificial-offerings
   -require-libations/.

5 For a survey on this offering, see William K. Gilders, *Blood Ritual in the Hebrew
   Bible: Meaning and Power* (Baltimore: Johns Hopkins Univ. Press, 2004), 109–41.

6 See also Lev 6:27 (6:20 Heb.).

7 Jacob Milgrom, "Israel's Sanctuary: The Priestly 'Picture of Dorian Gray,'" *Revue
   Biblique* 83 (1976): 390–99; Milgrom offered parts of this thesis in his earlier
   "Sin-Offering or Purification-Offering," *Vetus Testamentum* 21 (1971): 237–39.

8 Milgrom, "Israel's Sanctuary," 398.

9 Milgrom, "Israel's Sanctuary," 394.

10 Jacob Milgrom, *Leviticus 1–16*, Anchor Yale Bible 3 (New Haven: Yale Univ. Press,
   2009), 1011.

11 Milgrom, *Leviticus 1–16*, 1079–84.

12 See, e.g., Milgrom, *Leviticus 1–16*, 239.

13 Yitzhaq Feder, *Blood Expiation in Hittite and Biblical Ritual: Origins, Context, and
   Meaning*, Writings from the Ancient World (Atlanta: SBL Press, 2014), 1.

14 Pamela Barmash, *Homicide in the Biblical World* (Cambridge: Cambridge Univ.
   Press, 2005), 111.

15 For surveys of the significance of blood in the Hebrew Bible, see B. Kedar-

Kopfstein, "דָּם," *TDOT*, 3:234–50; Christian Eberhart, "Blood: I. Ancient Near East and Hebrew Bible/Old Testament," *EBR*, 4:202–12.

16 Gilders, *Blood Ritual*, 178–79.

17 On ransom language in the New Testament, see Nathan Eubank, *Wages of Cross-bearing and Debt of Sin: The Economy of Heaven in Matthew's Gospel*, Beihefte zur Zeitschrift für die neutestamentliche Wissenschaft und die Kunde der älteren Kirche 196 (Berlin: de Gruyter, 2013).

18 Gilders, *Blood Ritual*, 178–79.

19 See Gilders, *Blood Ritual*, 22, 169.

20 See discussion, with references to various arguments, in Craig R. Koester, *Hebrews*, Anchor Yale Bible 36 (New Haven: Yale Univ. Press, 2001), 432–33.

21 Other examples of divergent Septuagint readings and discussion in Jan Joosten, "Divergent Cultic Practices in the Septuagint: The 'Shoulder' (βραχίων) of the Priest," *Journal of Septuagint and Cognate Studies* 48 (2015): 27–38.

22 William H. C. Propp, *Exodus 1–18*, Anchor Yale Bible 2 (New Haven: Yale Univ. Press, 1999), 400–401.

23 Jon D. Levenson, *The Death and Resurrection of the Beloved Son: The Transformation of Child Sacrifice in Judaism and Christianity* (New Haven: Yale Univ. Press, 1993).

24 Gili Kugler, "The Cruel Theology of Ezekiel 20," *Zeitschrift für die alttestamentliche Wissenschaft* 129 (2017): 47–58.

25 See Marc Zvi Brettler, "Interpretation and Prayer: Notes on the Composition of 1 Kings 8.15–53," in *Minhah le-Nahum: Biblical and Other Studies Presented to Nahum M. Sarna in Honour of his 70th Birthday*, ed. Marc Zvi Brettler and Michael Fishbane, Journal for the Study of the Old Testament Supplement Series 154 (Sheffield: Sheffield Academic Press, 1993), 17–35.

26 NJPS is cited for the end of this verse.

27 "Zevachim 6a:15," Sefaria, https://www.sefaria.org/Zevachim.6a.15?lang=bi& with=all&lang2=en. For similar rabbinic texts, see Feder, *Blood Expiation*, 167n4.

28 Feder, *Blood Expiation*, 167n4.

29 David A. Lambert, *How Repentance Became Biblical: Judaism, Christianity, and the Interpretation of Scripture* (New York: Oxford Univ. Press, 2016).

30 Ephraim E. Urbach, *The Sages: Their Concepts and Beliefs*, trans. Israel Abrahams (Jerusalem: Magnes, 1975), 464, and, more broadly, 462–71. Contra Urbach's claim, it is not clear that the rabbis coined the term *teshuvah*; see its use in the Cairo Geniza copy of the Damascus Document (CD) 19:16.

31 Guy Stroumsa, *The End of Sacrifice: Religious Transformations in Late Antiquity* (Chicago: Univ. of Chicago Press, 2009), 64–65. This idea may have precedents at Qumran.

32 See Jeff Hoffman, "A Linguistic Analysis of the Phrase *Ma'avirin et Ro'a HaGezeirah*," TheTorah.com, September 2014, https://thetorah.com/linguistic -analysis-of-maavirin-et-roa-hagezeirah/.

33 David Biale, *Blood and Belief: The Circulation of a Symbol Between Jews and Christians* (Berkeley: Univ. of California Press, 2007), 65; Stroumsa, *End of Sacrifice*, 68.

34 E.g., Moed Katan 28a; Midrash Tanchuma (Buber), Acharei Mot 7:1; 10:1.

35 Jonathan Sacks, *The Koren Siddur* (Jerusalem: Koren, 2015), 1018, modified slightly.

36 Moshe Greenberg, *Ezekiel 1–20*, Anchor Yale Bible 22 (New Haven: Yale Univ. Press, 1983), 275.

37 Propp, *Exodus 1–18*, 233.

38 Propp's suggestion (*Exodus 1–18*, 234–38) that Moses is being punished here for killing the Egyptian (Exod 2:12) is inventive.

39 Lawrence A. Hoffman, *Covenant of Blood: Circumcision and Gender in Rabbinic Judaism* (Chicago: Univ. of Chicago Press, 1996), 113–14.

40 Gilders, *Blood Ritual*, 39.

41 William H. C. Propp, *Exodus 19–40*, Anchor Yale Bible 2A (New Haven: Yale Univ. Press, 2006), 295. See Gen 15:10; Jer 34:18.

42 So, e.g., Carol L. Meyers and Eric M. Meyers, *Zechariah 9–14*, Anchor Yale Bible 25C (New Haven: Yale Univ. Press, 1993), 139.

Chapter 8: "A Virgin Will Conceive and Bear a Child"

1 On Isaiah 7, see H. G. M. Williamson, *Isaiah 6–12* (London: Bloomsbury T&T Clark, 2018); John J. Collins, "The Sign of Immanuel," in *Prophecy and Prophets in Ancient Israel*, ed. John Day (New York: T&T Clark, 2010), 225–44.

2 Ruth Sheridan, "Scripture Fulfillment," in *JANT*, 727–30.

3 The classic study is by Jane Schaberg, *The Illegitimacy of Jesus: A Feminist Theological Interpretation of the Infancy Narratives*, expanded ed. (Sheffield: Sheffield Phoenix, 2006).

4 See Brigit Katz, "Is This the Seal of the Prophet Isaiah?," Smithsonian SmartNews, February 26, 2018, https://www.smithsonianmag.com/smart-news/seal-prophet-isaiah-180968255/.

5 See S. A. Irvine, *Isaiah, Ahaz, and the Syro-Ephraimitic Crisis* (Atlanta: Scholars Press, 1990), 159–71.

6 New American Bible available online at the Vatican website, http://www.vatican.va/archive/ENG0839/__PNQ.HTM. The footnote to the verse reads, "The Church has always followed St. Matthew in seeing the transcendent fulfillment of this verse in Christ and his Virgin Mother. The prophet need not have known the full force latent in his own words; and some Catholic writers have sought a preliminary and partial fulfillment in the conception and birth of the future King Hezekiah, whose mother, at the time Isaiah spoke, would have been a young, unmarried woman (Hebrew *'almah*). The Holy Spirit was preparing, however, for another Nativity which alone could fulfill the divinely given terms of Immanuel's mission, and in which the perpetual virginity of the Mother of God was to fulfill also the words of this prophecy in the integral sense intended by the divine Wisdom."

7 See "Isaiah, Chapter 7: The Syro-Ephraimite War," United States Conference of Catholic Bishops, http://www.usccb.org/bible/isaiah/7. We thank Jonathan Homrighausen for this reference.

8 For details on these and other miraculous conceptions, in relation to the Matthean and Lucan infancy accounts, see Charles H. Talbert, "Miraculous Conceptions and Births in Mediterranean Antiquity," in *The Historical Jesus in Context*, ed. Amy-Jill Levine, Dale C. Allison, Jr., and John Dominic Crossan (Princeton: Princeton Univ. Press, 2006), 79–86.

9 See Marc Zvi Brettler, "Who Was Samson's Real Father?," TheTorah.com, May 29, 2017, https://thetorah.com/who-was-samsons-real-father/.

10 George W. E. Nickelsburg, "First and Second Enoch: A Cry Against Oppression and the Promise of Deliverance," in Levine, Allison, and Crossan, *Historical Jesus*, 87–109 (93).

11 Philo, *Allegorical Interpretation* 3.219.

12 James E. Kiefer, "Justin Martyr, Philosophy, Apologist, and Martyr," Biographical Sketches of Memorable Christians of the Past, http://justus.anglican.org /resources/bio/175.html.

13 Justin Martyr, *Dialogue with Trypho* 67, in *ANF*, 1:232.

14 Jerome, *Commentary on Isaiah*, and discussion in Adam Kamesar, "The Virgin of Isaiah 7:14: The Philological Argument from the Second to the Fifth Century," *Journal of Theological Studies* 41, no. 1 (1990): 51–75 (62–75).

15 Kamesar, "Virgin of Isaiah 7:14," 64, citing Exodus Rabbah 1.25, "Shemot Rabbah 1," Sefaria, https://www.sefaria.org/Shemot_Rabbah.1.25?lang=bi&with =all&lang2=en.

16 The place of this prophecy in Judaism is summarized in Gerold Necker, "Immanuel (Emmanuel)," *EBR*, 12.994–97.

17 Barry Rubin, ed., *The Complete Jewish Study Bible* (Peabody, MA: Hendrikson 2016), 497.

18 M. Friedländer, *The Commentary of Ibn Ezra on Isaiah* (London: Society of Hebrew Literature, 1873), 1:41–42.

19 For more on Panthera, see Daniel J. Lasker, "Mary in Jewish Tradition," in *JANT*, 744–47.

20 Marc Zvi Brettler, Peter Enns, and Daniel J. Harrington, *The Bible and the Believer: How to Read the Bible Critically and Religiously* (New York: Oxford Univ. Press, 2012), 101.

21 Ben Witherington III, *Isaiah Old and New: Exegesis, Intertextuality, and Hermeneutics* (Minneapolis: Fortress, 2017), 79.

Chapter 9: Isaiah's Suffering Servant

1 Much of the material in this chapter is based on Marc Zvi Brettler and Amy-Jill Levine, "Isaiah's Suffering Servant: Before and After Christianity," *Interpretation* 73 (2019): 158–73. That article contains fuller discussion of the scholarly literature. See also Bernd Janowski and Peter Stuhlmacher, eds., *The Suffering Servant: Isaiah 53 in Jewish and Christian Sources*, trans. Daniel P. Bailey (Grand Rapids: Eerdmans, 2004); Darrell L. Bock and Mitch Glaser, eds., *The Gospel According to Isaiah 53: Encountering the Suffering Servant in Jewish and Christian Theology* (Grand Rapids: Kregel, 2012).

2 For the multiple textual variations, see Eugene Ulrich, ed., *The Biblical Qumran Scrolls*, vol. 2, *Isaiah–Twelve Minor Prophets* (Leiden: Brill, 2013), 434–35.

3 God is being spoken of in the third person in v. 10 ("Yet it was the will of the LORD"), but God speaks of the servant in the first person beginning in 11b ("The righteous one, my servant"). This change of person may suggest that the prophet is quoting God in 11b and so that half verse should be put in quotation marks.

4 Matthew, like the other Gospels, uses the Greek term "saved" (*sōzō*) in two ways. First is in reference to healings from physical infirmities. For example, to the woman cured of vaginal or uterine hemorrhages, Jesus says, "Take heart, daughter; your faith has made you well," and Matthew records, "instantly the

woman was made well" (Matt 9:22 NRSV). The translation "made well" masks the Greek *sōzō*, "saved." Second is the more familiar usage in terms of "saved from sin." Matt 1:21 speaks of the angel's message to Joseph concerning Mary, "She will bear a son, and you are to name him Jesus, for he will save [*sōzō*] his people from their sins."

5 See Richard I. Pervo, *Acts*, Hermeneia (Minneapolis: Fortress, 2008), 225–26.

6 Christopher R. Hutson proposes that Jesus is engaging in an "impromptu, late-nite performance" in arranging to have his disciples carry swords: Hutson, "Enough for What? Playacting Isaiah 53 in Luke 22:35–38," *Restoration Quarterly* 55 (2013): 35–51 (43).

7 Ben Witherington III, *Isaiah Old and New: Exegesis, Intertextuality, and Hermeneutics* (Minneapolis: Fortress, 2017).

8 Richard B. Hays, *Echoes of Scripture in the Letters of Paul* (New Haven: Yale Univ. Press, 1989), 63.

9 Dale C. Allison, Jr., *Constructing Jesus: Memory, Imagination, History* (Grand Rapids: Baker Academic, 2010), 414n98. Conversely, Hays, *Echoes of Scripture*, states, "it is very difficult to make a case that Isaiah's Suffering Servant texts play any significant role in Mark's account of Jesus's death—at least at the level of Mark's text-production" (87).

10 Tryggve N. D. Mettinger, *A Farewell to the Servant Songs* (Lund: CWK Gleerup, 1983), 45.

11 Bentzion Kravitz, "Isaiah 53," Jews for Judaism, https://jewsforjudaism.org /knowledge/articles/isaiah-53-the-jewish-perspective.

12 See, e.g., Tovia Singer, "Who Is God's Suffering Servant? The Rabbinic Interpretation of Isaiah 53," Outreach Judaism, https://outreachjudaism.org /gods-suffering-servant-isaiah-53/.

13 See John Goldingay and David Payne, *A Critical and Exegetical Commentary on Isaiah 40–55*, International Critical Commentary (London: T&T Clark, 2006), 2:159.

14 H. Simian-Yofre, "עבד," *TDOT*, 10:387.

15 Jeremy Schipper helpfully summarizes arguments for and against reading Isa 53 in sacrificial terms in "Interpreting the Lamb Imagery in Isaiah 53," *Journal of Biblical Literature* 132 (2013): 315–25 (325).

16 Intergenerational vicarious punishment is found in the following sources, among others: Exod 20:5; 34:7; Deut 5:9; 2 Samuel 12; Lamentations 5:7. It is rejected in Deut 7:10; Jer 31:29–30 (for the future); and Ezek 18:1–20.

17 Mettinger, *Farewell to the Servant Songs*, 45. For a helpful summary of Christian scholars' identifications of the slave, see Kenneth D. Litwack, "The Use of Quotations from Isaiah 52.13–53.12 in the New Testament," *Journal of the Evangelical Theological Society* 26 (1983): 385–94.

18 See, e.g., John J. Collins, "A Messiah Before Jesus," in *Christian Beginnings and the Dead Sea Scrolls*, ed. John J. Collins and Craig A. Evans (Grand Rapids: Baker Academic, 2006), 15–36 (21–23).

19 Contra Israel Knohl, *The Messiah Before Jesus: The Suffering Servant of the Dead Sea Scrolls*, trans. David Maisel (Berkeley: Univ. of California Press, 2000); see the counterclaims by John J. Collins, *The Scepter and the Star: The Messiahs of the Dead Sea Scrolls and Other Ancient Literature*, 2nd ed. (Grand Rapids: Eerdmans, 2010), esp. 164–70; Collins, "The Suffering Servant at Qumran?," *Bible Review* 9,

no. 6 (1993): 25–27, 63; and Torleif Elgvin, "Eschatology and Messianism in the Gabriel Inscription," *Journal of the Jesus Movement in Its Jewish Setting from the First to the Seventh Century* 1 (2014): 5–24. See also James Tabor, "A Pierced or Piercing Messiah?—The Verdict Is Still Out," *Biblical Archaeology Review* 18 (1992): 58–59.

20 James C. VanderKam, *The Dead Sea Scrolls Today*, 2nd ed. (Grand Rapids: Eerdmans, 1994), 219.

21 James H. Charlesworth, "Suffering Servant," *EDSS*, 2:901.

22 The following discussion draws substantially from D. Jeffrey Bingham, "Justin and Isaiah 53," *Vigiliae Christianae* 53 (2000): 248–61. See also Daniel Bailey, "Our Suffering and Crucified Messiah (*Dial.* 111.2): Justin Martyr's Allusions to Isaiah 53 in His Dialogue with Trypho, with Special Reference to the New Edition of M. Marcovich," in Janowski and Stuhlmacher, *Suffering Servant*, 324–417.

23 Bingham, "Justin and Isaiah 53," 251.

24 Origen, *Against Celsus* 1.55, in *ANF*, 4:420.

25 Bruce D. Chilton, *The Isaiah Targum*, Aramaic Bible 11 (Wilmington, DE: Glazier, 1987), 103.

26 Many of the examples in this section are drawn from S. R. Driver and A. Neubauer, *The Fifty-third Chapter of Isaiah According to Jewish Interpreters*, 2 vols. (1876; repr., New York: Ktav, 1969). For an overview, see Elliott Horowitz, "Isaiah's Suffering Servant and the Jews: From the Nineteenth Century to the Ninth," in *New Perspectives in Jewish-Christian Relations: In Honor of David Berger*, ed. Elisheva Carlebach and Jacob J. Schacter, Brill Reference Library of Ancient Judaism 33 (Leiden: Brill, 2012), 429–36; Michael L. Brown, "Jewish Interpretations of Isaiah 53," in Bock and Glaser, *Gospel According to Isaiah 53*, 61–83.

27 The description of this midrash and its discussion of messianism is based on Rivka Ulmer, "The Contours of the Messiah in *Pesiqta Rabbati*," *Harvard Theological Review* 106 (2013): 115–44. See also p. 375–77.

28 Ulmer, "Contours of the Messiah," 118; Ephraim E. Urbach, *The Sages: Their Concepts and Beliefs*, trans. Israel Abrahams (Jerusalem: Magnes, 1975), 687–88.

29 See Raymond Brown, *Death of the Messiah: From Gethsemane to the Grave—A Commentary on the Passion Narratives in the Four Gospels*, vol. 2 (New York: Doubleday, 1994), 1458.

30 See Joel E. Rembaum, "The Development of a Jewish Exegetical Tradition Regarding Isaiah 53," *Harvard Theological Review* 75 (1982): 289–311 (299).

31 The *Revised Common Lectionary* is followed by several mainline Protestant denominations. The three-year cycle appears on Vanderbilt University's *Revised Common Lectionary* site: https://lectionary.library.vanderbilt.edu/.

32 Robert Lassalle-Klein, "Voice of the Suffering Servant, Cry of the Crucified People," *Explore Journal* 18 (2015): 32–35, available at Ignatian Center for Jesuit Education, https://www.scu.edu/ic/media--publications/explore-journal /spring-2015-stories/voice-of-the-suffering-servant-cry-of-the-crucified-people .html, quoting Ignacio Ellacuría, S.J., rector of the Universidad Centroamericana (UCA) in El Salvador.

33 Mary Frances Reis, "Good Friday Reflection by S. Mary Frances Reis," *Visitation Monastery of Minneapolis* (blog), March 2016, http://www .visitationmonasteryminneapolis.org/2016/03/good-friday-reflection-by-s -mary-frances-reis/.

Chapter 10: The Sign of Jonah

1   Sources consulted for this chapter include Fay Elanor Ellwood, "Jonah (Book
    and Person)," *EBR*, 14:568–80; Yvonne Sherwood, "Jonah," in *The Oxford
    Encyclopedia of the Books of the Bible*, ed. Michael D. Coogan (Oxford: Oxford
    Univ. Press, 2011), 1:477–81; Jack M. Sasson, *Jonah*, Anchor Yale Bible 24B (New
    Haven: Yale Univ. Press, 1990); and Uriel Simon, *Jonah*, JPS Bible Commentary
    (Philadelphia: Jewish Publication Society, 1999). For Christian reception history,
    see, inter alia, A. K. M. Adam, "The Sign of Jonah: A Fish-Eye View," *Semeia* 51
    (1990): 177–91; S. Chow, *The Sign of Jonah Reconsidered: A Study of Its Meaning in
    the Gospel Traditions* (Stockholm: Almqvist & Wiksell, 1995); and especially
    Yvonne Sherwood, *A Biblical Text and Its Afterlives: The Survival of Jonah in
    Western Culture* (Cambridge: Cambridge Univ. Press, 2000).

2   J. William Whedbee, "Jonah as Joke: A Comedy of Contradictions, Caricature,
    and Compassion," in *The Bible and the Comic Vision*, ed. J. William Whedbee
    (Cambridge: Univ. Press, 1998), 191–220; Mark Biddle, *A Time to Laugh: Humor
    in the Bible* (Macon, GA: Smyth & Helwys, 2013), 57–72.

3   Stephen J. Davis, "Jonah in Early Christian Art: Allegorical Exegesis and the
    Roman Funerary Context," *Australian Religion Studies Review* 13 (2000): 72–83;
    more broadly, see Robert C. Gregg, *Shared Stories, Rival Tellings: Early Encounters
    of Jews, Christians, and Muslims* (Oxford: Oxford Univ. Press, 2015), 369–407. See
    also Scott B. Noegel, "Jonah and Leviathan: Inner-Biblical Allusions and the
    Problem with Dragons," *Henoch* 37 (2015): 236–60.

4   Anna L. Grant-Henderson, *Inclusive Voices in Post-Exilic Judah* (Collegeville,
    MN: Liturgical Press, 2002), esp. 85–107.

5   Gabriel H. Cohn, "Flight from Himself—The Book of Jonah," Bar Ilan Univ.,
    Parashat Hashavua Study Center, Parashat Ha'azinu-Shabbat Teshuva 5770 /
    September 26, 2009, https://www.biu.ac.il/JH/Parasha/eng/haazinu/cohn
    .html.

6   Avigdor Shinan and Yair Zakovitch, *Once Again: That's Not What the Good Book
    Says* [in Hebrew] (Jerusalem: Yedioth Ahronoth, 2009), 300–303.

7   The targum renders "Hebrew" as "Jew," perhaps to prevent now-competing
    Christian claims that see Jonah as a Christ figure. See Sherwood, *Biblical Text
    and Its Afterlives*, 107.

8   See Emanuel Tov, *Textual Criticism of the Hebrew Bible*, 3rd ed. (Minneapolis:
    Fortress, 2012), 238–39.

9   The most detailed study of this pattern is Yair Zakovitch, *"For Three . . . and for
    Four": The Pattern for the Numerical Sequence Three-Four in the Bible* [in Hebrew]
    (Jerusalem: Makor, 1979).

10 Sherwood, *Biblical Text and Its Afterlives*, 117.

11 Robert W. Wall, "Peter, 'Son of Jonah': The Conversion of Cornelius in the
    Context of Canon," *Journal for the Study of the New Testament* 29 (1987): 79–90.

12 See Nicholas J. Schaser, "Unlawful for a Jew? Acts 10:28 and the Lukan View of
    Jewish-Gentile Relations," *Biblical Theology Bulletin* 48 (2018): 188–201.

13 Louis Ginzberg, *Legends of the Jews*, trans. Henrietta Szold and Paul Radin (repr.,
    Philadelphia: Jewish Publication Society, 2003), 2:1034.

14 So Pseudo-Chrysostom, *Quod Mari* 22, cited in Sherwood, *Biblical Text and Its
    Afterlives*, 15.

15 Sherwood, *Biblical Text and Its Afterlives*, 15, summarizing Ambrose of Milan.

16 See John B. Friedman, "Bald Jonah and the Exegesis of 4 Kings 2.23," *Traditio* 44 (1988): 125–44.

17 Sherwood, *Biblical Text and Its Afterlives*, 23, citing Martin Luther, *Lectures on Jonah*, in *Minor Prophets II: Jonah, Habakkuk*, ed. H. C. Oswald, Luther's Works 19 (St. Louis: Concordia, 1974), 94.

18 Janet Howe Gaines, *Forgiveness in a Wounded World: Jonah's Dilemma*, Studies in Biblical Literature (Atlanta: SBL Press, 2003), 131.

19 James Bruckner, *NIV Application Commentary: Jonah, Nahum, Habakkuk, Zephaniah* (Grand Rapids: Zondervan, 2004), 61, citing J. D. Douglas, ed., "Jonah," in *The New Bible Dictionary* (Leicester: Inter-Varsity, 1962), 652–54.

20 Bruckner, *NIV Application Commentary*, 61, quoting J. A. Bewer, *Critical and Exegetical Commentary on Jonah*, International Critical Commentary (Edinburgh: T&T Clark, 1912), 64.

21 For the Jewish readings of Jonah, see Ellwood, "Jonah (Book and Person)," *EBR*, 14:573–80. Exactly when and where the custom of reading Jonah on Yom Kippur started is debated; it may not have been read in the land of Israel in late antiquity because of its significance to early Christianity. See Rachel Adelman, *The Return of the Repressed: Pirqe de-Rabbi Eliezer and the Pseudepigrapha*, Supplements to the Journal for the Study of Judaism 140 (Leiden: Brill, 2009), 217n18.

22 "Sanhedrin 89b:6," Sefaria, https://www.sefaria.org/Sanhedrin.89b.6?lang =bi&with=all&lang2=en.

23 "Taanit 16a," Sefaria, https://www.sefaria.org/Taanit.16a?lang=bi.

24 Adelman, *Return of the Repressed*, 234.

25 Adelman, *Return of the Repressed*, 233.

26 "Taanit 16a," Sefaria, https://www.sefaria.org/Taanit.16a?lang=bi.

27 "Yalkut Shimoni on Nach 550," Sefaria, https://www.sefaria.org.il/Yalkut _Shimoni_on_Nach.550?lang=en, translation by the authors.

28 Translations that follow of the standard critical edition of the Rabbinic Bible are by the authors.

29 Aryeh Wineman, "The Zohar on Jonah: Radical Retelling or Tradition?," *Hebrew Studies* 31 (1990): 57–69.

30 Kristin Romey, "Man-Eating Fish, Tower of Babel Revealed on Ancient Mosaic," *National Geographic*, November 15, 2018, https://www .nationalgeographic.com/culture/2018/11/jonah-tower-babel-huqoq -ancient-synagogue-mosaic/.

31 See David Marcus, *From Balaam to Jonah: Anti-Prophetic Satire in the Hebrew Bible*, Brown Judaic Studies 301 (Atlanta: Scholars Press, 1995).

Chapter 11: "My God, My God, Why Have You Forsaken Me?"

1 See Brown, *Death of the Messiah*, 2:1455–65, esp. 1460–62. See also Richard B. Hays, "Christ Prays the Psalms: Israel's Psalter as Matrix of Early Christology," in *Conversion of the Imagination* (Grand Rapids: Eerdmans, 2005), 101–18 (105–6); Joel Marcus, *The Way of the Lord* (Louisville: Westminster John Knox, 1992), 172–86. Mark 15:34 reads, in what is mostly an Aramaic transliteration (Aramaic words spelled with Greek letters), "Eloi, Eloi, lema sabachthani," which the evangelist translates for Greek-speaking readers as "My God, my God, why have

you forsaken me?" The translation is close to the Septuagint, "God, my God," although (like the Hebrew) it repeats "my"; it also includes an extra phrase, "pay attention to me" or "hear me." Matt 27:46, "Eli, Eli, lema sabachthani?" also doubles "my God, my God" in Hebrew rather than Aramaic, though the last word is in Aramaic.

2 Some early Latin manuscripts of Matthew's Gospel include a similar direct quotation of Ps 22:19 after the notice of the soldiers' actions. Catherine Brown Tkacz, "Esther, Jesus, and Psalm 22," *Catholic Biblical Quarterly* 70 (2008): 709–28 (716).

3 Joel Marcus, *Mark 8–16*, Anchor Yale Bible 27A (New Haven: Yale Univ. Press, 2009), 1051.

4 The verse does not appear in all manuscripts, and the NRSV prints it in brackets to indicate the insecure textual history. The same line appears in Acts 7; see the discussion of Stephen's speech, below.

5 The Greek is *pneuma*; see discussion of this term in Chapter 3. Old English translates the Latin *spiritus* as "ghost," and hence "Holy Ghost" enters the English language.

6 See Esther M. Menn, "No Ordinary Lament: Relecture and the Identity of the Distressed in Psalm 22," *Harvard Theological Review* 93 (2000): 301–41 (334).

7 St. Jerome, *Commentary on Matthew*, trans. Thomas P. Sheck, The Fathers of the Church, vol. 117 (Washington, DC: The Catholic University Press, 2008), 326. See also Tkacz, "Esther, Jesus, and Psalm 22," 716, following Menn, "No Ordinary Lament," 334–35.

8 Tkacz, "Esther, Jesus, and Psalm 22," 717.

9 Proposed famously by Rudolf Bultmann, *The History of the Synoptic Tradition*, trans. John Marsh (Oxford: Basil Blackwood, 1963), 313. See discussion in Allison, *Constructing Jesus*, 648.

10 For a good example of how Mark's initial readers may have understood the Marcan use of Ps 22, see Holly J. Carey, *Jesus' Cry from the Cross: Towards a First-Century Understanding of the Intertextual Relationship Between Psalm 22 and the Narrative of Mark's Gospel*, Library of New Testament Studies 398 (London: T&T Clark International, 2009).

11 The Mishnah (ca. 200 CE) speaks of the Hallel (e.g., Pesachim 5:7) but does not delineate its contents, and neither Philo nor Josephus mentions it.

12 Marc Zvi Brettler, *How to Read the Jewish Bible* (New York: Oxford Univ. Press), 219–29, and in greater detail, William P. Brown, ed., *The Oxford Handbook of the Psalms* (New York: Oxford Univ. Press, 2014).

13 Alan Cooper, "Some Aspects of Traditional Jewish Psalms Interpretation," in Brown, *Oxford Handbook of the Psalms*, 253–68 (254–57), and Rolf Rendtorff, "The Psalms of David: David in the Psalms," in *The Book of Psalms: Composition and Reception*, ed. Patrick D. Miller and Peter W. Flint, Supplements to Vetus Testamentum 99 (Leiden: Brill, 2004), 53–64. Regarding Ps 22, Karl Friedrich Keil and Franz Delitzsch are among the few scholars of the past two centuries to defend Davidic authorship, in *Psalms*, Keil and Delitzsch Commentary on the Old Testament (Grand Rapids: Eerdmans, 1971), 303–6.

14 On the Levites' role in composing and preserving psalms, see Nahum M. Sarna, "The Psalm Superscriptions and the Guilds," in *Studies in Biblical Interpretation* (Philadelphia: Jewish Publication Society, 2000), 335–56.

15 See Klaus Koch, *The Growth of the Biblical Tradition: The Form-Critical Method*, trans. S. M. Cupitt (London: Adam & Charles Black, 1969), 159–82; William H. Bellinger, "Psalms and the Question of Genre," in Brown, *Oxford Handbook of the Psalms*, 313–25.

16 Hermann Gunkel, *Introduction to Psalms: The Genres of the Religious Lyric of Israel*, trans. James D. Nogalski (Macon, GA: Mercer Univ. Press, 1998).

17 Gunkel, *Introduction to Psalms*, 122 (Gunkel's italics).

18 On the structure of the lament of the individual, see Gunkel, *Introduction to Psalms*, 131–98; Claus Westermann, *Praise and Lament in the Psalms*, trans. Keith R. Crim and Richard Soulen (Atlanta: John Knox Press, 1981), 64–81; Carleen Mandolfo, "Language of Lament in the Psalms," in Brown, *Oxford Handbook of the Psalms*, 114–30.

19 Samuel S. Balentine, *The Hidden God: The Hiding of the Face of God in the Old Testament* (Oxford: Oxford Univ. Press, 1983), esp. 49–56 (on Psalms).

20 See Gunkel, *Introduction to Psalms*, 140n203, for dozens of cases; see, e.g., Ps 6:10, "All my enemies shall be ashamed and struck with terror."

21 Richard J. Clifford, *Psalms 1–72*, Abingdon Old Testament Commentaries (Nashville: Abingdon, 2002), 123.

22 Davida H. Charney, *Persuading God: Rhetorical Studies of First-Person Psalms* (Sheffield: Sheffield Phoenix, 2015).

23 Philip Nel, "Animal Imagery in Psalm 22," *Journal of Northwest Semitic Languages* 31 (2005): 75–88; Nel, "'I Am a Worm': Metaphor in Psalm 22," *Journal for Semitics* 14 (2005): 40–54; Göran Eidevall, "Images of God, Self and the Enemy: On the Role of Metaphor in Identity Construction," in *Metaphor in the Hebrew Bible*, ed. P. Van Hecke (Leuven: Leuven Univ. Press, 2005), 55–65.

24 Noted, e.g., in A. F. Kirkpatrick, *The Book of Psalms*, Cambridge Bible Commentary (Cambridge: Cambridge Univ. Press, 1902), 115; W. O. E. Oesterly, *The Psalms* (London: SPCK, 1959), 176.

25 John S. Kselman, "'Why Have You Abandoned Me?' A Rhetorical Study of Psalm 22," in *Art and Meaning: Rhetoric in Biblical Literature*, ed. David J. A. Clines, Journal for the Study of the Old Testament Supplement 19 (Sheffield: JSOT Press, 1982), 172–98.

26 In addition to the commentaries, see Brent A. Strawn, "Psalm 22:17b: More Guessing," *Journal of Biblical Literature* 119 (2000): 439–51; Kristin M. Swenson, "Psalm 22:17: Circling Around the Problem Again," *Journal of Biblical Literature* 123 (2004): 637–48.

27 Swenson, "Psalm 22:17," offers an exhaustive history of research and follows Strawn's suggestion that Near Eastern iconography—depictions of lions—might help resolve the problem; Strawn, "Psalm 22:17b."

28 Roger Aus, *Barabbas and Esther and Other Studies in the Judaic Illumination of Earliest Christianity*, USF Studies in the History of Judaism 54 (Atlanta: Scholars Press, 1992), 13–14, claims, "the original Hebrew certainly is reflected in the LXX, Syriac, [Origen], and Jerome, who have 'they have pierced my hands and feet.'" The claim is cited, approvingly, by Tkacz, "Esther, Jesus, and Psalm 22," 724. Tkacz gives several other examples of scholars who find "pierced" to be original.

29 See discussion in Swenson, "Psalm 22:17."

30 Cited in Swenson, "Psalm 22:17," 639, with reference to John Calvin, *Commentary*

on the Book of Psalms, trans. James Anderson (Edinburgh: Calvin Translation Society, 1845–1849), 1:373–75.

31 Mark H. Heinemann, "An Exposition of Psalm 22," *Bibliotheca Sacra* 147 (1999): 286–308 (302).

32 Frag 1–10 3.15–16, as translated in James H. Charlesworth and Henry W. Rietz, eds., *The Dead Sea Scrolls. Hebrew, Aramaic, and Greek Texts with English Translations*, vol. 6b, *Pesharim and Related Documents* (Tübingen: Mohr Siebeck, 2002), 17.

33 Uriel Simon, *Four Approaches to the Book of Psalms: From Saadya Gaon to Abraham Ibn Ezra*, trans. Lenn J. Schramm, SUNY Series in Judaica: Hermeneutics, Mysticism and Religion (Albany: SUNY Press, 1991), 187.

34 "Pesachim 117a:12," Sefaria, https://www.sefaria.org/Pesachim.117a.12?lang =bi&with=all&lang2=en.

35 Jesper Høgenhaven, "Psalms as Prophecy: Qumran Evidence for the Reading of Psalms as Prophetic Text and the Formation of the Canon," in *Functions of Psalms and Prayers in the Late Second Temple Period*, ed. Mika S. Pajunen and Jeremy Penner, Beihefte zur Zeitschrift für die alttestamentliche Wissenschaft 486 (Berlin: de Gruyter, 2017), 229–51 (234).

36 Menn, "No Ordinary Lament," 317n73.

37 Menn, "No Ordinary Lament," 316.

38 Michael V. Fox, "Additions to Esther," in *OTB*, 1:103–5; Menn, "No Ordinary Lament," 317n74.

39 Menn, "No Ordinary Lament"; Tkacz, "Esther, Jesus, and Psalm 22."

40 Midrash Tehillim 22.6, cited in Menn, "No Ordinary Lament," 320. See also William G. Braude, *The Midrash on Psalms* (New Haven: Yale Univ. Press, 1959), 1:305. The Hebrew terms for "hind" (*'aylit*) and "my strength" (*'ayloti*) are similar, as Menn points out ("No Ordinary Lament," 320n84).

41 Menn, "No Ordinary Lament," 320.

42 Tkacz, "Esther, Jesus, and Psalm 22," 726. Tkacz follows Menn, "No Ordinary Lament," 317, who is following Chana Safrai, "De Psalm van Esther en de Psalm van Verlossung: Een exegese van psalm 22," in *Mijn god, mijn god, waarom hebt gij mij verlaten: Eeen interdisciplinaire blindei over psalm 22*, ed. Marcel Poorhuis (Baarn: Ten Have, 1997), 81–93; we did not have access to this Dutch publication.

43 Tkacz, "Esther, Jesus, and Psalm 22," 719.

44 So most recently in Anat Reizel, *Introduction to the Midrashic Literature* [in Hebrew] (Alon Shevut: Tevunot-Herzog Institute, 2011), 283.

45 Braude, *Midrash on Psalms*, 1:322.

46 Ulmer, "Psalm 22," 119.

47 See p. 307.

48 Ulmer, "Psalm 22," 117.

49 Ulmer, "Psalm 22," 121.

50 Ulmer, "Psalm 22," 116, 106.

51 "Rashi attempts to defuse or neutralize teaching to the effect that Hebrew Scripture prophesizes the passion, the death, and the resurrection of Jesus of Nazareth," Mayer I. Gruber, *Rashi's Commentary on Psalms* (Philadelphia: Jewish Publication Society, 2007), 130n14, 131.

52 The translations of Rashi follow Gruber, *Rashi's Commentary on Psalms*.

53 Simon, *Four Approaches*, 71–97.

54 Menn, "No Ordinary Lament," 303.
55 Abraham Jacob Berkovitz, "Jewish and Christian Exegetical Controversy in Late Antiquity: The Case of Psalm 22 and the Esther Narrative," in *Ancient Readers and Their Scriptures: Engaging the Hebrew Bible in Early Judaism and Christianity*, ed. Garrick V. Allen and John Anthony Dunne, Ancient Judaism and Early Christianity 107 (Leiden: Brill), 222–39 (239).
56 Midrash Tehillim 22.16, translated in Braude, *Midrash on Psalms*, 1:311.

Chapter 12: Son of Man

1 *Cambridge Dictionary*, s.v. "idiom," https://dictionary.cambridge.org/dictionary/english/idiom.
2 Geza Vermes, *Jesus the Jew* (Philadelphia: Fortress, 1981), 160–91.
3 See George W. E. Nickelsburg, "Son of Man," *ABD*, 6:137–50; Adela Yarbro Collins, "Son of Man," in *New Interpreter's Dictionary of the Bible*, ed. Katharine Doob Sakenfeld, 5 vols. (Nashville: Abingdon, 2006–2009), 5:341–48. When the phrase is a technical term, it appears, by convention, as "Son of Man"; when it refers to any human, it is written as "son of man."
4 Moshe Greenberg, *Ezekiel 1–20*, Anchor Yale Bible 22 (New Haven: Yale Univ. Press, 1983), 61, 62.
5 See John J. Collins, "The Son of Man in Ancient Judaism," in *Handbook for the Study of the Historical Jesus*, ed. T. Holmén and S. E. Porter (Leiden: Brill, 2011), 2:1545–68; M. Müller, *The Expression "Son of Man" and the Development of Christology: A History of Interpretation* (London: Equinox, 2008).
6 1QHa 12:31, following the translation of Martin G. Abegg, Jr., on Accordance Bible Software.
7 H. Haag, "בֶּן־אָדָם," *TDOT*, 2:161–62; Mark S. Smith, "The 'Son of Man' in Ugaritic," *Catholic Biblical Quarterly* 45 (1983): 59–60.
8 On Dan 7, see John J. Collins, *Daniel*, Hermeneia (Minneapolis: Fortress, 1993), 274–324; Carol A. Newsom with Brennan W. Breed, *Daniel*, Old Testament Library (Louisville: Westminster John Knox, 2014), 212–52. The length of their comments reflects both the chapter's difficulty and its significance.
9 See esp. Larry W. Hurtado and Paul L. Owen, eds., *"Who Is This Son of Man?" The Latest Scholarship on a Puzzling Expression of the Historical Jesus*, Library of New Testament Studies 390 (London: Bloomsbury T&T Clark, 2012).
10 See John Day, *God's Conflict with the Dragon and the Sea: Echoes of a Canaanite Myth in the Old Testament* (Cambridge: Cambridge Univ. Press, 1985), 167–77.
11 On the development of Jewish angelology, see Saul M. Olyan, *A Thousand Thousands Served Him: Exegesis and the Naming of Angels in Ancient Judaism* (Tübingen: J. C. B. Mohr, 1993).
12 Daniel R. Schwartz, "Jewish Movements of the New Testament Period," in *JANT*, 614–19 (619).
13 See esp. Loren T. Stuckenbruck and Gabriele Boccaccini, eds., *Enoch and the Synoptic Gospels: Reminiscences, Allusions, Intertextuality*, Early Judaism and Its Literature (Atlanta: SBL Press, 2016), 1–18.
14 Matthew Goff, "1 Enoch," in *The Oxford Encyclopedia of the Books of the Bible*, ed. Michael D. Coogan (Oxford: Oxford Univ. Press, 2011), 1:230. For the uses of this

term in Ge'ez, see George W. E. Nickelsburg and James C. VanderKam, *1 Enoch 2*, Hermeneia (Minneapolis: Fortress, 2012), 113–14.

15 See, e.g., Goff, "1 Enoch," 230; Nickelsburg and VanderKam, *1 Enoch 2*, 330–32; W. E. Nickelsburg and James C. VanderKam, "Enoch and the 'Son of Man' Revisited: Further Reflections of the Text and Translation of 1 Enoch 70.1–2," *Journal for the Study of the Pseudepigrapha* 18 (2009): 233–40.

16 See Darrell D. Hannah, "The Elect Son of Man of the Parables of Enoch," in Hurtado and Owen, *Who Is This Son of Man?*, 130–58.

17 See Lorenzo DiTommaso, "2 Esdras," in Coogan, ed., *Oxford Encyclopedia of Books of the Bible*, 1:248–52.

18 Michael Edward Stone, *Fourth Ezra*, Hermeneia (Minneapolis: Fortress, 1990), 383–85.

19 Simon J. Joseph, "'His Wisdom Will Reach All Peoples': 4Q534–536, Q17:26–27, 30, and *1 En* 65:1–67:3, 90," *Dead Sea Discoveries* 19 (2012): 71–105 (73–74).

20 Shelly Matthews, *Perfect Martyr: The Stoning of Stephen and the Construction of Christian Identity* (New York: Oxford Univ. Press, 2012).

21 See Günter Stemberger, "Daniel (Book and Person): III. Judaism B. Rabbinic Judaism" and Robert Chazan, Barry Dov Walfish, and Michael G. Wechsler, "Daniel (Book and Person): III. Judaism C. Medieval Judaism," *EBR*, 6:99–108.

22 See Peter Schäfer, *Jesus in the Talmud* (Princeton: Princeton Univ. Press, 2009), 109.

23 Alinda Damsma, "From Son of Man to Son of Adam—the Prophet Ezekiel in Targum Jonathan," *Aramaic Studies* 15 (2017): 23–43; see also Joel Marcus, "Son of Man as Son of Adam," *Revue Biblique* 110 (2003): 38–61, 370–86.

24 Damsma, "From Son of Man to Son of Adam," 36.

25 Damsma, "From Son of Man to Son of Adam," 33.

26 See Daniel Boyarin, "Beyond Judaisms: Metatron and the Divine Polymorphy of Ancient Judaism," *Journal for the Study of Judaism* 41 (2010): 323–65 (340–41).

27 Boyarin, "Beyond Judaisms," 342.

28 Craig Evans, *Ancient Texts for New Testament Studies: A Guide to the Background Literature* (Peabody, MA: Hendrikson, 2005), 202.

29 For the best collection of medieval Jewish individual sources in Hebrew and English, see Arthur J. Ferch, *The Son of Man in Daniel Seven* (Berrien Springs, MI: Andrews Univ. Press, 1979), 9–12.

30 Martin Lockshin, "Jesus in Medieval Jewish Tradition," in *JANT*, 735–36 (735).

31 Damsma, "From Son of Man to Son of Adam," 34n40.

32 See Bart D. Ehrman, "Brian and the Apocalyptic Jesus: Parody as a Historical Method," in *Jesus and Brian: Exploring the Historical Jesus and His Times via Monty Python's Life of Brian*, ed. Joan E. Taylor (London: Bloomsbury T&T Clark, 2015), 141–50 (142).

Chapter 13: Conclusion: From Polemic to Possibility

1 Merriam-Webster Dictionary, s.v. "jeremiad," https://www.merriam-webster.com/dictionary/jeremiad.

2 Michael Carasik, *Theologies of the Mind in Ancient Israel*, Studies in Biblical Literature 85 (New York: Lang, 2006), 24, uses the analogy of God replacing Israel's logic board.

3 Menachem Cohen, *Jeremiah* [in Hebrew], Mikra'ot Gedolot 'Haketer' (Ramat Gan: Bar-Ilan Univ. Press, 2012), 173, authors' translation.

4 Dialogika, an online library sponsored by the Council of Centers on Jewish-Christian Relations (CCJR) and the Institute for Jewish-Catholic Relations of Saint Joseph's University in Philadelphia, offers a cyber archive of such statements from Roman Catholic, Protestant, and Eastern Orthodox groups. See https://www.ccjr.us/dialogika-resources/documents-and-statements. See also "Documents, Declarations, and Speeches," Center for Christian-Jewish Learning, Boston College, https://www.bc.edu/research/cjl/cjrelations/backgroundresources/documents.html.

5 Commission of the Holy See for Religious Relations with the Jews, "'The Gifts and the Calling of God Are Irrevocable' (Rom 11:29): A Reflection on Theological Questions Pertaining to Catholic-Jewish Relations," 2015, 2.14, http://www.vatican.va/roman_curia/pontifical_councils/chrstuni/relations-jews-docs/rc_pc_chrstuni_doc_20151210_ebraismo-nostra-aetate_en.html.

6 Sponsored by the Center for Jewish-Christian Understanding and Cooperation (CJCUC) in Efrat, Israel: "To Do the Will of Our Father in Heaven: Toward a Partnership Between Jews and Christians," Orthodox Rabbinic Statement on Christianity, Center for Jewish-Christian Understanding and Cooperation, December 3, 2015, http://cjcuc.org/2015/12/03/orthodox-rabbinic-statement-on-christianity/.

7 For further discussion see Amy-Jill Levine, "*Nostra Aetate*, Omnia Mutantur: The Times They Are a Changing," in *Righting Relations After the Holocaust and Vatican II: Essays in Honor of John T. Pawlikowski, OSM*, ed. Elena Procario-Foley and Robert Cathey (Mahwah, NJ: Paulist, 2018), 226–52.

8 E.g., "Bible Version Comparison," Bible Study Tools, https://www.biblestudytools.com/compare-translations/.

Author Index

Note: Bold page numbers refer to discussions in the text. Regular page numbers refer to citations.

Abahu, **408**
Adam, A. K. M., 459n1
Adelman, Rachel, 440n54, 460n21, 460nn24–25
Aitken, James K., 431n27, 437n59
Akiva (Aqiba), **48, 191, 193, 409, 424**
Alexandri, **409**
Allen, Garrick V., 464n55
Allen, R. Michael, 433n11
Allison, Dale C., Jr., **294,** 448n1, 455n8, 456n10, 457n9, 461n9
Amit, Yairah, 433n23
Amram, David Werner, 452n54
Anderson, Gary A., 432n39, 438n12, 450n24
Ando, Clifford, 450n19
Appel, Kurt, 431n30
Aqiba. *See* Akiva
Aristotle, **173**
Aschim, Anders, 442n19, 442n29, 443n30
Augustine, **73, 101, 128**
Aus, Roger, 462n28

Bailey, Daniel P., 458n22
Bal, Mieke, 441n7
Balentine, Samuel S., 462n19
Barbiero, Gianni, 446n34, **446n34**
Barmash, Pamela, 453n14

Barnard, Jody A., 448n80
Barr, James, 441n4, 442n25
Barton, John, 431n27
Baskin, Judith R., 451n36
Batto, Bernard F., 445n15
Bauckham, Richard, 441n8, 447n71
Baumgartner, Walter, 445n16
Beale, G. K., 432n39
Bellinger, William, 462n15
Bellis, Alice Ogden, 441n11, 443n40, 453n2
Belnap, Daniel L., 448n2
Ben Ezra, Daniel Stökl, 448n81
Benovitz, Moshe, 434n29
Ben Reuben, Jacob, **58**
Berger, David, 435n37, 436n58
Berkovitz, Abraham Jacob, **378,** 464n55
Berkowitz, Beth A., 449n9
Bernstein, Moshe J., 430n25, 432n3
Berrin, Shani L., 430n24
Bewer, J. A., 460n20
Biale, David, 454n33
Bialik, Hayim Nahman, 440n52
Biddle, Mark E., 459n2
Billerbeck, Paul, 448n82
Bingham, Jeffrey, **306,** 458nn22–23
Black, David Alan, 449nn7–8
Blake, Lillie Devereux, **110**
Blidstein, Moshe, 436n53
Boccaccini, Gabriele, 443n36, 464n13
Bock, Darrell L., 456n1, 458n26
Bockmuehl, Markus, 438n12, 441n8
Böttrich, Christfried, 443nn32–33

467

Primary Texts Index

Subject Index

Abraham (Abram): angelic visitation, 395; army equipped by Melchizedek, 165; circumcision of, 250; guilt of, 300; as noble warrior, 148; priestly line and, 137, 139, 144–45, 149, 151, 152–53, 167, 168–69; sacrifice of Isaac, 35, 238; supernatural aid in conception, 274

Acts of Paul and Thecla, 103

'adam, 387, 389, 441n6. *See also* Adam; Garden of Eden story

Adam: creation of, 106–7; Eve created from, 109–10; in Hebrew Bible, 119, 441n6; Lilith and, 132; marriage and, 111, 123; New Testament readings of, 36, 101, 103; sin of, 113, 126–27; "son of man" and, 387, 389; work of, 108, 116–17. *See also* Garden of Eden story

adultery, 188–91

Against Julian (Augustine), 128

Against Praxeas (Tertullian), 72–73

agricultural work and hardship, 106, 108, 115–17

Alexander Jannaeus, 50–51

allegorical readings, 35, 36, 225, 281

'almah, 266, 269, 271, 272, 278–79, 280, 455n6

Alphabet of Jesus ben Sira, 132

Amidah, 177

anagoge, 37

anagogical readings, 35, 37

angels: appearance of, 395; in creation story, 23, 72–73, 94–95, 96–97; Jesus distinguished from, 70–71, 137, 141;

"one like a son of man" as, 398–99; revelatory exegesis by, 22–23, 37

anger, righteous, 188, 449n7

Antiochus IV Epiphanes, 21

antitheses, 182, 183, 184–85, 205, 216, 448n2

Apocrypha, 7–8

Apostolic Constitutions, 95–96

Aquila (translation), 367

atonement: in ancient Israel, 229–30, 231–33, 234, 240, 245; blood and, 146–47, 230–33, 240, 245, 253; Christian understanding of, 253; circumcision and, 248, 250, 251; death of righteous and, 247; nonsacrificial, 176, 232, 241–44; repentance and, 176, 232, 241; respect for traditional claims, 176; supersessionism and, 174–75; vicarious, 301–2, 305, 311, 457n16. *See also* sacrifice

Atrahasis, 109, 441n9

Babylonian Talmud, 12, 28, 94, 338, 373

Balaam, 389

Barcelona Disputation (1263), 58

Bar Kosiba, Simon, 48

ben 'adam, 387–92, 394–98, 408, 409, 410–11. *See also* "son of man"

Ben Amittai, Jonah, 329–30

Ben Ephraim, Messiah, 375–76

betulah, 267

Bible, Christian, 3, 9–11, 12–13. *See also* New Testament; Old Testament